WI...N

R. Thames

Goodwin
Sands

Thanet

Dover
Folkestone

Deal

Winchester

The Weald

R. Rother

Rye

STRAIT OF DOVER

Calais

Southampton

R. Arun

R. Adur

Brighton

Hastings

Dungeness

Boulogne

SOLENT

Chichester

Portsmouth

Selsey Bill

Newhaven

Pevensey

Beachy Head

dles

Isle of
Wight

CHANNEL

Dieppe

Cherbourg

Havre

R. Seine

Caen

THE
ENGLISH CHANNEL

Scale of Miles

0   25   50   100

THE ENGLISH CHANNEL

The English Channel

A History

BY

JAMES A. WILLIAMSON

THE WORLD PUBLISHING COMPANY

CLEVELAND AND NEW YORK

Published by The World Publishing Company

2231 West 110th Street, Cleveland 2, Ohio

Library of Congress Catalog Card Number: 59-11535

FIRST EDITION

61334

Contents

CONTENTS

CONTENTS

Illustrations

(The following illustrations will be found in sequence after page 160.)

1. The Needles *(Aerofilms Ltd.)*

2. Standfast Point *(Aerofilms Ltd.)*

3. Portchester *(Committee for Aerial Photography)*
   University of Cambridge. Photo by J. K. St. Joseph.
   Crown Copyright reserved.

4. Pevensey *(Aerofilms Ltd.)*

5. Ships from the Bayeux Tapestry

6. The Gokstad Ship *(Universitetets Oldsaksamling. Oslo)*

7. Rye *(By permission of Country Life)*

8. The Dart Entrance *(Reginald Green)*

9. Dartmouth *c.* 1540 *(British Museum. Cotton MSS. Aug. I. i. 38)*

10. Plymouth *c.* 1540 *(British Museum. Cotton MSS. Aug. I. i. 18)*

11. Edward III's Royal Cog *(Water-colour by Gregory Robinson)*

12. French Raid on Brighton *(British Museum, Cotton MSS. Aug. I. i. 18)*

13. Ship of 1490 *(British Museum, Cotton MSS. Jul. E. iv. 6)*

ILLUSTRATIONS

Maps

Preface

THE SCOPE of this book is the English shore of the Channel and
the activities upon it of nature and man, from the shaping of the
coast in ancient times to the making of the holiday resorts in modern.
In so large a subject, which touches upon all the history of England,
omissions have been inevitable; and I would ask those who miss
the inclusion of some interesting topic to consider that if all had
been brought in, the book would have expanded to prohibitive
length. The subject has fascinated me for many a year and I hope
will appeal to some who may not have given much thought to it.

There are two chief ways of knowing a coast, walking along it
and sailing past it. Walking gives the most intimate knowledge
of the geography and economic development, but from the wrong
point of view to appreciate the problems of the sea-going people
who have made their livings through the centuries upon the coastal
waters. Wheeled transport, even by the pedal cycle, is not nearly
so good: it is too fast to permit reflection or the absorption of
detail, it seldom takes one along the water's edge, and it concen-
trates attention on the road rather than the scene. To know a
country one must walk; and in most parts of our coast it is still
possible to walk along cliff-edge or beach-bordered marsh, or on
miles of firm sand when the tide is low. But looking out to sea
does not reveal much of the things that have concerned the workers
on the sea. Sailing does some of that, even yachtsmen's summer
sailing, for it enforces thought on tides, winds, dangers and weather
prediction, and anchorages and harbour approaches. Even with all
the modern aids of coastal lights and handy yacht rigs and hulls
such as no working boat could have employed, there remains much
of the unforeseeable which governed the lives of the coasters and
fishermen of the past. And the coast as it appears from the sea is

different from the coast as seen from within, and at times much more beautiful. I have tried to combine the fruits or both views without attempting lyrics of description such as I could not achieve in the written word. Some are present in my mind, and perhaps the relevant facts may help to transfer them.

The illustrations are a selection from a much larger number that have been considered. Some excellent ones have had to be rejected because they are so large that reduction to book-page size would eliminate most of their value, and some smaller ones because their delicate quality would not survive the process of reproduction. Here my gratitude must be expressed to the care and experience of numbers of the publishers' staff in controlling the enthusiasm of the author.

I have many other obligations, as readers of the book will note. I have indicated some in the List of Illustrations and others in the pages on which they are apparent.

J. A. WILLIAMSON

CHAPTER ONE

The Making of the Channel

AT A very late stage in geological time, after protracted ages in which the rocks and the soil—the hard stuff, the coal measures, the chalk, the clays, the gravels and flints—had been laid down and overlaid and heaved up and denuded away, into something like the surface we know, the country now called England found itself physically part of the continent of Europe. And at that time a few stragglers of human kind, now known as palæolithic men, equipped with flint-bladed tools and weapons, were wandering through Europe and England pursuing for food the wild animals produced by the landscape and the climate—strange animals, some of them, such as we see no more in life. In the broadest sense the natural layout of the country had reached what we think of as its final shape ; although it is not final, but merely the temporary stage on which our brief history is being enacted. The general lie of the surface was not quite horizontal, but slightly inclined from west-north-west to east-south-east, towards, that is to say, northern France and the Netherlands, with unbroken land connection all the way from farthest Scotland to those regions of the Afro-Asian junction where the earliest civilisations were about to begin. In our country the hardest and most ancient rocks came to the surface in the higher western parts, and thence dipped more sharply than the general surface towards the east, where they were overlaid with softer materials more recently deposited.

All this had been effected by waves and ripples in the crust of the earth, alternate crests and troughs, slowly upheaving and sub-siding, so that parts were covered deep by the sea and afterwards uplifted high into the winds and the rain. Remaining to our scene is the present condition of the earth waves, an alternation of ridges and valleys running across the country, in southern England roughly on an east-west system, in northern England on a north-south, and in places as radiants from a central plateau such as Salisbury Plain. The east-west foldings concern our present subject, for they created it. One of the longest and deepest valleys lay between present England and present France, and it was to become La Manche, the Sleeve, the English Channel. Only less fundamental to this same subject was the next-but-one valley to the northward, for it was to produce in its time the estuary of the Thames and the port of London.

Climates rose and fell like surfaces, and there were the warm periods when the ancient hunting men killed sabre-toothed tigers, and the cold periods when great sheets of ice, the deposit of unmelted snows, covered the major part of England, grinding-off the summit rocks in resistless horizontal movement and depositing the debris, when at last the thaw came, far from its places of origin. The glaciations (there were more than one) did not actually invade southern England, but they had great effects on its climate and water-movement and thus on surface and ultimately coastline.

The Channel position after the last glaciation seems to have been as follows. There was already a long gulf reaching in from the Atlantic to form what is now the western part of the Channel. Its shore on the English side probably followed a line not very far removed from the present one, although the detail of cliffs, coves and forelands must have been different.[1] The coast of Cornwall, Devon and part of Dorset was formed by ancient erosion, and the rocks in most places are old, hard and resistant; but the hardest material does yield in time to the attack of the sea waves, some significant alterations are historically attested in the past two thousand years, and minor encroachment of the sea can be visually observed in the region to this day. The romantic story that between Cornwall and Scilly stretched the fair, rich land of Lyonesse, peopled and prosperous, but overwhelmed by a sudden tempest, is

---

[1] See A. H. W. Robinson, *The Floor of the British Seas, Scottish Geographical Journal*, Vol. 68, No. 2, 1952. The thirty-fathom contour is close to Land's End, the Lizard and Start Point. From mid-channel south of the Isle of Wight it makes a long narrow tongue eastwards, ending at a point about seven miles south of Beachy Head.

fabulous, and any such connection must have been long before the advent of mankind. There is however the possibility that the Scillies themselves were in early human times a unit rather than an archipelago, and that the Seven Stones, now a group of rocks between the Scillies and Land's End were perhaps an inhabited island ; for there has been a lowering of land levels here as farther to the east.

It is up Channel that the great change commonly known as the neolithic subsidence produced its most radical effects. Here the starting position was that the east-probing Channel gulf ended against a broad land connection between England and the Continent, so broad that not only was England joined with France but also across a great low-lying plain with the Netherlands and Germany. Across that plain the Rhine flowed north to an outfall far beyond its present mouths, and the Thames, by one account, flowed east to join it as a tributary ; although, by another interpretation, the Thames may have turned south round the Kentish upland and have found its way through a valley to the Channel gulf already described in the west.

Thus the scene was set for the last great subsidence. There had been at least one such subsidence before, followed by a re-emergence, but they had been in pre-human times and do not concern us here. This one took place within the human record, as warmth was returning on the heels of the last glacial retreat, and a new sort of man, who tilled fields and grew crops and kept his animals under control, was coming north to find his habitation in England. Neolithic man, he is named, by reference to the quality of the stone implements he used, after a transition period of primitiveness now called the mesolithic. The neolithic period is a short one compared with the long millenniums of the palæolithic, for the human mind was on the move and other revolutionary changes were to come. It was somewhere in this mesolithic and neolithic age that the geographical breach took place and Britain became an island. Some attempts have been made to date it in terms of calendar years. We may perhaps take it as an average of findings reached by different lines of approach that the pronounced main subsidence occurred chiefly in a period at least eight thousand years ago, and possibly much more. The big subsidence was probably not continuous, but showed halts and even small reversals ; and there is no date at which it can be said to have ended. The shores of the lower Thames and the estuary have sunk considerably since the Romans built Londinium ; for parts which they inhabited are now below tide level. It is possible that the flood tide from the sea reached only to their London Bridge, although now it flows for many a mile up

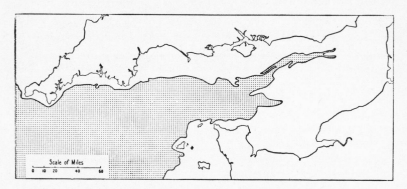

A possible early stage in the formation of the Channel.
The shaded portion is that enclosed by the
present 30 fathom line

through Greater London to the west. On the flat coastline of West Sussex the indications are that subsidence too slow for measurement may still be proceeding ; for out on the sea bottom stand the stumps of forest trees, and the erosion that is actively eating Selsey Bill may be due to something more that the attack of the waves, although that undoubtedly is its principal cause. We may perhaps justly think of the neolithic subsidence not as one continuous widespread sinking but as the sum of numerous local ones of restricted local durations. The practical result is the same.

The result was that the great Anglo-German plain was flooded and became the southern part of the North Sea. The Channel gulf bit eastwards along its valley and broadened as it did so. Finally the chalk ridge across from Kent to Picardy was breached, most likely through some rift cut by fresh water. There must have been a date for that, a year in which the first salt tide, however small a trickle, flowed through between south and north ; but we do not know it, though it marked the beginning of the island's history. The gap must have widened very quickly in its early stage, for there was a difference in the time of the high water coming round Scotland into the North Sea and that of the high water direct into the Channel from the Atlantic ; and the effect of the difference of level in the narrow passage must have been torrential. Soon, comparatively, it swept the opening wider and the wild tide-race diminished ; but still to-day, with twenty miles to work in, the tides of Dover Strait are swift and complicated.

The broadening to the full twenty-one miles of our time is a difficult thing for a realistic imagination to compass. Allowing that it began, say eight thousand years ago, the over-all rate is a mile in four centuries. But the rate must have been very much greater in the early stages than it has now become. The chalk cliffs of Dover are still falling, but not to the extent that these figures would indicate. Neither have they been doing so since the Roman invasion. The Romans built a lighthouse at Dover, the pharos which still stands not quite on the margin of the sea.[1] They would not have put it very far inland at a time when the best lights had a limited range of visibility ; and so we have a suggestion of a very moderate loss of ground in the past nineteen hundred years. Taking the over-all rate as constant, and the erosion equally divided between the English and French sides of the Channel, both highly arbitrary assumptions, the loss of ground at Dover since Cæsar's time would be about two and a half miles, which the position of the pharos must negative as a fact. When we add to this that the base-date of 8000 years ago is only a guess, we see that arithmetical calculations yield us little. We must be cautious about the rate of erosion in the historical period.

This chapter's main concern is the rough outline of the coast at the time of the Roman incursions, which mark the beginning of our recorded history. Details, often of a fascinating kind, are left to treatment in their bearing on human fortunes at later stages. One broad point must be established here, that for the purpose of

[1] There were two lighthouses, of which one now stands.

this book, which is historical, the Thames estuary must be included with the Channel. Geographically, they are obviously separate; but historically they are inseparable. The shores of the estuary converge to London's river. And London ever since it was built has been England's greatest economic seaport, sending all its westward trade (save in special crises of war) through the Channel and for the most part close to the Channel's English coast. The westward trade, it is true, has not been the whole of London's trade, nor in most times the major part of it, but it has been the most important single element in the stream of Channel traffic. So our historical Channel must be considered as running up past the Dover Strait and round the Forelands to Gravesend Reach, where to this day the Channel pilot disembarks from the incoming ship and hands her over to his brother "mud pilot" to conduct to London's docks.

The coast produced by the subsidence naturally followed the land contour which at any given time had sunk to sea-level, and at most places the land surface would shelve steeply or gently into the water. We may see this in the tidal reaches of a river like the Thames or on the shores of an enclosed natural harbour such as Portsmouth or Chichester; the land slopes into the water, usually with a fringe of soft mud between high and low tide levels. But on the open sea coasts another factor acted concurrently, the action of the sea waves driven by the winds. These had the effect of erosion, eating horizontally into the shelving land and creating a perpendicular wall or cliff. Leaving out for the moment other factors, also concurrent, the effect of the subsidence was to produce a coast mainly of cliffs, high or low—and a cliff in the geographical sense may be only a few feet high—interspersed with gulfs and long channels penetrating inland through drowned valleys. These penetrations were not cliff-edged, since they were out of reach of wave-action. They owed their outline simply to the run of the contour which the subsidence had brought down to high water level. At the time we are considering, two thousand years ago, the Channel coast conformed roughly to the above description, and west of the Isle of Wight it does so still. Up Channel, east of the Wight, there have been great subsequent changes, owing mainly to the fact that nature and man have had softer materials to work on. Between Hythe in West Kent and the Fairlight upland near Hastings in East Sussex one can easily discern the old cliff coastline sweeping round in a curved bight or open bay. That was the line the sea touched, probably as late as Julius Cæsar's incursion, but now it is many miles inland from the present coast, and between the two lines is a dry, fertile and populated strip of country. We shall see in a later chapter of this book how the large-scale recovery of ground was partly natural and partly man-made, and very much bound up with the rise and decline of the Cinque Ports. There has been another large recovery in Pevensey Bay between the Hastings upland and Beachy Head, another between the Isle of Thanet and the mainland of Kent, and a variety of minor ones. Down Channel we do not see these recoveries. Erosion of the hard cliffs has been slow, but it has gone on, and there are no large areas that were water-covered in Cæsar's time and are now dry land.

Wave erosion not only creates cliffs but destroys them. The waves eat into the base of the cliff they have made until they cause an overhang, which falls with a crash into the sea. For a time the debris acts as a defence to the new cliff formed behind the line of the old. But in time the sea washes away enough of the debris to expose the new cliff to the waves, and the process begins again. The time is long or short in accordance with the nature of the debris : if soft, it soon goes, if hard, it long remains. So down Channel there are hard rocky ledges, which seem immutable in the human time-scale, running out from the cliffs and the lofty headlands, and new falls of cliff are rare. These outlying ledges cause violent commotion of the surface water as the tide races over them, particularly when the winds are strong; and the races off the Lizard, Start Point, Portland Bill and St. Albans Head are well known to coastal sailors and dangerous to small craft. Up Channel the material is softer—chalk, clay or sandstone—and the fallen debris is comparatively soon dissolved or eaten away, so that the recession of the cliffs continues rapidly. The material of the Fairlight cliffs, east of Hastings, is very soft, and in a lifetime the edge of the cliff-top may move more than fifty yards inland. The old coastguard path along which in Victorian days one might meet a bearded middle-aged bluejacket with a telescope, has gone down into the sea, and buildings that had gardens between them and the edge now have none and are approaching their time of destruction. Chalk is of varying qualities, and that of the Dover region is soft. The cliffs there also are falling at a rate that is obvious. Cliff-falls are not due solely to erosion. Rain waterlogs and washes down the faces and fills faults and crevices in the rock, and frost causes it to burst them asunder as it bursts domestic water-pipes.

When an undulating landscape is drowned by subsidence the effect is unequal and islands are left above the surface of the water. The neolithic subsidence created numbers of small islands near the Channel coast, of which few remain. For, as the subsidence continued, they degenerated into patches of tide-covered rocks, or, if of soft stuff, were altogether eroded away. Three large islands, Wight, Thanet and Sheppey in the estuary, have had a different history, or rather, are still in an early phase of their history, and remain. The Eddystone Rocks, ten miles south-west of Plymouth Sound, have always been rocks as far back as we have mention of them, but they must once have been an island, too early, probably, for habitation save by those palæolithic ghost-men who flit in the mists of long ago. The Owers, a larger rock-patch off the West Sussex coast, have sunk deeper, although probably more rapidly ; and they may once have supported sheep and men. The Royal Sovereign shoal, east of Beachy Head, is another ex-island. It does not show above the surface, but comes near enough to it to be a danger to shipping. East of the Fairlight coast was the island on which stood the old port town of Winchelsea. It lasted until the thirteenth century, when island and town were washed away, so completely that the site is not now identifiable. Down Channel, Portland is an island, although now permanently connected to the mainland by a shingle beach. Farther west Looe Island is a very interesting little formation, a circle of high ground only just isolated by the later stage of the submergence. Large slabs of fallen rock form the bed of the intervening strait, and it is locally said that at low tide on Good Friday one may walk across.

The great headlands, Dungeness excepted, all pushed farther out into the sea than now. They have remained headlands instead of being levelled off largely because they consist of high ridges running out into the submerged area, and therefore have produced more debris, which it takes the sea longer to remove. Dungeness is a cape of an entirely different kind, not receding but actually growing seaward ; and probably in Roman times it was hardly prominent enough to deserve to be called a cape. But Dungeness is the product of an accretion of shingle washed along the coast from erosions elsewhere. Selsey Bill, in course of erosion like the rest, is not a high-standing cape. It is a peninsula of the low-lying coastal plain of West Sussex, and its cliffs (in the geographical sense) are hardly more than a dozen feet high. For a mile and a half out to sea stretches shallow water, and then there is a deep channel between the shoal and the former island of the Owers rocks. The Mixon beacon on the edge of the shoal may well mark the point of Selsey Bill in earlier historical times, for it is known that Saxon Selsey was an important town with a large church that served as the cathedral of the region before that of Chichester took its place in 1075. All of that old Selsey is now gone, and the succeeding village has had to extend continuously inland as its seaward side has been continuously washed away. It is now entrenching itself behind expensive sea-walls, which will not be permanent unless expensively maintained.

The question of erosion leads naturally to the sand and shingle beaches of the Channel coast, for they are its products. Various kinds of eroded material, from hard ancient rocks to soft recent clays, have fallen into the sea, and in places they have included much gravel, sand and flint. The breaking waves work on them unceasingly, pounding and rolling them and wearing them down. The result is that the shores are fringed with fine sand and shingle consisting of pebbles of various sizes and origins. In the far-western Channel the process has yielded much sand and rather less shingle, and the typical west-country beach along the cliff-foot consists of fine clean sand interrupted by rocky ledges and covering a general sub-stratum of rock not far below its surface. The sands are not stable and may alter rapidly.

From the Dorset coast eastwards we have more shingle. The Chesil Beach, the longest uninterrupted straight beachline in the country, runs from Bridport to Portland. It is eighteen miles long, of which the last twelve are not resting on the main coast but are separated from it by a long inlet called the Fleet. The shingle itself lies on a bed of clay. Chesil Beach is an ancient and stable formation. The shore of the Fleet within it has never been eroded by the waves, and this suggests that the whole thing took shape and achieved finality in the course of the great subsidence, the shingle being cast up on a sinking platform of clay in time to defend from wave-attack the inner shore, presumably the other side of a valley. But perhaps the chief mystery of Chesil is its uncanny straightness. Why should a line of submergence, which commonly follows a winding contour, be almost dead straight for eighteen miles ?

From the Wight to the Dover Strait there is shingle in many places, save at the bases of cliffs, which in this half of the Channel occupy less of the mileage than do the low shores. The usual beach consists of steep shingle from above high water mark down to the half-tide level, and below that sand sloping much more gently into the sea. In fact the sand runs right up the beach, but is overlaid by the shingle in its higher portions. Some of the shingle accumulations owe their density to human intervention, for sea-coast towns have their buildings at stake, to be defended against erosion ; and the best defence is not only a sea-wall, which can itself be breached by storm-waves, but a series of groynes running perpendicularly from it into the sea and so entrapping and stabilising a bank of shingle as an advanced line of defence for the wall itself. The ideal aimed at by the big towns like Brighton and Hastings is a sea-wall that is normally not under attack.

The shingle owes its origin to continuous erosion from the time when the subsidence began. It owes its disposition in long beaches to the fact that there has been a continuous tendency for material between the tide-marks to drift eastwards up Channel. The action of waves breaking on the shore is the cause of the eastward drift. The waves are driven by the winds, and in the Channel there are more and stronger winds from south-west and west than from the eastward. The great gales in which more material may be shifted in a day than in six months of calmer weather nearly all rage in their full strength from the south-west. Thus the wind-driven waves do not break on the beach perpendicularly, but obliquely. The swash of broken water carries the pebbles up the beach, but also along it to the eastward. The corresponding backwash when the wave has spent its force carries them down again, perpendicularly, but not in the place at which they went up. A given pebble may be shifted several feet eastward by the action of one quite ordinary wave. And this has been going on for centuries. One may ask then, why is there anything left ? Why has not all the shingle accumulated at some eastern corner of England where the south-wester does not blow obliquely on the coast ? The answer is that a great part of it has, at the remarkable growing promontory of Dungeness ; that projecting headlands, even small ones, farther west have acted like man-made groynes, holding up masses of shingle pressed against them ; that erosion is continually producing new material ; and finally, that the spectacular daily progress of some marked pebble under observation is by no means typical of all the pebbles on the beach. At any given time it is only an infinitesimally small portion of the material that is subject to wave-action. Below high-water mark it is only the surface stones that are being shifted, and under them is a thick layer of static stones ; while nearly all beaches rise well above high-water mark, their pebbles having been hurled up there by the waves of some mighty storm that occurs only once in a generation, aided by some demoniac wind that far exceeds the normal Channel gale. There is good reason for suspecting also that another force raises the topmost shingle banks above the reach of the waves ; and this force is the pressure caused by the lateral push of the sea against the lower banks. It is thought to have a squeezing action that thrusts the whole mass upwards.

The action of the tidal currents has been claimed by some to be a component force in the eastward drift. It is true that a current running along the sea-bed can shift small grains by direct pressure, and larger stones by undercutting the sand from their bases and causing them to roll over. But the theory does not take account of the fact that the tides are reversible and in most places flow as hard in one direction as the other. The tidal water carries much very fine material in suspension, and where there is an eddy or prolonged slackening of the current this material tends to be pre-cipitated to the bottom in the form of silt or alluvium. This has had an important effect in filling up the shallow gulfs and lagoons formed by the subsidence—in fact it has ultimately created hundreds of square miles of dry land. But it has very little bearing on the eastward drift of the shingle beaches. There the wind is clearly the dominant factor.

A comparatively late and very extensive change effected by the great subsidence was that in the region of the present Isle of Wight. Part of southern Hampshire and the coastal plain of West Sussex and the northern half of the present Isle of Wight together formed a continuous basin of low-lying land traversed by a fairly large river flowing eastwards out of Dorset. The river valley followed a line that is now covered by the sea in Poole Bay and by the salt waters of the Solent and Spithead straits, and it went farther east still, past the Owers and out to some estuary now unknown in the lost coastline of the Sussex plain, then far more extensive that it now is. This ancient river, conveniently called the Solent river, received as its tributaries the smaller streams that now flow separately into the present sea, including one that ran through the deeper valley that is now Southampton Water. Even more interesting was what lay to the south of the Solent river. The Wight was not an island ; and now, as an island, it is a mere remnant. It stretched eastward up Channel and southwards out into the present sea. The backbone of what is left is a central ridge of chalk running from Culver cliff in the east to the Needles at the western point. This chalk ridge ran westwards all the way, probably at a lower elevation, to the so-called Isle of Purbeck in Dorsetshire and formed the southern crest enclosing the valley of the Solent river. Outside it to the south and south-west lay lower land whose extent we do not know. Then came the great subsidence. The sea lapped over the low plains, cutting back that of Sussex to something like the line we know, isolating the Owers as an island, encroaching on the south of the·Wight till it met more steeply rising ground, flowing through Spithead up the Solent river and the Southampton river. But still the chalk connected the Wight with Dorset to the west, and the Solent was a tidal estuary and not a strait. The rising waves

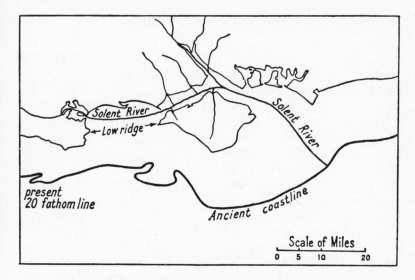

The formation of the Isle of Wight and adjacent coasts.
The present 20 fathom line in the Channel is indicated
as the approximate location at one stage of
the early coastline

from the south bit into the chalk ridge, cliffing it, eating through its
height and depth, until at last they breached it and the tides burst
through the gaps. The Solent river became the Solent strait, and
its western valley part of the main Channel. The last stage, the
breaking down of the chalk into reefs, and then their complete
removal, was probably comparatively swift, for it would seem that
the chalk was soluble. The whole thing was similar on a somewhat
smaller scale to what happened in the Straits of Dover. The findings
of geographers seem to indicate that the break-through was quite
late in the period of the subsidence, perhaps only a few centuries
before history began with the arrival of the legions. To-day the
tall chalk-stack or pillar named Old Harry, standing out from the
white cliffs of Standfast Point in East Dorset, looks out across
fourteen miles of salt sea eastward to the chalk pinnacles of the
Needles, the point of the western Wight. Old Harry and the

Needles are the surviving flanks of a line pierced and carried and overrun by a frontal assault. They will not long remain as its monuments. The Needles, although of a hard quality of chalk, are not what they were in the eighteenth century, as we know from drawings of that time. Old Harry is within danger of collapse.

The late occurrence of such great geographical events, and the fact that they took place on a scene inhabited by people of whom we know something, recognisable ancestors of ours, carries a dramatic quality transcending that of cool science.

Diodorus Siculus, a writer of Cæsar's time, repeating statements made by much earlier authorities, asserted that the islands now known as British were called the tin islands because they exported that metal to the continent. He said that the inhabitants brought the tin to the coast and thence took it to an adjacent small island named Ictis, whence the ships of the Phœnician traders carried it to Europe ; and further, that the transit to the small island was effected in carts crossing by a causeway at low water. The tin was evidently that of Cornwall and West Devon, the only British area of supply.

Much argument has turned on the interpretation of this statement, some holding that Ictis was St. Michael's Mount by the shore of Mount's Bay in Cornwall, still approachable in this manner, some that it was the Isle of Wight, named Ictis or Vectis by the Romans, to which there may have been some low-tide causeway before the Solent had reached its present breadth and depth, some even that it was the Isle of Thanet off eastern Kent. There are objections to all three interpretations. Thanet seems practically absurd, involving as it did a difficult and tedious land-transport across the whole breadth of southern England, only to end in a shipment that could have been made from the metal's place of origin. The Wight involves the same difficulty, to a lesser but still prohibitive extent ; and it may have been named Ictis by the Romans merely because they had heard the story. St. Michael's Mount is thought by some not to have been insular at all at the period but to have been a hill surrounded by low ground, although others find no evidence for this. Probably some Cornish or South Devon islet, not necessarily St. Michael's Mount, may be the origin of the story, although it is not altogether likely that the whole of the tin export was conducted from any single place. The mining area was widely spread, and natural harbours on the coast are numerous. But the island story is in itself credible, for a small island would be defensible and therefore a good site on which to accumulate the valuable tin whilst awaiting the advent of the traders. Looe Island would have fitted the conditions as well as St. Michael's Mount, and there were others.

In general, as we have indicated, there is a broad difference between the formation of the coast up Channel, east of the Wight, and down Channel, west of it. The outline of the eastern half takes its existence from the last submergence, the so-called neolithic subsidence. With the western half this is not so valid a statement. The subsidence occurred there also, but a coastline already existed ; the Channel gulf entering from the Atlantic was already there. We do not know its eastward extent or its breadth between England and France. But on the coasts of Dorset, Devon and Cornwall the sea may have touched approximately its present margin long ages previously. The west country is high-lying, and the subsidence dipped it vertically without involving a general overflow as in the east. Undoubtedly every cliff-face has been changed in detail and pushed back, and the softer cliffs have yielded more than the harder. Undoubtedly also the rising waters have entered the river valleys and turned them into estuaries, the natural harbours of the west country as we see them now. As the sea waves reached new rocks and soil the erosion produced new pebbles and sands, and with them the character of the sea beaches we know. But to the large view it is the same coast with modifications, not a radically new one as we see up Channel.

We have now to turn north of the Dover Strait to the Thames estuary. The chalk cliffs of Dover continue round the South Foreland and decline to sea-level near Kingsdown. Here the coast faces east across a channel of deep water towards the great Goodwin Sand. The water close in to the Kentish shore has, ever since ships have existed, formed an anchorage in which to await a fair wind for passing south and west into the English Channel. The anchorage is the Downs, a name which may occasionally cause confusion with the hills so named, and the present town of Deal on its shingle beach fairly overlooks it. From Deal the old coastline, following the contour of submergence, trended north-west through a broad strait named the Wantsum out to the northern coast of Kent; and the other or north-eastern side of the strait was formed by the Isle of Thanet. Thanet is low-lying on its Wantsum side—the Wantsum was simply a flooded valley—and towards the North Sea it turns a face of chalk cliffs. The Thanet chalk is a mass quite distinct from and less lofty than that of the North Downs. It is a surviving remnant of which the lost part has been eroded away. The shores of the Wantsum strait were very irregular and extended up two estuaries, those of the Great and Little Stour rivers, which flowed out of the higher interior of Kent. The Wantsum was open as a ship channel in Roman times. Then silt and reclamation gradually choked it, and it has been entirely closed for the past five hundred years. To-day it is firm dry land. Round its southern entrance there have been great changes, involving the rise and fall of ports.

From the Wantsum westward towards London river the north coast of Kent is a product of subsidence and erosion. The cliffs are low and soft, and are washed down by rainfall and eaten away by the waves; and on this coast the operative winds are those from between north and east. Erosion has been severe and still goes on. The twin spires at Reculver, a seamark always spoken of as "the Reculvers," are now the last relics of the medieval church which collapsed with the fall of the cliff a hundred and fifty years ago. In the sixteenth century Leland recorded that it was more than a quarter of a mile from the sea.

The off-lying sea is shallow, and farther out is obstructed by the great sandbanks that alternate with deeper channels to fill the Thames estuary. As we go farther east towards London it is evident that the subsidence had by no means ceased in Roman times. The Isle of Sheppey has suffered loss of area, subsequently made good by reclamation, and much of it is artificially preserved by embankments. On the Essex shore of the Thames below London are areas similarly safeguarded. But the embanking dates from the medieval centuries, and the Romans inhabited this land without the need for defending it. Great off-lying sands in a shallow sea are characteristic of Eastern England once the turn round the Dover salient has been passed. The Goodwins were supposed to represent an island that was overwhelmed as late as the eleventh century, and in parts it has been stated that clay underlies the sand. But there is no real evidence for the island theory, and that for the clay is very unsatisfactory.[1] The sands and channels of the Thames estuary, with a general trend towards the north-east, may represent the drowned slopes and valleys of a gently undulating plain. But the idea must not be too closely pressed, for some of the sands shift rapidly, and channels deepen that once were shallower. The two or three centuries of accurate charting that lie behind us indicate that while the main disposition of the great banks is stable, there are important minor instabilities. The factors producing them are so intricate or so untraceable as to defy calculation.

The English Channel coast was formed by a process that had no beginning and has had no end, a process of continuous change. In its creation nothing ever really began ; it evolved from one stage to another from the formation of the earth. We take for con- venience the last great subsidence as the prelude to the geographical- cum-human story, but only because at that stage the story is about to enter the late pre-historic zone in which men's movements begin to be discernible and human migrations appear dimly through the mist. It is like watching a ship sail the last ten miles into port after a voyage of ten thousand miles beyond our ken. The opening of the Roman era is an approximate basis for the most recent story, in which the human element predominates over the natural ; but even there we have really not a fixed point but a moving phase. We choose it because about there the dateless human pre-history, in which there are no personalities and no events, merges gradually into a recorded history of increasing detail. That history covers but an inch on the great wall-chart of time.

[1] See R. L. Cloet, *Hydrographic Analysis of the Goodwin Sands*, etc., *Geographical Journal*, CXX, Pt. 2, June 1954.

CHAPTER TWO

Briton and Roman

I. PREHISTORIC

UNTIL the past four hundred years the Channel and the Narrow Seas served less as a defence of this country against invaders than as a path by which invaders came. The idea of using the sea as a defence was early formulated and sometimes applied from Roman times onward, but it was never ultimately victorious until Tudor England created the regular Navy which has had a continuous and successful history from the sixteenth century to the twentieth.

Prehistoric newcomers probably met with little human opposition before they landed. Mesolithic or early neolithic men may have crossed by the land connection before the Channel and the North Sea had broken through it. Later incursions had to come by water. The area of origin of the ideas, if not of all the peoples, constituting the neolithic movement was in the Middle East, where cultivation of crops, settled habitations, and the use of domestic animals are traceable at much earlier periods than in the north and west. It is not necessary to suppose that all the people came from the Levant ; a way of life could spread by contact as well as by migration. Be that as it may, we can discern that the new way of life entered Britain from the south in the long slow centuries after the ice sheets had melted off the high grounds, and the tundra conditions of swamp and scrub on the plains had given place to forested valleys and dry upper slopes, and an Atlantic climate of mild summers and wet but not too frostbound winters had produced the conditions from which modern England was continuously to grow.

The Channel shores received many successive waves of immigrants. There were some who came across the narrower part of the sea from northern France and the Netherlands, short, long-skulled men with improved stone implements, notably axes for felling trees, which the palæolithic hunters had not needed, and hoes for turning the soil for their crops. These people also made earthenware pots for holding drinks and grain. Others came up from the Mediterranean through Spain and along the Biscay coast of France and thence across the wider Channel to Cornwall and Devon ; and not stopping there, went on to Wales and Ireland and the coasts of the northern narrow sea that has Ulster on one side and Scotland on the other. Their outspread through all the highland half of Britain is traceable by their burials, which collected many bodies in great common tombs walled and roofed with huge stone slabs and covered by a mound of earth—the megalithic type of monument. It is supposed that this was done on the compulsion of some powerful religious or magic motive and that the cohesion it gave to its votaries enabled them to dominate the more materially minded folk who had come across the upper Channel. The megalithic people used to be emphasised as the Iberians, on the assumption that Spain was the cradle of the race, but we hear less of this name now that it is realised that they were immigrants into Spain as they were into Britain. It was also considered that the black-haired, dark-eyed strain still noticeable among the people of Cornwall and Devon was a result of Iberian ancestry. It may well be so. Their bones tell us that these immigrants were short and long-skulled, although we can only assume that they were dark because they came from the Mediterranean. The ancestry of all modern men is extremely mixed, and many physical types must be latent in the blood of all of us. It may be that in a given region it is the environment—the soil, climate, food, water—that brings out one type in preference to others.

All this was stone-age life, before the general adoption of metal tools and weapons. But it was comparatively settled agricultural life, far different from that of the wandering hunter with his rudimentary flint knife and spearhead. Settled communities give rise to trade in the things that some produce and others lack. There is reason to suppose that the megalithic immigrants were growing interested in metals even before the definable bronze age set in

33

In highland Britain there were deposits of copper, tin and lead, and in Ireland copper and gold. As the settled way of life developed these things were in demand on the continent, and it seems likely that they were the basis of the earliest cross-Channel trade. If so, that trade was rather across the broader western Channel than across the Narrow Seas.

This brings us to the kind of shipping used. Dug-out canoes carved from a single solid trunk have been preserved; but the tree-trunks of western Europe were not so large as, for instance, those of the American tropics, which yielded fleets of sea-going dug-outs to the Carib adventurers of the West Indies. The British dug-out canoe was small and narrow, more suited for inshore fishing than for long-distance trade. An early idea for something larger was the curach, a frame of wicker or light timbers fastened together and covered with sewn hides. The curach is still made and used in western Ireland, a small fishing craft nowadays, although there is good evidence that the Irish once made larger ones that were capable of serious voyaging. It is possible that large curachs carried the cargoes and the emigrants of neolithic mankind. The curach is light and rides high, drawing little water, very suitable for easy landing on beaches in reasonable weather. The coracle was a diminutive of the curach, a very small one-man boat usable only in sheltered waters. Later still, in the age of metal tools, came the all-timber ship, with planking strongly fastened to a stout keel and frame. In such ships, with tall masts and leather sails, Cæsar found the Veneti of western Gaul carrying on an organised trade with distant countries. How long they had been doing it we do not know. The growth of shipping was concurrent with the growth of all the equipment of life among the metal-users; but there had obviously been some useful shipping available to those megalithic men who came to Cornwall from the southward.

The making of bronze tools and weapons began on the continent, spreading northwards, even though some of the tin and copper may have come from stone-using Britons. Soon after 2000 B.C. the first of several waves of bronze-using invaders crossed the Channel, and the bronze-age civilisation—for such it became in comparison with earlier primitiveness—made remarkable progress

34

for fifteen hundred years. There was regular trade out of Channel ports, and the metals from western Britain made the long passage to the Biscay coast to connect with a land route through south-western France to the Mediterranean. The use of iron spread northwards from the Balkans, by the Danube, and into Germany and France ; and about 500 B.C. iron-using invaders entered Britain to assert an ascendancy in their turn. The later bronze and earlier iron people were Celts, of a different physical type from the neolithic and megalithic men, taller and round-skulled ; and all went into the melting-pot to fuse as the Britons of Cæsar's time. One more invasion and settlement preceded the Romans, that of strong iron-using Belgæ, Celts with a Teutonic infusion, who conquered south-eastern and southern Britain, used improved iron ploughs, and founded towns. With them prehistory merges into history ; and dated history with named heroes begins with Cæsar's first incursion in 55 B.C.

In all the later centuries of metal-using prehistory the Channel witnessed trade, migration and invasion. Cornish tin we know by written record to have been carried to western France from the fourth century B.C., and it certainly had been much earlier. Numerous products, by archæological evidence, passed either way across the upper Channel. Migrants and invaders were set in motion by great folk-movements in interior Europe, Teutons pressing inland Celts westward, they in turn extruding coastal Celts across the sea. Fair-sized wooden ships were built. An iron anchor and an iron chain-cable of this period found near the Dorset coast do not consort with coracle-shipping ; the craftsmanship that could make them belongs to a higher order that that of the skin-coated boat. We do not know what ports were frequented or whether there were any settlements at them that could be called towns. Two thousand years of coast erosion have in most parts obliterated whatever there may have been. There is no hint of any naval defence, although there were hill forts and promontory forts for opposition after invaders had landed. The main body of the Belgæ sailed into the Thames estuary and took possession of the country north and south of it. Theirs was clearly an invasion in force, not a piecemeal infiltration. It was not only in Kent that the Belgæ played their part in Channel history. From the fresh-water Thames they spread southwards to come down to the coast of Hampshire and Dorset. Their sea trade was active, and they were in full communication with their Belgic brethren in north-eastern France. Add to this the trade between south-west Britain and western France, and we have a picture of the late prehistoric Channel as a sea traversed by hundreds of stoutly built ships operating their sectors of the long trade-routes that circulated goods between remote Britain and Ireland and the farthest eastern end of the Mediterranean.

II. CÆSAR'S INVASIONS

On this scene came Julius Cæsar, to explain much for us and to fill in many details, a great man of action with a talent for concise objective writing. From our point of view also he had the luck that his writings have been preserved, while those of earlier and later observers have perished. Three hundred years before his time, another literate pioneer, Pytheas the Greek of Marseilles, had come by the tin route to our south-western coast and had described what he saw; but his work has perished save in fragmentary allusions to it made by other writers.

In 58 B.C. Julius Cæsar was appointed to a command which included the Roman province on the Mediterranean coast of Gaul. The threat of German invasion from across the Rhine convinced him that the safety of the Roman state demanded the taking-over of the whole of Gaul and the establishment of the Roman frontier upon the Rhine. In six years he accomplished the task, and in the course of it he acquired and recorded first-hand knowledge of the sea coasts of France and of the south-east Belgic corner of Britain.

First, in 56 B.C. he had occasion to overthrow the Veneti, the principal tribe of a confederation of sea-going peoples of Biscayan France, centred about the mouth of the Loire. What he tells us of the shipping of these folk shows the following facts.[1] The vessels were built of oak with heavy beams and frames fastened with iron

---

[1] I rely on the translation by S. A. Handford in *Cæsar: The Conquest of Gaul*, Penguin Classics, 1951.

bolts. They were of comparatively light draught and flattish bottom to enable them to take the ground in tidal waters. Above water they were high at bow and stern, which Cæsar says was for safety in the big seas of the Atlantic. They were pure sailing ships, without oar propulsion, and the sails were of thin leather or raw hide. They had iron anchors and iron chain cables. Cæsar was impressed by the bulk and the strong construction of these ships of the Veneti, of which in the final battle they were able to bring no less than two hundred and twenty into action. His basis of comparison was the lighter, oar-driven fighting ships, no doubt of Mediterranean model, which he had had constructed on the occupied coast of Gaul for the purpose of his campaign. Aided by a highly fortunate calm, his galleys were enabled to attack and capture one after another the motionless sailing ships and achieve a complete obliteration of Venetian sea power. He nowhere gives any absolute figures of the size and proportions of the ships. The cultured ruling class of Rome, for whom Cæsar wrote, took little interest in maritime affairs or the details of ships, and their thoughts on a sea battle did not instinctively fly, as ours would, to tonnage, dimensions and propulsion. We are fortunate that Cæsar's account shows as much realism as it does. We have at any rate something impressive on the shipping of the Atlantic coast and the western Channel at the close of the prehistoric age.

In his campaign in northern France Cæsar found that Britain served as a place of refuge for defeated Gallic chiefs. He determined to investigate Britain with a view to conquest. In 55 he brought round his successful fighting squadron to the Straits of Dover, and collected Gallic shipping as transports for an expeditionary force. His base was Portus Itius, generally identified with Boulogne. It is remarkable that in spite of the trading and political relations between Gaul and southern Britain, and the close intercourse between the Belgic tribes on either side of the Channel, Cæsar learned in advance virtually nothing of the country he was to attack. He questioned traders about the coast, the harbours and the people, and they professed ignorance of all he wanted to know. The Gallic seamen told him nothing of the tides, and he did not even learn that at the full and change of the moon they rose higher than in the intervals.[1] The Romans were newcomers in northern France and had only just subdued the Morini, the Belgic tribe from whose territory the expedition was to start. It is evident that Cæsar had not their good will. Not knowing where to steer for a landing-place, he sent out an officer in a fast galley to make a reconnaissance. After four days this man returned with a report on a very limited stretch of coast, apparently that between Dover and Deal, with the latter recommended as a good landing beach.

The military force consisted of two legions, which might in practice amount to about 8000 men, and the auxiliary troops, light infantry and cavalry, were probably as many more; but in the outcome the cavalry failed to achieve the Channel crossing. The bulk of the troops went in 80 sailing transports, Gaulish ships, but apparently not like those used by the Veneti. The oared galleys carried the senior officers and their staffs. We have a faint clue to the size of the native Channel ships. A very rough calculation is alone possible, and it points to the accommodation of 150–200 troops per ship. Cæsar in one allusion backs this when he speaks of two ships carrying 300 soldiers. The expedition took no heavy baggage nor large food-stores, and we must picture the men as tightly packed for a passage of a few hours duration. The ship that emerges from these considerations must have had something like the capacity of 70 to 100 modern measurement tons. We know that she drew about four feet of water and that she had no oars; and that is about all we do know.

In late August or early September the expedition sailed by night and next morning was off the Dover cliffs. The cavalry, sailing at a different time, were foiled by the weather and returned to port. At Dover the Britons were assembled on the cliffs, and Cæsar saw that the place was unsuitable for a landing. When the tide ran fair he rounded the South Foreland and anchored off the shingle beach of Deal with relatively low ground behind it. The Britons followed the movement and were ready to resist the landing. The transports were taken in as close to the beach as they could go, in water whose depth allowed the armed men, with great

[1] So Cæsar tells us, although it is strange that his people had not learned this in the course of their prolonged campaign against the Veneti.

difficulty, to jump overboard and wade through the surf. They did not like the look of it and plainly hesitated. Then occurred the famous exploit of the standard-bearer of the Tenth Legion, who leapt into the sea with the eagle and struggled alone to the shore, calling on the legion not to see its emblem lost. The men followed and the beach was won. Fighting and negotiations with the British chiefs ensued, and Cæsar did not get far inland. The weather turned bad and the September equinox was approaching. On the night of full moon a strong wind blew from the east, and the tide rose high. The transports, close to the shore, dragged their anchors, were stranded, and smashed against one another. The galleys had already been hauled up the beach in apparent safety, but the high water and heavy seas damaged them also. There were no materials available for repair, and Cæsar was obliged to break up twelve of the worst damaged vessels and use their timber and metal-work to patch up the others. He then took the first opportunity of fine weather to sail safely back to the continent.

He had made a reconnaissance in force and had learned the requirements for a serious invasion. But it is evident that he still underestimated the difficulty of conquering Britain. He had seen and respected the fighting power of the Kentish Belgæ, but he thought that beyond them there were mere savages who would give little trouble. It is evident also that his geographical probings had not gone far enough to reveal the Wantsum channel between Thanet and the mainland. For there would have been the best landing-place for his next attempt, and the fact that he did not use it was to lead to the same shipping disaster as on the first occasion. One is struck by the inability of the Roman officers to get any useful information out of the natives, and by their lack of enterprise in surveying the coast on their own account.

Cæsar determined on an invasion for conquest in the year 54. Before he left for Italy in the winter of 55-4 he gave instructions for complete preparations. The sailing transports, the Channel merchantmen of the period, had not been satisfactory. He ordered the construction of a large fleet of new vessels to his own requirements. They were to be of a flatter and shallower model, with greater breadth, and they were to be provided with oars in addition to the sails. The Roman legions contained numbers of skilled craftsmen. Their campaigns involved much heavy timber work in fortifications and the bridging of rivers, and for river-crossings they also built boats. All such work was done by the legionary soldiers, in whose ranks there were undoubtedly woodmen, carpenters, smiths and shipwrights. Consequently, when Cæsar returned for the campaign of 54 he found over 600 new vessels constructed and the old ones repaired, yielding him a fleet of some 800 in all. This was achieved by an army of not more than 40,000 legionaries, not all of whom could be quartered in regions where shipbuilding was possible, in winter weather, with their own food to be collected, and with full military precautions to be maintained against hostile action in a country that was only superficially conquered. However much native labour was impressed, it was on all counts a wonderful achievement. Cæsar warmly praised his officers and men for the job they had done.

The invasion of 54 was by a fully equipped army, not a raiding force. There were five legions, 2000 Gaulish cavalry with transport for their horses, many other auxiliaries, a number of distinguished guests, chiefs of doubtful loyalty whom Cæsar did not think it wise to leave behind, a great quantity of heavy baggage, ballistic machines, foodstuffs and fortress material. About midsummer the expedition sailed at sunset from Portus Itius with a south-west breeze. In the morning it was apparent that the unpredictable tide had set the fleet eastward into the North Sea, so that the British coast appeared in the distance away on the port beam. The wind had dropped, and the men in the transports had to get out their oars and row hard. And so they all came to land about midday not far from the previous year's location, although perhaps a little to the north of it, since the account records that the shore was of soft sand. This track must have taken the fleet somewhere near the Goodwin Sand or the island that is supposed to have been its predecessor, but Cæsar says nothing of it.

The landing was unopposed although not unobserved. The local defenders saw that the great expedition was too big for them to tackle, and evacuated the coastal area, sending word to their kings in the interior. Although the Belgæ of Britain presumably

40

owned ships as did their brethren in Gaul, there was no attempt at
naval hindrance to these invasions, and there is no mention of
British shipping. Cæsar disembarked the whole force and set out
forthwith to seek the enemy, leaving the fleet at anchor and a camp
guard of ten cohorts on the beach. How those legionaries worked!
A crowded night passage, an eight-hours spell of heavy rowing, a
gigantic disembarkation fatigue and the construction of an en-
trenched camp, and immediately thereon a twelve-mile night march
in roadless country ; all in two nights and the intervening day.

For that was where Cæsar was in the morning, twelve miles
inland, when bad news reached him from the coast. He was
fighting his first action with the Kentish Belgæ, storming one of
their woodland strongholds, when word came that there had been
a great on-shore wind in the night which had driven the fleet with
much damage upon the beach. He halted the army and himself
went back, to find forty ships a total loss, and the rest stranded and
battered. He decided that every vessel of his huge armada must
be hauled up clear of the highest tides and the whole surrounded
by a great entrenchment. It took ten days to accomplish, and we
are left to imagine the labour it entailed, dragging hulls of possibly
a hundred tons measurement up a sloping beach with only the gear
brought in them and the traditional know-how of Mediterranean
centuries, the experience won of block and tackle, lever and wedge,
since the heroes of antiquity had sailed a thousand ships to Troy.

Then, leaving the skilled tradesmen of the legions to work at
the repairs, Cæsar went on with the campaign. We are concerned
here with the Channel and not with details of the inland proceedings.
He crossed the Medway and the Thames, and in modern Hertford-
shire fought the main strength of the Belgæ under their supreme
king Cassivelaunus. He knocked them about lustily, but there was
no point on which the conquest could rest, and the summer was
ending. He could not remain in Britain for the winter, with Gaul
too lightly held behind him. Cassivelaunus had also had enough
of it, and the result was a negotiated peace, with acknowledgement
of Roman overlordship, hostages and promise of tribute. Before
the dreaded equinox Cæsar launched his ships and sailed with many
prisoners back to Gaul, never to return. The tribute was not long

paid, and the overlordship was an empty phrase. But he had not altogether failed, as the long outcome was to prove.

III. THE ROMAN CHANNEL

A spontaneous development-process of north-European mankind had been interrupted. Pressure from the Teutonic and ultimately from the Slavonic peoples had pushed the half-Teutonic Belgæ into the Low Countries and northern France and across the Channel, where they had imposed themselves upon the earlier Celts of south-eastern Britain. They were already the ruling element for fifty miles north of the middle Thames and as far west as Hampshire and Wiltshire. It was a repetition of what had happened several times before in prehistory. Then in four years the Roman military power took possession of central and northern Gaul and undertook to stabilise the Rhine frontier against the Germans. Belgic Britain had been made forcibly aware of a new and formidable civilisation. Its reaction was to assert its independence, but it was also attracted by what it learned. In the century after Cæsar the British Belgic aristocracy consolidated its power under the house of Cassivelaunus, and developed its wealth and cross-Channel trade, a coinage on the Roman model, and a hankering after the ways of life of the great imperial power. There were intrigues and revolts among the chiefs and nobles, and exile of the unsuccessful to the continent, so that Cæsar's 'successors had much more information about Britain than he had possessed.

In that century there was talk in Rome of the mineral wealth and the surplus corn produced in Britain, and of the island's desirability as a conquest. But the Emperor Augustus had laid down a conservative policy on projects of expansion, and nothing was done until A.D. 43, the year after the death of Cunobelinus, the most powerful of the kings who followed Cassivelaunus. Then the Emperor Claudius decided on conquest, and his generals in Gaul made very competent preparations. Unlike Cæsar, they based themselves on a thoroughly romanised Gaul, which gave no anxiety at their rear or time-limit to their operations. They now had a fair idea of the map of south-eastern Britain, the Wantsum channel was well known, and very possibly a trading centre already existed on the site of London. In 43 Aulus Plautius led the invasion in three divisions, which are said to have landed at Lympne on the south side of the chalk promontory, at Dover on its salient, and at Richborough in the shelter of the Wantsum. Local historians claim that the Selsey and Chichester region in West Sussex was one of the landing-places, but of this there is no evidence and no inherent likelihood. In four years the Romans were in possession of lowland Britain, and they were to remain for four centuries.

What did the Romans do with the Channel coast? First, we must be clear on the meaning attached to that embracing phrase " the Romans." The orders were given and the great officers appointed by the imperial government in Rome, and its general policy was followed. The large majority of the persons who entered Britain in its service were not Romans in any national sense, although some had the status of Roman citizens. There was not from the outset any homogeneous racial infiltration. The legionary soldiers were of citizen status. In the early days they seem to have been recruited chiefly in northern Italy, where the people were mainly of Celtic stock. The legions which made the conquest remained as a sedentary garrison, generation after generation taking their wives from the people among whom they lived and being replaced by their sons in the service. After a century they were British legions under the Roman discipline. The more numerous auxiliary troops came from anywhere, Gaul, the Low Countries, the Rhineland, Spain, Illyria, the Levant. In the end they predominated, and were being recruited from the Teutonic Franks and Goths outside the imperial allegiance ; and so also were their commanding officers. But in any case the troops made little contribution to the southern British scene until the period of decline and fall, for they were stationed in the highland north and west. The civilian infiltration was important and equally inchoate. In the first years of the conquest merchants, slave-dealers, financiers, land agents, economic adventurers of all sorts and all races, flooded in. London, with its safe sea passage to Boulogne, sprouted as a mushroom city, like Kimberley or Johannesburg in the nineteenth century, in careless unfortified security for its first hectic years, until the insurgent Iceni wiped it out in massacre in 61. London soon grew again, but it grew within strong walls. There it remained, the economic capital, the principal meeting-place of Britain and the Continent, as cosmopolitan as the Empire itself.

There were three routes from the continent to London, all starting from Boulogne or Gesoriacum, probably Cæsar's Portus Itius. The shortest sea passage was direct to Dover, to be made with luck in a few hours. The Roman port of Dover was the small estuary of the river Dour in a cleft between the cliffs, now all silted up and built over. Here, once in, the shipping could lie in safety, although to make it in bad weather was a dangerous adventure. The twin lighthouses helped at night. But we must imagine Dover as a port for officials with state galleys at command, and rich business men pressed for time. Either class, with good horseflesh, could push rapidly to London. For merchandise Dover was unsuitable, since the land transport would add to the expense. Richborough or Rutupiæ, at the southern opening of the Wantsum Channel, was an alternative passenger port, at the end of a longer sea passage but with a much safer approach in the south-westerly weather that made Dover dangerous ; and here again there was a good road, opened in the days of the conquest, to Canterbury and on to London. For merchandise and all slow traffic the ships went through the Wantsum into the Thames estuary and up-river to the port of London.

It may seem that the Wantsum, cutting off the Thanet salient, is too much emphasised as a facility. It saved only a few miles in a voyage of many, but the mileage on the map was not the whole consideration. The North Foreland made an acute angle in the outer course, and a wind favourable for reaching it was likely to be adverse after passing it; and off the chalky promontory there was no safe anchorage in which to wait for a change. In the Wantsum the laden merchantmen could anchor in security, and there were good harbours at Richborough and Reculver, at either end of the channel.

There was another harbour, Portus Lemanis, the modern Lympne, on the southern side of the chalk mass running out to Dover and the South Foreland. It was formed by the issue of a river from the interior, and with progressive silting and the building up of shingle beaches it is now some way inland from the sea. The anchorage shifted down-river to become in Saxon times the port of Hythe.

It was during the Roman occupation that the first great reclamation of tidal marsh took place in the triangle between Hythe, Romney and Appledore. The later English word for this process was "inning," and it is convenient to use it throughout. The Roman inning of Romney Marsh was the largest single operation of its kind on the Channel coast. We have seen in the previous chapter that the cliff line formed by the great subsidence swept in an arc far inland of our present coast. A large area at the foot of it was only shallowly covered by the sea, leaving a string of low islands running as the chord of the arc from the high land at Hythe to the next high land of the modern coast towards Hastings. Shingle banks were piled up along this line by the eastward drift, interrupted by openings through which the tides poured in and out of the shallow lagoon within. The lagoon itself was only a phase in a succession of changes, for sand brought in suspension by the salt water and muddy sediment washed down by the rivers were deposited as an alluvium. The bottom of the lagoon was thus raised, although it could never be raised in this way above high-water level, and threading the alluvial flats were the courses of the tidal and river water.

This was the scene on which the old engineers set to work, an expanse of wet banks, above water at low tide and covered at high, with a range of twenty feet between the high and low-water levels. Their problem was to convert it into dry land, the reclaimed alluvium which produced excellent pasture. Along the open Channel coast they linked up the shingle banks into a wall composed of timber piles, tree branches, faggots and earth, the Dymchurch Wall that has stood in one form or another ever since. Its present form is of masonry and concrete, but it is essentially the wall the Romano-Britons made. Its seaward end rested on the island that was afterwards to form the site of New Romney. From this end they made another wall of the same material straight inland to the old erosion-coast at Appledore. This wall still exists, seventy to

eighty feet wide, not so high as it once was, but still standing up
markedly above the marsh, and on it runs the high-road from
Appledore to Romney. It has been called the Rhee Wall through the
centuries to this day. Having made the walls, the engineers had
still to get rid of the water enclosed within them. They dug
ditches to canalise it and made sluices through the walls. At low
tide the sluices were opened to drain the enclosure. At high tide
they were closed to keep out a new influx. The twenty-foot tidal
range was the key factor in the process. So in the course of years
Romney Marsh was drained. And there it is to-day, most of it
below high-water level, and still defended from the open Channel

The coast in Roman times from Thanet to the Isle of
reached by the highest tides.

by the miles of Dymchurch Wall. There is no written record of the doing of this work in the Roman period, although finds of coins and pottery within the area show that it could not have been post-Roman. Some have guessed that it was pre-Roman, but it seems unlikely.

A caution is necessary on the name Romney Marsh. Strictly used, it means the area above described, the triangle enclosed by the Dymchurch and Rhee Walls and the ancient coast. But it is sometimes loosely used to include also the greater marsh area westwards to the Hastings salient. All this was not inned until long after Roman times, neither was the work done in one big

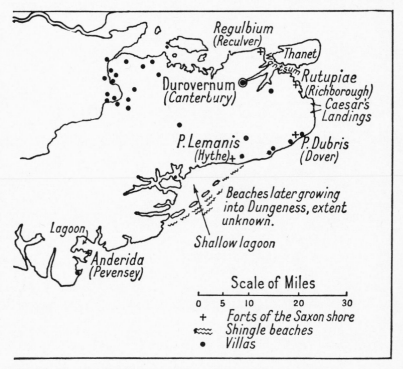

Wight. The coastline is intended to represent the contour
Some details are conjectural

47

operation, but piecemeal in successive centuries. These later western innings have all their separate names, and it confuses truth to include them under the designation of Romney Marsh.

Westwards down Channel some towns and seaports come into view in the early Roman period, although some were and others may have been in existence before it. There was a port at Selsey, but it was the older Selsey that is now beneath the sea. The Celtic people of the West Sussex coastal plain had a hill stronghold overlooking it on the Downs four miles north of present Chichester. This is close above Goodwood race-course, and the entrenchments are still plainly visible. The hill is now called The Trundle. Before the Roman invasion the inhabitants had made a new town on the plain near where the little River Lavant flows into the great submerged basin of Chichester Harbour. The new town of Chichester had thus a good fresh-water supply and was close to port facilities, at least for small craft. The Roman invaders found it as the capital of the Celtic coast kingdom, whose king Cogidubnus made instant submission to them and was allowed as their satellite to continue reigning over his " regnum." The word Regnum was loosely used as the name of the city, but its true name seems to have been Noviomagus. Under Roman rule it enclosed itself in walls, afterwards improved with bastions, whose bases still exist, with medieval fortification superimposed. Chichester was therefore a slightly pre-Roman port, and it has always since been a seaport, although never one of the first rank.

Portsmouth was geographically a more attractive harbour, but it apparently had no settlement in the early Roman period. At the head of Southampton Water there was the port of Clausentum on a peninsula bordered by a loop of the River Itchen inland from the dock area of modern Southampton. Poole was a likely place for a seaport, but we hear nothing of it at this time, nor do we of Portland or Weymouth as seaports, although traces of Roman occupation exist there. It must be remembered that there are no comprehensive geographical or economic surveys of Britain surviving from the Roman occupation, no administrative documents (with one unsatisfactory exception), and only incomplete mentions of political events. In seeking to reconstruct the truth the archæologist still dominates with his digging and his dating of coins and potsherds, as in the prehistoric ages ; and his enterprise is heavily restricted. Farther west down the coast the Roman influence grew thinner. Fine harbours were apparently unused ; we have no Roman Dartmouth, Plymouth, Fowey or Falmouth. Exeter was a Roman city. It has been described as the frontier outpost looking westward to the wild unsubdued uplands of Dartmoor and Cornwall; and Exeter was also a port, although we know little of the nature and extent of its trade. Topsham, its present outport, four miles down the Exe towards the sea, was also used for the trade of Roman Exeter.[1] The above conception of farther Devon and Cornwall as a Wild West must, however, be modified by the fact that tin was mined and exported, although by what ports and routes we do not know ; and that there are a few evidences of romanised residents. The Dumnonii appear to have lived in peaceful co-existence with the Roman power.

Behind the coast were towns, some of which had been tribal strongholds or capitals, especially in the parts dominated by the Belgæ. Roman rule utilised them and founded others as the administrative centres of districts and also as centres of attraction for the more influential Britons, tempted by the amenities of baths, forum, shops and amphitheatre, to be broken in to the Roman way of life. Canterbury (Durovernum) served this purpose in the Kentish interior and was also a traffic centre, no doubt with horses and vehicles obtainable, where the London-going roads from Lympne, Dover and Richborough converged. At Rochester (Durobrivæ) there was a small ferry-town where the London road crossed the Medway. The hinterland of the marsh coast to the westward and also of the Hastings cliff salient and the farther marshes between it and Beachy Head was the Weald, the Anderida Silva, between the lines of the North and South Downs ; and here the human settlement was scanty and there was no town, although there is evidence of Roman working of the iron deposits. Chichester was the town centre for the population of the West Sussex coast plain. North of Southampton Water was a peopled district where the Belgic intruders had founded a town as the successor to a hill

[1] W. G. Hoskins, *Devon*, London, 1954, pp. 37-8.

stronghold; and this, as Venta Belgarum, the Romans developed, the later city of Winchester. In Dorset again they developed Dorchester (Durnovaria) as the regional centre. Thence westward among the near-coast towns there is only Exeter.

But these towns, always to native minds a somewhat artificial and unnecessary excrescence of social life, do not complete the picture of the romanised Channel coast. The villas were the essence of the provincial civilisation. Landowners built themselves houses, some large some small, on their own estates; and there installed the civilised amenities of baths and central heating, plastered and decorated walls, glass windows, tiled and pictured floors, sculpture, and no doubt books and furniture of which all trace has perished. It has often been noted that after the Roman period it was not until the Victorian England of the nineteenth century that the middle and upper classes again began to enjoy such warmth and cleanliness in their dwellings. The villa was the nucleus of an agricultural estate which tended to concentrate the livestock and the working dependents close to the owner's mansion. Some large villas show evidence of production of corn for export, and of manufacture of woollen cloth. They are numerous along the south coast, but the distribution is uneven. Of the villa sites recorded in the Ordnance Survey Map of Roman Britain there are many in Kent, but none on or near the long stretch of coast between the two chalk salients of the Dover area and Beachy Head. This is the coastline of the Weald, the Anderida Silva then uncolonised and visited only by the iron miners. The West Sussex coastal Regnum was thickly settled, and on and south of a line from Beachy Head to Winchester some forty villa sites are known, together with five in the Isle of Wight. In Dorset and extreme East Devon there are ten, mostly near the coast. West of Exeter there are none. The villas constituted the wealth and enterprise of southern Britain. There were also in patches interspersed with them the more primitive Celtic villages dating from the pre-Belgic and pre-Roman period; and their inhabitants were adopting on their poor scale some of the Roman amenities.

Teutonic adventurers from the North Sea coast of Germany were soon taking stock of the British shores with plunder in their minds. Here in the south-east quarter of the province was attractive booty for the seamen of the hard-living coastline of Schleswig, Saxony and Frisia, and it was all undefended by forts or troops, for the garrisons were on the northern and western frontiers. There was Channel shipping indeed, most of it merchantmen carrying the booty, and the government vessels must have been mainly for transport since there had hitherto been no one for them to fight. It was a beautiful raiding area, like the Spanish Main to the Elizabethans, and as the second century merged into the third the raids of Saxon pirates grew prominent. All central Europe was under pressure, pressure of new racial movements from the East, pressure of populations with inadequate living space ; and the direction of outlet was westwards. The people on the North Sea coast of Germany lived in peculiar conditions, in a half-submerged belt of flat land, fringed by a string of surviving islands, not very fertile, compelling them to live mainly by fishing and the sea. They could not expand into the agricultural areas inland, and they must even have been dependent on them for shipbuilding timber such as did not grow on the sandy coastline. Necessity drove them to plunder the civilised West for such goods as were merchantable throughout uneasy Germany and the dim areas behind it.

In the third century the pirates became an increasing nuisance on the coast of southern Britain and northern Gaul. They were collectively known to their victims as the Saxons, but a great many of them must have been those later known as Frisians, from the islands fringing modern Germany and Holland. The imperial government stationed an armed fleet in the Channel, based on the continental as well as the British coasts. There are inscriptions naming the *Classis Britannica* and the *Classis Sambrica* or fleet of the Somme. Towards the close of the century their commanding officer Carausius, perceiving the strategic value of these fleets to his personal ambition, rebelled against Rome, seized control of Britain, proclaimed himself emperor, and carried on a successful career as an independent sovereign for several years, defending his position by means of his Channel fleet. It is the first occasion in history of sea power being used for the defence of the island. His defence was successful until he was murdered by one of his officers, who usurped his position. Meanwhile the legitimate Roman government was preparing a strong naval and military expedition in Gaul, which it launched in 296 against Allectus, the usurper. He lacked the ability of Carausius and was invaded, overrun and slain, and Britain was reunited to the Empire. The Carausius affair was not a patriotic revolt of the Britons. They were and had long been Romano-Britons, and had little national sentiment. Carausius himself was not one of them, but a Netherlander, and he succeeded because he governed well and cut off the flow of taxation to Rome. His professed aim was to become ruler of all the Empire, and in supporting him the Britons had no notion of separation from it.

All this did not solve the pirate problem, and most likely intensified it. The restored imperial government was obliged to take new measures. Their dating is uncertain, but it seems to have been about 300 and the following years that the system of defence known as the fortresses of the Saxon Shore took shape. It provided for the first time a series of fortified harbours and mobile garrisons to guard southern Britain against savage invaders. There were certainly ten of these fortresses, four of them north of the Thames [1] and six in Kent, Sussex and Hampshire, with a possible eleventh near Carisbrooke in the Isle of Wight. The whole was under the unified command of an officer known as the Count of the Saxon Shore. The scantiness of written evidence about Roman Britain is illustrated by the fact that the only list of the forts and of the troops in garrison is from a document of date 428, written when the system was in fact collapsing, although embodying information of the previous century. This certainly gives us the names of the forts, but apart from that almost everything we know of them is based on examination of their existing ruins above ground and on archæological digging and dating of the buried material within them. The list of 428 names the regiments in garrison, but says nothing of ships. But that there were fighting squadrons based on them is more than a guess, it is a certainty. Of the forts with which we are concerned, from the Wantsum round to the Solent, every one

---

[1] The four north of the Thames were at Branchester in Norfolk, Burgh Castle in Suffolk, Walton Castle in Suffolk (the site now entirely lost by erosion), and Bradwell in Essex.

was sited at the water's edge of a sheltered anchorage. The light troops mentioned, some of them cavalry, were no doubt for rapid strokes along the shore at raiders who might have landed for plunder; but that there were also squadrons of fast galleys for punishing the Saxons by sea admits of no doubt, especially after the career of Carausius. It is only the loss of all the written evidence about the system that has deprived us of direct knowledge.

Two of the forts, at Reculver and Richborough, were at the northern and southern ends of the Wantsum. Reculver is for the most part lost by the erosion of the low cliff on which it stood. It was placed on the western side of the Wantsum entrance, overlooking a secure anchorage just within. Richborough is more largely preserved. Only its eastern wall has entirely gone, again by the fall of low soft cliff. The sea may have caused this erosion, but it has since retreated far to the eastwards owing to the deposit of sand and silt on the shallow bottom. The causes are complex and hard to disentangle, probably complicated with the growth and shifting of the Goodwin Sands and changes in the tidal streams and the crooked course of the river Stour. Richborough, when built, was on a small island with an anchorage north-west of it within the Wantsum. It has been more closely searched by archæologists than any other of the forts, and much valuable evidence obtained. It should be noted that there was a port here, as there was at Reculver, before the fortress was erected about the beginning of the fourth century. The ports dated from the Roman conquest. So also did those of Dover and Lympne, the next Saxon Shore fortresses down the coast. There is now no trace above ground of the fortress at Dover, which has been covered by the later town; but it has been located on the south-western shore of what was then the Dour estuary, now dry ground. The walls at Lympne (Portus Lemanis) are still visible, although much broken and ruined by the slipping of the soil on which they stood. The modern name for the ruins is Stutfall Castle. These four stations are fairly close together, and between them they must have provided a naval force for watching the Narrow Seas.

But evidently they guaranteed no positive stopping of the Straits. For, a long way down Channel we find the great fortress then called Anderida, now Pevensey Castle.[1] It is placed on the seaboard of what was very sparsely settled country, with no town near and no Roman road leading inland. It was not a land defence, for there was little to defend, nor a commercial port, for there was no trade, but simply a naval station, with its garrison most likely intended to provide fighting men for its ships. Ten acres are enclosed within the walls, which still stand in parts 30 feet high and more than 12 feet thick, an eloquent testimony to the strength in which the Saxons were expected to appear in the Channel. Pevensey as built was on a low spit projecting eastwards to form one arm of Pevensey Bay, a broad tidal basin extending four miles inland, now all reclaimed and turned into sheep pasture, with the modern shore itself a mile to seaward of the castle. In later times the Normans built a taller stone castle inside one end of the great oval circuit of the Roman walls.

Portchester, to-day less damaged than any of the other forts, stands on the northern edge of the submergence that created Portsmouth harbour. It is not known that there was any previous port here, or that the site of modern Portsmouth was occupied. It is believed, but not conclusively proved, that Portchester was the Portus Adurni of the 428 list. As at Pevensey, the Normans built a castle within the Roman walls. Portchester provided a perfect anchorage for a galley fleet, and the natural conditions of shore and water have been less changed by the passage of sixteen hundred years than at any other of the fortress sites. The possible eleventh fort of the series has been revealed by excavation close to the river Medina at Carisbrooke in the Isle of Wight. It does not appear in the list, and its Roman name is unknown.

The massive nature of these defences shows how seriously the later emperors took their responsibility of protecting the province. It shows also the weight of the attack that they had to meet. In the fourth century the Saxons were already out for something more than smash-and-grab raiding. The defences justified their creators by yielding the province a century of survival. They were coupled

[1] It is possible that a natural harbour then existing at Hastings was fortified and used by the fleet. But erosion here has been very extensive, and all trace of the works (if any) has gone. On the surviving shore some trace of occupation has been found. Hastings may have been a signal station keeping a lookout to the sea.

with the Wall against the Picts in the North and the Welsh forts against the Scots from Ireland. Substantially these measures gave lowland Britain peace and prosperity for most of the fourth century. The villa civilisation reached its zenith in the south, with profitable export of corn to the Continent. The first breakdown occurred in 367, when Picts, Scots and Saxons all attacked together and broke through the defences into the rich south. It looks like a grand alliance of the barbarians; but whether it was pre-concerted or coincidental we can only guess, for we know nothing of the mentality of their chiefs or their capacity for widespread and forward planning. But they certainly did fall on simultaneously, and the Count of the Saxon Shore was killed in action in the south while his colleague the Duke of the Britains, the senior land commander, died fighting in the north. Next year 368 the Emperor Valentinian sent reinforcements, which landed at Richborough and systematically cleared the province.

All the defences were restored, but Roman Britain had lost something that it could not regain. Not only had devastation weakened its economy, but a precedent for successful invasion had been set. Britain deteriorated. Its polity slowly went down and lost cohesion, just as in the great subsidence the lost lands of northern Europe had been slowly overflown by the advancing sea, cut first into islands, and they in their turn sinking into mere shoals and sandbanks. In Britain the parallel is fairly exact, and in Europe too, for the Empire was going under like its outermost province. In Britain we used to date the end at 410, the so-called " departure of the Romans." We now know that date to have little significance. No " Romans " departed then, for the Romans were and had long been the Romano-Britons, the people of the province, who remained to endure their destiny. War-bands and marauders ranged the country, villa estates were broken up, slave-labour dispersed, the decaying towns abandoned, the Latin language lost among the Celtic peasantry, who could survive longest because capable of the lowest standards of living. It was very slow, a century and more, nearly two centuries, no one can assign fixed dates, for there is hardly any written record. Archæology, never so active as in our generation, is busily recovering the fragments, and almost yearly some preconception has to be modified, but the overall picture is far from coming clear. No one knows the detailed fate of the Channel coast civilisation or when the forts of the Saxon Shore were left empty of defenders. Of only one of them we hear the end, Anderida the most isolated, where the wealden forest ran out to the coastal lagoon. Anderida, by a tradition fixed long after into writing, fell to the Saxons by siege and massacre in 491. Of the others, nothing.

CHAPTER THREE

The Saxon Centuries

I. THE SAXON CONQUEST

THE EVENTS to consider in the first part of this chapter are important because they fixed upon the Channel coast the population which has there predominated ever since, broadly Anglo-Saxon from Kent to Hampshire, mixed Saxon and Celtic down Channel to the westward, almost pure Celtic in Cornwall. There is a real distinction between Saxon and Celt. It was naturally at its greatest in the period of invasion and conquest, a distinction of language, customs, religion, ethics and emotional temperament, vividly expressed in the writings of the Welsh priest Gildas in the sixth century, the Christian Celt who regarded "the heathen" as unclean beasts with whom no communication could be held save at the sword's point. The racial hatred did not altogether last, and in the period of settling down, after the conquest had reached its limits, there was a Saxon-Celtic fusion in a broad belt of the nearer West country which left no conscious memories of former difference. Only beyond the Tamar river did the Cornish Celt remain pure-bred and self-conscious, retaining his separate language for ten centuries and his view of the English as the foreigners beyond the frontier for much longer still. Only in our day is Cornish nationalism being overrun and conquered, with money and not with swords, by the swelling flood of detribalised people from no particular region, hotel-keepers, *rentiers*, holiday-makers, who constitute the amorphous society of modern England ; and the process is not yet complete.

We have seen something of the Romano-British Channel coast, thickly peopled and prosperous in Kent and again in West Sussex, with an almost unoccupied intervening gap in East Sussex, peopled and rich again in Hampshire and the Isle of Wight, less intensively so through Dorset to Exeter, and thence to Land's End peopled indeed but little romanised. The actual numbers of the population present a puzzle. Modern scholars, working on very faint statistical clues, have estimated the population of the entire province right out to the Welsh coast and the northern wall, at from half a million to one and a half millions, the latter figure being regarded as extreme. But when we consider what this population achieved, the support of some 50,000 troops, the massive masonry defences, some sort of naval service, the upkeep of the roads, the export of surplus corn and other things, and the high standard of living in the towns and villas, all without the fluid capital and mechanisation of industry known to our time, we are moved to wonder how so tiny a working force could have done it, however enslaved and regimented. One answers that average million of the estimates with a query. Perhaps the truth was two or three times as much.

However that may have been, Britain was a rich prize to the Teutons across the North Sea, first for portable booty, second as a good soil for settlement; and on the second ground they would have occupied it even had there been no Roman civilisation, just as the several waves of former migrants had done. As the fourth century merged into the fifth all Germany was on the move into the decaying Western Empire—Goths, Burgundians and Vandals, and Franks crossing the lower Rhine into northern France. Although probably in small numbers as compared with the inhabitants of the Roman provinces, they were moving as whole peoples, their women and families all included. With most of them there was a pretence of legitimacy in the process, for the distracted Roman government accepted them as allies and confederates and set them to fight one another where it could. Rome had long been recruiting barbarians into its armies, but this later movement was not like that. The incoming warriors were not organised into disciplined Roman regiments, but came in their own tribes under their own chiefs, who were in time to found dynasties ruling new kingdoms. It was all slow, much extended in time, with spasmodic advances and long halts, more than a century elapsing before anything like a new layout of political Europe appeared.

The men of coastal Germany moved with the rest, but they moved across the sea, for they were bred to it. In other respects their migration was different. The Teuton chiefs who entered by land were converts to Christianity, or became converts before they had proceeded far. They did not regard themselves as destroyers of the Empire but as prospective members of it. The continental barbarians looked kindly on the Empire, where they considered that a better time could be had by all than in primeval Germany. It was far otherwise with the Teutonic sea-goers. They were heathens without the slightest leaning towards the Christianity that was now the major religion of Britain. They had no respect for the existing province or desire to qualify as its citizens or to inhabit its towns or villas. They wanted first all the plunder it would yield, and then the soil itself, for use according to their own methods and social practices. Their German coast had always been remote from imperial influence, and their nearest contacts on the main continent were the Franks, the most barbarous and the last christianised of the land-invading Teutons.

We hear traditionally of three nations attacking Britain, the Angles, Saxons and Jutes. There is a distinction of place between the first two, since the Angles have been located in the Schleswig corner between Denmark and Germany, and the Saxons on the north-facing coast between Schleswig and the Netherlands; but otherwise they were broadly similar. The origin of the Jutes is mysterious. There is no early evidence that they came from northern Denmark, later named Jutland. Roman writers speak vaguely of tribes of Eudoces or Euthiones, without any certain location, but there is nothing to show that they were the invaders of Britain. After these invaders had settled in Kent two or three generations elapsed before they are found describing themselves as Jutes, and we do not know whence this title came. In some matters of law and land custom they differed from the Saxons and are thought to reflect Frankish influence. One suggestion is that they were a distinct tribe of unknown provenance who had resided in Frankish territory in the Netherlands. Another is that they were a war-band of mixed origins, most likely including Frisians from the Netherland coast. Their first leader Hengist appears to have been an Angle.

In the early fifth century Britain still survived intact as a recognisable Roman province, and was in better shape than Gaul across the Channel. Then, towards the mid-century, Pictish incursions grew again from the north, and bands of plunderers penetrated far southwards. Vortigern, a South Welsh prince who aimed at supreme sovereignty, made a bargain with Hengist, a rover from overseas, to supply a Teuton war-band and help in clearing the country. Hengist's price was possession of the Isle of Thanet, so it seems probable that his followers were not very numerous. The Picts were duly quashed, and fade out of the story, and Hengist's people occupied Thanet. Others came over to join them, and soon Thanet was insufficient for their needs. Hengist undertook the conquest of Kent, and after several years of sporadic fighting achieved it. His people, whoever they were, settled in as the Cantwaras, the Kentish Men, later the Jutes. His successor Oisc, who may not have been his son, founded the dynasty of Kentish kings. Kent contained four fortresses of the Saxon Shore with Romano-British towns adjacent to them, and two other towns, Canterbury and Rochester, and numerous villas with their estates. There is no record of the forcible capture of any of them, but the Romano-British owners disappeared. How and when is an untold story. The storming of such a stronghold as Richborough would have been a glorious victory likely to be long remembered in the traditions of the victors. There is not a hint of any such thing, neither does archæology find trace of it. Perhaps, with the decay of British government, the garrisons had been discontinued in all these strong places before ever Hengist appeared. We do not know what happened to London. Its history too is a blank.

While the Jutes were still fighting in Kent a body of Saxons distinct from them invaded the coastal plain of West Sussex. Here and up to the north-facing escarpment of the Downs the villa civilisation was thickly established and the area was probably one of the richest parts of the whole province. The Saxons, afterwards distinguished as the South Saxons, conquered it, not, it seems, in one rush but in an expansion that covered several years. The first party were said to have landed at Cymen's Ora, which may mean Selsey. Chichester was a fair-sized walled and bastioned town. How it fell, or whether it fell at all, are unknown. The alternatives are defence and storm, a non-fighting evacuation, or some co-existence of the Romano-British townsmen and the agricultural Saxons. If the last, it is probable that the town quickly died, for its people depended on its being the economic and administrative focus of a wide district—they still so depend to-day—while the more primitive Saxons wanted the land for subsistence-farming and had no use for a capital or a shopping and marketing centre.

The downland, not a single chain but a tumbled belt of hills, formed the northern zone of the new kingdom of Sussex. The down-land belt runs into the sea at Beachy Head, the coast plain narrowing to disappearance at Brighton. On the eastern side of the ridge running out to the promontory the wealden zone also found its border in the sea. From the foot of the ridge low ground sloped eastward into the tidal lagoon of Pevensey Bay, and on a very low spit projecting into the lagoon the Roman government had built, as we have seen, the fortress of Anderida. Evidently Anderida was an annoyance to the South Saxons. It may well have been if a fleet was still based on it, and in any case it prevented the Saxon king from extending his authority eastward along the wealden section of the coast, where the high ground around Hastings was at least worth having. Anyhow, in 491, according to the Anglo-Saxon Chronicle, King Aelle took Pevensey "and slew all that were therein." We can believe the fact, although we need not precisely accept the date, for the Chronicle was not written in its present form until the close of the ninth century, and the earlier entries represent the oral tradition of time long past. Whether those slain in Anderida included a still-existing regular garrison or whether they were just a concentration of fugitives we cannot say.

The South Saxons did ultimately colonise the Hastings district, although we do not know when. They also made a thin occupation of the Weald, not much for ploughing, but rather for wood-cutting and iron-smelting. The populous part of the kingdom lay between the northern edge of the Downs and the sea coast. On the map it does not look very large. But as to-day one stands on the crest above Amberley and looks northwards over what was the forested and swampy Weald and then southwards across the diminishing hills to the plain and the distant sea, one can understand what a tight little kingdom it was, compact, fertile, and defensible, strategically almost an island, where the Saxon way of life, co-operative agriculture, self-contained and needing neither trade nor towns, could work itself out in seclusion. The Sussex men, it is likely, were the most purely Saxon of them all, without British infusion, and slow to be touched by the new influences that were to sweep the whole country in the centuries to follow.

While the Saxons were creating their Sussex kingdom, the Jutes in Kent were finding themselves overcrowded, and some of them passed along the coast and invaded the Isle of Wight. It was, so far as archæological evidence indicates, a prosperous Romano-British island. How and exactly when the Jutes took possession are unrecorded. All that is known amounts to the fact that they were there when Anglo-Saxon records scantily begin in the late sixth century. A few of these Jutes also seated themselves on the northern shore of the Solent and around Southampton Water. They were thus the western neighbours of Sussex.

The small settlements already described, with others on the east coast, did not represent the whole of the Anglo-Saxon activities. Towards the end of the fifth century fighting bands of the invaders traversed all lowland Britain in search of plunder. They were not settlers but pirates. How great damage they did cannot be assessed, although it seems possible that they put an end to what remained of the villa estates and the effective life of the towns. Marauding bands probably did not storm fortified towns, but they ruined them none the less by destroying the economy of the countryside on which the town lived. The resistance concentrated in the highland west of the province, whose people, never so much romanised as in the lowland, became increasingly Celtic in language and outlook, the Welsh of modern history. These Christian Britons at length produced an administrator, Ambrosius Aurelianus, capable of welding them together, and a soldier, Artorius or Arthur, with a genius for the field of battle. Arthur won a culminating victory, a little before or after the year 500, at a place recorded as Mons Badonicus or Mount Badon. The site of Mount Badon has been disputed. Colonel A. H. Burne in his *Battlefields of England* gives good reasons for placing it at Liddington Hill, five miles south-east of Swindon. Arthur routed the raiding army so decisively that, we are told, the whole plundering process was stopped and the land had comparative peace for fifty years. Although all details are vague, we may regard the victory itself as an established fact. It is a parallel to the victory of Alfred over the Danish plundering army four centuries later. The result, in the earlier as in the later conflict, was that the invaders, having found that crime did not pay, withdrew to the eastern region where their colonies were already established, and devoted themselves to land settlement. It is however a little difficult to imagine that a defeat in the field, however bloody, had a deterrent effect lasting half a century. A likely contributory factor was that there was not much left to plunder in the British plain. The rich Romano-British upper-class life was gone. Only British peasants, clinging for subsistence to the soil that was their only possession, were left. This most likely accounts for the long interval, in which the eastern kingdoms consolidated and developed. When they had done so they resumed the advance, this time for land rather than booty.

The old songs of the Teutonic twilight, before the dawn of real history, ranted about Thor and Odin and the glory of long ships and bright-sworded heroes; but they were romantic minstrels' work for enjoyment in hours of ease. The men who conquered Britain did not sail with all that in their heads. They went to sea to escape the evils of not going; starvation through excess of numbers on the barren North Sea coast; oppression (meaning enslavement) by stronger powers in the German interior. The sea-raiders had their wives and children to feed. So long as it could be done by plunder, that was the simplest way. When plunder ran short, there was a better land than their own to settle and plough, and a peasantry they could oppress instead of remaining in Germany to be themselves oppressed. All this, admittedly, is deduction and inference. The old chronicle entries are in terms of military invasion. They say nothing of the wives and families and the colonisation which nevertheless took place. They give no clue to the length of the emigrating period, or how many people followed in the wake of the pioneers. It is all dark, and we are left to judge from the results.

In the southern England of the Channel coast, Wessex, the greatest of the Saxon colonies, took shape when the advance was resumed. The Chronicle says that Wessex was founded by Saxons landing on the coast and penetrating inland, northwards through the New Forest and Dorsetshire. The findings of archæology indicate very strongly that the kingdom of Wessex resulted partly from a Saxon invasion through the Wash and the Fenland rivers, advancing along the line of the Icknield Way to the upper Thames, and thence expanding southward. There is no reason why both these movements should not have taken place, the southern one founding a colony that afterwards joined up with the northern. The united West Saxons became a formidable power under King Ceawlin towards the close of the sixth century. In or about 577 he won a decisive victory over the highland Britons at Dyrham near Bath, and overran the country to the Severn estuary and the shore of Somerset. The Celts of the south-west were thus severed from the Welsh, with whom they never rejoined. Thenceforward Wessex had all the south-west as its field of expansion.

The results were as follows. In the century and a half after Dyrham the West Saxons developed a strong military power in excess of their ability to colonise. They did not eliminate the west-country Britons, but made them their vassals, chiefs as well as peasants. They evolved a system whereby tribute to the king enabled him to support a permanent war-band of professional soldiers. He could still in a crisis call out the fyrd, the men of the working population, but his small regular army greatly strengthened his position. His thanes or companions were the officers of a force always available for aggression or police work. In the latter half of the seventh century West Saxon rule extended along the Channel coast through Devon as far as the Tamar. Nationally the western people became a mixture of Saxon and Briton, with the Saxons in control and their language prevailing, everywhere short of Cornwall. Based upon this wide-spreading Wessex, the kings could react eastwards. They took over the Jutish settlements on the Solent and the Isle of Wight. They made the kings of Sussex and Kent their subordinates. By the end of the eighth century the word Wessex stood for everything south of the Thames. The Channel coast was the coast of Wessex.

II. THE ANGLO-SAXON CHANNEL COAST

Christianity was the official religion of the Roman Empire during most of the fourth century, and it was well established in Britain before the final troubles of the province set in. As Roman Britain perished and Celtic Britain survived in the west, the Celts became fervent Christians. The Saxon invaders did not. They were pagans when they came, and pagans they remained for more than a century after their establishment ; and when those of southern England became Christians they were converted, not by the Britons, but by a mission sent from Rome. This fact should be a deterrent to a now fashionable magnification of the British element in the resulting population of southern England. For wherever in the Empire Christian and pagan mixed on anything like equal terms, Christianity prevailed and paganism died out. The Franks, our nearest neighbours, are an example, adopting Christianity concurrently with their movement into France. The inference is that the British-Saxon intermingling was of slight effect. In this connection however, it is pertinent that we do not know whether in the fifth or sixth centuries Christianity did actually prevail among the Celts west of Exeter. We do know that the Welsh were Christians, and the Britons of the nearer west ; but the south-western peninsula was very isolated even in Roman times, and may not háve been much affected. There is evidence of Celtic Christian activity in the sixth century, but it was an evangelising activity,[1] which implies that the field was pagan. The great Cornish outburst of Christian fervour, which dots the map to-day with the names of Cornish saints, came largely through missionary work from Ireland, Wales and Brittany.

With Christian missions to the Anglo-Saxon heathen we enter at last the era of established dates. There is no doubt that the

---

[1] Hoskins, *Devon*, pp. 218–22.

Roman missionary Augustine arrived in Kent in 597, well-nigh the first undisputed date in the history of the Channel coast since the fourth century. Augustine landed at Ebbsfleet on the Thanet side of the Wantsum entrance and converted Ethelbert the Jutish King of Kent. The landing-place is a little curious. It may have been simply an accident of weather or some such factor, but it does carry a suggestion that Richborough was no longer the port of entry. Were the sands already banking to bar approach to it ? Was the town itself a deserted ruin ? It certainly enjoyed no future in the history of Kent. Ethelbert had a dwelling-house in the centre of Kent, close to the ruins of Roman Durovernum or Canterbury. He allotted this house to the missionary and his attendant monks. Among the ruins Augustine found those of a church of Roman times, and this he rebuilt as his cathedral, for he had been consecrated archbishop of the English. For his monks he built a modest house outside what was left of the town, and this grew and flourished as the monastery of Saint Augustine, a dominant house in later days. Augustine established a subordinate bishopric at Rochester and another in London, whatever its condition may then have been. The London site belonged to the East Saxons of Essex. In a few years they turned hostile, and the first London bishopric came to an end.

We are concerned only with the Christianising of the Channel coast, not with the great work of the Celtic missionaries in the north, and their resultant controversies with the Romans. Augustine's success was limited to Kent, whose Jutish people were in some ways, not all definable, different from the Saxons. Perhaps the distinction arose partly out of Kent's position on the best line of communication between England and the Continent, and the consequent prevalence of overseas trade and a money economy. That there was some continental influence we know from the fact that Ethelbert's wife was a Frankish princess. The Wealden coast to the west was still a dead area—its time was to come later, and the effective kingdom of Sussex began at Pevensey or even Beachy Head. The insulation of Sussex is evidenced by the fact that it was the last English kingdom in the whole country to be converted to Christianity, although Kent, the first, was separated from it only by thirty miles of desolate coast. Wilfrid, a notable churchman of the seventh century, began the conversion of Sussex in 681, working from Selsey. A few years later the Jutish Isle of Wight, not a separate kingdom, but a highly conservative region, also submitted to missionaries, and their work in outline was complete. Wessex had fallen to Christianity half a century earlier. Birinus, a monk from Rome, began work there in 635 and converted the king.

All these dates merely mark beginnings, for among the Anglo-Saxons it was a general rule that conversion began with the kings and nobles and spread downwards. Among the peoples there was a good deal of paganism surviving long after the missions had begun. The missionaries worked from a few monasteries established by favour of their royal converts. They made preaching tours through the countryside, with a great many baptisms and almost as many subsequent backslidings, for there was no organisation to maintain the convert's interest and gradually alter the pattern of his life. This came only with the parish, its church, and its resident priest. The parishes were developed in the centuries after the seventh, which was that of the pioneer conversions, and it was only then that Christianity as a way of life really possessed the country. But Saxon village church-building was fairly thorough in the end, and in southern England a great many of the parishes and church sites, although few of the now existing churches, date from the Saxon time.

We may regard the Anglo-Saxon Channel coast as complete by the middle of the ninth century, Christian from end to end, with monasteries increasing in numbers, half a dozen bishoprics, and parish churches arising in the villages ; the kings of Wessex supreme from Cornwall to Kent ; a few up-Channel fishing harbours changing slowly into ports with foreign trade, and a merchant class growing numerous enough to be recognised by law ; London regaining its place in the economic system ; and a sense of cohesion as a kingdom developing in time to withstand the strain that the Danish invasions were about to impose.

Westward from Dorset the population grew progressively thinner. Exeter was the only west-country port ; Dartmouth and Plymouth did not yet exist. In all their western territories the West

Saxons colonised less intensively than did their blood-brothers in the east, and their relations with the Britons were less exacerbated by passion and religion. There were fighting campaigns, but also a good deal of peaceful penetration and a substantial balance between the two nationalities. Exeter came under West Saxon rule about the end of the seventh century. Unlike the other Romano-British cities, it was occupied after the invaders had become Christians, and a mixed population seems to have co-existed within the walls. Going on westward, the Saxons found Devon very thinly peopled by the Britons, and the expansion consisted less in fighting than in the unopposed colonisation of a waste land in which there was plenty of room. Saxon ploughs could make prosperous village settlements on soils potentially rich but too heavy for more primitive cultivators to use. Left to themselves, the Celts had always been dwellers on bare uplands, and those of the west had not been intensively romanised. Conquest in Cornwall did not entail much colonisation, but rather the establishment of jurisdiction over the local chiefs.

Up Channel, developments were taking place which are dateless and unrecorded and known to us as facts only after they had been slowly accomplished. A population began to grow in the wealden region between the North and South Downs, and ports were founded on its coastline from Beachy Head to Romney Marsh. The Weald was by no means a uniform jungled swamp. It was diversified undulating country, most of it wooded, much of it good arable soil when cleared, and its swamps consisted in the courses of its rivers and brooks, which were obstacles to travel and transport but did not account for a great proportion of the area. The coastline was, from west to east, in three sections ; first Pevensey Bay, the tidal lagoon east of Beachy Head ; next the cliff coast of the moderately high ground behind and on either side of Hastings ; third, the tidal lagoons from the Hastings cliffs to the Rhee Wall and the nascent promontory of Dungeness. Into these lagoons flowed the rivers Brede and Rother, with estuaries of tidal marsh reaching far up into the land. In the period of conquest both Jutes and South Saxons neglected this wealden area and coast. Now, probably in the seventh, certainly in the eighth and ninth centuries, they began to occupy it.   Pevensey, if it had been left desert after Aelle's mas-sacre, became a port again, although never of the first rank.   The Hastings peninsula, for such it was as the coast ran then, many square miles of good hilly soil, was colonised, presumably by Sussex men, for the present boundary between Sussex and Kent lies a dozen miles east.   The seaport of Hastings,[1] sheltered like that of Dover, in the estuary of a little river in a depression between the cliffs, appeared as an entirely new foundation ;   for anything Roman that may once have been there had disappeared.   On an island or a peninsula on the seaward edge of the lagoon into which the Rother debouched the port of Winchelsea came into existence, and on other islands of the tidal marsh, Rye, Romney and Lydd. The last two belong to the mid-Saxon period.   Rye and Winchelsea are dateless but apparently later ;   they first appear in history in the late eleventh century and have become " the two ancient towns " in the twelfth, presenting us with a long-accomplished fact.   It may be thought that this proliferation of new seaports would have been hard pressed to find trade.   But trade and shipping were reviving, one might almost say booming, all over northern Europe as the debris of the Roman Empire was rebuilt into a new civilisation.

The Channel coast was not heavily attacked in the Danish in-vasions of the ninth century.   Wessex indeed was assailed and hard hit, and delivered by the genius of Alfred ;   but its invaders entered by land from east and north, having disembarked most of their forces on the North Sea coast of England.   Along the Channel coast there were raids and landings which did not amount to the deadly peril of the Great Army which came south across the Thames. There was never any Danish colonisation in southern England. Some of the so-called Danes were Norsemen, who had come by way of the Scottish islands to the Irish Sea.   They reached the Channel coast by rounding the Land's End.   Others were invaders coming down Channel from the east.   In practice their victims found no more distinction between them than there had been in earlier centuries between Angle and Saxon.   Their first raid on

[1] The name Hasting, that of a kindred, not of a topographical feature, is of an early type not bestowed after the seventh century.   The final " s " is a late addition to the name.

South Devon was in 851. Almost a generation later, in 876, they captured Exeter and wintered there, but in the following year Alfred rooted them out. More raids and landings took place in the Channel. Alfred created a naval force to counter them. His ships were built to be stronger than those of the Danes; but the Saxon chronicler gives an unintelligible account of them, and evidently did not understand the details himself. So we have to leave it at that, simply that Alfred's were the better ships. He enlisted Frisians to man them. This naval defence was not entirely successful in preventing raids on the coast. Probably it was too costly to keep a fleet always ready for enemies who came by surprise; for Wessex must have been desperately poor after the devastations committed by the Great Army which entered it by land.

For the greater part of the tenth century the Danish peril diminished, while Alfred's successors reacted against the Danelaw and compelled it to submit to them. This was the golden age of Saxon England, in prosperity, defence and much besides. The kings were rich enough to maintain a permanent fleet, and the disappointed Vikings transferred their efforts to the French side of the Channel. There they created a French Danelaw, the Duchy of Normandy, after forcing the Frankish king to recognise their settlement by a treaty made in 912. It is notable that it was the Norse element which gave its name to the new state.

In the last twenty years of the tenth century the troubles of England began again with the long unlucky reign of Ethelred the Redeless, the first incompetent king of Alfred's line. The story followed the earlier outline, first plundering raids, then invasion for conquest; and this time the conquest was carried out. In 981, 982 and 997 there were serious attacks on the Wessex coast. In the latter year the enemy came from the Irish Sea, began with Cornwall, and ravaged all the way up Channel to Kent. Four years later they attacked Exeter, failed to take it, but burnt everything in the countryside adjacent. In 1003 the Danish king Sweyn took and burnt Exeter in spite of its fortifications. We see here the function of a walled city in the Saxon period. Exeter, with its small population—as late as the Domesday survey it had only 1500 inhabitants—had not yet any great economic importance.

Its permanent manpower could hardly have defended the extent of the walls. But it served as a refuge against invasion. We must picture the country people of a large area crowding in, driving their victuals on the hoof, and manning the defences until the peril was past. The walled city of the eleventh century traces its descent, through the Roman towns and forts of the Saxon Shore, to the hill strongholds of the prehistoric Celts, entrenchments like those on the Sussex Downs and the great Maiden Castle near Dorchester. Alfred used this technique for defence when he founded the midland burghs on the borders of the Danelaw ; for they were not in origin trading towns. The Danes used it for offence when they were able to seize a strong place. They quartered themselves in it, and lived by plundering and foraging in an ever-widening circle until they had devastated a whole shire, and then they moved on to new fields.

One feature of Ethelred's Danish wars is of great interest as a new development in Kent after a silence of five hundred years. When that ill-doing king did succeed in collecting a fleet to oppose the Danes, he assembled it at Sandwich. It was a new port, built where the river Stour found outlet through the sandy flats two miles south-east of Richborough. But the sandy flats were new since the great days of Roman Rutupiæ, whose harbour was at the entrance of the Wantsum, into which the Stour debouched. The Wantsum was still open in the eleventh century, but it was evidently too much silted and choked to accommodate a fleet. The new Sandwich, in what had been open sea in Roman times, had taken its place, destined to be left behind in its turn as the vast sand accumulation pushed the water's edge ever eastwards. What caused all this sand to gather so suddenly ? For sudden it was in the scale of geographical time. No doubt the great Goodwin bank out in the sea had some connection with it. But we know nothing certainly of the origin of the Goodwin or its history. The story is that it was an island overwhelmed in the time of Earl Godwin, a generation after Ethelred. Perhaps it had been disintegrating and releasing sandy debris in the previous centuries. But there is no earlier record of such an island. Local tradition is apt to connect a well-known personal name with a similar name of a geographical feature, even though there may have been no connection in fact.

The last half-century of Saxon England was a time of political insecurity, minor civil war, and a breakdown of the morale of the ruling class, particularly noticeable in the twenty-four years reign of Edward the Confessor, which ended in 1066. Godwin, the ambitious half-English, half-Danish Earl of Wessex, who died in 1052, was responsible for much of the public deterioration. He left several sons, all of them able and some unscrupulous. Harold was the best of them, for he at least mingled patriotic feeling with his self-seeking. In the Channel the picture is of increasing traffic with the Continent and growth of the new up-Channel ports. England was becoming, more than it had ever been since the Roman period, a part of Europe, with Normandy, Flanders and Scandinavia as its especial contacts. The Channel shipping was not only mercantile but played a part in political action. Godwin used fleets from his Kentish and Sussex ports to back his insubordinate moves, and on one occasion to sail up the Thames and force his way into control of the government. The Confessor, son of Ethelred and a Norman princess, and in his early days himself a refugee in Normandy, favoured his overseas friends, and an ominous Norman influence grew up in England, with the house of Godwin as its opponents.

Down Channel, the advance of shipping is not so obvious. There was as yet no great contact with the French and Spanish coasts of the Bay of Biscay, none with Portugal or the Mediterranean. Exeter was the only notable west-country seaport and, to judge from its population, its economic importance cannot have been great. To describe Exeter as the only port does not mean that there were no boats or people in all the havens with which nature had endowed the coast. There must certainly have been fishing, and no doubt coastal trade in fish. When we first hear of it, somewhat later, " dried fish " had grown to be an article of export. It is impossible to believe that the men of Cornwall's Channel coast did not take the ample shoals of pilchards which in later times formed a principal part of their country's food supply. That in itself involved some trade, for it needed salt, which Cornwall did not produce.

CHAPTER FOUR

1066

IN THE explanation of matters of action two questions, why then? and why there? are generally found to need answer, and unless both are dealt with a true understanding of the event is prejudiced.

Why then? has been thoroughly answered in the numerous accounts of William the Conqueror's invasion, and since the answers are generally familiar they need not be recapitulated in this book. It is enough to say that William determined on invasion in 1066 and to take his reasons as known. Why there? on the other hand, has scarcely been posed. Why the Battle of Hastings, and not some other place on the south coast? There is no real answer in any standard history in the ninety years back from our day to Freeman's *Norman Conquest*. It seems to be assumed that Hastings would do as well as any other place on the coast facing Normandy and that there was no special reason for landing there; it just happened. But this is wide of the truth, and the Hastings landing was deliberate. William had an invasion plan which he prepared in advance and followed right up to the day of the battle; and then, the result of the battle being much more fortunate than he could have expected, the plan ceased to serve, and he went forward on another, which yielded a more speedy success than he had originally counted on. That is the story which the following pages will seek to make good.

First, the reader should know something of the direct evidence. It is of poor quality. It consists of poems and chronicles, mainly of Norman origin and some written long after the event, and of the pictorial record of the Bayeux Tapestry. There is, as one expects for this period, an absence of administrative documents, lists of ships, payrolls, victualling accounts, the trustworthy evidence which warrants positive statements. There is no narrative of the campaign known to have been written by an eye-witness, although it is possible that one of the chroniclers, William of Poitiers, was present. He does not claim to have been there, but he is known to have been appointed a chaplain of the Duke's. He probably had good opportunity of gaining information, but if so he cannot be said to have made the best use of it. The soldiers are entirely silent, for the fighter of those days was not a writer. The writers were the priests, and they in the course of their profession had formed a style that was emotional and rhetorical and did not produce a sober story based on sifted evidence. The writers who provide the account of 1066 were interested in individual personalities and moral judgments. They were sentimental and prejudiced, retailing the picturesque anecdote and the rumour of the camp, and not above embroidering and inventing should the moral lesson demand it ; and this approach diverted them from the hard facts which the historian would like to know. The Bayeux Tapestry stands by itself as the best of the primary authorities, for its pictorial nature compelled its designers to visualise some things that the writers have left vague. As far as it goes it tells an objective story that makes sense ; but its scope is very limited, and it leaves large fields untouched.

With such unsatisfactory material modern writers have striven to build a passage of true history. If one may be permitted a criticism, it is that some have taken their material too seriously, not admitting that a good deal of it is rubbish, and have left out of account some illuminating facts derivable from a wider survey, which have a considerable bearing on Duke William's undertaking. They tend to overlook the governing influence of geography—not indeed that of the battlefield, which they have studied intensively— but that of the Channel coast and its East Sussex sector as it stood nine centuries ago. Yet, in the present writer's opinion, a wide survey of the geographical situation of 1066 must form the setting for a true appreciation of what took place.

When Professor E. A. Freeman published the third volume of

his *Norman Conquest* in 1869 he set going a long bout of controversy on the handling of his subject, for in due course his critics found things wrong in his version of events. Freeman was not greatly addicted to seeking inspiration from the landscape, but he did have a look at the neighbourhood of Hastings. He saw it as it existed in the nineteenth century, and transferred the vision to the eleventh. For him Hastings suited William because it commanded the London road and " the great roads east and west." He might as well have added the South Eastern Railway, for the great roads east and west were as non-existent in 1066, and the London road was, in William's eyes at least, hardly worth " commanding." J. H. Round, whose hobby was the baiting of Freeman, had much to say of the errors of Freeman's battle. But Round's own preoccupation was mainly with the verbiage of the Norman scribes and not with the geography of Sussex. In 1892–4 Round, T. A. Archer and Miss Kate Norgate carried on a literary brawl about the Battle of Hastings in the *Contemporary Review* and the *Quarterly*, afterwards being moved on to the more secluded pages of the *English Historical*. So earnestly did they hurl those medieval poets at one another's heads that a principal subject of the row became the question whether the Saxons did or did not build a palisade in front of their lines ; and one of them, taking up an obscure phrase in a chronicle, suggested that it could have been made of cottage window-frames. Hilaire Belloc was an out-of-doors man with an eye for the meaning of landscape, but he had hobbies of his own to ride and so missed what might otherwise have occurred to him. One of them was to attribute to Frenchmen as many of the great deeds as possible, and therefore he considered that William must have been all French. You can see, says Belloc, from his figure in the Bayeux Tapestry, that William had the round bullet head and square shoulders of the Gaul and that his supposed Norse element is negligible. This led Belloc wrong, for it was in the Viking tradition that William planned his campaign. Another subject on which the controversialists strove vigorously was the name of the battlefield. The unlucky Freeman opted for Senlac and thereby incurred extensive sneers from Belloc. To Freeman, no doubt, Senlac had a good old Anglo-Saxon sound, and probably Belloc thought so too, and would not have it at any price. The name seems after all to be one of the less important features of the event.

All this was somewhat characteristic of the age of history-making that ended in 1914—Belloc's *Bayeux Tapestry* was published just as the Great War broke out. Since then the battle of the Battle of Hastings has quietened down, and recent historians have made their contributions without being manhandled. Sir Frank Stenton and Professor F. Barlow have given comprehensive and objective accounts of the events of the year, and Colonels A. H. Burne and C. H. Lemmon [1] two commonsense and convincing stories of what befell on the fatal field and day. But still the question remains, why that field?

Before passing to the geography, a very useful collection of the historical material may be noted. In 1909 Charles Dawson published his *History of Hastings Castle*, and as an appendix to the second volume he printed in English translation the relevant parts of the eleventh- and twelfth-century chronicles and poems which narrate the campaign of Hastings. Here the reader who cannot tackle the Old French of the period may see for himself the nature of the written evidence. Dawson has recently come under detective inquiry, with damaging results to his reputation, in the Case of the Piltdown Skull; but this revelation of his character does not detract from the value of his collection of authorities, since in this matter he had no reason to pervert the truth.

Just as the two great chalk ridges of the Downs run out into the sea at the South Foreland and Beachy Head respectively, so the Weald country between them pushes out a lower ridge, not of chalk but of clay and sandstone, which reaches the sea at the Fairlight cliffs east of Hastings. The Fairlight ridge runs through Battle in a direction east-south-east, somewhat obliquely to the main coastline. From its southern side it sends out spurs ending in minor cliffs, and between two of these spurs the estuary of a little river created the Saxon port of Hastings, now entirely obliterated by the cutting-back of the projecting cliffs and`the silting-up of the estuary, over which are built the main shopping streets of nineteenth-

[1] Burne, *Battlefields of England*; Lieutenant-Colonel C. H. Lemmon, *The Field of Hastings*, Budd & Gillat, St. Leonards, 1957.

century Hastings. The old Hastings was presumably an important place, since it became the senior member of the Cinque Ports and for a time contributed the largest contingent to their joint fleet.

But our main purpose is with what lies on either side of the Fairlight ridge and the Hastings coastline. We have already noticed the great tidal lagoon of Pevensey Bay. East of it comes a spur of

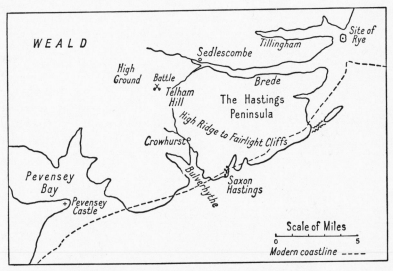

The Hastings coastline in the eleventh century.
The shore-lines are shown as at high water

higher ground on whose seaward face has arisen the modern town of Bexhill. Eastward again, between Bexhill and Hastings was a smaller tidal lagoon known as Bulverhythe, into which fell streams issuing from the main Fairlight ridge and its spurs. The largest of these streams, the Asten, rises close to the scene of the great battle. The former tidal area of Bulverhythe may be discerned to-day by the billiard-table smoothness of the grassland that has replaced it, through which runs the river between containing banks. The level reaches nearly as far north as Crowhurst, two miles from Battle. From the level on its eastern side the slopes are steep to the high ground of the main upland. A good point from which to survey the whole scene is the viaduct built at the opening of the present century to carry the branch railway from Crowhurst across Bulverhythe to Bexhill. Bulverhythe has long been reclaimed, its surface now lying below high-tide level and its waters passing through a sluice in the beachline to the sea. But the reclamation has taken place since the Conquest, and the haven was open for centuries after that event. Here we have established the south-western shore of the eleventh-century Hastings peninsula.

The northern shore was provided by the estuary of the river Brede, one confluent of which rises also close to Battle but flows off in the direction opposite to that of the Asten, the Battle ridge being the watershed. The Brede estuary merged in the sea between the present sites of Winchelsea and Rye. It led inland in a westerly direction keeping an average width of about half a mile for several miles until it narrowed to two hundred yards as it approached the site of the present village of Sedlescombe. It is now all reclaimed, but the tell-tale billiard-table flatness reveals the surface of the ancient mud banks up to and a little west of Sedlescombe bridge. The sea tides are said to have reached up to Sedlescombe as late as the sixteenth century. The Brede is now a fresh-water stream below the land level at that place, but it is kept low by the sluice arrangements at the outfall near Rye. Most of the Brede valley is still below the level of the highest tides.

These two lost geographical features, the Bulverhythe lagoon and the Brede estuary, made the Hastings region a peninsula. The neck, measured from sea-level to sea-level (at high water), from near Sedlescombe to near Crowhurst, was about four miles wide, the line of measurement passing close to Battle. But the effective isthmus for military purposes was much narrower, since the upper courses of the streams were swampy, and slopes descending to them steep. For the use of armies the only way into or out of the peninsula was by the trackway that ran along the Fairlight ridge from the sea to Battle and thence north-westward into the wooded country of the Weald. The passage was at its narrowest in the dip between Telham Hill and Battle Hill, where the swampy courses of the Asten and the Brede diverged from the watershed. Battle Hill

78

looked across the dip to the peninsula. Telham Hill was the defence of the peninsula against incursion from the Weald.

To complete the geographical picture we need to mention another and somewhat longer estuary, that of the Rother, which runs roughly east and west about five miles north of the Brede and parallel to it. The Rother was tidal from Rye well up to Bodiam, and certainly a broad swamp, if not tidal, as far west as Roberts-bridge. The Rother did not form a boundary of the Hastings peninsula, but was an obstacle to approaching it from any direction east of north. The Ordnance Map of Roman Britain (3rd edition) marks a Roman road from Rochester through Kent to a point north of the Rother, and thence probable though untraced to Hastings. One circumstance raises a doubt whether this road was in any useful condition in 1066 ; and it is that William after his victory did not use it. The road had very likely sunk to the status of a forest trackway, and may even have been as unknown to the Saxons as it was until recently to us.[1] The Weald must have contained a number of tracks and trails, for the simple reason that people lived in it.

Such being the geographical position on the English side of the Channel, we take up the question of William's purposes. First, we may state one thing which he did not mean to do. In going to Hastings he did not intend to make an immediate advance north-wards from that place to London. We can be quite sure of this, not only because he made no move for a fortnight after landing, but also because, even after gaining a decisive victory, he still did not go that way to London. Instead, he turned eastwards to Dover and thence towards the Thames by the good going along the high ground of the North Downs. It was a much longer way round. The direct northern way from Hastings was the track, whichever it may have been, by which Harold's Saxons had come from London. Any road through the Weald led through wooded undulating coun-try, with sharp little hills covered with thickets, and swampy bottoms that the passage of an army would not improve. William evidently did not find it attractive.

Even if we do not accept the statement of one authority that

[1] For this road see I. D. Margary, *Roman Roads in Britain*, London 1955, pp. 38–40.

William had himself made the journey to London in the reign of the Confessor, we can be sure that he was well informed of all the above. There were numerous Norman sympathisers in England, some Norman landowners, and much cross-Channel traffic. The Hastings district was included in the large manor of Rameslie which King Canute had granted to the Norman abbey of Fécamp, whose servants must have been regular visitors on the abbey's business. There were seamen in the Norman ports who knew the Sussex coastline in all its convolutions. Topographical information was amply available.

Another kind of information William also had, the inherited knowledge of what had taken place in the prolonged Scandinavian invasions of England and the ultimate conquest by Canute. No single battle had gained England at one stroke. With fight after fight up and down the country it had been the work of years, even against so poor an English leader as Ethelred the Redeless. Administration was so primitive, and a public economy so almost non-existent, that it was impossible to concentrate the fighting strength of the country into one campaign or upon one battlefield. To beat the English in one battle, therefore, had never been enough, for there was always another English army to come on. Canute's conquest had been the end of a long war of exhaustion. All this was known to a Norman chief of Viking stock, related and discussed since his boyhood, a passage of history which he knew intimately.

In the purely military aspect William had therefore a long war in prospect when he formed his plans. In his strategy he adopted the Viking practice, to land an army, seize a strong defensible position, send out parties to forage and ravage in a widening circle, with plenty of killing and the levy of harsh tribute on thane and peasant, beating the life out of a whole countryside ; and then to advance into a new one, and so forward. That had been Viking warfare in England, merciless and long drawn out. That was how William meant to begin his conquest, without any intention of a quick dash on London from his landing-place. The Hastings peninsula was the ideal invader's camp, fifty square miles of it, fit to feed him while he was settling in, fit to support the cattle he would collect from far afield, with a good seaport, and a narrow isthmus as the only means of access. There was nothing else on the whole coastline so good for his purpose.

There were other things in William's mind besides the traditional Viking outlook. In France the Normans had learnt much. Although pagan at the outset, they had become strong adherents of the Christian church, imbued with its ideas of authority, and realising how they served in the creation of a strong state. The reconstruction of Europe owed much to the Church, and all peoples were at one in the doctrine that to offend its principles was a deadly sin. William appealed to this feeling in skilful propaganda against Harold Godwinson. Harold, he said, was guilty of breaking a solemn oath, sworn on holy relics, to support the Norman claim to the English throne. The propaganda campaign worked on all levels, at Rome itself, where the Pope conferred his blessing and a consecrated banner ; among the barons, knights and men-at-arms of France ; and among the English, who were told that their king was a moral outcast doomed to disaster. William was an astute politician, for there was ground in England ready for this seed. The great men were jealous of Harold, one of themselves who had jumped above their heads. He was an earl's son, not a king's son, and they felt no natural loyalty. The mass of the people were more faithful to Harold, as a fine soldier who would defend their soil from the stranger ; but the past century had weakened the mystic quality of English kingship, and if he did not win immediate and continued success their support would be likely to weaken. This was a situation in which William could play politics with brilliant promise. It fitted with his use of Hastings as a camp of observation, a bridgehead from which, with harshness to the people and cajolement of the great, he might undercut Harold's position and soften up his realm to the point of collapse. The Viking war promised to be a long one. The politician's war held good hope of something shorter, in months perhaps instead of years. Not even William looked for an end in a matter of weeks. The Hastings camp did not promise that.

William's armament was not all Viking in its tactics, for it relied largely on the new cavalry arm of the European continent ; and the old Vikings, like the Anglo-Saxons, fought always on foot. But in another sense it did resemble the innumerable North-Teuton forces which had crossed the North Sea and sailed down the Channel since the Roman Empire had begun to weaken. For it was a war-band of the traditional constitution, not the new feudal turn-out of the Duchy of Normandy. In the feudal levy the tenants-in-chief led their vassals, as a legal obligation, to a service of limited duration, an arrangement suitable for home defence but not for adventuring overseas. There was nothing feudal about William's army. There were some great barons with him, but they seem to have been volunteers, serving not in discharge of an obligation but in quest of fortune for themselves. The same was true of all the rest, picked knights and men-at-arms, professional bowmen and slingers. It was an army of great quality but not of overwhelming numbers, like the war-bands of old; for like them it would have to cross the sea in a limited number of ships. The men were eager for a paying adventure. William recruited them not only from Normandy but from Brittany and central and north-eastern France. The common man may have served for pay, although of that we know nothing; the financial side is completely unrecorded. There may have been no cash transaction at all, for the barons and knights undoubtedly served for booty in the form of English estates, and the same motive may have acted in descending scope for all the soldiery. It was in the Viking tradition, an investment in violence.

Two things at least needed financial resource, ships and victuals. We know that William provided large numbers of the first, and we may infer that he made provision of the second; for he and his people would not have endured the disorder of a cosmopolitan force pillaging all over Normandy. Some of the ships were contributed by the great vassals, perhaps in lieu of their feudal obligation, and other supplies may also have been yielded.

The Bayeux Tapestry is our authority for the type of ship. Its authors seem to have taken pains to get their details right, and we may put some trust in them. Vessels with both oars and sails had been used for centuries in northern Europe. The authors of the Tapestry, however, show William's fleet as consisting of sailing vessels without any oars, save the single steering-oar over the starboard quarter, always employed before the invention of the hinged rudder. This exceptional delineation is good evidence that the Tapestry shows sailing vessels of deliberate purpose, because they were the ships used on this occasion ; if the designers had been careless about detail they might have shown oared ships.[1]

The ships are open and undecked, fit for beaching and therefore of light draught. They look as if they might have been about forty feet long, broad in the beam, and perhaps four feet deep in the water, elongated saucers with a very flat floor. Each had a single mast and a square sail on a yard. Their small size is further attested by the practice, as the Tapestry indicates, of unstepping the mast after beaching. The picture shows the seamen lifting the mast by heaving it up with their hands as the vessel lies on the beach, which could have been done only with a very light stick. These ships or open boats were specially built for a particular service, the conveyance of an army across the Channel. The Tapestry has a picture showing the timber-felling and building in progress. They had to carry the maximum number of men and horses, and probably for this reason oars were not used, since to work them would have taken up space that could not be spared. With the single sail and light draught these boats would not work to windward or perhaps even make good a course at right angles to the wind, for there would have been much leeway. A rough sea would have caused injury to the horses. The required conditions were a fair wind and not too much of it, and for these the expedition had to wait.

The number of William's ships is not established. Medieval writers had little sense of exact statement, and their figures are seldom to be trusted. Thus William of Jumiéges says there were three thousand ships, and Geoffrey Gaimer eleven thousand. Only Robert Wace gives us something with what may be a realistic check. He says he had heard his father told by another man that the ships were " seven hundred less four," or 696. If this number is wrong the truth is more likely to have been lower than higher.

[1] The only oared ship in the Tapestry is that which conveyed Harold to France in 1064. Its delineation make the absence of oars in the 1066 pictures the more certainly deliberate. Some of the vessels have what may be oar ports, but there is not the least sign that oars were actually carried. The latest and best edition of the Bayeux Tapestry is that edited by Sir Frank Stenton and six assistant editors for the Phaidon Press, London, 1957.

Allowing the 696, and allowing for some other factors, the baggage and stores and that perhaps a third of the men were mounted, we have some faint clue to the numbers of the army, although the possible reasoning can yield only the vaguest estimate. The Tapestry appears to indicate vessels that might, for a short passage, accommodate about forty men in addition to the crew. But a horse needed more transport space than a man, say five times as much. Thus the numbers transportable in the seven hundred ships would work out at something under 12,000 men and 4000 horses. In addition, some bulky baggage was shipped, including a timber castle taken in sections for erection at Hastings; and there must have been some victuals and fresh water. Thus 12,000 must be regarded as an outsize and rather improbable figure for the total of the army. Most modern historians tend, with reason, to put it lower.

William concentrated his expeditionary force at the mouth of the river Dives, on the Norman coast west of the Seine estuary. He had everything ready by the middle of August, but then he waited for a month. The chroniclers say that he was waiting for suitable weather, but there was certainly another reason.

In England Harold was aware of the peril and took measures to counteract it. As the summer advanced he called out the fyrd or militia of the southern counties and disposed them to guard the coast. He had also his house carls, the small regular army of the Saxon crown, than whom, by their foes' admission, there were no better troops in Europe, tough, disciplined, and wonderful marchers. It is a pity that we do not know their numbers. His first defence was his fleet. He concentrated near the Isle of Wight the ships from London and the south-eastern ports, ready to strike along the Sussex coast. The ships are unlikely to have been as numerous as William's, but they were unencumbered with horses and would have done something towards breaking up the expedition. In the next century the standard ship of the Cinque Ports was to be manned by a crew of twenty-one, which accords roughly with the capacity we have guessed for William's ships, of carrying forty passengers.

By late August there was a pause, the English ready for the invasion, the invasion not taking place. William knew how to wait. The main difficulty on either side was economic, the strain of victualling and possibly paying large forces doing nothing, and meanwhile the summer passed. For William it was a nice calculation, of postponement until the defence disintegrated, but not until the weather broke up. There were probably spies at work on either side. William at least had early news of what was happening in England. At the beginning of September Harold's seamen were near starvation, and he had nothing to give them save leave to depart. The ships dispersed eastwards along the coast and round to London. The men of the fyrd, with a neglected harvest behind them, had reached the limit of their service, and they also had to be allowed to disperse. There remained the house carls, for whom we can well see the king finding victuals when all others starved.

At that juncture, in mid-September, William put to sea. He sailed from the Dives, but he did not reach England. Instead he went into St: Valery on the French side of the Channel, farther up to the eastward, in the territory of his ally the Count of Ponthieu. Freeman says that he did this with the purpose of obtaining a shorter passage when he should cross to England. St. Valery is in fact about 60 miles from Hastings, while the Dives is about 100 miles. But it needed a preliminary voyage of a hundred miles thus to shorten the eventual passage by forty, which does not seem an attractive proposition ; for it must be remembered that for the crowded troops, and especially for the horses, a long passage in open boats was one of the crucial risks of the undertaking. Between the two French ports the coast projects, with Cap d'Antifer as its salient point. A wind which would have allowed William to round Cap d'Antifer from the Dives would have been a fair wind for sailing on to East Sussex. There can be little doubt that when he left the Dives he was bound for England. Then something went wrong after he had started, no doubt the wind veering too much to the westward. He could not make Sussex, and he gave the word to rendezvous at St. Valery. Before he reached it the weather had become bad. Ships were lost—we do not know how many, and the bodies of the drowned came ashore in such numbers that the Duke had them buried quietly in order not to depress the spirits of the army. It does not look as though this unlucky voyage was according to plan. If William had intended to go to St. Valery he could have sent the army round by land. However, there they were at St. Valery, with sixty miles to go, say twelve to fifteen hours sailing with a fair wind.

An independent event now intervened decisively in William's favour. About mid-September Harold had news that the King of Norway, Harold Hardrada, had landed with an army in Yorkshire. It was an invasion promoted and accompanied by Tostig, Harold Godwinson's mutinous brother, who had been expelled from his earldom of Northumbria. The Norsemen had defeated the northern earls, Morcar and Edwin, at Fulford outside York, and were negotiating for a settlement detrimental to Harold Godwinson. He was a man of speed and energy. He started northwards with the house carls and surprised the invaders at Stamford Bridge on 25th September. There he ruined them decisively in a battle in which Tostig and the Norse king were both killed, leaving the survivors to take their ships and sail home. Harold thus illustrated the long-established principle that it was not sufficient for invaders to win their first battle, since other English armies would then come forward to tackle them. But in so doing he had left the south coast open to William. Three days afterwards, on 27th September, William set sail from St. Valery, knowing that the Norsemen had landed, not knowing that they were already done for. He did not know in fact whether he had to conquer England from Harold the Englishman or Harold the Norseman. A camp of observation and a waiting game until the situation grew clear was more than ever his policy. The immediate aim was to get himself established on the English side of the Channel, and this he could now do without opposition.

The Norman fleet entered the wide basin of Pevensey Bay, and William placed a garrison in the Roman walls of Pevensey Castle. He landed the army on the eastern side of the bay and entered the undefended Hastings peninsula, occupying the town and moving many of the ships into its sheltered harbour. He threw up an earthen rampart on the hill overlooking the harbour from the east, and surmounted it with the timber walls brought from Normandy. The rampart and palisade constituted a Norman castle at that date —the massive stone keeps came later. And there he sat tight for

86

the next fortnight, and was prepared to sit for half a year. But he was not idle. He had strong parties out in the thinly peopled Weald foraging for corn and cattle, and displaying the heavy hand to impress on southern England that his mastery was formidable. Guy of Amiens wrote : " Your people, not getting much land, but obtaining peace, invade the country and devastate and burn it with fire ; and no wonder, because the foolish people refused you as their king, they therefore perished utterly and were annihilated." This passage, and more to the same effect, relates to the period after the landing and before the battle. William lost no time, either, in opening the political offensive. An envoy went northwards to remonstrate with Harold for seizing the throne, and to set forth William's right. The arguments were designed to appeal to Harold's people, since it was plainly futile to appeal to Harold himself. Their invocation of divine displeasure upon Harold as an oath-breaker had some effect in shaking faith in his fortune ; for Gyrth, his younger brother, asked to be given the command of the army, saying that he had broken no oath. If this could result from the first breath of the political war, we can imagine the rot that might have set in if Harold had postponed the day of battle. This envoy probably met the Saxon chiefs in London.

A local thane who saw the landing rode northwards to warn Harold. The English king acted instantly and by some almost incredible feats of marching brought the house carls from York to London, and thence through the Weald to the gate of the Hastings peninsula. He sent out orders for the fyrd to assemble and join him. When he reached Battle [1] on the afternoon of 13th October an unknown number of them had done so, and others were on the way. All the numbers are unknown, of Saxons and Normans alike. If William's army had originally been of 12,000 men, a very liberal estimate, it had been reduced before it fought. Some had been drowned on the passage to St. Valery, a garrison had been left at Pevensey, and another undoubtedly in the castle at Hastings. Some Normans had also been lost at an unknown date at Romney, for, when passing that way after his victory, William took vengeance on the townsfolk for having slain his men who had landed there by mistake.

[1] There was no village then, and the site was uninhabited.

Colonel Burne estimates that 9000 was the probable strength of William's army in the actual battle. The Saxons were not substantially more numerous, and may have been less. On the fortune of such small forces, it might seem, turned the future history of England. Really, it was not on their fortune, but on that of three individual men—or perhaps four.

Harold halted his men that October evening on the hill where Battle Abbey now stands, facing south-eastward across a valley towards Telham Hill. Harold, having lost his kingdom and his life, has ever since been criticised for rashness in thus trailing his coat before the Normans ; the loser is always wrong. He took a risk, as did his adversary, the risk of battle. If he had held off, his army might have grown stronger in numbers but weaker in spirit. For William's political offensive was a deadly threat to a nine-month king with a smirched character and a half-disloyal aristocracy, a threat that would grow daily. The northern earls had been inclined to make a bargain with Harold Hardrada before Stamford Bridge. They were quite likely to make one with William, a much more able diplomatist. Time was on William's side. There would have been parleys, plausible arguments delivered in open council, insidious speeches by smooth ecclesiastical envoys deploring the war and the effusion of blood, with the pitiless ravaging of Sussex to point the moral. To all men in that year it seemed that William would be simply another king, another Canute from overseas : none imagined that he would be a new sort of king, who would uproot the existing society. Harold had to fight without delay. And about the battle of Hastings itself there was no foregone conclusion. It was anybody's victory until the closing hour.

William was in Hastings when his patrols and foragers fell back on the peninsula and told him that the Saxons were coming. The chroniclers allow it to be thought that his army was in Hastings too, but we must remember that when these lyrical gentlemen spoke of the army they had really in mind the Duke himself and the great few who surrounded him. Their confused narratives are not indeed positive on the point. The geographical situation makes it highly probable that a substantial force was already holding Telham Hill, the gate of the peninsula. On the morning of the 14th William decided to fight that day, for time had gone over to Harold's side, and delay would make the Normans grow hungry.

At dawn he rode up to the front—about seven miles—and was ready to begin at nine o'clock. No one has denounced him for rashness, because he lived and won. But if he had been killed in any of that day's combats he too would now be set down as brave but foolhardy, and there would be a romantic sigh for the gallant Normans making their last stand about the castle and the port, and the few survivors taking ship for France.

The facts and deductions set forth in this chapter have seldom been jointly considered. The battle itself has been fully and variously described in many books. It is the best known medieval battle in English history, doubtful though the interpretation of many of its incidents may be. There will be no attempt to re-tell it here or to paraphrase the two excellent recent accounts that have already been cited.

Of its significance there is something to be said. The fate of England was decided not by the defeat of the Saxon army but by the extinction of the house of Godwin. Harold's two surviving brothers, Gyrth and Leofwine, were killed with him. He seems to have had illegitimate children, but they were too young to be of any account. Gyrth was a young man of great promise, loyal and active. Of Leofwine we know little. After them there was no one left to bring on the other English armies which, in the light of previous history, might still have driven the diminished Normans into the sea. Fulford in the north had been retrieved by Stamford Bridge. Hastings in the south was followed by no other effort. To lead it there was not one man of high rank who combined courage, talent and public spirit. They shifted and shirked and acquiesced. So it fell out that Hastings was unique among the battles of invasion, in that by itself it decided that the invasion should succeed.

William had no need to stay in Hastings. The waiting policy had served its turn. In five days he was on the move. He took no chances with the Weald, a bad country for mounted knights and probably holding many Saxons. He turned east, skirting the great tidal lagoon into which the Brede and Rother debouched, to

Romney and thence to Dover. From Dover he went north-westward to London. It was not ripe to submit, and he did not seek to force a crossing of the river. It was all politics now, and he did not wish to provoke another battle. After Hastings he could not have had with him much more than half of the army that had sailed from St. Valery. He turned westwards and then down into Hampshire, where he secured Winchester and the royal treasury; then northwards again across the Thames at Wallingford and on to Berkhamstead. All these marches left a trail of devastation and showed that there was no one, not even Morcar the Earl of Northumbria or Edwin Earl of Mercia, with the heart to raise an army against him. The two earls were in London deliberating with the bishops and the citizens. Their talk ended in nothing, and at Berkhamstead they came to make submission. William was in London without a fight before the year's end.

CHAPTER FIVE

The Cinque Ports

I. ORIGIN OF THE CONFEDERATION

THE ACTIVE history of the Cinque Ports as an organ of national importance lies within the three centuries after the Norman conquest. At a time when the shipping produced by the coasts of Sussex and Kent ranked as the first-class shipping of the period, the Crown applied the feudal principle to sea service. It granted to the ports of the up-Channel coastline rights, privileges and immunities in return for the service of specified numbers of ships and seamen to be furnished by the contracting towns, acting at first individually and afterwards jointly as a confederation. The ports throve upon their privileged position. The Crown was sure of sea service quickly available at a predictable strength to defend the coast and to maintain its communications with its territories in France. The latter was undoubtedly the prime consideration, for after the conquest the territories of the Crown were on either side of the Channel, which had to function as a bridge rather than a barrier between England and France.

The conditions changed. Less than a century after the Conquest Henry II married Eleanor the heiress of Aquitaine, and the wine-growing region of south-western France with the great wine-shipping seaport of Bordeaux came into his possession. Half a century after that his son John lost Normandy to the King of France. The emphasis upon communications shifted down Channel, to the western seaports which had never hitherto been prominent. The longer passage needed larger ships, decked ships to keep the sea for weeks instead of days, in place of the open boats in which men dodged bad weather for the short voyage across the upper

Channel. These larger ships were not freely able to use the shallow havens of the Cinque Ports, whose native shipping thus sank from the first to the second class. The loss of Normandy did indeed bring forward the motive of defence of the coastline against a France that had not before been hostile. But it was a local defence ; for the Anglo-French wars ranged all over the Channel and the Bay of Biscay and involved principally the greater ships of the growing western ports. If Chaucer had lived a hundred years earlier he might have made his typical English shipmaster a man of Rye or Winchelsea, but in the fourteenth century he described him as a west-countryman of Dartmouth. Side by side with the contract fleet of the Cinque Ports, the Crown developed a navy completely of its own, a sporadic growth, it is true, and not consistently maintained ; but we do hear of galleys belonging to King John at Southampton, and a Clerk of the Ships to supervise them ; an ominous portent to the future of the up-Channel ports.

But most of all it was geography that determined the history of the Cinque Ports. They came into being at a certain stage in the evolution of the coastline. Geographical change then supervened at a very rapid rate, and, for the most part, it killed them. In the eleventh century the coastline was deeply indented, and the ships were small. By the sixteenth century the inlets and the havens had filled up and the coast was almost as smooth as it is to-day. Sandwich almost choked, Dover striving desperately to keep its entrance open, Rye available only for small craft, Hythe, Romney and Winchelsea completely closed by obstructions, Hastings obliterated (as a port) by erosion. Five hundred years saw their zenith and then their long-drawn decline. What we see now is, of some the fascinating, still beautiful remnants, of others, the ugly things that cover them, as in a palimpsest an illiterate scrawl might cover a once fine script.

About the origin of the confederation the finding of historians has changed. It was formerly thought that the whole structure was created at one stroke by Edward the Confessor, before the Conquest. This belief rested on the phrasing of a charter issued more than two hundred years later by Edward I, in which it was formally recorded that he had inspected and now confirmed the grants of his predecessors, going back to that of the Confessor. Here it seemed was evidence that the Saxon king's charter to the whole confederation had indubitably been granted, although now it does not exist. The more modern view is that it never did exist, that there was no pre-Conquest confederation, and that Edward I's "*inspeximus*" was only a conventional phrase, not to be taken literally. No doubt the Portsmen, negotiating with the chancery of the Plantagenet king, did claim that their privileges went back to the Confessor, but they could not have produced his charter for inspection. The run of the known facts does not permit of it.

The Domesday survey in 1087 shows that Dover, Sandwich and Romney had certain privileges, varying in each case, on account of rendering sea services to the Crown. It does not mention Hastings or Hythe. Among the services, Dover undertook to convey a messenger of the King across the Channel for twopence in summer and threepence in winter. Thus by the end of the Conqueror's reign the Crown had separate contracts with three ports of the Five who were to be the founder-members of the confederation. Rye and Winchelsea had not yet attained the same importance. Neither is mentioned in Domesday, but there is an un-named " new burgh " in the region, which may be Rye. That town was a recognised borough in the middle of the following century. Of Winchelsea—the Old Winchelsea on the now lost island—there is likewise no clear mention until 1130; although the King, returning from Normandy in 1067, landed at " *Vincenesium*," which might be Winchelsea.

It is in the reign of Henry II, a hundred years after the Conquest, that the Cinque Ports begin to be described under that collective name.[1] Their contracts with the Crown were still individual, not collective, but they began to take certain common action, such as sending representatives to an annual court at Shepway to watch over the functioning of the privileges. Hence arose a customary law of the Cinque Ports, at first spontaneous, later confirmed by

[1] K. M. E. Murray, *Constitutional History of the Cinque Ports*, Manchester, 1935. The author shows that the Confederation in its essentials took shape under Henry II.

authority, the germ of the recognised confederation. From the outset each of the Five admitted minor havens to a share in their privileges on condition of contributing to the quota of men and ships. The minor members were known as limbs. Ultimately there were thirty-two of them. One, Seaford, a limb of Hastings, lay west of Beachy Head. Another, Brightlingsea, a limb of Sandwich, was on the Essex shore of the Thames estuary. All the others were in East Sussex and Kent. Rye and Winchelsea were originally limbs of Hastings, but rapidly flourished until they were able to take senior rank. In 1206 King John issued six charters, varying in detail, one each to the original Five, and one jointly to Rye and Winchelsea, which had to supply two ships between them to make up the total of twenty due from Hastings.

In and after the middle of the thirteenth century, by charters of Henry III and Edward I the Cinque Ports and the Two Ancient Towns (Rye and Winchelsea) were fully recognised as a confederation having some of the legal position of a shire of the realm. The combined ship service was of 57 vessels each with a crew of 21, the evolved legal customs were consolidated into a code administered by the Court of Shepway and not subject to the King's judges, and the very considerable exemptions from the payment of dues throughout the King's dominions were declared common to all. The whole is summed up and rounded off in the great charter of Edward I in 1278. By this time Rye and Winchelsea were on a complete equality with the old Five. Winchelsea in fact was now richer and more populous than its former patron of Hastings.

The military aspect of the Ports' duties, especially prominent after the loss of Normandy, necessitated a commander-in-chief. Dover Castle was the greatest military stronghold on the Ports' coastline, and its Constable was inevitably an important servant of the Crown. The Constable of Dover Castle thus became gradually identified with the commander and administrator of the Ports' sea service, under the title of Lord Warden of the Cinque Ports. The arrangement was long in evolving, and became solidified only in the mid-thirteenth century. The great Hubert de Burgh, Constable of Dover Castle in the troubled time after John's death, is held to have been the first effective Lord Warden, although he did not formally hold the title.[1]

II. INFLUENCE OF GEOGRAPHY ON HISTORY

This constitutional summary has been necessary. We may now leave charters and seek material of another kind in the open air, the towns themselves, the cliffs, marshes and beaches, and what the winds and the sea did to them, the living record spread before the eye. It is best to work up Channel with the south-west wind and the eastward drift.

First, some West Sussex harbours may here be noted which did not belong to the Cinque Ports system. Chichester, like its Hampshire neighbours Langstone and Portsmouth, is an excellent example of the effect produced by the neolithic subsidence in the flooding of a basin of low-lying land by the advancing sea. It consists of four distinct flooded depressions, with intervening tongues of slightly higher ground, all diverging from one entrance from the main sea. This was simply the accident of the run of the contour line which the sea-level reached in the subsidence. The single main entrance, and the shores on either side of it, have been modified by wave action, although this has been mitigated by the shelter afforded by the Isle of Wight against the full force of south-westerly gales. But, once inside, the outlines of the firm ground and the ramifying channels have been little changed, and the ordnance map of to-day would probably need little alteration to conform with a similar survey that might have been made at the time of the Norman conquest.

Numerous small streams flowing from the chalk downs a few miles inland provide the excess of outflow over tidal inflow needed to keep the channels scoured. Silt, covered at high tides, edges the channels; and the equilibrium between silting and scouring depends on the flow of the rivulets of fresh water. The growth of population

---

[1] A succinct account of the constitutional developments is given by F. W. Brooks, *The Cinque Ports*, in *The Mariner's Mirror*, Vol. XV, No. 2 (April 1929). But it should be compared with K. M. Murray already cited.

in all this area is causing the fresh water to be tapped off from its sources in the chalk and used in various ways that lead to its ultimate loss by evaporation, and this may in time so diminish the outfall into the harbour as to result in further silting ; but up to the present the change is not seriously evident.

The town of Chichester appears not to have been a markedly active port in the period we are dealing with. It probably owed its rise in importance after its post-Roman eclipse rather to the transfer of the bishop's see from Selsey in 1075. Bosham, a much smaller place at the head of another channel of the harbour, has received more historical mention because great persons were connected with it. Its church was one of the earliest built in Sussex, and has been claimed to be superimposed on a building of the Roman period. The late Professor R. G. Collingwood told the present writer that he did not think there was any good evidence of a Roman Bosham, and that the Roman bricks interspersed in the masonry of the Saxon church tower were probably included in material brought from Chichester for its construction. Medieval Bosham appears to have been a flourishing small-trading and fishing port. Canute had a residence there, and his young daughter is said to have been drowned in the creek. Edward I knew the story long afterwards and placed a memorial to the child in the chancel of the church. In the nineteenth century, when the floor of the nave was lifted, a stone coffin containing the bones of a girl was discovered. Harold sailed from Bosham in 1064 on the visit to Normandy that resulted in the oath to assist the Duke to the English throne.

The old port of Selsey has long gone under the advancing sea, and the present village on the tip of the Bill has no harbour. An Elizabethan map [1] shows Selsey as very nearly an island, with a long flooded depression almost cutting it off from the mainland. The depression is now reclaimed, but its position is easily recognised. Pagham harbour, just east of the Bill, consisted of a small flooded basin. In more modern times the shingle beaches drifted across the entrance, and its trade was not enough to warrant the expense of keeping it open. The basin was therefore reclaimed and converted to pasture. At the beginning of the present century storm-waves

[1] British Museum Map Room, photostats of maps at Hatfield House, Vol. II.

broke through the beach and again flooded the basin, which has since been derelict.

Going east, the first considerable Sussex river is the Arun, which cut its valley southwards through the Downs in the far distant age when the Weald was an uplifted area above the level of the present chalk ridge. In its natural state the Arun had a wide tidal estuary, and on rising ground on its western edge there grew the port of Arundel, approached from the sea through a channel amid the maze of silt-banks that filled the estuary. Arundel was a quiet little port for the local trade of the countryside, open until quite recent times for small sea-going vessels.

The Arun estuary has been inned by the land-owning interest, and converted into a wide pasture, all below sea-level, through which the river winds between enclosing banks. Littlehampton at its mouth now does the port business. The next eastward port, Shoreham, is at the mouth of the River Adur, which cuts through the high ground much closer to the sea, and thus has a narrower coastal plain to traverse. The name Adur dates from the seventeenth century, the result of an antiquarian guess that Bramber Castle was identical with Portus Adurni. The river's early name was the Bremer or Bremre. The outfall is of the type which the growing shingle banks push eastward until some breach occurs and the river again finds exit at the starting-point of the process. In modern times the alternation has been stopped by the construction of jetties to keep the entrance steady in one place.

With the outflow of the Sussex Ouse we come to the first Cinque Port, Seaford, a limb of Hastings. The connection of Seaford and the Ouse is not apparent to-day, neither is there any harbour at Seaford. In medieval times it was made a port by the deflection eastward of the river mouth, which was pushed as far as Seaford by a long shingle beach accumulating between the river and the open sea. The river itself led inland through its gap in the Downs to Lewes, with tidal marsh along its course, spreading wider as it approached the town. The present high road from Seaford to Lewes follows fairly closely the eastern border of the former marsh, now inned and reclaimed. Seaford ceased to be a port, probably in the fifteenth century, when the usual thing happened to the deflected river-mouth and the outflow burst a new and direct opening two miles back to the westward. This became the port of Newhaven, since stabilised by artificial works. Newhaven was only struggling into existence in the Tudor period, when its name was scarcely known to topography. In Henry VIII's time an Englishman speaking of the New Haven did not mean the English port at all, but the new seaport of Le Havre at the mouth of the Seine, founded by Francis I.

When the Weald was gradually cleared and peopled, Pevensey, as we have seen, became the port for that part of it that lay close east of Beachy Head. As one goes eastward along the Sussex coast the tidal range increases, the difference between low and high water level being about fourteen feet at Chichester and rising to twenty-two feet at Hastings. These are the figures of ordinary spring tides, but the rise may be two or three feet more on exceptional occasions. The effect of the big tidal range was to create the wide-spreading tidal lagoons on the low-lying parts of the coast, covered by the sea at high water, an expanse of mud banks with intersecting channels at low. The original Pevensey Bay was one of the largest of the lagoons, fringed to seaward by shingle beaches spread out by the eastward drift.

Four main factors attacked the permanence of these lagoons, two natural and two of human agency. First, silting tended to raise the mudbanks nearly to high-water level, the silt consisting of mud washed down by streams from the interior and of fine matter carried in suspension by the tide water and precipitated in the lagoon. Second, the shingle beaches tended to increase until they obstructed the entry of tide water and its free exit as a scouring agency, and so made the lagoon more stagnant and subject to silting. The growth of the shingle beaches resulted from the erosion of headlands to windward of them. Thus the chalk promontory of Beachy Head has been cut back by the fall of its cliffs to a considerable, though not measurable, distance since the Norman conquest nine centuries ago. It formerly held up on its western face an accumulation of shingle resulting from the continuous erosion of the low West Sussex coast to the westward. With the fall of the Beachy Head cliffs this shingle was washed round the point by the eastward drift to form a new coastline across the entrance of Pevensey Bay. The more important of the human agencies above noted was the inning of marsh lands by the agricultural people who wanted to increase the area of usable soil. They narrowed the channels by embanking their courses and so cut off the tide water from flowing over wide areas. This, more than anything else, has accelerated the effect of natural agencies in transforming the ancient Pevensey Bay into a broad area of grassland still for the most part below high-water level. But still the fresh water streams needed exit to the sea between their artificial banks, and their outfalls were invaded by salt water at every tide to a depth of many feet. Thus they still allowed port facilities to the small shipping of the coast. The improvident conduct of the mariners themselves—and this is the final factor—helped to complete the extinction of the havens ; for shipmasters making room for cargo dumped overboard their ballast of stones in the very anchorages best suited for their work, and the accumulation on the bottom formed lodgment for silt that would otherwise have been scoured out by the ebb tide. So the channels rapidly silted up, and the volume of tide-water diminished, and the breaches it maintained in the outer shingle line shrank to an extent that no longer permitted the access of ships. All this extinguished Pevensey Bay in the medieval time, and the little port of Pevensey itself by the seventeenth century ; and to-day the fresh-water outflow passes to the sea through sluices in a continuous shingle beach which leaves only the name but not the fact of a bay on the smooth modern coastline.

This process has been described in detail for Pevensey, which was never of itself an important haven, because the same factors in varying combinations moulded the fortunes of all the marsh ports eastwards. We shall meet with them in the history of Winchelsea and Rye, Romney and Hythe, and finally in the far Kentish region of Sandwich and the Wantsum channel. The marsh ports sprang into vigorous life with the growth of population and civilised intercourse. After a brief zenith of prosperity they were destroyed less by natural silting than by the action of the people whom they served, the landowners inning the marshland, and the seamen dumping ballast in the anchorages or abandoning worn-out craft to decay on the banks of the channels.

Two of the seven senior members of the confederation, Hastings and Dover, were not marsh ports but fell into a different category. They owed their harbours to clefts eaten down through a cliff-line by small rivers. So much they had in common, but in their subsequent fortunes not a great deal else. At Hastings there have been three distinct towns. The first was the Anglo-Saxon port which was prominent in 1066, and which continued active as a Cinque Port for the next two centuries. It has now utterly disappeared. The second began to grow up before the loss of the first, and was sited at the mouth of another river-valley a little to the eastward. It had smaller port facilities and was more a fishing settlement than a place of trade. It now exists as the Old Town of Hastings, with a small fishing fleet still active from its beach. The third Hastings was built for the most part during the middle decades of the nineteenth century, its central business quarter on ground which had been the inner shallower portion of the haven of the first Hastings. This is the big town of to-day, spreading westwards along the shore on ground not previously built upon, and inland up slopes which were farm land a century ago.

The river of the first Hastings was known as the Old Roar, or more commonly in later times as the Priory stream. The cliffs projected much farther out to sea than now, possibly a quarter of a mile or more. Their erosion has been extensive. On the west side of the river the cliff was called the White Rock. On the east side the high ground was the hill on which the castle is built, and some of its debris out in the sea is exposed at low water as the Castle Rocks. The White Rock may have been hooked somewhat to the eastward at its point, and within on a low-lying shore it gave shelter to the strand and the houses of the first town. All of the site is now open sea. How large the town was we do not know, but at the beginning of Cinque Ports history it rivalled Dover in shipping and population. Its ruin was caused by the erosion of the White Rock, exposed to the full force of south-westerly gales, and the corresponding erosion of the Castle Hill on the other side. As the protecting cliffs were lost the storm waves gained access to the

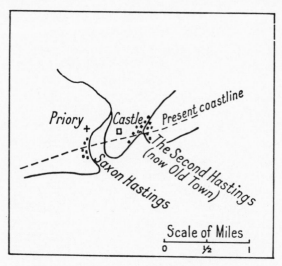

Early Hastings; a conjectural sketch of
the coastline

low-lying town. The strand was eaten away, the streets and churches fell one by one. Nor was this all, for the White Rock had been a groyne holding up the eastward drift of the shingle along the coast. With its fall the shingle drove across the entrance of the port, natural scouring was diminished, and silting increased in the inner part of the estuary which had not been lost. It seems to have been not worth while for the townsmen to retreat and rebuild up the estuary. Perhaps indeed they could not, for the land down to the water's edge belonged to the Priory of the Holy Trinity, there established. Instead they developed the settlement in the valley of the little Bourne stream on the other or eastern side of the Castle Hill; and this, lacking the natural features of a good seaport, became the essential Hastings of the fifteenth century and onwards, with fishing as its chief activity.

The dates of the changes at Hastings are not exactly known. Charters and other documents refer to Hastings without specifying which harbour was meant, and both were within the limits of the town's rights. The port was certainly flourishing until and during the thirteenth century, and in distress in the fourteenth. In the former, it contributed, with its limbs, its full quota of 21 ships to the Ports' fleet. In the latter its contingent fell to six and even three. The late thirteenth century is on record in the story of other Channel ports as a period of violent storms so devastating as to cause permanent alterations in the coastline. These may well have included the destruction of the original port of Hastings. We may tentatively, although it is little more than a guess, regard the close of the thirteenth century as the crucial time, after which the little town in the Bourne valley never recovered the old position which the lost Hastings had formerly occupied.

The area of the marsh ports begins five miles east of Hastings, where the Fairlight cliffs descend to sea-level. There were undoubtedly low islands, representing a slight undulation in the land covered by the advancing sea of the neolithic subsidence, prolonging the line of the cliffs, and the eastward drift had thrown up a line of shingle beaches based on these islands. On one of the humps, probably not at first an island, but a peninsula, forming the eastern end of a shingle spit jutting eastwards from Cliff End, arose the first port of Winchelsea.[1]

Its location may be given as somewhere between Cliff End and the present western shore of Dungeness. The life of the first Winchelsea was short but vigorous. It probably existed in the eleventh century, is discerned as a limb of Hastings in the twelfth, and was rich and populous and a senior Port in its own right in the thirteenth. But the sea was its enemy. The line of low islands and shingle banks was essentially unstable, and the continuing fall of the Fairlight cliffs uncovered it to the gales from the south-west. In 1250 a storm did great damage, destroying 300 houses, and another followed two years later. The fact that the place remained economically strong even after that shows that it must have been a port of unusual size and energy. But the attacks of the sea continued, and the abandonment of the site had to be faced. It was already being carried out when the great storm of 1287, one of the most violent in our history, drove its waves over the place and

[1] See Capt. H. Lovegrove, R.N., *Old Shore Lines near Camber Castle*, *Geographical Journal*, CXIX, Pt. 2, June 1953.

washed nearly everything away. After that, if not before, there remained only an island, rapidly diminishing, although for some years there may have been a few habitations left. The exact locality is not now identifiable.

Edward I made the Cinque Ports one of his personal concerns, and before the final disaster he had been for some years directing the construction of a new Winchelsea. For its site he chose a peninsula projecting eastwards into the tidal lagoon, two or three miles inland of the probable position of old Winchelsea. On the northern side of the peninsula ran the estuary of the Brede, on the southern that of a little brook now represented by the Pannel Sewer. At its extremity the peninsula rose fifty feet above sea-level in a roomy plateau large enough for a full-sized medieval town. At the foot of its steep sides the sea flowed deep enough for the up-Channel shipping of that date. The anchorage was well within the great tidal lagoon and defended by the shingle beaches which formed its outer boundary. On the King's orders the Lord Warden laid out a large town, with a rectangular street plan, a great church, and a strong surrounding wall ; and plots and properties were assigned to the inhabitants of the old town in process of abandonment. All promised well, and for over a century Winchelsea flourished, although its built area never filled the whole of the ninety acres enclosed within the walls.

It would seem that the great storms had thrown back the whole line of the outer shingle and that a new beach was formed running north-eastwards to the point where Camber Castle (built long afterwards) now stands. The access to the new Winchelsea was probably round the knobbed end of this spit and then back westward to the anchorage under the town walls. The defect of the new port was that the channel was subject to silting. After a century of prosperity we begin to hear of it. Shipmasters, we are told, were dumping ballast, and the anchorage was threatened. A modern port authority would make short work of this offence ; but a medieval port was ruled by its own oligarchy, and among the principal offenders were the principal inhabitants ; and ballast-dumping could not be stopped. After another century Winchelsea was no longer approachable, and in the reign of Henry VII it was reported that all merchants were quitting the town. But it would be disproportionate to attribute the whole of the result to one cause. Silting was a natural process until it reached a condition of equilibrium with the scouring agency, the concentration of a huge volume of tidewater into a powerful ebb through the deeper channels, aided by the fresh water of the rivers. The progressive inning of the

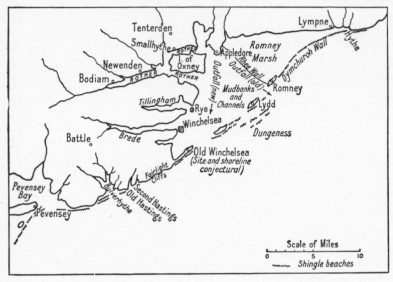

Hastings and the Marsh Ports in the 13th century

tidal marches, perhaps miles away up the Brede estuary, was diminishing the volume of the tidal water, and we can only guess what the eastward drift was doing in constricting the entrances which allowed it to fill the lagoon. Then again shipping was increasing in size. A channel which would serve very well for open boats of the Bayeux Tapestry type might be too shallow for the deepdraught decked ships of the later time, capable of bringing a hundred or two hundred tuns of wine from far Bordeaux.

After the fifteenth century Winchelsea was no longer a port, and during that century its growth had been arrested. The planned town-plots were never all occupied. The great church of St. Thomas was never finished. The chancel was built and stands to-day, too large for the congregational needs of the village that now surrounds it. Work on the nave was begun but not completed. Sheep now graze on most of the acres within the line traced for the walls [1] of a substantial town. Planners may plan, but the future does not always subserve their purposes. Winchelsea to-day is a beautiful reverie. It was never much more than an unfulfilled dream.

Rye, not three miles away across the lagoon, had better fortune. It arose on a small domed island where the estuary of the little river Tillingham merged in the tidal lagoon. Rye is now thought to be " the new burgh " mentioned in Domesday Book. We become conscious of it as a growing seaport in the following (twelfth) century. From then until the sixteenth century the port was active and kept up with the times, its business gaining benefit from the decline of Winchelsea. The marshes around Rye were among the last to be inned, and the water flowed freely on three sides of the town, while the shallow depression to the northward gradually filled up so that the island became a peninsula.[2] On the eastern and southern sides there was sufficient exposure to open water to cause erosion and the formation of cliffs ; and some of this certainly took place after the town had been fortified and walled in the fourteenth century.

A mile to the southward there was a deep anchorage called the Camber [3] within the spur of shingle beach which, after the storms of the thirteenth century, extended past Winchelsea from Cliff End. The Camber was important enough for more than local energies in its defence. Henry VII placed a battery on the shingle spit, and Henry VIII built Camber Castle, one of his standard coast defence works, with five circular bastions grouped round a central tower, all in thick masonry and embrasured for the heavy guns of the period.

[1] The walls of Winchelsea have now almost entirely disappeared. It has been suggested that the masonry was used for the construction of Camber Castle under Henry VIII.
[2] The railway now runs through the depression.
[3] " Camber " meant a small enclosed anchorage separate from a wider stretch of harbour water. The name is found elsewhere on the coast. There is a modern Camber at Dover and an old one at Portsmouth.

A French force intending the capture of Rye would apparently have been obliged by the run of the channels to pass close to Camber Castle and use the anchorage between it and the town; and the eighteen-pounder culverins already coming into use would have made the castle a strong deterrent. So far as we know, they never needed to come into action. All this is not immediately obvious to the modern observer, for the Camber is filled up, the marshes inned, and the Channel west to Winchelsea a mere faint depression in the grass. But from the castle walls one may still trace the line of the shingle bank, now also grass-covered, and of other banks thrown up subsequently to seaward of it.

Rye, although outclassed for the larger ships, kept its coastal and cross-Channel traffic long after the Tudor period, and it does so in a very limited sense to this day. It was an active passenger port for France in the seventeenth century, and had already received a settlement of refugee Huguenots, augmented after Louis XIV's revocation of the Edict of Nantes. It was always a fishing port from the days when fishing was done in long, oared vessels; a twelfth-century document mentions twenty-six-oared fishing-boats. Much later, when the fore-and-aft rigs were developed, the Rye luggers and ketches worked the rich fishing-ground between Hastings and Dungeness. The yards on the river-bank south of the town were turning out wooden fishing-craft in the present century.

It is not the purpose of this book to enthuse over scenic beauties, because the emotions they arouse cannot adequately be expressed in words, and many have done what they can in the matter for the great marsh and its ancient ports. But about Rye one thing may usefully be said. Its unique quality cannot be experienced simply by entering the town on wheels and gazing on its streets and buildings, rewarding though they are. Too many visitors are always doing that, and pleasure is alloyed by irritation. A show-place, as Rye is now, has an unhappy effect on its own legitimate inhabitants. A snatch of conversation, overheard on a busy summer day, may illustrate the point: "I'm sick of all this," said one, "they swarm everywhere and say we're quaint." It was a terse comment on what is called the tourist industry, the sale of the country's charms for money, a species of harlotry that is not to the taste of many who find themselves involved in it. No, all that is now the worse part of Rye. To see it with delight one must walk, far and wide over the marsh land, to west, to south and to east, by narrow tracks and footpaths. From every point Rye stands up like a jewel. The hill rises from the levels, the streets slope up the hill, the big church stands on its top, the low-pitched roof of the tower forming the apex of a flattened pyramid. In any light it is a harmony of tone and soft colour. On a day when the wind chases broken cloud across the face of the sun it is a swiftly changing picture of enduring elements re-combined. Rye seen from afar is a foundation of England. Seen from within, it sometimes suggests a dissolution.

Lydd and Romney may be considered together, for the first was a limb of the second, and their geographical fortunes were inter-linked. Both arose in the mid-Saxon period on sites that had been insular when the Roman conquerors first saw them. But the island which became Romney was linked to the mainland by the inning of Romney Marsh, of which it formed the southern point ; and from Romney the Rhee Wall ran north-westward to Appledore and formed a coastline looking out over the tidal lagoon towards Lydd and Rye. Lydd, some three miles south-west of Romney, remained insular, and on its seaward shore the shingle beaches built up, an inner beach and then an outer one some distance away ; and between them the late Saxons inned the Denge Marsh, the first work of the sort accomplished after the Roman inning of Romney Marsh. Still the shingle accumulated, until its seaward growth took shape as the promontory of Dungeness, which has continued to grow ever since, fed by the eastward drift with material from the erosion of Sussex to the westward. Up to the early thirteenth century the position was that Romney was a port at the junction of the Rhee and Dymchurch walls, and that Lydd coupled with Denge Marsh and Dungeness formed an island ; and that between Lydd and Romney flowed a great volume of tidal water in and out of the big area stretching all the way to Rye and Winchelsea and northwards on either side of the Isle of Oxney. The continuance of Romney as a port depended on this sea-gate of the lagoon being kept open. It seems that the opening was maintained against en-croaching shingle by the outflow of the Rother, the largest of the rivers entering the lagoon. As the tide ebbed the Rother water flowed along outside the Rhee Wall and between the ports of Lydd and Romney

The thirteenth century saw this arrangement upset. First, the monks of Canterbury, influential landowners in the region, began new innings outside the Rhee Wall, taking about seven square miles in one operation, of which Brookland is the central village. The effect of this was to push the Rother's course rather westward, outside the new innings ; but it still flowed out between Lydd and Romney. Then the great storms culminating in 1287 destroyed the position. Westward, as we have seen, Old Winchelsea went altogether. Eastward, towards the Rhee Wall, some displacement of material appears to have dammed the outflow of the Rother. The river left its old course and cut a new one round the eastern side of Rye. By so doing it ensured the permanency of Rye as a port. But it also cut off the hope of permanency for Lydd and Romney. Deprived of the scour of the Rother water, this gate of the lagoon was gradually choked, by silt within and by shingle without. The silting shallowed the water in the channel and rendered reclamation easier. The Walland and Agney innings extended that of Brookland; and finally inning was carried across from Lydd to Romney, and Lydd with Dungeness ceased to be an island. All this was completed in the fifteenth century, leaving the lagoon still unenclosed only in its western area round Rye. Romney as a port had its death sentence. It fought gallantly to keep open a direct channel to the sea, but the drift was too much for it. Dungeness, be it remembered, had not then reached its present extension, which now causes some denudation of the shore along the Dymchurch Wall. By the early sixteenth century the shingle had triumphed over Romney,[1] and John Leland in his travels recorded that the sea was two miles from the town, although he spoke with old men who remembered when the ships came up to the houses.

At the far eastern end of Romney Marsh, where the slopes of the North Downs begin to rise, stands Hythe. It is a head port, an

---

[1] The town is fully named New Romney, as distinct from Old Romney, a village two miles away near the Rhee Wall. It does not appear that there is in fact much difference between the ages of the two places. Old Romney was never important.

important early member of the confederation, and yet its history is curiously empty as compared with that of its brethren. It began as the Roman Portus Lemanis on what was then the estuary of the river Limen, flowing to the sea along the base of the rising ground and protected, before the inning of Romney Marsh, by an outer shingle bank. The position of the Roman port is indicated by the Saxon Shore fortress whose remains are now called Stutfall Castle. The great inning may or may not have prejudiced the Roman port, but in any case the estuary began to silt, and the port moved down-river, first to the early Saxon site of West Hythe and then to the late Saxon position of present Hythe. Here, until the late fourteenth century there continued to be a roomy haven, separated from the open sea by a great bank of shingle and kept open by the scour of the river. In the early fifteenth century decay was setting in. The causes are not on record, but one may suspect ballast-dumping as one of them, operating as it did at Winchelsea at the same time. Whatever the reason, Hythe silted in the fifteenth century, and the shingle inevitably drove across its entrance : nothing but a powerful in-and-out flow of tidal water could prevent that. The invaluable Leland records that small boats were still using Hythe in the time of Henry VIII. A century later, under the Stuarts, it was a port no more.

In an earlier chapter some notice has been given of Dover as a Roman port. It lay within the estuary of the Dour, then navigable as far in as the present Market Square. This seems a little incredible unless we remember that nineteen centuries of human occupation, with innumerable buildings and rebuildings of houses and the accumulation of rubble, have raised the land surface by several feet ; but this happens on all old town sites, and near the sea the process is often aided by blown sand. As the estuary opened seaward it tended to divide into two channels, with a bank of silt between them. In late Saxon times the port seems to have used the eastern channel, and not long before the Norman Conquest a castle was built on the height above it, where the pharos stood as a relic of the Roman age. The Saxon and early Norman castle consisted of an earthen rampart surmounted by a wooden palisade. It was more than a hundred years after the Conquest that the great walls and

keep of masonry were first constructed. It is a mercy that the un-
sentimental utilitarians of the Norman period spared the pharos,
which they might well have taken as building material; but no
doubt it was useful as a lookout tower.

The physical history of the port is at this point obscure, but it is
evident that at some time its users shifted over to the western
channel, to scour which it would have been possible to direct the
course of the Dour stream. By the opening of the fifteenth century,
if not earlier, the eastward-drifting shingle was a grave threat to the
value of the port. Its natural entrance was being blocked, and the
townsmen built a harbour arm outwards from the shore to hold
up the shingle on the western side and provide a sheltered anchorage
within. The remedy was only temporary. In the reign of Henry
VIII the pier was being overthrown, the shingle was sweeping
through and round it, and the anchorage was becoming firm ground,
which has since been built over. In this Tudor period the government was alive to the value of Dover as a naval port. There were
successive reconstructions or extensions of the harbour arm and,
under Elizabeth I, a new undertaking known as the Pent, an exca-
vated basin to retain the water of the Dour, which was released
with a rush at low tide in order to scour the channel.[1] The Pent
still in part exists as one of the inner docks of Dover. There were
official congratulations that at last the problem was solved and the
port was fit for Her Majesty's ships. But there was no permanent
solution. Soon the shingle drift found the end of the pier and
lapped round it, and successions of crisis and remedy continued
until the nineteenth century undertook gigantic works; and even
these have provided a great harbour which steadily silts up in
default of continuous dredging. Dover was kept alive through these
centuries of expensive struggle by its necessity as a port for the
continental traffic. The shortest sea passage was the predominant
inducement in the days of small sailing packets, whose passengers
grew richer and more numerous and more intolerant of delay.

The last of the head ports of the confederation, round the

[1] An Elizabethan water-colour sketch shows the design of the Pent, either before
or after its construction, and also a general view of the town and its surroundings in
the 1580's. It is in Additional MSS. 11,815 b.

corner and looking east, was Sandwich. Its geographical fortunes are linked with those of the ancient Wantsum channel between Thanet and Kent. As we have seen, the Romans found the Wantsum open and placed the ports and fortresses of Reculver and Richborough at either end of it. Into the Wantsum, and helping to

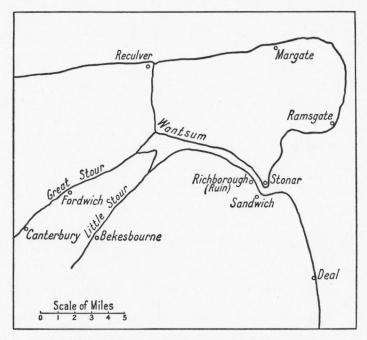

Sandwich and the eastern ports in the 13th century.
The drawing of the Wantsum is conjectural

keep it open, flowed the Great Stour and the Little Stour from the central parts of Kent. During many centuries the Wantsum was slowly being choked, from the usual causes, no doubt, among them the inning of the broad valley. There is no detailed record, but we know that the process was complete by the fifteenth century, so far as the utility of the channel for shipping was concerned. Late Elizabethan maps, however, show a drainage system, the last remnant of the Wantsum, finding exit northwards at Reculver. The fresh water of the Stours turned southward and sought its outlet past Richborough, from which we may infer that the northern part of the Wantsum silted up first. The first step in choking the southern end seems to have been the formation of a sand and shingle spit pushing southwards from the coast of Thanet near Ebbsfleet and deflecting the river past Richborough to the site of Sandwich. Here the combined Stour turned east and entered the sea. At this point there was in late Saxon times a broad anchorage where large fleets are known to have assembled ; and the town of Sandwich grew and flourished on its southern bank. Stonar, on a site a little north of it, was also a port, but did not last long enough to be a serious rival.

The harbour of Sandwich remained in good condition until the fifteenth century, by which time new masses of sand were coming in to the east of it. They had the effect of deflecting the river once more to the northward, completing a U-bend, but they do not at first seem to have had a closing effect on the port. But silt-banks were forming and the water was growing shallower. That this happened in most of the marsh ports at about the same time points to a cause arising out of the growth of trade ; and that cause was most likely ballast-dumping. It was laborious to carry the stone ballast ashore, and easier to throw it overboard when a full cargo made it redundant. The deterioration of Sandwich is testified by the cessation of the visits of the Flanders Galleys of Venice. These were fleets of great merchantmen, over 1000 tons in burden, belonging to the Venetian State. They sailed annually in convoy to carry the goods of the Levant and the Mediterranean to northern Europe. Their main terminal was in the ports of Flanders, but some of them were detached to trade with England. At first they used both Southampton and Sandwich, but in the late fifteenth century they ceased to enter Sandwich. The port was no longer safely approachable by great ships, and the Venetians thenceforward dealt only at Southampton. Leland, about 1540, recorded that the port was silting up, and said that one of the causes was the wreck of a great ship in the haven " in Pope Paulus time," a wreck on which a sandbar had accumulated. The actual Pope when Leland wrote was

Paul III (1534–50), but the phrase does not read as though it applied to him. Paul II had reigned from 1464 to 1471.

The port of Sandwich was not closed, but it was losing rank by becoming unsuitable for the greater ships. These also found London more accessible in the early Tudor period, for Henry VIII reorganised the pilot service, and buoys and beacons were placed to mark the shoals and channels of the Thames estuary. It followed that cargoes which might formerly have been handled at Sandwich were now laded or unladed in London. East of Sandwich the broad sandbanks continued to grow, and the exit of the Stour was pushed farther northward in a winding course that brought it ultimately out into Pegwell Bay. By the end of the sixteenth century the exit eastward into the sea was at Pepper Ness, approximately opposite Richborough and about a mile south of the present position.[1] The port maintained its business with minor shipping and has never quite ceased to do so. Its later activities, save in the special circumstances of modern war, have resembled those of Rye.

III. THE PORTS IN WAR

The activities of the Cinque Ports were trade, fishing, piracy and war; and they were so intermingled that it is difficult to treat them separately. In legitimate trade they were never great in comparison with London at one end of their coastline and Southampton at the other. Either of those two had a commerce far exceeding that of all the Cinque Ports together. Half a dozen ports on the east coast of England north of the Thames, from Ipswich up to Newcastle, each did much more medieval trade than did any individual member of the Cinque Ports confederation. Old Winchelsea had a name for great wealth and energy, but its history fell in a time for which statistical records are almost nil, and there is no real means of assessing its position. The second Winchelsea enjoyed a century of good fortune before its haven began to fail, and in that time its position was roughly equal to that of Sandwich. The life of Sandwich was much longer. It was a leading seaport long before the confederation was formed, and it kept its full vigour until the

[1] This is shown in a map preserved at Hatfield House.

close of the fifteenth century. On a long survey its trade was greater than that of any of its fellow members ; and the result in the creation of a fair-sized town may be seen to-day in the extent enclosed within the still visible line of the medieval walls. Sandwich was not only well placed for voyages to the Netherlands and Germany, but it was also an entrepôt for business originating in London. Until almost the end it attracted large ships which found the intricate navigation of the Thames estuary too risky. Their cargoes were transhipped at Sandwich into smaller vessels from the capital. But even so the total shipping using the port of London was infinitely greater, and the entrepôt service of Sandwich was the exception rather than the rule.

Dover, it seems, was never important for its cargo-carrying. Its hinterland was almost identical with that of Sandwich, which had better facilities. Dover, consistently throughout its history, has been a passenger port, with intermittent use as a naval station. Winchelsea, Old and New, had a special trade of its own, the shipping of timber from the Weald. The medieval Weald, long before and long after the Norman Conquest, must have been thickly forested, or it could not have supplied the great quantities of timber (mostly oak), which we know were taken from it. Charcoal for Sussex iron-smelting and oak for the local shipbuilding were only two of the uses. Much timber probably went to London for fuel and building. A large export went through Winchelsea, mainly to the Low Countries for fuel, shipbuilding and house-building : but the records, when they begin, show that it was mainly conducted in foreign ships. Exhaustion of timber supplies became nationally threatening in the Tudor period, when increasing population and demand for fuel, improving standards of housing, and increasing shipbuilding and iron-smelting produced a general shortage. Wool might be expected to figure as a Cinque Ports export. Romney Marsh was famous for its sheep ; but it was comparatively a small area, and the uncleared Weald was not a sheep country. For fiscal reasons also the wool export was canalised into tracks which facilitated the levy of duties. Sandwich, therefore, appears to have been at most times the only legitimate Cinque Port for the trade, although there was often a smuggling-out of uncustomed wool—owling, it was called—through Rye and Winchelsea. Generally speaking, the trade of the Ports suffered by the restriction of their hinterland to a fairly shallow coastal belt, beyond which the attraction of London drew off business to the northward.

Fishing, it is fair to say, was more important than the foregoing trades. Trawling for white fish or netting mackerel in the Channel was not the chief aspect of the portsmen's fishery. The herring dominated, and for herrings the Ports' fishing fleet sailed into the North Sea when the season began in the autumn, and there they made Yarmouth their headquarters. The herring was more valuable than most other fish because it could be salted and preserved, transported long distances, and sold for consumption in England and all neighbouring countries to relieve the winter shortage of fresh meat ; and, it may be added, to create the thirst that caused our ancestors to drink quantities of beer incredible to us. Cod came into the same category, but the great cod fishery lay farther north in the Iceland seas, and the English resort to it began only in the fifteenth century. The Iceland fishery was never, except for Sandwich, a Cinque Ports activity. The North Sea herring trade certainly was.

Before the Cinque Ports confederation was formed the men of ancient Hastings were resorting to the herring fishery and making their local headquarters at Yarmouth in Norfolk, where a broad clean beach and a sheltered anchorage afforded facilities for curing the fish [1] and repairing the nets. Up to about 1100 there was no permanent habitation, but only a temporary occupancy of the shore during the fishing season. But Yarmouth grew with the industry, from a small unknown place into a large one. A herring fair was established, to be held in October, and buyers attended from far and wide ; and there were the subsidiary trades attracted to fairs, and amusements in the shape of minstrels and drink-shops, a noisy and disorderly scene of trading, drinking and quarrelling, amid the

---

[1] Curing on shore seems to have been the practice, while the fishing was done close to the East Anglian coast. In later times the herring fishery was in larger vessels that could keep the sea for weeks at a time, and the crews salted the fish as caught. They went north to the Shetlands at mid-summer and followed the shoals of herring southwards. Dutch sailing fishermen were still doing this at the opening of the present century, long after the advent of the steam drifter.

screaming of gulls and the stink of fish. It was such a concourse as medieval man delighted in, for his life at most times was apt to be dull and solitary. Hastings obtained chartered rights at Yarmouth, and the other Ports received them also as the confederation took shape. The rights of " den and strond " amounted to legal occupancy of the beach and anchorage under the jurisdiction of the Ports' own officers, with prohibition of building on the strand by the inhabitants. But Yarmouth was itself growing rich on the fishery, and its people increasingly resented the intrusion. Other east coast ports took part, and supported Yarmouth. For a century (the thirteenth) there were intermittent outbreaks of rioting and fighting, not only in Yarmouth but on the high seas, where piracy became endemic. Even the strong kingship of Edward I was powerless to control its violent subjects. The Cinque Ports did, or failed to do, their own justice, and the Portsmen could not be called to answer in the King's courts.

In 1297 Edward I, in pursuance of his French war, prepared a strong expedition to land an army in Flanders. At Winchelsea he concentrated a fleet composed of Cinque Ports and east coast ships, with those of Yarmouth a leading element. In Edward's presence the seamen behaved well and did their duty to their sovereign. But no sooner had the King and his last soldier been landed at Sluys than the Yarmouth men and the Portsmen fought a general battle, not out of some chance provocation but by deliberate appointment. According to one account the King heard of the intention and forbade it, but to no effect. The Ports had the best of it. Yarmouth lost seventeen ships burnt and twelve taken and plundered, and 165 men killed. There were commissions and inquiries and awards, but to little purpose, and the feud went on into the following century. After fifty years it could still flare up, and it never really died until the whole maritime set-up of the country altered.[1]

The Cinque Ports had other feuds, as violently pursued, with the men of Bayonne in Aquitaine, who were also the King's subjects, and with the Norman seamen on the opposite side of the Channel,

[1] See *The Cinque Ports' Feud with Yarmouth* by F. W. Brooks, in *The Mariner's Mirror*, Vol. XIX, No. 1 (January 1933).

who were not. A pitched battle with the Normans in 1292 had indeed pushed the King into his war with France. Mr. F. W. Brooks, whose research has enlightened Cinque Ports history, remarks : " If modern historians recognise as the cause of these wars the anomalous position of the English monarchy in France, it is more than their contemporaries did. To them, it was the rivalry of the sea-faring communities of the English Channel."

The French wars had indeed begun out of kingly policies when John lost Normandy to the French at the opening of the thirteenth century. The Channel had been fairly peaceful in the previous period, when both its shores had lain under the same strong rule. But from John's time wars were frequent, and inter-war revenges and reprisals filled in the intervals with a growing record of piracy until, by the end of the century, the seamen had become in a sense the dictators of policy. The Cinque Ports were the strongest organised force on the English side, stronger than the King's own ships, of which we have intermittent glimpses. They won their first fleet action in 1217, when Hubert de Burgh, Constable of Dover Castle, called them out to attack a French expedition bringing aid to Louis of France, who was then in England contending for the crown. In a running fight in the Downs the Portsmen routed the French, and summarily executed the French commander, Eustace the Monk (and a noted pirate), on the deck of his own ship. From the windward position the English cast a cloud of blinding quick-lime over the French and followed it up by boarding. A contemporary illustration shows one method of delivering the quicklime. A bowman is seen in an English ship in the act of shooting a heavy arrow, on the point of which is fixed an earthenware crock or jug. The crock broke on the enemy's ship and distributed some noxious substance, probably the lime.[1] In the Baron's War half a century later the Ports sided with Simon de Montfort, but Edward I tamed them and, as we have seen, took the lead in founding New Winchelsea and confirmed the whole system by new charters.

During that century we do not hear much of French landings on the coast, but in the fourteenth-century wars of Edward III

[1] I owe this detail to a lecture delivered to the Historical Association at Chichester by Dr. L. F. Saltzman, who exhibited a lantern slide showing the picture.

—again precipitated by the seamen's initiative—the story was different, and it was then that Winchelsea, Rye and Sandwich, unprotected by dominating castles like those of Hastings and Dover, began to wall themselves in. It was not altogether effective, for in an emergency it often happened that there were not enough men in port to hold the walls. Rye suffered heavily in the Hundred Years War, being taken, sacked or burnt by French raiders in 1339, 1377, 1385 and 1448. It is worth noting that in the later French wars of the sixteenth century, when the battery and then the castle had been built at the Camber, Rye was never attacked. Camber Castle never fired a shot, which demonstrates, not its futility, but its effectiveness as a measure of defence. Hastings was burnt by raiders in 1339 and again in 1377. Winchelsea was sacked in 1360 and again in 1380, but in the bad year 1377 it was saved by the Abbot of Battle, who sent reinforcements in time to beat off the French. All this was cross-raiding, and the Portsmen were doing much the same over on the French coast. At times there was something like the spirit of modern international sport, "bringing home the ashes," and that kind of thing. Frenchmen might raid a Port and carry off the church bells, and next year their former owners might organise a party to fetch them back again. In Brookland church there is a font with half-obliterated inscriptions which suggest that they might have been cut in Normandy. But it was not all fun, and the general mood was that of atrocity and merciless killing.

As the thirteenth century passed into the fourteenth it is evident that the small open "ship" was giving place to something heavier. The quota of vessels due from the Ports for royal service fell from 57 to 27, but at the same time the number of men remained unaltered at 1,197, which can only point to larger ships. In 1340 the Ports sent 21 ships to Edward III's fleet which won the Battle of Sluys, and they also contributed to the national effort for the blockade of Calais in 1346–7. But by this date the Crown was drawing ships from every part of the country and the Cinque Ports fleet was no longer supreme. Edward III's continual requisitioning of ships and neglect to pay for them ruined many of the merchants and caused the decay of England's sea power which was shown in the great French raids of the latter years of his reign. He styled himself Lord of the Sea but did not maintain a regular navy, and in the end exacted too great an effort from the private shipowners. Piracy, it is needless to say, flourished as never before.

By the fifteenth century the Cinque Ports as a master element of England's power at sea were in decline, and the focus of strength in the Channel had passed westwards to the newer seaports from the Solent to Cornwall which had meanwhile been making sensational progress.

CHAPTER SIX

The Rise of the Western Ports

I. TRADE WITH WESTERN EUROPE

As WE have seen, the up-Channel history of the medieval centuries had been largely governed by changes in the coastline, erosion on the one hand, and the solidification of shallow lagoons on the other, with a very bulky drift of material eastwards. The down-Channel coast, including that of the sheltered Solent, was much more stable. It remained broadly what it had been at the opening of the historical period, with minor changes insufficient to control the main record of human activities. The appearance of the coastal waters illustrates the difference to this day. Up Channel the sea is somewhat clouded by the amount of dissolved material which it carries in suspension. Down Channel the water is much clearer, and it is possible to see the bottom at considerably greater depths, because there is less mud and more sand in the detritus of the shore. The change from thick to clear is observable, sometimes with the sharp definition of a frontier line, off the coast of east Dorset in the neighbourhood of Swanage and Anvil Point.

The ports of the western Channel had always existed ready for use, but they did not begin to be fully used until a century after the Norman Conquest, and even then their growth was gradual. The external relations of the country had a good deal to do with it. The Second Crusade (1147) opened up a new and distant objective for English trade, and so also, and more substantially, did the Aquitaine marriage of Henry II. The loss of Normandy in 1204 opened a period of frequent war with France which had an even greater effect on the western ports than it had on the Cinque Ports and their neighbours. Internal development also assisted. The south-west had been thinly peopled and devoted mainly to agriculture and fishing for its own subsistence. Exeter may have had some worthwhile foreign trade, but in the period before customs records began to be kept (about the end of the thirteenth century) it is not possible to be sure. From the inadequate information available it looks as though Exeter's importance had been rather that of a fortress and a city of refuge. There is no probability of any other port west of Southampton having had a substantial position in foreign trade before the twelfth century. But by that time conditions were changing. The English wool export was finding one of its exits through Southampton. The population of Dorset was increasing, and that county, with Hampshire, Wiltshire, Gloucestershire and Somerset, became an area of growing activity in wool production, leading to a valuable cloth industry in the fourteenth century. Bristol and London handled much of the west-country cloth, but some found its way to the Channel coast. It was a small and slow development. It is probably true that piracy and war were more effective factors than peaceful trade in the early growth of the down-Channel ports. But the piracy itself is a testimony to the general increase of Channel traffic, for the robber needs someone to rob. The economic life of northern Europe was pulsing more strongly in each succeeding century, and England had her share in it.

The north-European troops in the First Crusade had for the most part marched southwards by the land routes to the Holy Land. In the Second Crusade (1147) their going was by sea. From northern Germany, Flanders, England and Normandy they took ship, and the whole fleet of 164 vessels concentrated at Dartmouth for the final departure, the intention being to pass the Straits of Gibraltar and on to the Levant. In the English contingent there were Londoners, East Anglians and Cinque Ports men. We have no information about the ships, but for such a voyage they must have been larger than the boats of the Bayeux Tapestry. They duly sailed from Dartmouth in May and reached northern Spain in time to spend Whitsuntide at the shrine of St. James of Compostella. The Peninsula was then in process of reconquest by the Christians from the Moors. Oporto in northern Portugal was in Christian hands, but Lisbon was still to win. Alfonso, the first King of

Portugal, persuaded the Crusaders that they might as dutifully fight the infidel in Portugal as in the Holy Land, and they joined him in an attack on Lisbon. After a siege of four months the city fell, to become the capital and greatest seaport of the new kingdom of Portugal. A priest from Hastings became the first bishop of Lisbon regained. An informal alliance of sympathy and mutual interest arose between English and Portuguese, to endure, with one long Elizabethan intermission, through all the centuries to the present, perhaps the longest international friendship in European history. The mutual interest lay in trade, cloth and corn from England, wine and fruits from Portugal—dried fruits such as dates, figs and grapes, and even the one fresh fruit that would endure a long voyage : it is possible that the first orange was eaten in England when the captors of Lisbon came home.

Whether there had been a small trade with the Peninsula before, we do not know. Probably there had, for in the record of such things nothing ever begins, since trade is older than history. But with the foundation of Portugal the trade became important enough to be viewed as something new, and it concerned the merchants and shipping of western England. Spain in this connection came a little later. Northern Spain was in Christian hands long before the twelfth century, but it was a rugged country whose products did not at that time offer the elements of a valuable trade with England. Later it did so, and from the fifteenth century there was an export of iron from North Spain to England, with English manufactures and foodstuffs in the other direction. But the English commercial interest, when it grew important, was always greatest with Andalusia, the south-western province of Spain with an ocean coast ; and this did not come under Christian rule until the thirteenth century. We may take the capture of Seville from the Moslems in 1244 as a central date. After that, English trade with Andalusia grew prominent, and the English sailed regularly, many of them down Channel from London, the merchants for Seville and the ships for its sub-port of San Lucar, nearer the mouth of the Guadalquivir. At Seville the English obtained the wines, fruits and oil of southern Spain, soap and fine leather, and a variety of costly things forwarded from the Mediterranean and transhipped at Seville. In

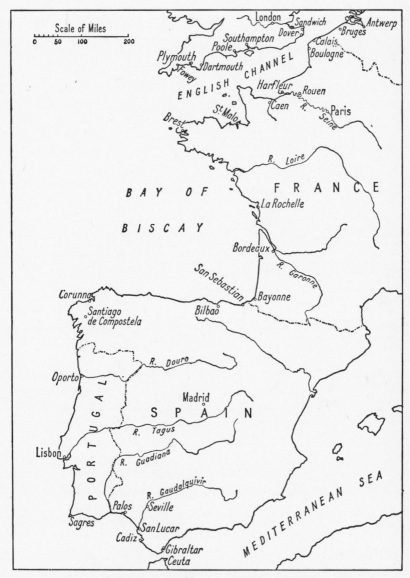

The opening of trade with Western Europe. The places named
are those prominent in the 15th century

these early days English merchantmen did not regularly enter the Mediterranean themselves, and Seville was their entrepôt. Taken altogether, the Christian reconquest of Spain and Portugal was a great stimulus to the trade of southern England.

Henry of Anjou married Eleanor of Aquitaine in 1152, two years before he became King of England. The marriage brought all south-western France under the practical governance of the English Crown, not indeed in full sovereignty, since the holder of these provinces was in law a vassal of the King of France so far as they were concerned. But as long as the arrangement lasted the English commercial position in them was very strong; and in Bordeaux, the economic capital of the region, English control endured for three hundred years. There were three leading seaports, Bayonne in Gascony, on its river estuary close down to the Pyrenees; Bordeaux in Guienne, a river-city eighty miles up the broad tidal Gironde; and La Rochelle, a coastal harbour farther north in Poitou; and these provinces, with others stretching far into the interior, formed the Aquitaine inheritance at its greatest extent. Bayonne shipped woad, a dyestuff for the cloth industry, and Rochelle shipped wine and salt, in that age of salt-preserved flesh and salted fish a commodity relatively more important than it is now. Nearly all the salt was produced by allowing sea water to overflow into shallow pans on a low-lying coast, to be evaporated by the heat of the sun. The Rochelle region had such a coast and a hotter sun than that of England. The English indeed had some coastal salt-pans, and they also produced salt by evaporating sea water with fuel, and by similarly treating brine-springs or " wiches " occurring here and there; although not until centuries later did they exploit the salt mines of Cheshire. But the English supply did not meet the demand, and the " bay salt " from the Bay of Biscay was essential. Bordeaux was the centre of the greatest wine area of the time. In the city itself and in the wide country round everyone lived by making and selling wine, so much so that they did not grow all their own foodstuffs, and the region bought some of its corn from the foreigners who came for the wine. The coastal belt was not fertile, and it was the position of Bordeaux far up the river in the rich interior that made it the monopoly port of the wine trade.

That position also meant that the Bordelais were landsmen and did not run many ships. The buyers of the wine took it away in their own ships, English, Norman, Flemish, Germans of the Hanseatic League. The political connection favoured the English, who were doing business in a place where the local government was under the control of their own king. Prospering England developed a taste for Bordeaux wine. The trade was seasonal. The ships went south in the late autumn when the year's vintage was ready, and stayed until the new year completing their cargoes ; and in the average winter there were thousands of Englishmen in Bordeaux. It was like the incursion of the Cinque Ports men into Yarmouth for the herring season. The tun of Bordeaux wine, a huge cask holding 252 gallons, became the unit of measurement of the stowage of an English merchantman. It is reckoned to have occupied sixty cubic feet in the hold, and various formulæ were evolved for calculating the tonnage of a ship without the actual experiment of lading her with tuns of wine. But the measurements were elastic, and one finds the same ship recorded at different times with different tonnages.

II. MEDIEVAL SOUTHAMPTON

In Roman times there was a port (Clausentum) at Southampton, with boat communication up the Itchen to Winchester, but there is no evidence that this port was at all prominent in war or trade. Saxon Wessex made Winchester its capital, and when the kings of Wessex became kings of England Winchester continued in some sense as an alternative capital to London and the permanent location, so far as there was one, of the treasury. In spite of this Southampton did not take rank as a leading port of Saxon England, probably because it was too far down Channel and the trade with western France was slight. The Norman Conquest brought into the region new landowners who also had interests in France, and in the ensuing century Southampton developed a cross-Channel traffic and evidently became of some consequence as a port. There are no records of its progress, but we find it accomplished by the reign of John at the opening of the thirteenth century.

It is said in many books that Southampton as a medieval port enjoyed a valuable facility in the shape of its double tide, and on that account became a focus of commerce. The phenomenon is as follows : the stream of flood tide coming up Channel from the westward forks at the Needles, one branch flowing up the Solent and the other past the outer coast of the Isle of Wight. The Solent tide gives Southampton its first high water. Before, however, this has fallen more than a few inches, another high water begins to arrive, caused by the outer stream doubling the eastern end of the Wight and coming back westward past Portsmouth and Spithead. Since this second flood-stream has farther to go than the direct stream up the West Solent, it makes the second high water at Southampton about two hours after the first ; and between the two there has been only a slight fall of level. After the second high water there is a very rapid ebb. Now, how did this benefit the port in medieval conditions ? First, it yielded a prolonged period of slack water from just before the first high to just after the second, during which ships and boats could be handled without the complication of a tidal current. Second, before quays and jetties were developed, ships had to lie at anchor away from the shore and could not lade or land goods across the soft mud when the water was low ; and the prolonged high water thus yielded more working hours. This seems to be the sum of the advantages. Whether it was the determining factor in the rapid growth of Southampton is another matter, and it seems possible that it has been exaggerated. The mud difficulty could be simply overcome, as it is now in many small ports, by tipping loads of stones or gravel to form a causeway or "hard" down to low-water mark.

Southampton had other natural advantages which were probably more important. Its water was as safe an anchorage as was to be found anywhere on the Channel coast. It had a uniquely safe approach in bad weather, when there was no need for ships from the westward to use the risky Needles passage, since they could pass outside the Wight and arrive through sheltered water round its eastern end. The position of Southampton well up into the land with twenty miles and more of observed approach gave some guarantee against surprise by enemy raiders. The same position gave easy access to a wide surrounding region of productive country.

The Southampton hinterland was richer than that of any other south coast port. The Itchen provided boat-transport to Winchester, which itself stood on a medieval main road running one way to Salisbury and Exeter and the other way through Guildford to London; and in fact a good deal of Southampton's mercantile prominence depended on this easy route to London.

In the second century after the Norman Conquest the Middle West country of Hampshire, Dorset, Wiltshire, Gloucester and Somerset began to produce more people and more goods, raw wool, lead, corn, and later cloth. Italians were keen buyers of wool, Spain and Portugal and the Bordeaux country were always glad of corn, and cloth would sell anywhere. For distribution in its hinterland Southampton attracted not only the things that came from Bordeaux and the Peninsula and Italy, but English goods coming coastwise, herrings from the eastward, other fish from the west, tin, and even building-stone from Purbeck and Portland. The place was made for a great commercial port, and the customs records show that it became one.

In the warlike reign of John, Southampton becomes prominent as a naval port, with Portsmouth as a minor haven subsidiary to it. John kept royal galleys, together with naval docks and storehouses, at Southampton, and assembled considerable fleets there and at Portsmouth for his French wars. Later in the thirteenth century Edward I did the like. At the same time commerce became considerable. In John's time Southampton was the leading English port in the wine trade, and for long afterwards was only just second to London. In 1272 Southampton imported 3,147 tuns of wine, and London 3799.[1] Southampton obtained from John and Henry III the farm of its own customs and those of Portsmouth for a fixed payment of £200 a year, then a large sum. In this century the Bordeaux wine import was almost entirely in the hands of the merchants of Bayonne, who contrived to dominate the Biscay trade routes. In the fourteenth century English ships obtained a large share of the import, and in the season of 1372 no less than 200 of them arrived to lade at Bordeaux. The great Italian trading connection with England was chiefly located at Southampton. In the

[1] *Historical Geography of England*, ed. H. C. Darby, Cambridge, 1936, p. 274 n.

thirteenth century cargoes were entering the port from Genoa and Venice.

In 1319 occurred the first visit of the Flanders Galleys of Venice, great vessels owned by the state, with their cargo space for the voyage sold at auction to individual merchants. This date however is somewhat deceptive, because the first visit ended in an affray between the Venetians and the townsmen, in consequence of which the galleys did not come again for a long time. It was not until the latter part of the fourteenth century that they called regularly. At first they used Sandwich and London as well as Southampton, but latterly Southampton only, until conditions changed and they ceased to run in the reign of Henry VIII. There were commonly from three to five of them on each voyage, staying for two months at Southampton and billeting their large crews ashore. These galleymen had a recognised burial place of their own in the church of St. Nicholas. In the fifteenth century, after Florence had acquired the seaport of Pisa, Florentine galleys also came regularly for a time. The galleys were expensive to operate and suitable only for the most valuable cargoes. The more bulky stuff was commonly brought in Italian carracks, the large sailing ships that superseded the cogs. " Carracks of Jeane " (Genoa) were well known in Southampton.

The imported goods were forwarded by road, mostly to London, where an influential colony of Italian merchants dwelt and radiated their business over the country. The Italians brought the oriental spices which they obtained from Arab traders at Alexandria, other eastern goods from all the ports of the Levant, sweet malmsey wines from the Greek islands, superfine cloth and silks, glassware and armour from the Italian cities, and dyes, vegetable oils and alum, all necessary materials to the growing English cloth industry. As compared with the period of the Norman conquest all these things were new to England and testify to the growing amenities of the later medieval age. In return the Italians took away chiefly raw wool, the richest trading product of thirteenth and fourteenth-century England. It was superior to any wool produced in continental Europe, and an absolute necessity to the luxury cloth trade of Italy. English kings were well aware of its value, and levied very high export duties. To facilitate collection the wool export for northern Europe was made the monopoly of the Merchants of the Staple and canalised through certain staple towns, concentrating ultimately at the great wool market at Calais, to which all north-European buyers had to resort. The Italians were placed on a different footing. They were exempt from the Staplers' monopoly and free to buy their wool wherever they liked in England, provided that they sold none of it north of the Alps and the Pyrenees. Thus the Italian colony in London was the centre of a web of travelling agents, seeking wool all over the country, dealing largely with the great monasteries which concentrated the wool of their districts, and forwarding the sacks by road or by coastal shipping to South-ampton. The sack of wool contained 364 pounds. Rammed hard and smoothly sewn up, it must have been an awkward package to handle for cartage and ferrying in small boats.

In the fourteen century the wool export began to diminish, not because there were fewer sheep, but because English cloth-making was on the increase. By the fifteenth century the cloth export had gone ahead of raw wool as the country's leading trade. There was a cloth industry at Winchester soon after the Norman conquest, and there may have been one before. In the next century it began to grow. It grew even more at Salisbury, the new city founded in the twelfth century, when Old Sarum on the hill was being abandoned. Salisbury in the fourteenth century became the greatest cloth-making centre in England, and there were others in the country west of it. Much of this cloth found exit through Southampton, to pay for the increasing shipments of wine from Bordeaux and of wines and luxuries from Portugal and southern Spain.

Southampton, as we shall see, was by no means the only port for all this western trade, but in its great days it was the chief of them. Its great days culminated in the fifteenth century and lasted into the early Tudor period. We have a monument of them in that large but comfortable town house built in the reign of Henry VIII, the " Tudor House," still standing miraculously intact in an area devastated by Hitler's bombs. Southampton declined in the early sixteenth century, partly by reason of Portuguese empire-building in the Indian Ocean. The

Portuguese diverted the spice trade round the Cape of Good Hope to Lisbon. The Venetians, suffering also from Turkish aggression, found their richest business cut off at its source in Asia ; and the Flanders galleys came no more to Southampton after 1532. Much else died out with them, the carracks of Genoa and the argosies from Florence and Ragusa. The Portuguese sent all their eastern wares for northern Europe up Channel to Antwerp, so that London took the place of Southampton as the English distributor. In another and perhaps more important way London's trade grew at the expense of Southampton's. Under Henry VIII the reorganisation of the Trinity House yielded a better pilot service and a better marking of the Thames estuary channels by buoys and beacons. The London merchants who had been using Southampton as an outport therefore changed over to the Thames and worked their ships from London direct.[1] By 1530 Southampton was in distress, and many merchants were forsaking the town.[2] It obtained an Act of Parliament to release it from some of the dues to the Crown which it could no longer pay, one stated reason being " that the King of Portugal took the trade of spices from the Venyzians at Calacowte."

Although rich, medieval Southampton was not a place of large population, for it had no industry save shipbuilding. It was a town of merchants, financiers and shipowners, and to the end its most valuable imports were brought by foreigners. Its customs receipts made it the second port to London, and far ahead of Bristol. The actual bulk of merchandise may have been proportionately lower than the money collected, for the wool was very highly taxed, and on other things the foreigners paid higher duties than did the English merchants. On the other hand the entrepôt trade in wares brought coastwise from other English ports was not dutiable, and so does not make its mark in the records. All early customs figures, moreover, have an unassessable element of falsity, since there was generally a good deal of smuggling and evasion. The customs work was not done by a national service but by local men who were usually merchants themselves.

[1] For much valuable information on these matters, see Alwyn A. Ruddock, *Italian Merchants at Southampton*, Southampton, 1951.
[2] The customs receipts of Southampton in the years 1504–9 averaged £10,341 a year ; in 1533–8 they averaged £3,232.

Portsmouth, as distinct from the ancient Portchester higher up its harbour, was a place of later growth than Southampton, to which it was for long a subordinate annexe. The early mentions of it are post-Conquest and relate to the arrivals of great persons from overseas. From the energetic thirteenth century onwards the spacious harbour was used for the assembly of fleets and expeditions, but the town itself was comparatively insignificant. To the fleet of 1345, for example, Southampton contributed 21 ships with 576 men, and Portsmouth 5 with 96. In naval history the two ports are closely linked, Southampton providing most of the construction and fitting-out, and Portsmouth the place of concentration. Henry V's armament of 1415, which led to Agincourt, started from both ports, and is said to have used 1400 ships, a number which looks exaggerated and may have been inflated by the counting of every cockboat and tender. After Agincourt Henry began the creation of a powerful royal fleet to keep the Channel while he systematically conquered northern France. Several great ships were built at Southampton and had moorings in the deep Hamble river which enters Southampton Water from the east. The bones of one of them lie in the Hamble mud and are seen at exceptionally low tides, oak timbers still hard after more than five hundred years. Under Henry VI the naval effort died completely, and the ships were sold off, a prelude to a period of shame and disaster. Adam de Moleyns, Bishop of Chichester and a minister of the Crown, wrote *The Libelle of English Policy*, a powerful argument for reviving the Navy and keeping the sea. His end was to be murdered at Portsmouth by clamorous seamen whom he had no money to pay. There was no revival until the Tudor century, and only then did Portsmouth become great for a time as the chief base of the permanent Navy.

Smaller ports in the sheltered water covered by the Isle of Wight formed parts of the same shipping system of which Southampton was the head. Indeed the whole of the Solent, Spithead and Southampton Water comprised one great medieval harbour, the most useful creation of the neolithic subsidence on the Channel coast. On the Island side lay Newport at the head of the Medina river and Cowes at its entrance, Yarmouth on the West Solent, with a good anchorage in the mouth of the little river Yar, and the somewhat mysterious Francheville on the shore of a similar flooded depression midway between Yarmouth and Cowes. Francheville is said to have been a considerable trading port until in the late fourteenth century the French sacked it so thoroughly that it never recovered. On its site stands now the little village of Newtown, and the anchorage is used only by yachts and occasional barges lading gravel. On the Hampshire side were the river ports of Lymington, Beaulieu and the Hamble, all serving their respective small areas of the countryside, with the trade of Beaulieu intensified by the presence of the great Cistercian monastery founded in 1204. If Romano-British and Saxon England had been originally colonised by immigrants coming in across the western Channel instead of the Narrow Seas to the eastward, all this great port area would have been the natural centre from which the occupation of the country would have extended. If we could imagine our island to have been as isolated as nineteenth-century New Zealand, Southampton would have become almost inevitably its capital, for it was much more convenient to shipping than the estuary of the Thames.

III. EXETER, DARTMOUTH, PLYMOUTH, FOWEY

West of the Isle of Wight the new trades and the new warfare brought seaports into being in every sheltered bay or river mouth of Dorset, Devon and Cornwall. Exeter excepted, none of them are known to have had important business or shipping before the thirteenth century, but thereafter their growth was rapid. Poole harbour is a wide flooded basin formed by the neolithic subsidence, serving not only Poole but Wareham, its channels kept open by the scour of rivers and a strong ebb tide. It is the last lagoon port of its kind as we go westward. Edward I tried to make a new planned town on Poole harbour, as at Winchelsea, but inhabitants did not come forward, and the attempt was a failure. Weymouth is a narrow river mouth which could have admitted a fair tonnage of medieval shipping, and outside it, even before the modern construction of the great artificial harbour of Portland, there was an anchorage sheltered in most weather for larger vessels. Lyme Regis and Bridport were two little breaks in the high-lying coast of Lyme

Bay, used with danger and difficulty, but contriving to carry a small trade for their hinterland.

Exeter, as we have seen, had a much older history. Whatever its trade may have amounted to in earlier times, it grew greater with the establishment of the cloth industry, which yielded an export to balance the import of southern wines and luxuries. Exeter was in origin a fortress city and then the seat of a great bishopric, and its trade perhaps came third in the reasons for its existence. Trade nevertheless grew prominent, although the port facilities were on the whole poor. Originally the small ships went up the Exe to the city. The river must always have been difficult, and it was closed to shipping when in 1282 the landowning interest constructed the Countess Weir to serve a water mill. Topsham, where the estuary begins four miles seaward of Exeter, then became the port. It was an inconvenient arrangement, and Leland in the early sixteenth century recorded that the Exeter people wished to restore the navigation up to the city. Before the century was out they did so by constructing the small-ship canal which continues to function to this day. In spite of its difficulties Exeter's position in the West Country gave it a share of the cloth trade which was approximately half that of Southampton in the mid-fourteenth century. But, lacking a big safe anchorage of ready access, Exeter was never one of the ports of assembly for the war and pirate fleets that grew prominent in the later Middle Ages. From causes which it could not overcome, Exeter was the most respectable seaport of that disorderly time. To the south of the Exe estuary, on the coastline that looks eastward across Lyme Bay, the small river-mouth port of Teignmouth, with a shallow bar at its entrance, and the fishing villages on Tor Bay, were in the minor class.

Round Berry Head and southwards to the opening of the Dart, the lofty cliffs and jagged coastline were less dangerous than impressive to approaching shipping, for the tidal rocks lie close in to the shore. The Dart, with an approach of sheer beauty unsurpassed by anything else on the Channel coast, leads inland through a narrow and crooked pass between high grounds and broadens into a roomy anchorage of deep water sheltered from every wind. Had the country around it only been open and easy for transport, Dartmouth might well have grown to the position that Plymouth was later to attain, as the greatest naval and commercial port of the south-west, for it was a much safer and more commodious harbour than was Plymouth in its earlier days. But instead, the Dart country was difficult by reason of its steep heights, making wheeled and even packhorse traffic slow and expensive, and the port had to grow mainly as a place of assembly and entrepôt business. Even in the engineering nineteenth century the town of Dartmouth was never reached by a railway line, and passengers and goods had to arrive

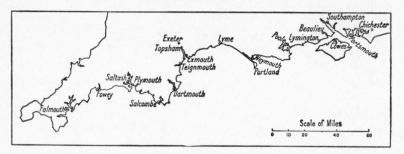

The Western Channel Ports

at Kingswear on the other side of the haven and cross by ferry. Higher up the river at Totnes, where an early bridge existed and the country grows a little easier, the water becomes shallow and the channel almost dries at low tide.

In the first two centuries after the Norman Conquest Totnes was the port for such trade as existed, while on the site of Dartmouth there dwelt only a few fishermen without even a village church.[1] At a later stage, when the cloth export began, many of the merchants still lived at Totnes on account of its better road connections, although the ships, becoming larger, were handled at Dartmouth. The wine import, beginning with the Crown's acquisition of Bordeaux, and balanced by the export of dried fish collected along the whole western coast, set going the progressive development of the Dart estuary; and Edward I, always careful of his seaports,

[1] *Dartmouth*, by Percy Russell, London, 1950, is one of the best port histories for the Channel coast.

134

gave facilities for the growth of Dartmouth itself. In his time it began to change from a hamlet into a town.

The fourteenth and early fifteenth centuries witnessed Dartmouth's first period of prosperity. In 1341 the town was incorporated as a borough, with an obligation to find two ships of 120 tons each for the King's service. Five years later, for the siege of Calais, it did much more, collecting from itself and its smaller neighbours 31 ships and 700 men. The long voyages across the Bay of Biscay evolved the big ship of the period, up to 200 tons, such as the up-Channel ports could not easily harbour. John Hawley, a seaman and shipowner prominent in the Dartmouth records from 1372 to 1408 and ten times mayor of the town, was evidently an architect of its wealth.

Mr. Percy Russell, the recent historian of Dartmouth, suggests that Chaucer's famous shipman is probably a portrait of Hawley. Chaucer visited Dartmouth on official business in 1373, and there was a Dartmouth ship named the *Magdalen* in that decade. If Hawley was in port when Chaucer was there the two men must have met. It may be added that Hawley is quite likely to have been personally a member of the pilgrims' band at Canterbury. There was a pilgrim route outwards through Dartmouth to St. James of Compostella, and a corresponding inflow of foreigners to Canterbury is indicated by the dedication of the church at Kingswear to St. Thomas Becket. Perhaps Hawley conducted a party of his passengers. Medieval pilgrimage was the counterpart of modern touring with a spiritual addition to the pleasure motive. Imagination may play upon southerners in holiday mood, Gascons, Spaniards, Italians, riding pleasantly through the countryside from Devon up to London, there to see the sights and congregate for the final stage to Canterbury. It is something to set against the gruesome record of war by land and sea that forms the chief material of Channel history at this time.

Dartmouth began to decline, or perhaps more properly to halt in its progress, in the mid-fifteenth century. Channel wars and piracies were not the reason, for the port flourished on them. The chief single cause was the loss of Bordeaux in 1451, which tended to shift the wine trade into the hands of the Flemings and the Germans

Dartmouth

of the Hanseatic League, the carriers of northern Europe; and these were in the habit of taking their English cargoes to London. Another new development was the rise of the Iceland fishery from about 1420. The east coast ports worked it, and Bristol took part, but only occasionally any ships from the Channel coast. It cut into the dried fish industry of Devon and Cornwall, which thenceforward became less prominent. Yet another century, and the Newfoundland fishery was to provide a new oceanic employment for the south-western ports.

Westward round the Start and Prawle Point and close to the cliffs of Bolt Head opened the river entrance to Salcombe, a place which never became a considerable port. It had better access than Dartmouth to the interior, but it had also an outer bar that could be dangerous in any but fine weather. This, however, was not so bad

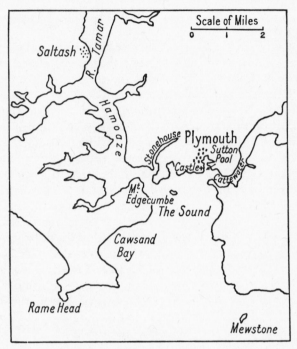

Scale of Miles
0   1   2

Saltash

R. Tamar

Hamoaze

Stonehouse

Plymouth

Sutton Pool

Castle

Cattewater

Mt Edgecumbe

The Sound

Cawsand Bay

Rame Head

Mewstone

Early Plymouth and the Sound

as the natural disabilities of Bridport and Lyme Regis, and does not altogether explain the insignificance of Salcombe. Its inner anchorage, though safe, is not nearly so extensive as that of Dartmouth, and there was no adjacent manufacturing city like Exeter to bring the port to life.

The fortunes of the western ports depended, as we have seen, mainly on their suitability for the big ships of the later medieval time. In this respect Plymouth was well placed. It had not only a fair-sized anchorage in the Cattewater, and the completely landlocked Sutton Pool for lading and discharging cargoes, but it had a sheltered approach through the Sound. Before the enterprise of the nineteenth century constructed the Breakwater, Plymouth Sound, as the records show, could at times be a dangerous place for large ships, a mouse-trap in which they could be driven on the rocks and wrecked by a southerly gale. But these occasions were comparatively rare, and in most bad weather the Sound was reasonably safe ; and it was also completely sheltered from the eastward. The whole disposition of the shores therefore provided good commercial facilities and a large accommodation for the assembly of expeditions. The position of Plymouth lay also far westward down the Channel, so that expeditions and single merchantmen could sail for the Bay of Biscay and the Peninsula without so much chance of frustration by adverse winds as those departing from the ports farther east. Once home in Plymouth the large ship could disperse her lading by the small coastal shipping, and the land communications through South Devon were good. A practicable road existed all the way through Exeter and Salisbury to London. The Cattewater is the mouth of the river Plym, entering the north-east corner of the Sound. Into the north-west corner issues the Hamoaze, the name given to the lowest reach of the river Tamar, which forms the border between Devon and Cornwall. On the Cornish bank of the Hamoaze the little town of Saltash existed before the Norman Conquest. It became a borough and a recognised port, and was a considerably older place than Plymouth.

Plymouth, like Dartmouth, was a place of late medieval growth. There was a pre-Conquest monastery, later a priory, at Plympton, three miles to the eastward, but the site of Plymouth itself was agricultural land, most of it belonging to the manor of Sutton, which came into the possession of the priory. Hence the fishing settlement which grew on the shore of Sutton Pool was under the rule of the prior. The fishing hamlet slowly became a seaport, and in 1254 is first mentioned by the name of Plymouth. A generation later, still under the prior, it was a considerable town, with a bailiff as its chief officer ; and it sent two members to the Model Parliament of 1295. The growing maritime business of the western Channel had created another port. A century later it had a mayor and council and a population possibly exaggerated at the figure of 7000, being reckoned the fourth town in England, and was agitating for freedom from the rule of the priory. It achieved this in 1439-40 when an Act of Parliament and a royal charter annulled the priory rights and recognised Plymouth as a free borough.[1]

Meanwhile the usual port development had been going on. Royal expeditions assembled in the Sound—Edward I collected 325 ships there on one occasion. Plymouth itself contributed 26 ships and 603 men to the transport of the army that won the battle of Crécy in 1346. The Black Prince sailed from Plymouth to his victory of Poitiers, and returned there with his captive King John of France. In the late fourteenth and early fifteenth centuries there were damaging French and Breton raids on the town, which remained partially ruined for a time. There was fishing and a coastwise trade, and a big-ship trade with Bordeaux and the Peninsula. Old Plymouth lay mostly on the western side of Sutton Pool, with its streets sloping up to St. Andrew's church to the westward. It was not visible from the Sound, the high ridge of the Hoe intervening; and the Hoe was in early days unoccupied. The medieval town was walled, and had a castle overlooking the narrowest part of the entrance to Sutton Pool, across which a chain could be stretched to keep out assailants. Fragments of the castle can still be seen, and are not to be confused with the great citadel on the Hoe, which was erected in the seventeenth century.

The only medieval Cornish port of the first rank was Fowey, for Falmouth was much more modern in its growth. Fowey, about twenty miles west of Plymouth Sound, has an entrance somewhat resembling Dartmouth's, a river estuary unobstructed by a bar, leading in between high grounds and broadening within to a fairly spacious anchorage, with the town of Fowey on the western bank and the village of Polruan facing it on the eastern. Medieval Fowey rivalled and at times surpassed Plymouth in its maritime activities —it sent 47 ships and 770 men to the Crécy expedition. It was never so populous a town as Plymouth, and its shipping list was no doubt made up partly with small vessels from the minor havens lying on the coast on either side of it. Like Dartmouth, the town itself was not walled, but the narrow entrance was defended by a castle on either side. A document mentions that these castles were

[1] For the full story of the early growth see C. W. Bracken, *History of Plymouth*, Plymouth, 1931.

a bowshot apart. If one stands there to-day one has a measure of the range of the long-bow, some 220 yards, about equal to that of the muskets of Waterloo. The men of Fowey, lacking perhaps the elements of a genuine trade adequate to their energy, were notable for their piracies in the unruly time of the Hundred Years War. The south Cornish coast had numerous small ports, Looe and Polperro between Plymouth and Fowey, Par and Mevagissey between Fowey and Dodman Point, Falmouth between the Dodman and the Lizard, and others west of the Lizard in Mount's Bay. Every little cove had its fishing-boats, helping to feed the population of a somewhat barren hinterland, and finding cargoes of dried fish and salted pilchards for the ports to sell, together with Cornish tin, overseas and up the coast. Cornwall had probably a higher proportion of seamen among its people than any other county of England.

IV. WAR AND PIRACY

The whole period from the early fourteenth to the late fifteenth century, in which the western ports grew from adolescence to maturity, was dominated by Anglo-French warfare. There was occasionally a strategic purpose in the use of sea power. Edward III gathered a great fleet from every coast of England to cruise in the narrow seas and cover his long siege of Calais. Henry V created the first really powerful Royal Navy to make his control of the Channel absolute while he conquered northern France. All of them levied merchant shipping to transport their forces overseas on numerous occasions. But most of the sea warfare was not on any strategical plan. It was cross-raiding, the harrying of the enemy's coastline by spasmodic expeditions for the main purpose of obtaining booty, and for another motive, often seen, of pure retaliation, inflicting wrong for wrong. The war, as between governments, was not continuous, but interrupted by long periods of truce. But between the seafaring populations it hardly ceased. Legal means of obtaining redress for injury were inadequate, and the victims resorted to reprisal. Reprisal generally fell on innocent associates of the original offenders : if a Breton robbed a Dartmouth man, all Dartmouth men would rob all Bretons ; and so the irregular maritime war was never stopped. Yet, surprisingly, trade went on, as the customs records show. The reprisals cut only the fringes of it, for if they had killed it they would themselves have ceased. Even in the times of formal war the records show trade with France proceeding. Governments issued safe-conducts, and there are entries of ships from the Channel Islands so numerous as to show that Jersey and Guernsey formed an entrepôt for much more business than the islands themselves could have supported. Another conclusion is evident, that in spite of all the raiding there was never any threat of a serious invasion of England for military conquest. The raiders came, generally in small force, and withdrew even if successful. The invasions were all English invasions of France.

The Southampton and Portsmouth area formed the base of Henry V's regular Navy, although some of the ships were built on the Thames. Most, however, were built at Southampton under the charge of the merchant William Soper, who was Surveyor of the King's ships. The fleet was necessary to Henry's plans of conquest, for the French sought to dispute the Channel crossing. The Earl of Huntingdon with the King's ships fought a battle at sea in 1417 and captured four large vessels from the French before the army could cross to the invasion of Normandy. When Henry V died in 1422 the government in the name of his infant son was at first under the late King's brothers, John Duke of Bedford and Humphrey Duke of Gloucester. Bedford was a good soldier, and Gloucester, although erratic, a man of energy. It was not altogether feebleness that caused them to discard the Navy of Henry V, but rather, one must believe, a conclusion that it was superfluous and had nothing to do, since the French were by then offering no resistance at sea. The ships were sold or laid up to decay in the Hamble.

The decision was in the long run a bad mistake. But it was one of those mistakes whose consequences generate an enduring doctrine, a lesson which the nation learned and never forgot. By the 1430's its evil results were becoming apparent, and a political tract of first-class importance, the *Libelle of English Policy*, enunciated for the first time in a detailed argument the doctrine that England can live only by sea power. The *Libelle*, although written by a man of learning, was not in Latin for the few, but in rhymed English for the many. The rhyming was needed to assist recollection and repetition in the days before printing, when written copies could not be numerous and circulation of ideas was by word of mouth. Sea power, with legislation to promote the economic interests of English shipping and a royal fleet to " keep the seas," became the conscious aspiration of the growing mercantile class. It was to remain little but an aspiration for fifty years to follow.

The list of raids on English ports in these wars is impressive. But the damage was seldom of enduring effect. Houses were cheap, merchant shipping was cheap, and townsmen's lives were cheap. An abounding birth-rate soon filled the empty places of those who would mostly have died young in any case. We may take a generation to rebuild a bombed city, but the fifteenth century soon rebuilt a burnt one in which the sanitary conditions must often have made a good fire a blessing in disguise. At the opening of the Hundred Years War the French took the initiative in raiding, and in 1338–39 beat up the whole Channel coast of England : Rye and Hastings, Portsmouth and Southampton and Plymouth were all more or less damaged. The battle of Sluys in 1340 destroyed a good tonnage of French shipping, and after that the English were stronger at sea for over two decades. The closing years of Edward III saw a return of weakness, and the year 1377, his last, was one of disaster, when Dover, Rye, Hastings, Portsmouth and Plymouth were burnt or pillaged.

Plymouth experienced its most celebrated raid in 1403. The Sieur du Chastel with 1200 Breton men-at-arms sailed into the Sound. The castle and chain and stone-firing guns prevented the Breton ships from entering Sutton Pool, and the troops landed at Cattedown east of the Pool, marched round it, and invaded the " back half " of the town, where they burnt six hundred houses. In the remainder of the town, towards the castle, the Plymouth men held out until the enemy retired to their ships with a quantity of plunder. Many were killed on either side, and the town's guns were claimed to have had a range of half a league. This was in August, and in October Plymouth with the King's aid launched its counter-stroke with 4000 men. They did much laying waste on the Breton coast, burnt

40 ships, and captured 1000 tuns of wine.[1] Next year, 1404, it was Dartmouth's turn to be attacked. Dartmouth was fairly snug within its narrow entrance, where a castle already stood on the western side, and probably some defence opposite, where Kingswear Castle was afterwards completed. Du Chastel again commanded the raiders, and as before he did not attempt the entrance, but landed on the open Slapton beach to the westward with 2000 knights and men-at-arms. This necessitated an advance of some miles over the high ridge to come down upon the unwalled town from behind. The veteran John Hawley took command of the Dartmouth men, who drew bows, and the women, who threw stones. They did not wait in the town, but went out to a good defensive position at Stoke Fleming, where they routed the invaders. Du Chastel was killed and many distinguished men taken prisoner, and the survivors sailed home to St. Malo. A deputation of Dartmouth men took the prisoners up to London and received a handsome reward from the King. Well-to-do prisoners of course represented ransom money. Those who did not look well-to-do were not made prisoners.

Piracy made great strides during these long wars. Many of its practitioners could legally claim that they were not pirates, for reprisals was generally sanctioned, and some of the freebooters were even sent out with commissions to preserve order on the seas. This was often true after the extinction of the royal naval service in the weak reign of Henry VI. It was easy for the pirate, who was generally also a legitimate trader, to explain that he had been attacked by his victims and had " apprehended " them. In the fourteenth century it became the custom for peaceful shipping to sail in convoy with some heavily manned vessels as escorts. The pirates then took to hunting in large packs, and regular battles ensued. Poole in the early fifteenth century, under the leadership of the redoubtable Harry Pay, became notorious for its pirate squadrons. So also did Fowey, whose mariners, the " gallants of Fowey," roved the whole Channel and did not spare their own countrymen of the Cinque Ports—but the nationalist Cornishmen may not have admitted that Englishmen were their fellow-countrymen. Later in the century

[1] Bracken, *History of Plymouth*, pp. 42–3.

Fowey grew more formidable and was the recognised cock of the Channel. Edward IV, involved in foreign disputes by these operations, at length intervened by land process and chastened Fowey so severely that this form of maritime enterprise was abated. The other sea-going peoples, Spaniards, Bretons, Normans, Flemings, and the Germans (Easterlings) of the Hanseatic League, were all similarly occupied, and piracy and trade were inseparably mingled. The Easterlings, by the size and number of their ships and the wealth of their merchants, were the greatest power in the North Sea, and the English ports of the east coast suffered heavily from them. Although the English had treaty rights in the Baltic ports they were bullied out of using them, and their Eastland Company was in abeyance by the end of the fifteenth century.

Down Channel and in the Straits of Dover it was different. The Hanseatic League had developed a carrying trade in the products of Biscayan France and the Peninsula, which it transported to Flanders and London. Carrying trades have in various periods excited an almost moral indignation, owing to the notion long held that shipping should handle only the trade of the country owning the ships. The German convoys could be attacked in the Straits and the Channel as they could not be in the North Sea. Edward IV's Earl of Warwick (the King-maker) was for some time governor of Calais, where he was active in pulling in the hulks of the League on flimsy pretexts. Farther west the assaults on the Easterlings continued. In 1449 Robert Wennington, having received a general commission "to cleanse the sea of pirates," equipped a strong force mainly of Dartmouth ships. His purpose was to intercept a great convoy of Hanseatic and Flemish vessels carrying salt up Channel from the Biscay coast of France. Wennington met the convoy in mid-Channel abreast of Portland and hailed the admiral in its leading ship : "I bade them stryke in the Kingys name of England." The German made an obscene reply also involving the King's name, whereupon the Dartmouth men fell on and gave their foes a drubbing that resulted in the surrender of the whole convoy, about a hundred sail. Far from being embarrassed by this singular method of abating piracy, Wennington wrote a spirited account of the action to an official at court, claiming that he had brought in the biggest haul of prizes seen in the past hundred years. Under the unhappy Henry VI English government was then at its lowest depth of incompetence. It could do nothing to keep its own subjects in order, and in this case it closed the matter by paying compensation to the Flemish victims, but not, apparently, to the Germans.

Such was the Channel scene in these last medieval centuries, a pageant of swarming ships and striving men, set in the panorama of the beautiful coastline with its ports and villages on the shores of havens unblotted by the industrial ugliness of a later day. It is a picture fair to contemplate in the bird's-eye view of time, though often foul with blood and pestilence for those who dwelt in it. But these people were our forefathers. They lived with zest, and were no more nor less unhappy than we. They knew no other life, and do not call for pity. And they were on the move, going forward. The fifteenth-century Channel was no longer merely the obstacle one crossed to get to France. It was already the highway to the West, of Biscay and Portugal and Andalusia. There was promise of more also. A few pioneer captains were sailing through the Straits of Marrok into the Mediterranean, even to " Levant's End." A handful of new ocean men, from Bristol only as yet, were trading with Madeira and the Azores and groping for a new island out west of Ireland, and lading salt in anticipation of good fishing there ; and unnamed Englishmen were joining the Spaniards in the conquest of the Canaries and getting grants of land in them ; and certain English merchants under Edward IV were seeking to open trade with black Africa itself. There were probably Channel men in these dimly known enterprises. There certainly were not long afterwards, when Plymouth and Dartmouth and Southampton opened their eyes to a much farther West than the Middle Age had thought of.

Chaucer's " Shipman " yields a glimpse of the late fourteenth century at sea. Less known but more informative is a fifteenth-century verse description of a pilgrim voyage to Compostella. It has no title and is usually cited by its first line.[1]

---

[1] The MS. of *Men may leve all gamys* is preserved at Trinity College, Cambridge. The words have been printed in full in John Masefield's *A Sailor's Garland*, and in R. and R. C. Anderson's *The Sailing Ship*.

Men may leve all gamys
That seylen to Seynt Jamys
For many a man hit gramys
When they begyn to sayle.
For when that they have take the see
At Sandwyche or at Wynchelsee
At Bristow or where that hit bee
Theyr hearts begyn to fayle.

The master gathers the hands to hoist the great main yard with the hauling cry of "Howë! Hissa!" The boatswain and his men get the great boat on deck, and it serves as a refuge for some of the pilgrims. The bowline is hauled, the tack and sheet adjusted, and the ship gathers way with the wind abeam. The pilgrims soon begin to "cowgh and grone," though some with stouter stomachs "layde theyr bookys on theyr kne and rad so long they myght nat se." The master strides the deck, calling to the steward for a pot of beer and bidding him "cover the boorde" (with a tablecloth?) and set out bread and salt. The pilgrims, who play the part of a misery-chorus, "have theyr bolys fast them by, and cry aftyr hote malvesy, theyr helthe for to restore." They cannot face meat, but "som wold have a saltyd tost"; and altogether the master reckons that their keep will not cost him much for a day or two. "Then cometh owre owner lyke a lorde, and speketh many a royall worde," patronizing and comforting the poor wretches, and ordering the carpenter to build little cabins for them. The lucky ones get a straw bed, but the others have to curl up in their cloaks on the deck. The worst place of all was the cabin through which the bilge-pump was worked: "a man were as good as to be dede, as smell thereof the stynk." No wooden ship was entirely tight, and the salt water rotted in the bilges.

The pilgrimage to Jerusalem was still made by venturesome souls, although generally by the land routes as far as the Mediterranean. St. James of Compostella was the favourite English destination, and the pilgrim trade was a considerable business, with competition enough to secure some consideration and comfort for the passengers.

CHAPTER SEVEN

Channel Shipping

THE FOREGOING chapters have made passing mention of the ships that sailed the Channel in fifteen centuries of known history, nearly all the shipping types of northern Europe, and a few from the south. Here we may assemble some conclusions about them drawn from a great body of research on a subject that has never been so actively pursued as in the past fifty years. Numerous investigators have made certain of much, but much is still open to doubt, and much, we may believe, is yet to discover.

The material consists to a small extent of remains of actual ships, most of them fragmentary, buried and in later times exhumed. But to a much greater extent it is literary and pictorial, verbal descriptions, illustrations in medieval manuscripts, ship pictures on the seals of seaport towns, a few church carvings, scanty administrative documents with allusions to shipping, and in the fifteenth century a few inventories of gear and fittings. One or two contemporary ship models of the fifteenth century are known, but models, like drawings, are often unreliable for proportions, having been made as votive offerings for churches rather than as accurate records of dimensions. Measurements of dimensions are generally lacking, and tonnage begins to be mentioned only in the last two centuries of the period. Medieval illustrations are generally unsatisfactory. The ships shown on seals are obviously distorted by being squeezed into a circular frame, and wax is a material that cannot show the fine detail requisite in a small representation. Seals were not intended to be faithful illustrations of what were common objects to the eyes of their users : the intention was symbolic. So also was it in the manuscript illustrations, nearly all drawn by ecclesiastics to portray incidents in holy writ and the lives of churchmen, in which the vessels were merely accessory, and accuracy unimportant. Their portrayers were landsmen, and it is a fairly general truth that an artist is unable to draw from the round a complicated object with whose functions he is unfamiliar. We see the same thing in a modern time in the quaint drawings of locomotives and railway scenes made in the 1830's and even later : the proportions are wrong and the details distorted because the artist did not know how the things worked. Would that some medieval seaman had turned monk and shown a talent for drawing the ships he knew ! But probably the *scriptorium* committee would have disallowed his work as not being symbolic enough. Convention is a tyrant. It all amounts to this, that we have to disbelieve the medieval picture of a ship whose side elevation is shaped like a crescent moon, with a large battlemented platform perched upon either horn, and to reconstruct from its symbolism something that really was built and would sail.

The Celtic curach was one of the earliest northern vessels known to history. Cæsar briefly mentions them, but does not give dimensions. Small ones exist in western Ireland to-day and undoubtedly existed on the Channel coast in Cæsar's time. The present examples are about sixteen to eighteen feet long and five feet broad, and are used for fishing. They are always rowed, but can set a small sail as an auxiliary. They have a light timber frame, covered, until the last century, by hides, but now by tarred calico. They are cheap to construct, but do not last as long as wooden boats. Various evidence leaves no doubt that the Celts of former times built much larger vessels of this type and used them for voyages across the open sea. It was in such curachs that Scotic raiders and invaders crossed from Ireland to Great Britain in the Roman period, and it was most likely in one of them that St. Patrick made his passage to Ireland after being kidnapped from the shore of the Bristol Channel. The seagoing curachs did much the same work as the Norse longships, which are better known only because buried examples have survived almost intact.

The curach's development was arrested by its obvious limitation of size, and the future was with the wooden ship, which flourished wherever good timber was plentiful. The few details known about the native shipping of Gaul in Cæsar's time have been given in a previous chapter. These ships are interesting because they were apparently a good deal larger than vessels built centuries later on the same coastline. For the defence of the Saxon Shore the Roman administration seems to have used fighting galleys of the classical Mediterranean type, but almost nothing is known of the merchant-men which carried the Channel traffic of that time. The Saxon assailants of the province used open boats with oars and sails, but little is known of them. For the Norse and Danish shipping the position is much clearer. The Scandinavians used two types of vessel, one for war and raiding, another for trade and ocean dis-covery in the far north. The two occupations were equally impor-tant, and the same people were both traders and vikings, the word viking being not a national but an occupational description. To go a-viking meant to go on the warpath. The Scandinavian mer-chantmen which traded across the North Sea and on the route linking Norway, the Faeroes, Iceland, Greenland and North America have left no buried and exhumed examples and no pictorial representa-tions. Knowledge of them has been gleaned from entries in the Norse sagas. They were primarily sailing-ships, not of extreme length, and constructed for carrying capacity and long endurance at sea with comparatively small crews.

The viking ships, as we know from half a dozen examples still actually existing, were quite different. They were long, open boats of shallow draught, built for speed and the transport of a large crew on a short voyage. The primary means of propulsion was the oar, and the square sail on a single mast was rather an auxiliary to the rowing effort. They, and all the wooden ships of northern Europe from their time to the fifteenth century, were clinker-built. That is to say, the planks overlapped and were fastened one to another by nails or pegs driven through the double portion. Distinct from this was the Mediterranean method of planking by laying the planks edge to edge and ramming in caulking material to prevent leakage. The planks were not fastened to one another but to the ribs of the ship's frame. This was known as carvel-building, and it was not until the late fifteenth century that carvel-built vessels began to appear in English ownership. The method then rapidly ousted clinker-building for all large ships.

The Norman ships of the Bayeux Tapestry were essentially of the viking type in form, shallow and open, but since their purpose was to make one hop across the Channel on a favourable day they did not carry the oars and relied only on the square sail, thus giving more transport space for the soldiers. In the Tapestry some are shown with the round oar-ports in which oars could be worked, and others without any sign of them, and this may mark the distinction between existing ships which William requisitioned and the ships specially built for the expedition.

The essential economic distinction between oared ships and sailing-ships was that the former provided greater ultimate speed through not being obliged to await a fair wind, while the latter yielded greater carrying capacity, but suffered much more overall delay. The sailing-ships, being decked, were more seaworthy for long voyages in open water, but probably more likely to be wrecked when near the coast. They habitually carried a few long sweeps to assist in entering harbours and to keep them from drifting upon rocks or shoals when becalmed, but the relative smallness of their crews did not admit of regular oar propulsion.

In the two centuries after the Norman Conquest when the activities of the Cinque Ports and the narrower eastern part of the Channel were at their height it is evident that many oared ships were in use. They were good for inshore fishing, the passenger traffic to France, and the piracy which for the Portsmen was as much an occupation as the carrying of cargoes, all of which employments needed greater mobility independent of the direction of the wind than could be obtained from the single-masted sailing-ship. When the western trades developed and the western Channel ports grew with them the large sailing-ships became the predominant type. On all the European coasts the same process was evident. There was an immense growth of maritime trade. Longer voyages called for larger ships, and the fourteenth and fifteenth centuries produced them.

The large variety of names for the different types provides a puzzle for those who seek to establish their definite meanings. It seems likely that some of the names were not employed with technical accuracy, and also that the same name might mean different things in successive periods. To take three of the most commonly used words : the balinger appears to have been an oared vessel of small or moderate size ; the barge was larger and probably driven mainly by sails, but the word was very loosely used and might mean almost anything ; the cog has a clearer meaning, standing for the large sailing merchantman, broad and deep in the hold, with single mast and a great square sail. The fourteenth-century cog was the typical big ship in the long distance trades. Yet Chaucer, writing of his representative seaman bringing wine from Bordeaux in his ship the *Magdalen*, calls her a barge. It would seem that Chaucer used barge as merely another word for ship in general. Cogs of 200 tons were known in the fourteenth century, and they formed the main element in the fighting fleets of the time. As fighting consisted chiefly in boarding and the use of hand-propelled missiles (guns at sea were as yet exceptional), all the ships were built with raised poops and forecastles to accommodate the fighting men and make things more difficult for boarders. The superstructures were at first temporary, erected only for war service, but later were built as integral parts of the hull. For peaceful purposes they gave the better accommodation for crew and passengers that was called for by longer voyages. It is in the pictorial representation of these large cogs that the seals and manuscripts are most misleading. The ships' hulls are made too short and the superstructures too high. The curve of the sheer-line is exaggerated into a half-moon proportion. The ships are commonly shown as riding much too high in the water. The whole effect is that of an unstable construction that would hardly float upright for a moment. The only realistic picture of a cog occurs in a stained-glass window, date about 1400, at Bourges in France, which does look as though correct proportions have been observed.[1] For rationalisation of most of the artistic conventions we have to turn to the few moderns who are at once marine artists and nautical archæologists. A most satisfying modern picture of a fourteenth-century cog is to be found in Gregory Robinson's *Great Ships of History*, and it certainly is a real ship sailing

[1] R. and R. C. Anderson, *The Sailing Ship*, London, 1926, Plate IV.

on a real sea. Mr. Robinson has generously allowed the reproduction of his painting in this volume.

The foreign ships that came into the Channel were probably for the most part cogs, but there were some of types not built in England. The most remarkable were the Flanders Galleys, with their terminal ports at Sandwich and Southampton. In this connection the word galley is incorrectly used, for in the strict sense it meant the purely fighting vessel of the Mediterranean with a length of eight or more times its beam, propelled by as large a number of oars and rowers as could be packed into it, and using the ram as the principal weapon of offence. Soldiers (and later gunners) occupied the comparatively small forecastle and poop. The true galleys had no cargo capacity or ability to remain at sea for long periods, when it would have been impossible to feed the crowd on board. They were simply fighting machines, a sort of marine cavalry for charging at high speed with shock action. They were seldom seen in northern Europe, although in the sixteenth century the French and Spaniards occasionally brought galley forces round from the Mediterranean.[1] The so-called Flanders Galleys were quite different, and their Venetian owners did not call them galleys but galleasses. They had a length of about four and a half times the beam and a depth in hold to yield good cargo capacity. They were up to 1200 tons in burden and were driven by lateen sails on three masts. They had also a powerful oar equipment with 180 rowers. The rowers were paid men, not slaves as was usual in the fighting galleys. They were run like modern liners, visiting specified ports and, by virtue of the oars, keeping roughly to a time-table. They were no doubt expensive to operate, but they carried costly goods, eastern spices, rare fabrics, and a variety of luxuries, and, on the return passage, the highest qualities of wool that could be bought in England.

Genoa and other Italian ports also sent merchantmen to the Channel, many of them bound for Flanders, but some for Southampton and Sandwich. They were large sailing-ships, generally described as carracks. They were in the main a big development of the

[1] King John's galleys were probably not strictly so named. In English, " galley " might mean any oared vessel.

cog type, the large size being called for by the length of the voyage. A round trip between the Mediterranean and northern Europe, with long halts for the disposal of cargo, often occupied more than a year. It would appear that these great sailing-ships, requiring a port in the Channel as far west as possible in which to await a change of weather, sometimes used Falmouth for the purpose, and the name of the Carrick Road in Falmouth harbour commemorates their visits. The Germans of the Hanseatic League, also operating a long trade route between the Baltic and Portugal and Andalusia, increased the size of their ships, which were known as hulks.

These increases in the range and bulk of trade had their effects on English shipping. Early in the fifteenth century the simple cog type began to be superseded by longer ships, first with two masts and then with three. The evolution was rapid. Two-masted ships were built early in the century, and three masts followed during its middle years. The two-mast stage was so short that no satisfactory picture of the type has survived, and the information is derived from inventories of spars and sails. Soon after 1400 these make mention of a mizen in addition to the mainmast, and there has been some controversy on whether the new mast was before or abaft the original single mast; for although in English mizen now means the after mast, in French *misaine* still means foremast, and both English and French got the word from the Italians. Very soon, however, a third mast was established. The single-masted cog had long had a bowsprit, steeved up to a considerable angle above the horizontal, to which had been led the bowlines which kept the leading edge (the luff) of the great sail taut when sailing as close to the wind as she would go. It was an easy development to convert the bowsprit into a foremast and set a square sail upon it, so easy that it is surprising that it had not been done before. The Mediterranean merchantmen of ancient Rome, long centuries earlier, had had this raking foremast and a sail upon it, but the practice had somehow died out. By the mid-fifteenth century the foremast and foresail had arrived, together with the mizen at the after end, and the three-masted ship was complete. The chief sail was still the square mainsail, much larger than the other two together. The foresail was also square, small but destined to grow. The mizen was generally a lateen sail of Mediterranean origin,[1] which helped the ship to lie closer to the wind. Pictures become more realistic in the late fifteenth century and give us an intelligible notion of what these new ships were like. They had a decisive advantage over the single-masters in that they would, in good conditions, really work to windward, although that ability must not be exaggerated. It is doubtful if the cogs ever made good a course much better than at right angles (eight points) to the wind. The fine sailing-ships of the nineteenth century would make good a course five and a half points from the wind. The new ships of the Renaissance age were between the two in ability. This was in fair conditions. If a strong wind dictated a reduction of sail, with the permanent exposure of hull and gear remaining, the leeway was increased until " making good " to windward disappeared. But the windward ability of the new vessels, however small, made a great increase in their overall possibilities, and it is no mere coincidence that a new age of oceanic voyaging set in with their invention. One cannot imagine Drake getting round the world in a cog.

Up to about 1200 all northern ships were steered by an oar worked over the starboard quarter. Incidentally, this gives a mnemonic for the distinction between " starboard " and " port " as now used for the two sides of a ship : the starboard was the steerboard, on the right hand of the helmsman as he stood facing forward. In all vessels above the small boat size the steering oar was a heavy piece of timber and had to be carried on a pivot, the end of a beam projecting over the sides, with a hand-piece or tiller coming inwards across the deck. So long as this steering was in use the ships were built " double-ended," with the sternpost shaped like the stem, raking outwards and upwards in a curve. As a steering mechanism the oar was good, but it had the disadvantage of being exposed to damage. A heavy sea might wrench it from its pivot, since it was not supported at its blade end in the water ; and it might be broken if the vessel lay with her starboard side against a quay, or jostling among others in a crowded anchorage. The

[1] The lateen rig, with one, two or three masts, was a quite separate development, which seems to have begun in the Mediterranean at the time of the great Moslem conquests. No lateen sails are recorded in northern Europe before the fifteenth century.

hinged rudder set on the sternpost was therefore an improvement, and it was invented just before or after 1200.

This led immediately to a change in the shape of the hull whereby the stern was differentiated from the bow. The sternpost for the hinged rudder was best made straight, not curved, and its rake had to be reduced for the rudder to function at its best. The markedly curved and raking stem long remained. It had a functional value because it enabled the overall length of the ship to be much greater than the length of the keel. The keel, the foundation of the structure, was strongest if made from a single oak log. The length of a log was limited by nature, and for anything in excess of that length two or more logs had to be scarphed together, which was not only a weakness but a waste of good oak in the long overlap of the scarph. The stem had to be scarphed on in any case, and so it was made to rake forward in a long upward curve, a quadrant of a circle. The sternpost had been similar, but the new rudder caused it to be altered. The long curved logs for the stem must have been even more of a problem than the keel, for they were shaped from trunks that had grown naturally in that form, and were not easy to find. The wooden shipbuilding that went on in every port and creek of the coastline created an element of strength in the population by making men use their brains as well as their hands. There were few higher forms of craftsmanship than that of the shipwright.

Modern yachtsmen are sometimes accused of shirking the difficulties of sailing seamanship by using auxiliary engines. In fact, sailing men through the ages have used whatever auxiliary power was open to them. The most universal in northern Europe was that of the tide flowing through the port entrances and the estuary channels which were too narrow to be sailed with any but a fair wind. Until the advent of the steam tug London's trade came up the river in successive six-hour advances with the flowing tide, alternated with six-hour halts at anchor during the ebb. The tug was something better of the same essential sort; and the master mariners of the nineteenth century had their full-rigged ships towed out by tugs from London river through the Downs and the narrows of the Channel whenever the direction of the wind would have made it a long business to get through under sail. To serve thus as auxiliary power to the sailing-ship was one of the first uses of the primitive steam vessel that made its appearance about the time Napoleon fell. The medieval cog had two methods of applying auxiliary power, long sweeps and towing by the ship's boat. To look at the Dartmouth entrance now, one might suppose that there was hardly one day in five when a cog could have sailed through it even on a fair tide without some assistance from oars or towing. A harbour in which auxiliary power was not generally required must have been exceptional. In the sixteenth century we find the Spaniards keeping galleys at Cadiz for the express purpose of towing the great ships of the plate fleets out to sea. At the same time the English Navy also had one or two galleys at Chatham, undoubtedly for towing the big warships in and out of the Medway. Here was the steam tug with all but the steam.

Mention has been made of Henry V's Navy. It was for that time a force that may be called portentous. Not only did it decisively "keep the sea" for his conquest of northern France, but it dealt successfully with the pirate gangs of all nations which had infested the trade routes. So at least we may infer from the substantial cessation of complaints during his short reign. In numbers and tonnage the fleet was unprecedented. There were fourteen large ships of over 300 tons, ten of medium size, and fourteen small ones. Southampton was the headquarters, and most of the ships were newly built, or rebuilt from existing vessels acquired by capture or purchase, at yards close to the town. William Soper, a Southampton merchant and draper, took general charge of the business administration. He was appointed Surveyor of the King's Ships at a salary of twelvepence a day. The *Holy Ghost* was a great Spanish ship rebuilt for the King's service. Others were the *Jesus* and the *Trinity Royal*. The greatest of all was the *Grace Dieu* of 1400 tons, constructed in a "dok" surrounded by a defence of stakes and brambles to prevent theft of the materials.

The story of the *Grace Dieu* is a sad one. She was the greatest ship that had ever been built in England and, like other greatest ships—Brunel's *Great Eastern*, for example—she was too long a stride forward in a business whose advance has always been by moderate successive steps. The Venetian and Genoese great ships that came to Southampton were carvel built in Mediterranean fashion. The *Grace Dieu* was clinker built, and in that large size the method proved inadequate to provide a seaworthy hull. She made only one passage—the ten miles from Southampton to Bursledon, up the Hamble river, and there she remained afloat, we may imagine leaking like a basket, for some years until she was put aground on the mud, and in 1439 was struck by lightning and burnt. This is the ship whose lower parts are still extant at Bursledon and have been carefully examined in our time.[1] Undeterred by the failure, Henry V ordered another and still greater ship to be built at Bayonne, where perhaps they built carvel fashion ; but she was not finished at the time of his death and nothing more is known of her. To own a monster ship has been the fancy of several kings. Apart from this, Henry V's Navy was sensible and successful, and when it was dispersed after his death the Channel relapsed into anarchy. Adam de Moleyns wrote his *Libelle* in 1436 as the despairing cry of a man who saw his country going down :

> Four things our Noble sheweth to me,
> King, Ship and Sword, and power of the sea.
> Where be our ships, where be our swords become ?
> Our enemies bid for the Ship set a sheep.
> Alas our rule halteth, it is benumb.
> Who dare well say that lordship should take keep ?
>
> I will assay, though mine heart gin to weep,
> To do this work, if we will ever see,
> For very shame, to keep about the sea.
> Shall any Prince, what so be his name,
> Which hath nobles much like ours,
> Be Lord of Sea ?   And Flemings to our blame,
> Stop us, take us, and so make fade the flowers
> Of English state, and distain our honours ?
> For cowardice alas it should so be.
> Therefore I gin to write now of the sea.

[1] See *Mariner's Mirror*, April 1934, *The Bursledon Ship*, by R. C. Anderson ; and February 1954, *The Building of the Grace Dieu*, etc., at Southampton, by Mrs. W. J. Carpenter Turner.

CHAPTER EIGHT

The New Maritime Interests

I. ATLANTIC PROSPECTS

SOCIAL HISTORIANS tell us that the beginning of the Tudor period in 1485 brought in no appreciable changes in English life, that to those who saw him Henry VII was not a new kind of king but rather an unusually efficient example of the established kind, and that in general the ordinary man of the early sixteenth century was no more conscious of living in Modern Times than his grandfather had been of living in the Middle Ages. Yet there was a movement. European man, in his perceptions, his interests and his way of life, has never long remained static. Every century, as we look back, has its colour, its climate and its outlook, different from those of the past. Even the countrymen and the townsmen of the Tudor century were living a different life as time went on. The seamen and the people of the ports and the coastline saw some rapid changes and grew familiar with things that their forbears had never thought of.

To the minds of some men, independent and daring private adventurers for the most part, the Channel opened out as a path to the wide world beyond Christendom, to fruitful fisheries, tropical spice islands, lands " beneath the equinoctial " where the sun's heat engendered gold and gems. After Cabot and the Bristol men had found land two thousand miles across the ocean, as they did in 1497 if not earlier, none could look out from Plymouth Sound and think that westward was " nought but herrings." Coastlines grew solid, veiled in mist but known to be there, the New Found Land, the Land of America, the Islands of the West Indies ; and thought and action reached out together.

Merchants in the Channel ports, with their ambitions limited to

Europe, realised that they had kings with a policy to favour their advance, a relentless opportunist policy of using every twist of law and treaty to depress the foreigner and favour the Englishman. Henry VII was in that aspect a new kind of king, a business man intent on profit and the penetration of markets, on increasing his people's wealth, which meant his own. The southern trades, in which the Channel was concerned, saw his chief successes, the trades with Gascony and Spain and the Mediterranean. In these the goods which had been brought in principally by foreigners were increasingly handled by English merchants and their shipping.

Above all, the sixteenth century was the century of the Navy, the royal force which had had only a fitful existence in times past, but which now became a permanent service, with ships, men and administration renewed in an unbroken succession to our own day. Henry VIII was the author of that. If his father was a king of a new character he himself was a king of a new type, the magnificent embodiment of a nation-state ready to break with the past and take its place in complete independence in an expanding world where the old rules and conventions were ceasing to be accepted. The mood of the time was for greatness. England wanted a great king, not cool and subtle, but flamboyant and majestic, and Henry fulfilled the desire. The older kings had been " His Grace." Henry VIII was " His Majesty," and the word was not so well worn that men used it without noting its significance. With genius he perceived that the prime support of majesty in its dealings with Europe must be not an army but a navy ; and the Navy grew in strength and experience from his first year to his last. The principal scene of its service was in the waters of the Channel.

The immediately useful discovery made by the Bristol men in the West was that of the Newfoundland cod fishery. The ports of the western Channel began early to take a share in it, but not at first on a great scale. Fish caught by Englishmen was not dutiable, and so makes no mark in the customs records, and the information is scanty. We hear casually of the Newfoundland fishing fleet in 1522, and Acts of 1541 and 1548 recognised and regulated the trade. It was only later in the century that it became a leading business of the west country ports, Plymouth and more especially Dartmouth.

Salt was a problem, for English supplies were not abundant, and the importation of foreign salt cut into the profits. For this reason the English fishermen worked close to the Newfoundland coast and landed their catch on suitable beaches. There they set up wooden platforms or stages where they split the fish, lightly salted them, and completed the curing by drying in the wind. The result was " stockfish," a dry, leathery but durable product, unappetising as food but valuable for victualling ships on long voyages, and for European consumption during the Lenten fast and on fish days throughout the year. It was a useful cargo for sale in the growing Mediterranean trade. The English fishermen commonly used ships of fifty tons with a crew of twenty. Half of them fished with hook and line from the ship or its boats. The others did the splitting and curing on the stages. They sailed from the Channel in March or April, when there was generally a seasonal east wind to blow them across the Atlantic, and they returned about July and August when the westerlies prevailed.

The French and Portuguese were early in the fishery, and later the seamen of northern Spain. With better salt supplies they made less use of the shore, and fished out on the great Newfoundland bank, barrelling the cod in strong brine and bringing it home wet. Spain and Portugal, always deficient in agricultural foodstuffs, came to rely greatly on the Newfoundland fishery, a fact of strategic importance in the Elizabethan war with Philip II. The English seem generally to have preponderated on the shore itself, and it became the custom in the coves and harbours for the first skipper arriving in the season to assume authority as admiral of the port and regulate disputes about stages. Although they were there only in the summer months this was the germ of the true colonisation of Newfoundland in the following century. These summer residents saw the climate at its best, and the earlier colonial planners received little information of the winter conditions which awaited them.

So much for the fishermen, unlettered men who left no written record of what they saw and did, and probably speculated little on what lay in the continent on whose fringe they worked. It was not until an educated Elizabethan, Anthony Parkhurst, devoted himself to sailing each year with the fishermen and exploring the country

1, 2.   *The Needles,* Isle of Wight (above) ; looking westward to Standfast
Point, East Dorset, with its chalk pinnacle, Old Harry (below). Beyond
Standfast Point is the entrance of Poole Harbour.

3. *Portchester Castle*. The outer wall is that of the Roman Portus Adurni. The castle and the church within the walls are medieval

4. *Pevensey*. The medieval castle built within the Roman walls of Anderida, a fort of the Saxon shore.

5, 6. *Ships from the Bayeux Tapestry* (above). *The Gokstad Ship* (below), a Viking vessel buried in the ninth century and uncovered in the nineteenth.

7, 8. *Rye* (above), as seen from the river which is now embanked. (Copyright Country Life.) *The Mouth of the River Dart* (below).

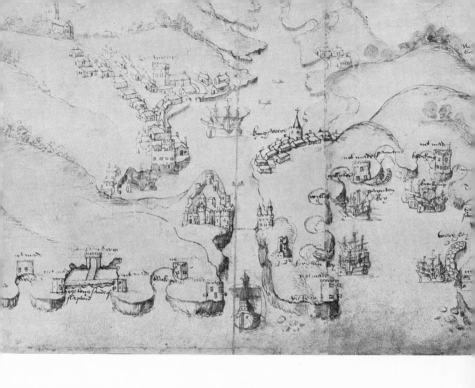

9, 10. *Dartmouth*, c. 1540 (above). The coastal defences were for an expected French invasion. They were not completed.
(below) *Plymouth in the Time of Henry VIII.*

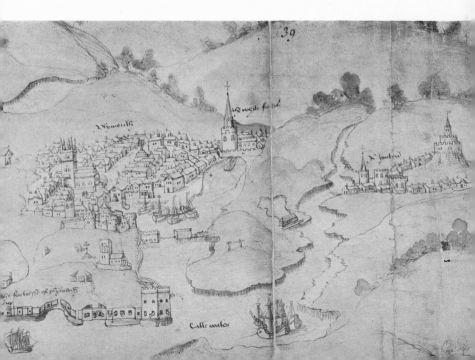

11. *Edward III's Royal Cog.* From a water-colour by Gregory Robinson.

12, 13. *A French Raid at Brighton, 1514* (above). The French are landing on the beach, firing the local ships, and the town is partly ablaze. (left) *A Ship of 1490.* From the manuscript *Life of the Earl of Warwick* in the British Museum.

14, 15. *The Great Harry* and *The Antelope*, 1545. The *Harry* (above)
of a thousand tons was the King's largest ship. The *Antelope* (below)
was of a low-built class called galleasses with auxiliary oars.
The oar-ports are seen beneath the guns.

16, 17. *Newfoundland Fishing Scene* (above). The cod are being landed and cleaned on the upper staging and dried off as stockfish on the lower. (below) *Elizabethan Galleon of the Armada Period.* The print is dated 1601.

18, 19. *The Royal Escape* (above). Formerly the *Surprise,* in which
Charles II escaped to France in 1651, and which he purchased after the
Restoration. (below) *Mayflower II.* A reconstruction of the ship of the
Pilgrim Fathers, built in Dartmouth and sailed to America in 1957.
(Beken & Sons, Cowes, Isle of Wight)

20. *The First Eddystone Lighthouse.* A contemporary painting in the possession of Viscountess Astor. This was the lighthouse destroyed in the great storm of 1703.

21, 22. *The Tudor House*, Southampton (above). *The Butterwalk*, Dartmouth (below), restored after severe damage in the Second World War.

23, 24. *Invasion by Napoleon.* Cartoons of 1803-5.

25, 26. *Hastings Luggers.* (below) *Deal Luggers,* 1872: from a
water-colour in the author's possession.

27, 28. *Hastings*, c. 1830 (above). The view is down the Bourne Valley through the present old town. (below) *Brighton*, c. 1830.

29, 30.   *H.M.S. Warrior*, 1860 (above), the first British ironclad.
(below) *H.M.S. Captain*, 1870.

while they worked, that any information about the interior became available.

English lawyers played an active and honourable part in spreading the light among their fellow-countrymen about the possibilities of enterprise across the ocean. In a sense Sir Thomas More takes rank with the pioneers, for his *Utopia* (1516), although primarily an essay in social planning, described a strange country in unknown South America, imagined before Pizarro and the conquistadores had revealed the truth. More and his friends, and by consequence King Henry, with whom they were influential, were certainly thinking in practical terms about the western mysteries. In 1517 More's brother-in-law John Rastell, also a scholar and a lawyer, led an expedition intended for the planting of a colony in the New Found Land. He probably also thought of using it as a base from which to press on to Asia, which he said was only a thousand miles beyond. Although Rastell had the King's approval his voyage was a fiasco. The seamen, instigated by a villainous purser, were determined not to cross the Atlantic. Rastell, only an amateur at sea, had no control. After leaving Gravesend, the mariners, alleging all sorts of deficiencies and leaks, insisted on putting into Sandwich, and then successively into Dartmouth, Plymouth and Falmouth. The summer was passing, and they said it was too late to cross the ocean. Rastell got them out of Falmouth and west to the Irish coast. There they found it necessary to visit Waterford, and finally Cork, where they pushed Rastell on shore and sailed back to London without him. Two years later Rastell printed a very interesting description of what was then known of North America and of what he had meant to do ; but he was never able to try again. Nearly twenty years afterwards, in 1536, there was another outburst of learned interest in America, when a party of London lawyers chartered a ship to take them to Newfoundland. They were simply tourists, without any colonising intent. They came to grief. Many died of hunger on the desolate coasts. The survivors at length victualled themselves by capturing a French fishing vessel, and struggled home. The Frenchmen afterwards turned up with complaint of piracy. The King personally investigated the affair and " was so moved with pity that he punished not his subjects, but of his own purse made full and royal recompense unto the French."

The true advance began with professional seamen, with whom were merged professional merchants. For the merchant often sailed with his own ship and goods to foreign markets, and the merchant's son learned the business of the sea as a mariner in his father's ships. This was particularly true of the west-country ports engaged in the Spanish and Mediterranean trades. It is illustrated in the story of the Hawkins family of Plymouth.

In the 1520's we hear of William Hawkins commanding his own ship in trading voyages to Portugal and Andalusia. He was a man good at making contacts, and he learned things about two tropical Atlantic coasts where Englishmen had not yet been. One was that of West Africa, the other of Brazil, and both offered fine possibilities of profit. Both had been discovered by the Portuguese, and had since been visited by the French. English exploiters came third on the list.

William Hawkins had a ship of 250 tons named the *Paul* of Plymouth. In her he sailed in 1530 to the West African coast, to the River of Sestos, in what is now Liberia. Its products included ivory and Guinea pepper, a variety inferior to the oriental pepper, and for them he traded knives, combs and hatchets, metal arm-rings, and English cloth. Thence he crossed the Atlantic to eastern Brazil, there to lade the brazil-wood which yielded a very costly dyestuff. Hawkins personally made the same voyage twice afterwards, and then sent out his ships under other captains. The only customs record surviving is that for a voyage by the *Paul* in 1540, which shows that the cargo brought home was twenty times the value of that taken out. Hawkins was well known to the King and to Thomas Cromwell, and in a letter we find him asking Cromwell to put his request to the King for a loan of money, guns and powder for the expansion of the business. On one of his voyages he brought back a Brazilian chief whom he exhibited at court, complete with barbaric adornments and a precious stone embedded in his chin. The poor savage died on the way home to Brazil. Martin Cockram, a sailor whom Hawkins left with the tribe as a hostage for their chief, was recovered in spite of the chief's death, and was living as an ancient man in Plymouth fifty years afterwards.

Soon after Plymouth had discovered the Brazil trade Southampton joined in it. Several Southampton merchants took part, including one Robert Reneger, who was to be well known later in another connection. These men, like Hawkins, were in business in the Spanish trade before they reached out over the ocean. By 1542 the Southampton men had a permanent station described as a fort on the Brazilian coast near Bahia. The customs indicate that they were selling brazil-wood in Italy, where the fine cloth woven required the finest dyes. Of all this we have only casual hints and the gleanings made long afterwards by Richard Hakluyt from mercantile ledgers and the memories of old men. They tell us almost nothing of what really went on in Brazil. But from Portuguese and French historians we learn that the brazil-wood coast was a scene of chronic violence. The Portuguese discovered it in 1500. Their main imperial interest was in southern Asia, and they had no force to spare for the occupation of Brazil. They proposed to treat it as a monopolised trading coast, leaving the natives to their own chiefs so long as they produced the necessary goods. The French very soon broke into this arrangement and seized a share of the trade, so that both peoples began to construct fortified posts. The warfare between them was ruthless, and in the 1520's the Portuguese were ordered to sink French ships and give no quarter. It was into this scene that the English intruded, but what their adventures were we do not know. In those times, unlike our own, adventurers in new directions did not seek publicity : if you found a good thing you kept it to yourself. One little pictorial fact comes out of the French records. The Brazilian natives classified Europeans according to the colour of their hair. One group, evidently the Portuguese, had dark hair ; the other, the French and English, had red hair. The French were mostly Bretons and Normans, but the distinction of national types would not be so obvious to-day. The melting-pot has supervened.

We have no record of the continuance of the English in Brazil after 1542, when they were evidently in full vigour. The trade may have died out owing to the outbreak of Anglo-French war in the

Channel, a war in which we know Hawkins and Reneger to have taken part. But the French certainly continued their Brazil business, and the English may have done. When we next hear of them in Brazil in the 1570's they appear as an established mercantile element rather than as newcomers. In the later period William Hawkins the second, the son of the man we have been dealing with, was certainly interested in Brazil ; and as he had been born in 1519 he may very possibly have served as a young man in his father's Brazil ventures.

The English merchants of Henry VIII's reign, and notably those of London, Bristol, Southampton and Plymouth, were strongly established in Spain, not only in the North Spanish ports from which they brought iron goods to England, but also in Andalusia with its mercantile capital of Seville, whence the rich trade of the Spanish western empire was conducted. Before 1485 the Anglo-Spanish trade had been mainly in the hands of Spaniards, and the Spanish colony in London had been predominant. By 1530 the balance had shifted to the English, and the English colony in Andalusia comprised some men doing business on a large scale. Some of them lived there permanently and married Spanish women. Others, not married, like Robert Thorne of Bristol, had half-Spanish children. Seville was the headquarters, but much of the shipping did its business at the down-river port of San Lucar, which was a feudal holding of the Dukes of Medina Sidonia. In 1517 the English at San Lucar obtained various privileges from the Duke, including the right to build a church of St. George for their special use. There is still a church of St. George at San Lucar, although it is not the original building of the sixteenth century. In 1530 Henry VIII chartered the Andalusian merchants as a regulated company, to elect its own governor and officers and rule itself as did the Merchants Adventurers in the Low Countries. Southampton was prominent in the Spanish trade. The Londoners also, using the good road communication, worked some of their ships from Southampton, which enjoyed a better position as a down-Channel port.

From Seville the English were able to trade with the Spanish Indies. There was nothing clandestine about their business, so long as they complied with Spanish regulations. These were that licence to trade had to be obtained and that goods had to be manifested at Seville and shipped only from and to that port in vessels sailing under the Spanish flag. English factors were in Hispaniola in the 1520's and at a later time there were several in Mexico. But direct trade between England and the Spanish colonies was not allowed, and an English ship which arrived at Santo Domingo in 1527 was fired on and turned away.

II. HENRY VIII AND THE NAVY

Henry VIII inherited a small fleet of seven ships in 1509 and immediately began to build and buy others. He entered his first French war in 1512 with nineteen royal ships and finished it two years later with twenty-four. He and his father were the creators of the permanent naval system, not only of ships and officers permanently in the service, but of dockyards and building yards and the Navy Board of experienced executives, which had developed by 1546 out of the one-man control of the medieval Clerk of the Ships. Henry VII made a beginning, using Portsmouth as his chief naval base and constructing there what was claimed to be the first dry dock in England. He also built two first-class fighting ships, the *Regent* and the *Sovereign*. Henry VIII continued to develop Portsmouth, which he guarded with heavy fortifications. There was not as yet much permanent population. Leland about 1540 remarked : "The town is bare and little occupied in time of peace," and "there is much vacant ground within the town wall." France being the enemy, Portsmouth was the best headquarters for a fleet intended to command the Channel, and it had not far distant the mercantile and man-power resources of Southampton. The great ships of Henry's fleet served only in the Channel, or on the Breton coast just beyond its entrance. Brest was their farthest limit in the one direction, and the estuary of the Thames in the other. They were commissioned only in the summer and laid up in the winter ; and in time of peace they were unrigged and laid up for years at a time. The smaller ships served on the east coast, where they had a sometimes decisive influence in supplying and supporting land expeditions against Scotland. Portsmouth, valuable as the base for the active fleet against France, was at the same time a cause of anxiety ; for it was open to a surprise stroke if the French should mobilise a winter force or get to sea earlier than they were expected in the summer. If the French had really got hold of Portsmouth outside the sailing season the best of Henry's fleet could have been destroyed without resistance. Hence the fortifications, coupled with small craft patrolling outside the Wight, and fire-beacons to give warning of attack. And gradually also Henry transferred the laying-up to Woolwich and Deptford on the Thames, where his chief building-yards were eventually located.

In naval policy Henry VIII, from his accession at the age of eighteen, was an alert and original thinker. His early councillors showed no interest in the fleet. This is true even of Wolsey, who could equip armies but badly fumbled the victualling of the Navy in the war of 1512–14. The growth of the Navy, in principle and in detail, was the King's own work. At the end he had an efficient naval staff, but it was of his own creation. The King's broad claim to credit is that he built up a strong fleet, not only for defence against invasion, but to make English policy effective in an age of new economic developments and powerful national monarchies. England's greatest mercantile connections were eastward with the Netherlands and southward with Spain, which itself was a step towards the rich Mediterranean trade that was beginning to develop. Henry VII had made treaty connections with the Netherlands and Spain, which were themselves dynastically linked with the Holy Roman Empire and the Hapsburg imperial family. These links solidified when in 1516 and 1519 the Habsburg prince, Charles V, became King of Spain and Holy Roman Emperor, a development that had been foreseen and expected. In the midst of the Emperor's dominions lay the hostile power of France, infinitely stronger and more aggressive than in the previous century. England's interest was with her best customers, and the new Navy was the keystone of the alliance, keeping open the Channel thoroughfare between the eastern and western seats of Charles's power and giving England's king a decisive voice in the high affairs of Europe. This effect was achieved by Henry's ships and guns and the Portsmouth base, which cost much less than did the armies with which Charles V and Francis I fought long campaigns on land.

The Channel situation called for strength, for the French were powerful at sea. In the 1490's the French crown had taken possession of Brittany, previously an independent duchy. The Breton coast had harbours, including the great port of Brest, and produced ships and first-class seamen. The Normans farther east were traditionally great seamen, since the days when they had fought the Cinque Ports men in endless raids and scuffles. Normans and Bretons were the maritime strength of the new French monarchy. They were more enterprising than the English in exploiting the western fisheries of the New Found Land, and as corsairs they were attacking Spain in the western tropics a generation before the English : it was here that the Imperial alliance held England back. The sort of enterprise that was to produce Drake and the Elizabethan captains was training vigorous French seamen half a century in advance of them. Francis I, becoming King of France in 1515, immediately set about creating the new naval base of Havre de Grace in the Seine estuary as a counterpart to Portsmouth ; but in the event his land campaigns prevented him from building up a royal fleet as strong as Henry's. He was himself a soldier, and he put his money into armies which he led to Italian conquests.

In detail also Henry VIII was a man of naval knowledge. He inspected ships and dockyards and conferred with captains, gunners and shipwrights. His personal interest in these men was keen. It was personal acquaintance, in one instance, that led him to intervene between a humble shipwright and a trial for heresy. The man's religious views were unsound, and he was haled before an ecclesiastical court. Henry told the priests that they might examine the man but were not to press him, for he was but a simple-minded fellow. It was a sign of the new age, a useful man not to be wasted : Henry V a hundred years before would have seen him burnt with pious satisfaction. Henry's first fleet was a mixed affair of various types and armaments, hardly one great ship being like another. An extraordinary variety of guns might be put into one vessel, specimens of all the sizes. But the guns represented a new policy. In a fight off Brest in the war of 1512 the *Regent* had grappled a great French ship, and both had caught fire and burnt together, with the loss of nearly all their men. This caused Henry to mount heavy guns low down in his ships, with the idea of sinking the enemy from a distance. To prevent his own ships from being sunk by gunfire he thickened their sides along the waterline with wales of extra timber ; and the age-long competition of guns and armour had begun. Ships had long been armed with small guns for the purpose of sweeping the enemy's decks, but the big gun policy was new. It entailed also the cutting of ports and their closure by hinged lids.

Henry VIII had one naval foible which he shared with other kings of his time, the desire to possess a monster ship which should make evident his majesty and prestige. When the *Regent* was lost he laid down the *Great Harry* of 1500 tons. She was finished in 1514, too late to take part in the war, but she was given a trial trip in the Channel and then laid up until the next war, 1522. We do not know her dimensions. She had four masts and a great variety of guns, some of them very heavy. A foreigner's description says that she had in her poop no less than *septem mansiones*, which has been translated as seven decks one above the other. More likely it stands for seven great cabins. Although the greater part of the oak timber was in free gifts to the King, she cost him an extravagant sum of money. The timber was unseasoned stuff, felled for the job and used immediately. This seems to have been the practice of early Tudor shipwrights, who were indifferent also to any distinction between summer and winter felling. Their ships began rapidly to be infected with rot, which was countered by cutting out and replacing the damaged members. When this was neglected in times of slack administration the whole fleet might become unseaworthy in a few years, as it did in the reign of Mary. This first *Great Harry* was a Channel portent, her base Portsmouth, and her sailing solely between Spithead and the Thames. She served for a month in 1522, when a new war broke out with France. The admiral paid due deference to the royal fancy by reporting that she sailed excellently, and then, although it was only the beginning of June, went on to speak of laying her up. She was an unhappy responsibility, and he wanted to be rid of her : she was seen afloat no more in this war. Thenceforward she quietly decayed at Portsmouth, and

John Leland, visiting the place about 1540, said that he had seen her remains lying in a dock.

The King was then building a second *Great Harry*, this time of 1000 tons. She was evidently a more practicable ship, with a more homogeneous armament. Henry was learning by experience, and was in fact creating a new and much better fleet with the money obtained from the dissolution of the monasteries. The second *Harry* was twice in action with the French in 1545 and received a lot of enemy shot without suffering much damage. She outlived the King and was accidentally burnt at Woolwich in 1553.

The Channel wars and the new ideas of national armament produced pictorial records of the coast such as do not exist for earlier times. The earliest picture now extant of any named and identified place on the coast is a coloured sketch showing a French attack on Brighton in 1514.[1] It depicts Brighthelmstone as a large village built round three sides of a square green, the shore forming the fourth. Hove appears as a distinct village to the westward. French galleys are seen thrust ashore on the beach, and French sailing-ships at sea covering the operation. The French have set fire to the local fishing-boats and the houses of Brighton. But the beacon fire smoking in "the town fire-cage," a sort of brazier hoisted on a signal spar, is summoning reinforcements, and the Sussex militia are shown in the background marching down to the scene. A written record tells us that they drove off the French, and that a few weeks later Sir John Wallop, a Portsmouth man, led a punitive force to commit satisfactory devastations on the other side of the Channel. He was claimed to have burnt twenty-one towns and villages.

The second Channel picture is topographically poor. It is a large painting at Hampton Court showing Henry VIII embarking at Dover in 1520. He was crossing to Calais to confer with Francis I at the Field of Cloth of Gold, a summit meeting in Renaissance costume which led only to renewed hostility. The picture shows the *Great Harry* and other large ships which in fact were not there,

[1] The picture bears the date 1545, but this is thought to have been added in error by a later hand. The French are known to have raided Brighton in 1514, and there is no record that they did so in 1545. In fact it is virtually certain that they did not. The picture is in Cotton MSS., Aug. I.1.18.

for the smaller vessels actually used are named in the records. All it shows of Dover is the castle on the height in the background and two unidentifiable forts on the shore—nothing of the town. There is however an undated picture of Dover which the details show to have been made under Henry VIII and probably in the earlier part of the reign. It shows very clearly the castle on the height and the town in the valley below. To the south-west of the town is the harbour with an entrance between two jetties. There are merchantmen in the harbour, and outside in the bay some ships of war, all very carefully drawn with plenty of detail.

Henry VIII's breach with the Pope in the 1530's brought in a period of danger and a risk of invasion by the strong Catholic powers. To counter it he used the wealth of the monasteries to rebuild the Navy and fortify the coast. The first acute crisis came in 1538–40, when it seemed likely that Paul III, having excommunicated Henry, would induce the two rivals Francis I and Charles V to combine to put an end to him. Henry met the threat with vigour. His dockyards were hard at work turning out new great ships, a new *Mary Rose* and others in addition to the new *Great Harry*, and turning out also new middle-sized ships of a design that was novel in England. These were of about 400 to 450 tons and were described as galleasses, although the word was not used with Italian precision. They had low super-structures, or none—the *Bull* had an upper deck flush from stem to stern—and they were fully rigged ships. But they had also auxiliary power, with a row of oar-ports for long sweeps close to the water-line. Above the rowing deck was the main gun deck with a few heavy weapons. The absence of superstructures and their multiplicity of light guns was due to the calculation that these ships could not be boarded in battle, since their oars would keep them mobile. Sir Julian Corbett in his survey of the Tudor Navy condemned this innovation as a retrograde step. It might also be argued that, for its purpose of fighting solely in the Channel, it was a very advanced one, anticipating the auxiliary full-rigged battleships of the mid-nineteenth century. It did not survive the King himself, for all the " rowing pieces " were disposed of after his death, or had the oars taken out

¹ Cotton MSS., Aug. I. 1. 22, 23.

of them ; but they certainly did good service in his last war with the French.

Not only did Henry modernise his Navy, but he also fortified the coast in such a manner as to end the long record of raids and surprise landings which had been an essential ingredient of past history. The east coast from Berwick to the Thames, and the Channel coast from the Thames to Falmouth were systematically provided with big stone castles at all the best anchorages and with lesser bulwarks and batteries at the minor ones, a thorough-going policy comparable to that of the martello towers in the Napoleonic War. Many of the castles still exist—Tilbury in the Thames, Walmer overlooking the Downs, Camber Castle at Rye, Calshot, Hurst and Yarmouth in the Solent, Pendennis Castle at Falmouth. Foundations of the castle at Deal can still be seen, and the remains of Sandgate Castle near Hythe were eaten away by the sea within living memory. Existing strong places were refortified, Dover, Portsmouth, Dartmouth, Plymouth and Fowey. All the little havens had their batteries. The guns and a few professional gunners were provided by the King, and the local men were enrolled to form full garrisons when the need arose, some local gentleman being appointed captain of the defences. The King had incurred the displeasure of the continent, and he met it unrepentant. So also did his people : they were with him heart and soul. They were nearly all Catholics, but they were quite clear that the King of England was not to be deposed by the Pope.

While this work was in progress the authorities had a thorough pictorial record made of the condition of the coast. Most likely it covered the whole Channel, but the only portions now surviving show the South-west and Calais. The view is drawn as from a position a mile or two out at sea and a few hundred feet up, looking on towns and coastline as one might see them from a high cliff. These coloured drawings give our earliest pictures of Dartmouth and Plymouth and the smaller ports adjacent. They are fascinating. Plymouth in particular is a gem. We owe the survival of this treasure to Sir Robert Cotton, the seventeenth-century collector, whose manuscripts are now in the British Museum. In his own library he had the items grouped in shelves and presses beneath busts of the Roman emperors, and the Museum has kept to the imperial arrangement. Most of the plans and drawings are under the name of Augustus.

III. THE INVASION THREAT OF 1545

The firm front shown in 1539 averted war, and before long the Emperor and the King of France fell out again. They came to blows in 1543, and the complications of politics, mainly Scottish, drew Henry VIII into the struggle. In 1544 he was seriously at war, in alliance with Charles V, against France and Scotland. In the summer of 1544 he led an army across the Channel to invade France through Calais. Charles was to join him in an advance on Paris. It did not come off. Henry laid siege to Boulogne, which he captured in September ; and at the same time the Emperor suddenly made a separate peace with Francis. Henry was left alone to fight France and Scotland, and among the English there was enormous indignation against Charles and his Flemish and Spanish subjects. This is the setting for some exciting transactions in the Channel and the western seas of Europe.

As soon as the war began Henry not only mobilised his whole Navy but requisitioned merchant shipping to transport his army to France. Shipowners whose ships were not so required received licences to put to sea and "annoy the King's enemies" as privateers. William Hawkins of Plymouth was among them, and he had half a dozen small wasps infesting the western Channel and snapping up French merchantmen. The conditions of this irregular warfare had altered since the previous century. The weatherly three-masted ship and the increased supply of guns made it unnecessary for privateers or pirates to combine in large squadrons. Instead they worked alone or in twos and threes and relied on speed. Their handy little craft were able to cut off stragglers even from guarded convoys and their guns compelled surrender without a hand-to-hand fight. They often did not keep possession of their victims, but removed the cream of the lading and let them go, sometimes to be captured again with some more good stuff. The essence of the game lay in the cheapness of the outfit. Small 50-ton ships cost very little, and the royal armouries at the Tower had plenty of light guns for issue to approved users.[1] The seamen were not paid wages but served for a share of the booty, one-third of its value going to the crew, together with the right to annex as individuals anything found above the main deck of a prize, for which purpose they stripped and searched the prisoners. It was all very rough and ready, but we do discern a more civilised attitude than that of the medieval centuries, far less wanton killing and the blackguardism of throwing men overboard to drown, as noted by Chaucer among the principles of his Canterbury shipman-pilgrim. The sixteenth-century freebooters did not do that.

When the Emperor made his separate peace Henry knew that he would have to face a French attempt at invasion. Francis I had considerable forces of trained professional soldiers, mostly Germans, Swiss and Italians, whose commanders made contracts with any government that would pay them. The mercenaries were equipped with armour and armed with field-guns and hackbuts, an early form of musket. Henry's own army consisted of civilian Englishmen enlisted for the campaign and armed with the bill and the longbow, which the new generation of officers considered to be obsolete. For defence Henry could call out the militia, consisting of every fit man between sixteen and sixty, also armed with bills and bows. It seemed that a French landing would be a very serious matter, and that all would depend on its prevention by the Navy. The French navy had probably fewer great ships than the English, but in the winter of 1544-5 Francis obtained a number of Italian carracks and armed them as ships of war. He also brought round twenty-five galleys from the Mediterranean, and by midsummer all this force, concentrated at Le Havre, had been welded into a formidable fleet exceeding the English in tonnage. Francis had plenty of fine seamen, the product of the ocean trades with Africa, Brazil and Newfoundland, and of twenty years of piratical attacks on the Spaniards in the Caribbean.

Meanwhile the English privateers were getting Henry into

[1] In the records of the Admiralty Court there are valuations of three privateer vessels of the Armada period, when prices were certainly higher than in Henry VIII's time. One of 35 tons was valued, complete with guns and all equipment, at £80 ; another of 45 tons at £50 ; and a third of 40 tons at £65. See K. R. Andrews, *Appraisements of Elizabethan Privateersmen*, in *Mariner's Mirror*, Vol. 37, No. 1, January 1951.

trouble. When the Emperor quitted the war his Spanish, Flemish and German subjects became neutrals. French merchants thereupon took to shipping their goods in the neutral ships, claiming that the flag covered the goods. The privateers contended that they had the right to take enemy goods out of neutral ships, and did so extensively. Sometimes they did more, for there was a high feeling that Charles V was a traitorous deserter. No doubt Henry thought so too, but he had to dissemble his feelings, for he did not want the Emperor to come in against him as an ally of the French. Towards that events were trending, owing to the exuberance of the privateers. Imperial protests became acrimonious, and in Spain the Inquisition was arresting English merchants and questioning them for heresy. Early in 1545 Charles arrested all English merchants in the Netherlands and Spain, pending satisfaction for the privateers' iniquities. It was the next thing to war.

But in England things were done according to law, and every maritime dispute had to be thrashed out in the High Court of Admiralty. The Court did its best, but it was choked with cases in which it had no true evidence for a decision. The litigants lied habitually. William Hawkins had captured some goods belonging to Juan Quintana Dueñas, who claimed to be a Spaniard. Hawkins said that the goods were French, and it did afterwards appear that the man had become a naturalised French subject under the name of Jean Quintanadoine. But Hawkins could not prove it at the time, and the court's decision went against him. He had already been selling the goods while the case was *sub judice*. Probably he had to, in order to satisfy his crews. The action made him guilty of contempt, and the Privy Council sent him to prison. He had been Mayor of Plymouth, doing good work for the Crown, and the King had a personal liking for him ; but with the Emperor in a threatening state an example had to be made. He was soon at liberty again.

Robert Reneger, the Southampton man who had traded in Brazil, and had also been a merchant in Andalusia, was now one of the privateers. The English merchants at Seville and San Lucar were going through a bad time, for the Inquisition not only racked its prisoners when examining for heresy, but confiscated their goods

on conviction. The more active spirits therefore became belli-
gerent at sea. Reneger cruised off the Spanish coast and there took
a prize which he alleged to be French. He carried her into a Spanish
port, where the authorities disallowed the capture. Spanish documents cast doubt on Reneger's story, but to his own satisfaction
he had an excuse for reprisals. In March 1545 he was off Cape St.
Vincent with four ships. There he met a Spanish ship from the
Indies carrying gold, silver, pearls and rich merchandise, worth
altogether 30,000 ducats. He captured her and brought the stuff
to England, letting the ship go. The Emperor was exceeding
wroth, and the case dragged on for years, ending in an only partial
restitution. Meanwhile Henry supported Reneger, who was
allowed to swagger with his wealth at court. He also provided
three or four armed ships for service with the Navy, and took part
in the summer's campaign. Dr. Connell-Smith, who has fully investigated this story, justly labels Reneger as a forerunner of Drake.[1]
He and the other privateers established a sense of confidence that
they could take any liberties they liked with Spanish power at sea,
so long as their own sovereign would back them.

Such was the general situation when the French were getting
ready to invade England in 1545. By midsummer they had 150
ships, large and small, concentrated at Le Havre, with an army to
be embarked in them. Henry collected 80 sail at Portsmouth, of
which about 40, not all of his own regular force, were described as
large. The French plan was to take Portsmouth and thence march
inland. They also counted on commanding the Channel and
starving out the garrison of Boulogne, which had shown itself
impervious to assault. Calais, a weaker place, would probably have
followed. This midsummer of 1545 was the high spot of Channel
history until the Armada year in 1588. Nothing of import so serious
to the country's destiny had occurred since the Norman conquest ;
for the stake was all or nothing, the overthrow or the triumph of
the Tudor rule that had already made England a great power.
Portsmouth was heavily fortified, and it may be asked why the
French should choose it as their point of attack. The answer is

[1] G. Connell-Smith, *Forerunners of Drake*, London, 1954, an illuminating account,
of English merchants in Spain in the reign of Henry VIII.

that its loss by the English would have meant the loss of the whole command of the Channel. The fleets of those days, crammed with men, needed constant supplies from the shore, and their brittle ships needed ready access to a dockyard. The *Great Harrys* and *Mary Roses* could not stand up to a summer gale. Portsmouth was the only English base on the Channel coast, and the Navy, having lost it, would have retreated to the Thames and left the Channel to the enemy.

Henry VIII was corpulent, old [1] and ill—he had only eighteen months to live. But he had personally directed the siege of Boulogne, and he now went down to Portsmouth to take command. On 18th July he was dining on board the *Harry* when the French were seen approaching. He went ashore to give orders for the calling-out of the militia and the concentration of all forces on the threatened point. The beacon fires flamed their message from hill to hill, and the men of southern England, who were ready for it, got instantly on the move, Londoners, peasants, yeomen and gentlemen, bowmen and billmen, petty-captains and captains, swarming along the roads under the command of Privy Councillors and the Lords-Lieutenants of the shires. Lisle,[2] the Lord Admiral, took over the Navy, to fight a first defensive action at Spithead with the aid of batteries along the shore. It was not the Nelson procedure, neither were the ships a Nelsonian fleet. The weather was hot, and the sun blazed upon grim and thirsty men. The militia meant business : one body asked the Duke of Norfolk to lead them between the French and the sea. It did not come to that, for the fleet was sufficient.

The French had anchored off Ryde and St. Helens. On the morning of the 19th, in a flat calm, D'Annebault the French admiral sent forward his twenty-five galleys. It was the galleys' perfect opportunity, smooth water, no wind, the English great-ships immobile at their anchors. For an hour the galleys fired at will into the fleet, making a special target of the *Harry*. They did no great damage, and evidently did not close to ramming distance. The

---

[1] He was 54, old for a Renaissance ruler. Not one monarch of his time lived to be sixty.
[2] John Dudley, Lord Lisle, afterwards Earl of Warwick and Duke of Northumberland, executed by Mary in 1553.

smaller English ships, the "rowing pieces," got under way and chased them off, while a breeze sprang up in the sultry air and the great ships made sail. But the odds were two to one, and Lisle did not press for a general battle away from the batteries. A sudden gust struck the *Mary Rose* with her gun ports open, the sills only sixteen inches above the waterline. She heeled and sank with the loss of nearly all her crew. The King saw it and cried out in anguish for his ship and his men. But the action was decisive for D'Annebault, who resigned the hope of taking Portsmouth. He landed some soldiers in the Isle of Wight, and in two days the native bowmen beat them out. He then withdrew his fleet eastwards and anchored off the shoals bordering Chichester Bar. The Sussex and Hampshire men were pouring into Portsmouth, but they were not needed, and the King stopped and dismissed the others on the roads.

The Channel privateers had been summoned to join Lisle and were coming in. Every seaman of the coast had been called up, and the women worked the fishing-boats that summer out of Sussex havens and Cornish coves. Lisle prayed for a south-west wind, for he saw the French in a bag between the Chichester and the Owers shoals. He got under way when it came, but D'Annebault saw the danger and withdrew in time. The French sailed eastwards and found a soft spot in the coast defences at Seaford. They landed some soldiers, but the militia quickly closed on them and few escaped to their ships. D'Annebault's hope was now to hold the Channel long enough for Boulogne to be taken, and he disembarked some of his troops to help in the siege. He then returned to the English coast. Lisle sailed to find him, and they met off Shoreham in mid-August. The weather was still hot and the wind light. D'Annebault again sent his galleys to the attack. The English galleasses were formed in a squadron separate from the sailing carracks, and, using their oars, dealt so roughly with the galleys that the great ships were scarcely engaged. It was then late in the day, and both fleets anchored, the English preparing for a decisive action on the morrow. But when day broke they saw the French sails disappearing over the horizon. D'Annebault had retired to Le Havre. He did not come out again. The hot weather had been doing deadly work in the overcrowded ships. Putrid food, fluxes and burning fevers, had killed great numbers in both fleets, and the French had suffered worst. An observer reported that the landing of their sick was a dreadful sight.

The campaign had lasted only a month, but it had vindicated Henry's care for the Navy. But for the Navy, the country would have suffered a first-class invasion by a professional army, and none can be sure what the issue would have been. The situation was to repeat itself in 1588, 1805 and 1940, with varying detail, and with the final question always left unanswered. Henry finished the war in the following year with an indemnity from France, and Boulogne was retained pending the payment of a heavy ransom. Before another year had passed both he and Francis I were dead and a different political situation was developing. The campaign of 1545 left its mark on the Navy almost until the Armada year. The success made doctrines and practices sacrosanct, although conditions and needs were changing, and John Hawkins as a naval reformer in the 1580's had a body of conservative diehards to overcome before he could get the fleet in order for the great struggle with Spain. Two of the men who served in 1545, William Holstocke and Sir William Winter, were members of the Navy Board in 1588.

There are some uncertainties on what took place in the action at Spithead, and there is difficulty in fitting the great numbers of ships into the restricted geographical setting. There is plenty of information but much vagueness and ambiguity, and the subject awaits investigation by a naval historian. One location is accurately fixed, the spot at which the *Mary Rose* went down, for her remains were found by divers in 1837, and some of her guns recovered.

CHAPTER NINE

The Elizabethan Scene

I. THE EDWARDIAN AND MARIAN PRELUDE

IN MARITIME affairs the death of Henry VIII in 1547 coincides with the opening of the new period which we call Elizabethan. Although Elizabeth I did not become Queen until 1558, some features of her reign are seen in growing importance during the short interval filled by Edward VI and Mary; and thenceforward they expanded through the remainder of the century. The essence of the change was that London became proportionately greater and the south coast ports smaller in their shares of maritime activity, and that the Channel grew increasingly to be London's channel to the west in predominance over its other interests. To this statement Plymouth stands in obvious exception, making its mark in English history as it had never done before. Plymouth at the mid-century was a small seaport so far as its trade and shipping were concerned. Its shining Elizabethan record was a series of incidents evoked by a handful of gifted leading men. They were great events that shaped history. They caused Plymouth to grow in wealth, size and population, yet they did not make it a materially great place in any comparison with London. The capital grew steadily throughout the half-century, and when it closed was only at the beginning of a further greatness that was not to cease.

Conditions, European and English, were changing. Protestantism was a rising force with a new quality, not the Lutheran type which had captured some German princes and become an accessory of their governments, but the more radical aggressive kind associated with the doctrines of Calvin. This fighting Protestantism was raising its head in Scotland, England, France, the Netherlands and the Rhineland. In the pre-Elizabethan decade it was a portent of revolution and an anxiety to rulers, but not yet victorious. But its growing strength in the Elizabethan age was to disrupt the traditional system of alliances, political and economic, and England's place in it.

The old home-waters trades were no longer to be exclusive of any others, but to share importance with new oceanic ventures, half warlike though almost entirely economic, their propagation in England governed by the fact that Catholic Spain ceased to be the great ally. And the oceanic ventures had illimitable expansion before them : American colonies, West Indian plantations, East Indian trade. The East India Company was created before Elizabeth died, and twenty years after that its capital was to comprise more than a million pounds, a sum that would have been impossible and incredible a generation earlier. That expansion was not Elizabethan, but it grew out of one that was, the Turkey Company of 1581 (from 1592 named the Levant Company), an exclusively London concern. This and many other undertakings needed capital, and capital for various reasons had to be raised in London. The merchants there had the highest financial experience, they had contacts with the European money-markets, especially Antwerp, and above all they were close to government, whose policies they could influence as none of the outports could. The close association of new economic adventures with government, the great mastery of Tudor government, and the concentration of the high courts of the legal system in London, with an importance greater than they had ever enjoyed before—these are some of the reasons for London's predominance in the new era of trade. Even the brilliant ventures that sailed from Plymouth, led by Plymouth men, were mainly capitalised from London.

The preponderance of the Crown's naval activity shifted from Portsmouth to the Thames estuary. After 1545 the French naval threat grew less intense. The French peace with the Emperor quickly expired, and Henry II, the new French King, was soon at war with him again, pursuing conquests on the Rhine and in Italy. The great French fleet of 1545 dwindled into a smaller one, as great fleets did in those times unless assiduously cared for. The ships rotted as a routine function of their being, and it was tempting to a land-minded government to sell off big ships for which it had no immediate use instead of paying expensively for their upkeep. Henry VIII had always done much of his building and laying-up on the Thames at Woolwich and Deptford. Portsmouth had been revealed as a somewhat risky location for the main base of the Navy. Henry's successors progressively withdrew the docks and store-houses to the Thames, and ended by creating a new naval base at Chatham in the Medway. Chatham was the headquarters of the Royal Navy during the Elizabethan age. It was in accordance with the new European situation. France lost strength, and degenerated into civil wars of religion. The Netherlands, in which Spanish armies appeared, became a threatening base for the invasion of England. The Medway looked towards them, and was also convenient for expeditions to Scotland, in which the Eliza-bethan government was increasingly interested. Naval interest shifted up Channel, and Portsmouth was almost abandoned by the fleet.

The events of 1544–5 had thrown a blight on Anglo-Spanish relations from which they never quite recovered. The new strength of Protestantism widened the rift. Even when the Catholic Queen Mary married Philip II, who succeeded his father as King of Spain shortly afterwards, the hostility between the English and Spanish peoples was increased. For Mary was unpopular, and her burning campaign against her Protestants was unjustly imputed to the influence of her Spanish husband. He in fact did not inspire the English burnings, but few knew that, and English opinion believed that he did ; for in his own Netherlands religious persecution was cruel and widespread, and in Spain the English had already suffered from the Inquisition. When Mary died the London bells rang peals of joy, as much for the end of the Spanish marriage as for that of the poor Queen herself. London had seen the fires of Smithfield. Its merchants had also been suffering in pocket from the views of the Spanish king. Anglo-Spanish enmity had set in. Yet for another decade the Anglo-Spanish alliance was none the less to continue, for its partners had the common interest that they both feared France. It was only when civil wars neutralised French power that England and Spain drew finally apart. Even then the contest was not between Elizabeth and Philip, neither of whom desired it, but between their peoples and their religions.

The Dukes of Somerset and Northumberland, who ruled successively in the name of the boy-King Edward VI, took steps for English maritime expansion in collaboration with the London merchants. The merchants were the prime movers, and they found the government helpful. The old seaman Sebastian Cabot, son of John Cabot who found North America, was invited to London and settled there with a handsome pension. He had been Pilot-Major of Spain and knew much that England did not know about world trade and ocean routes. A London syndicate at once employed Thomas Wyndham, a naval officer and privateer owner, to initiate a new trade with Africa. In 1551 he led an expedition to the Atlantic coast of Morocco, or Barbary without the Straits. He went again in 1552, and a regular trade was established at Agadir and other places in Southern Morocco. The promoters were nearly all merchants of London, and the ships were mostly of that port. Sometimes they took their departure from the south coast ports, Dover, Portsmouth or Plymouth, and returned to them; but it was essentially a London trade. The distribution of English goods and the collection of Moroccan goods were in the hands of Portuguese Jews resident in Morocco. In Portugal such men had to be conforming Christians, but in Morocco they practised their religion openly, and the English took out Hebrew Bibles for their benefit. The main trade was in English cloth, weapons and small metal goods, balanced by sugar, dates and molasses, all of which were somewhat rare in England. The Portuguese with their claim to a general monopoly of the African coast objected to the new English trade. They urged particularly the iniquity of supplying firearms to infidels and the impiety of providing Bibles for Jews. But the trade went on and governments supported it. The diplomatic factor in all the new trades which were to trespass upon Spanish and Portuguese monopolies was heavily in favour of London as against the outports, for the Londoners were close to the statesmen, and personal contacts counted for much.

In the summer of 1553, just as Edward VI died and Mary succeeded him, Wyndham was at Portsmouth fitting out a new expedition. It was on the account of the same influential group of London men, but it was for a new objective. It was to sail much farther south along the African coast, past Cape Verde and the River of Sestos, where William Hawkins had got ivory in the days of Henry VIII, and round Cape Palmas, where the coast ran eastwards for hundreds of miles into the great Bight of Benin. In modern terms, Wyndham was bound for the Gold Coast or Ghana, and for the coastal part of Nigeria. On the first he hoped to get gold, and on the second pepper. The Portuguese had been there for eighty years and had two or three fortified stations on the Gold Coast, between which were long stretches where the African chiefs and kings ruled with little interference. No Englishman had ever been there, and Wyndham took as his pilots two Portuguese renegades who knew the navigation. On 12th August he set sail with three London ships, the *Primrose*, *Lion* and *Moon*, and 140 men. One of them was young Martin Frobisher, then aged fifteen, an orphan from Yorkshire who was sent to sea by his London kinsman Sir John Yorke. For Frobisher it was the opening of a sea career of forty battling years, to end when he was shot by a Spanish musketeer at the storming of Crozon in 1594.

So Wyndham with his hundred and forty sailed down Channel in 1553, and next year the odd forty struggled back into Plymouth half dead with fever and scurvy. They told how they had robbed Portuguese ships on the way out (no new thing in Wyndham's record) and had fought on shore at Madeira. They had gone on to the Gold Coast and traded with the natives for gold dust. Then they had pressed on to a river in Benin to seek a lading of pepper. The African fevers smote them, Wyndham and the Portuguese died, most of the men died, and the forty survivors abandoned the *Lion* and made a terrible passage home in the other two ships. But they brought 150 lb. weight of gold, a very large sum for that time.

The merchants of the syndicate were greatly encouraged. In the manner of shipowners as viewed by seamen they paid the survivors twelve months wages for sixteen months service,[1] and immediately set forth a new and stronger expedition. This time there were five ships, and experience yielded better fortune ; for the fleet lost only twenty-four men and brought home 400 lb. of gold, probably the greatest amount that had ever come into England at one time, with ivory and pepper in addition. Here was another new trade established, and in spite of all opposition it went on. Various London syndicates tried their luck, and numerous expeditions went out, both in Mary's and Elizabeth's reigns. The Portuguese sent warships to the Gold Coast and ambassadors to London, both without avail. Mary indeed, urged by her Spanish husband, prohibited the voyages, but that did not stop them, for the Navy officials connived at them and even allowed the venturers to charter small ships belonging to the Queen. Elizabeth backed her merchants and refused to listen to Portuguese protests, and in her time Sir William Winter and other members of the Navy Board were themselves investors in the gold trade. This caused the only prolonged breach in eight hundred years of Anglo-Portuguese friendship. Plymouth, Portsmouth and London were agog with talk of gold and elephants' teeth, and with censure of the evil meanings of Philip II and his papal bulls.

II. THE ATLANTIC ENTERPRISES OF JOHN HAWKINS

At the beginning of Elizabeth's reign Plymouth, in alliance with London, became prominent in the opening of yet another ocean trade. Old William Hawkins, the Brazil pioneer, died in 1554, leaving his business to his two sons William and John. At that date William Hawkins the second was thirty-five, and John Hawkins was twenty-two. They appear to have been the chief shipowners of what was then the small port of Plymouth, conducting a general trade in various directions, mingled with privateering as opportunity arose. There was a sharp legal line between privateering and piracy. The privateer had a licence or commission from

[1] This was alleged by the men, who were greatly embittered. The case was examined in the Admiralty Court, whose documents were discovered by Professor J. W. Blake. The best and fullest account of all these African voyages is to be found in his *Europeans in West Africa*, 1450–1560, Hakluyt Society 1942.

government, whereas the pirate was just a criminal ; and the Hawkins firm always kept on the right side of the line. In contemporary minds the distinction was vital. John Hawkins expressed contempt for pirates and took pride in the honesty of his own proceedings. One of the Hawkins trades was with the Canary Islands, and John Hawkins made several voyages there. He became friendly with leading Spaniards in the islands and learned much about the trading prospects in the Spanish colonies in the West Indies. He also appears to have assisted in transporting Philip II to England for his marriage to Queen Mary, and to have done some particular service which made him favourably known to the King.

By 1559 Hawkins had plans maturing which required aid from London. He went there and married Katherine the daughter of Benjamin Gonson, Treasurer of the Navy and senior officer of the Navy Board. Thenceforward Hawkins kept a house in London as well as one in Plymouth, and was equally a citizen of both. His plans were involved in the international situation. The Anglo-Spanish alliance was still a dominant factor, for the power of France was yet undiminished, and both Elizabeth I and Philip II had reason to fear it. But Anglo-Spanish relations had nevertheless deteriorated, for reasons that have been noted in these pages. Responsible men on both sides desired to improve them and revive the vigour of the old connection that was the best guarantee of security. The French seamen, irrespective of formal peace or war, were raiding the Spanish West as they had been doing for thirty years past, and Spain was apparently unable to stop them. Most of the French raiders were now Huguenots, Calvinists of the French variety, and under Admiral Coligny the Huguenot party was growing strong in French politics and society. The Franco-Spanish feud was thus exasperated by religious offence.

What Hawkins had in mind was this : to offer to Philip II an English naval force in return for permission to trade in the western colonies. The trade especially in view was that of supplying negro slaves from Africa to the colonists. It was not an entirely revolutionary proposal, since the slave trade had long been on a system of contracts granted by the Spanish government to selected business firms, and these firms had not always been Spanish : some were

185

Portuguese and some were Italians of Genoa. If foreigners might hold the contracts, why should not the English be among them? But there was a big difference. Everything, slaves included, hitherto shipped to the Spanish west had gone through Seville under the Spanish flag. What Hawkins intended was to work direct from Plymouth in his own ships and under the English flag. He thought it a reasonable proposition, for Spain had evident need of the naval service he could offer. The Queen thought so too, and approved the plan, not only for its extension of English trade but for its creation of a new mutual interest that should prevent England and Spain from drifting apart. The decision rested with Philip, and for him religion was the main factor. His father had enjoined him to preserve the English alliance and to resist heresy. The two were now becoming incompatible. These English were evidently growing Protestant, and he positively would not allow any risk of heresy tainting his colonial empire. There were no negotiations before Hawkins began his venture. He did it on his appreciation of the facts, and the Queen approved on hers. Only after the venture had begun did Philip make his decision known : he had not been asked for it before. But Hawkins had connections in Spain and information of official opinions there which did not lead him to expect refusal. He started the western venture in the hope that his proceedings would demonstrate their own reasonableness.

With money put up by himself, his brother and members of the Navy Board he made a first tentative voyage in 1562-3. With three ships of his firm he sailed out of Plymouth and called first at Tenerife in the Canaries. This was his post-office for the West. His Spanish friends notified their associates in Hispaniola that he would soon be arriving with a cargo of English goods and slaves. Meanwhile he went on to Africa to collect the slaves. He then sailed across the Atlantic to Hispaniola. They were all ready for him there, planters eager to buy, officials prepared to connive. He sold his wares for some gold and pearls and a bulk lading of sugar and hides. He chartered a Spanish caravel to take some of the hides to Seville, and with his English ships returned prosperously to Plymouth. The cargo sent to Seville was a bold touch, showing how open and above board everything was and how Hawkins counted on Spanish approval. But it came at a bad moment. An Anglo-French war had broken out, and English privateers were committing the usual offences against neutrals. There was an out-break of anti-English feeling, and the Seville authorities confiscated the cargo. Hawkins appealed to Sir William Cecil and the Queen, who instructed the English ambassador in Spain to ask for its return; but he did not obtain it.

This, however, was considered to be only an incident, and the Queen gave further support to Hawkins. In his next expedition she invested a nominal £2000 by lending one of her ships valued at that amount, the *Jesus of Lubeck*. The *Jesus* was a high-charged ship of 700 tons which had been bought by Henry VIII in 1545 from the Hanseatic League. Twenty years later she was much decayed and had been condemned as beyond repair. Hawkins risked sailing in her because he needed an impressive-looking flagship and also because, as one of the great ships of the Navy, she advertised un-mistakably that the expedition had the royal sanction. Not only that, but the Queen summoned Hawkins to a personal interview before he sailed, and commanded him to display her royal standard as well as the Cross of St. George. Not unjustifiably he told the Spaniards in the west that his fleet was the Queen's and that he was sailing under her orders. The smaller ships were from Plymouth and belonged to the Hawkins brothers. Departing in the autumn of 1564, he made another successful voyage, with the call for liaison at Tenerife, the collection of slaves on the Guinea coast, and the middle passage thence to the West Indies. There he traded at various ports of the Spanish Main. It was the same story of willing purchasers and conniving officials. These men knew that they were breaking Spanish law by trading with unlicensed foreigners, but they did it nevertheless, and wrote home that Hawkins had com-pelled them by force. The violence was collusive. Hawkins landed armed men by private arrangement with the governors, who were then able to produce witnesses to testify to their King that they had been overcome. No one was killed, and the officials themselves bought slaves. Hawkins left the Caribbean by the Florida Channel. He visited and aided a Huguenot settlement on the North American coast, and passed on to Newfoundland, where he bought victuals from the fishermen. Thence he returned to Padstow in the autumn of 1565. Plymouth seamen were learning all the North Atlantic routes. It had been a fair weather voyage, but the *Jesus* was so strained as to be almost breaking up. She cost £500 in repairs.

Philip, who had not hitherto pronounced his decision on this business, now did so decisively. He instructed his ambassador in England to demand the Queen's prohibition of any more expeditions, and he had the governor of Borburata in Venezuela, one of the principal offenders, brought home for trial. Philip knew very well what Hawkins had to offer for his complaisance. Indeed, Hawkins had demonstrated it at that very place. For while he was trading at Borburata a noted French corsair, Jean Bontemps, arrived there. In the ordinary way the French would have sacked the port, but in Hawkins's presence they behaved meekly and took themselves off. An English captain and the guns of the Queen's great ship had preserved the peace. But Philip hardened his heart. To be defended in this way was a blow to his pride, and he positively would not allow even friendly heretics to go to his colonies.

The result was a diplomatic rumpus, and the Queen ostensibly gave way. In 1566 she exacted a bond for £500 from John Hawkins that he would not go to the Indies that year. The result was that Hawkins did not go but that three Plymouth ships did, under the command of John Lovell, one of his captains. Lovell did not make so good a voyage as Hawkins had done, for at Rio de la Hacha on the Main the governor deluded him into landing ninety negroes and then refused to pay for them. Elsewhere Lovell seems to have done fairly well. A young man named Francis Drake first appears in history as one of Lovell's company in this voyage. He was fervently religious, spoke much against the Pope and the priests, and converted lukewarm shipmates to Protestantism.[1]

Meanwhile Hawkins was ingratiating himself with Guzman de Silva the ambassador, dining with him, and talking hopefully of armed ships for the King's service in the Mediterranean. It did not much matter where the service was so long as the King would accept it—that was the thin end of the wedge. De Silva was half

[1] So said one of them, a Welshman named Morgan, when on trial in the Inquisition years afterwards.

convinced, and did not learn until next year that Lovell had slipped off to the Indies in November. Philip was cold, and returned no answer to the offer of service. But the Queen and Hawkins were determined on one more effort to establish the Indies trade.

In the summer of 1567 the biggest of these expeditions got ready at Plymouth. There were two ships of the Queen's, the *Jesus* and the *Minion*, and four Plymouth ships, and the combined crews amounted to 408 men and boys. De Silva knew all about it, since his people had seen the *Jesus* and *Minion* before they left London, taking in their guns from the Tower armouries, and also lading beans, which were the food for the slaves on the middle passage. The Spaniard protested, but got no satisfaction from the Queen and Cecil, only a story that the expedition was going to open up a gold mine in Africa and would go nowhere near Philip's Indies. The Queen could indeed produce a couple of Portuguese deserters with a tale of a gold mine, but we may doubt whether she believed them. De Silva wrote his doubts to his King.

Meanwhile Hawkins was in no hurry to leave Plymouth, since an autumn sailing gave the healthiest conditions on the Guinea coast, with the sun going south of the line. In August, while his fleet was lying in the Cattewater, seven Flemish ships sailed into the Sound under the command of one of Philip's admirals. They made straight for the Cattewater in a truculent fashion, not dipping their flags in salute. To refuse the salute was to declare hostile intent, as Hawkins well knew. He wasted no time with words, but instantly opened fire. The Flemings turned away and anchored off the Hoe. Their commander sent an officer with an indignant protest at his treatment in a friendly port. Hawkins answered that no doubt they were all friends, but that the rules of conduct were known, and he as the Queen's officer was there to see them observed. Everyone knew that Philip's ships had come in the hope of finding the English off their guard, to trump up a quarrel and destroy the expedition before it sailed. Hawkins was a man of genial good manners, but he could be " sudden and quick " if need arose. Young Drake was there on board the *Jesus*, aged about twenty-three, and Hawkins may have taught him something that day. The Queen for diplomatic reasons affected displeasure with Hawkins, but he told her that if he had acted otherwise she would have lost her ships, for the Flemings in the Cattewater would have been "proud neighbours."

At the beginning of October all was ready, and Hawkins assembled the crews in St. Andrew's Church for a last solemn service. It was a day Plymouth was to remember, for of all the four hundred not more than eighty were ever to see their native land again. St. Andrew's saw many such departures in the Elizabethan age. The wind came fair, and the fleet set sail.

III. THE PROTESTANT ROVERS IN THE CHANNEL

Sixteen months were to elapse before the remnants of the expedition struggled home. During that time an exciting period began in the Channel. In 1568 Philip's oppressed Netherlands rose in revolt and were savagely put down by the Duke of Alva and a Spanish army. The rebellion was partly caused by the violation of Dutch and Flemish rights of self-government, but its fire was due to the Calvinists who had suffered persecution for many a year. In France there had been already two short civil wars between Catholics and Huguenots, and now a third and fiercer one broke out. Coligny, the Huguenot leader, made La Rochelle the capital and headquarters of the Huguenot cause. Coligny, titular Admiral of France, although himself a soldier rather than a sailor, had an understanding of sea power. Cecil in England shared it. He was neither soldier nor sailor, but a statesman of penetrating views. And he was interested in the continental struggles, for he saw that victorious Catholics abroad would turn in their enthusiasm upon Protestant England. There was a third leader who was to join Cecil and Coligny, William of Orange, the commander of the defeated Dutch revolt, but he as yet was not a convert to the doctrine of sea power. He and his brothers were refugees in Germany, seeking aid from the Rhineland Calvinists and meditating another military attempt.

This was the scene in '68, when Coligny began to send out Huguenot privateers from La Rochelle. He did more, dispatching his brother to England to distribute Huguenot commissions to adventurous Englishmen; and there were plenty willing to take

them. By the summer there were fifty armed ships, Huguenot and
English, cruising in the western Channel, intercepting Catholic
shipping, whether Spanish, French or Flemish, taking their cargoes,
letting the plundered vessels go to lade themselves with more.
The cruisers financed the Huguenot cause; but they did more,
and here lay Coligny's genius. He had discovered something new
in warfare, the relentless pressure of sea power upon a military
supremacy. Every sullen rebel, cowed by victorious soldiery,
awaiting his turn to be haled off to a priestly dungeon, with the
stake as its ultimate sanction, took courage from the fact that there
upon the coast were the white sails of free men flouting the tyrant,
and that could he join them he would himself be free. It worked
most in the tormented Netherlands, where Alva was burning and
beheading thousands. The rest hung on, their thoughts on the sea,
biding their time.

Plymouth was a Protestant port, and it welcomed the privateers,
to sell their booty and buy their supplies. William Hawkins the
second was Mayor that year, and he had ships out with Huguenot
commissions. So had Sir Arthur Champernowne, the Vice-Admiral
of Devon, with his headquarters in the fort on Drake's Island (it
was St. Nicholas Island then). They were both representatives of
the Queen, and the Queen and her minister were not disposed to
censure them, for they were doing England's work as well as
Coligny's. That Spanish army in the Netherlands was a threat to
England no less than were the Catholic leaders in France who
declared Mary Stuart to be the rightful owner of Elizabeth's throne.

At that juncture, in the autumn of the year, Philip II committed
an incredible folly. He and his father for fifty years back had
regarded the Channel as a perfectly safe line of communication with
their Netherlands, for they had always had the alliance of England
and the safeguard of its fleet. Philip did not realise how the situation
had suddenly changed. Alva needed money to pay his soldiers,
and Philip borrowed it from the bankers of Genoa and dispatched
it up Channel in six small vessels, unarmed and unescorted—
£100,000 in silver coin cast naked upon a sea full of hungry sharks.
The Huguenots picked up the scent and chased the treasure-ships,
which turned for refuge to the nearest ports, one to Southampton,

and the rest to Plymouth and Fowey. The Spanish ambassador—a new one, Guerau de Spes—immediately asked the Queen to turn out her Navy and escort the wealth to its destination. She found it a somewhat impudent request, but promised to consider it. That money, if it reached Alva, might well finance an invasion of England, for Europe was now in a state of religious war. But there was little time for talk, since the Huguenots were gathering in Plymouth Sound and the Solent and nerving themselves to seize the treasure as it lay, in defiance of the Queen's sovereignty. For its own safeguard she ordered that it should be taken ashore and placed behind her guns and battlements.

A Spanish captain has described the scene at Plymouth as the Mayor supervised the unlading of the treasure. The Sound, the Cattewater, the Hamoaze, were full of armed ships discharging their booty to the town, buyers congregating for bargains, the townsfolk bubbling with excitement, the leading men presiding over what to Spain was wholesale robbery. So to the immediate view it was, legality preserved only by the somewhat hollow right of Coligny's commissions. But morally all Protestants were at war, for they were all threatened, the English ultimately, no less than the French and Dutch then and there. Coligny had called into being a Protestant Navy. Cecil aided him. William of Orange was soon to join, for he began to issue commissions to sea-cruisers next year. These three men saw through diplomatic fictions and struck a blow for the essential liberty of mankind.

The treasure went ashore, Guerau de Spes lost his temper and persuaded Alva to arrest all English goods in the Netherlands, Philip did the same in Spain, and Elizabeth, who had merely saved the money from the privateers, proceeded to borrow it herself from the Genoese. She did not spend it, and repaid it punctually when the debt fell due. What more could anyone expect of her, since to send it to sea again would have been to present it to the rovers, and to forward it with her own Navy would have been the action of a fool.

To this tempestuous scene, in January 1569, returned John Hawkins, with a tale to tell that raised excitement into hate. He had made the usual voyage to the Canaries, Africa and the Spanish

Main. At the colonial ports he had traded amicably with the planters, although the officials had been more reluctant, owing to the strict orders they had received from Spain. On the way out of the Caribbean a heavy gale struck the fleet and nearly sank the *Jesus of Lubeck*, whose age and rottenness had previously caused grave anxiety. She could not cross the Atlantic without repair, and Hawkins entered the port of San Juan de Ulua on the coast of Mexico to patch up the ship and buy victuals for the voyage home. Next day appeared thirteen Spanish ships, the plate-fleet arriving to take away the year's output of Mexican treasure, and on board was Martin Enriquez the incoming Viceroy of New Spain. Hawkins had control of the defences and could have kept the Spaniards out until he was ready to leave. But he considered that he must not involve the Queen in the diplomatic disturbance that would have been certain to be raised. He exacted solemn assurances of peace from the Viceroy and admitted him and his fleet. Enriquez had pledged his word and even written Hawkins a friendly personal letter. He was no sooner in than he concerted with his officers a surprise attack on the English and duly carried it out. Only the vigilance of Hawkins and the stout fighting of his outnumbered men saved a remnant of the expedition. Hawkins got away in the *Minion* and Drake in the 50-ton *Judith*, of which he had been made captain in the course of the voyage. Hawkins had 200 men and no food, save the hides in the cargo. He set a hundred on the shore of Mexico at their own request, and of these about seventy survived to become prisoners of the Spaniards. With the other hundred he sailed for England, and Guerau de Spes reported that only fifteen were alive when he anchored in Mount's Bay. Drake came in at about the same time, having parted company outside San Juan.

The treachery of Martin Enriquez caused an outburst of anti-Spanish hatred, and the Queen must have been glad that she had not been complaisant about the Channel treasure. She set Hawkins to write a short account of the affair, which was printed as a pamphlet for public information. The Channel cruisers continued their campaign, and this year (1569) the Dutch joined them with Orange commissions, the famous Sea Beggars, the real beginners of the liberation of the Dutch Netherlands. The Anglo-Spanish alliance was completely dead, and thenceforward it was cold war. Philip dared not make it a hot one, for that would have lost him the Netherlands. Elizabeth was beset with many difficulties, and she also allowed things to continue as they were. They continued for fifteen years, with one mild attempt at reconciliation in 1573–5, until the war became open and regular in 1585.

The Hawkins brothers set about retaliation for San Juan de Ulua. First, they were employed in 1569 on a relief of La Rochelle, which was besieged by the Catholics of France. John Hawkins almost certainly commanded the fleet of sixty London and Plymouth merchant ships which threw in the guns, powder, food and volunteers that helped to save the city. William Hawkins was at sea off the Spanish coast, capturing shipping ; but what in detail he did is unknown. The Channel itself was alive with activity. Huguenots and English cruised in its western approaches and landed their booty at Plymouth. Huguenots, English and Dutch had another base in the Solent, an anchorage they called the Medehole, near Cowes at the mouth of the Isle of Wight's river Meden.[1] Thence the captured goods went to Southampton and London. The Sea Beggars principally used Dover, for they preferred to operate near their own Netherland coast and stir up revolts there. At Dover also there was a mart of captured property and almost a concentration camp for prisoners who could pay ransom : the poorer sort were not murdered as they would have been in earlier times, but were let go with their ships.

In 1572 there was a development. Elizabeth apparently turned sour with the Dutch and friendly towards Philip. She sent John Hawkins to warn off the Dutch from using Dover and all the up-Channel coast to the Solent, and the Dutch leaders, a fierce unscrupulous lot, meekly accepted the dismissal and gathered their ships to depart. From what followed it is certain that this was not what it seemed, but one of those collusive jobs at which Hawkins was an expert. For the Sea Beggars concentrated at Dover and sailed off to their own country, held in the Spanish grip. There they

---

[1] Now Medina. The eighteenth century had a taste for refining place-names. St. Budoc near Plymouth became St. Budeaux, and there was a determined effort, visible in maps, to rename Porchester as Port Caesar.

194

surprised and captured the port of Brill, and shortly afterwards Flushing. And that set fire to the Netherlands, whose tortured people blazed into a general revolt. The Spaniards tackled it but never put it down. The Dutch cities rose against them, Leyden, Alkmaar, Haarlem, Zieriekzee, Gouda and Rotterdam, all the provinces of Holland and Zeeland. Some the Spaniards regained, but some they never regained. Flushing was strategically the prize of all, for it was a deep-water port commanding the issue of the Scheldt, up which lay the great city of Antwerp, the commercial heart of the Netherlands. Who held Flushing could strangle Antwerp's trade, and the Spaniards never held Flushing again. That fact, among others, was to decide the fate of the Armada in '88. Thus the Dutch were set on the long road to freedom, and the great war for it was to be fought on the continent and not on English soil. It was sea power as operated by the new statesmanship.[1]

John Hawkins and those Dutchmen at Dover must have grinned as he signified the Queen's displeasure to them and gave them their warning-off. He had not a ship to enforce it. It seems that he travelled round the coast by land, for his bill of expenses amounted to only £100. Edward Horsey, Captain of Carisbrooke Castle and the Isle of Wight, had previously been ordered to deny the Huguenots any facilities. He wrote Cecil a letter denouncing the privateers, and enclosed it in another saying that the first was written to be shown to the Spanish agent in London ; and at the time of these transactions he had a ship of his own out plundering the Spaniards in the West Indies.

Hawkins also had by no means finished with the West. In 1569 de Spes asserted that he and Winter sent several ships to the Indies, although we have no record of their doings there. Out of the profits of the Channel privateering he built up an armed squadron at Plymouth, ultimately of sixteen ships from 500 tons downwards. In 1570 he asked leave to intercept the returning plate fleets in order to recover his losses at San Juan. The Queen agreed, having her own bill for that affair to be satisfied ; but Alva equipped a Flemish armament to convey Philip's new Austrian bride down

---

[1] It must not be supposed that this was the whole story, but merely the Channel aspect of many interlocking problems and a complicated web of diplomacy.

Channel, and it was thought that this might give cover for a landing on the English coast. Hawkins had therefore to remain on guard until it was too late to catch the plate fleets. The Queen saw the utility of the Hawkins fleet and incorporated it into the national defence. The Navy at Chatham was on watch for the Spanish army in the Netherlands. Hawkins with his western squadron at Plymouth looked out for a possible invasion from Spain. This arrangement held good for several years and was the reason why Hawkins could make no ocean voyages in the seventies. He could not be spared. There was a Spanish plan to invade England in 1571 in co-operation with the conspiracy known as the Ridolfi Plot. Hawkins made remarkable use of his ships by offering them to Philip to facilitate the invasion. He did it, needless to say, with the Queen's knowledge, and by so doing obtained the whole invasion plan, which included arrangements for Hawkins to procure traitors to burn the Queen's ships in the Medway. Meanwhile Cecil, now Lord Burghley, was tracking down the domestic plotters, and with their arrest the whole thing was off. Philip granted Hawkins a patent of nobility and a pardon for his offences in the Indies. He was never allowed to know that Hawkins had deluded him. Besides the nobility Hawkins got something worth having. Some of his men captured in Mexico had been transferred to Spain. Philip, as part of the bargain, released them and sent them home to Plymouth. Philip was a somewhat gullible king, but he had an even more gullible ambassador in Guerau de Spes. This poor man had several interviews with Hawkins and assured the King that the Plymouth seaman held the key to the conquest of England. So he did. Held was the operative word.

IV. DRAKE AND THE OCEANIC ADVENTURERS

From 1570 privateering extended across the ocean to the Caribbean. Plymouth had the principal share in it, but London and the smaller Channel ports were concerned. Drake early set forth as an independent captain, specialising in fast-moving raids with small ships and small crews. He has been called a pirate, but reprisals were legitimate, and he had been one of those attacked at San Juan.

Most likely he had a Huguenot or an Orange commission. They all had, and these commissions were recognised by the English government. Moreover Drake was a deeply religious man, and he was convinced that Spain meant to extirpate his religion not only in the Netherlands but in England too. In a cold war there is no sense in slinging names like pirate and spy at those who do effectively serve their country. Drake achieved his first great success in 1572–73, when with seventy men and two little Plymouth ships he landed on the Isthmus of Panama and captured a gold-train (of pack-mules) outside Nombre de Dios. He did much more in that raid, the full story of which, from his own narrative, was printed by his nephew thirty years after his death.[1] Plymouth remembers his return on a Sunday morning when the people were in church, but slipped away from the parson and out to the Hoe when the news was whispered round.

Such expeditions became a Channel industry, and there were many of which little is known. Spanish agents were continually reporting the departure of ships for the Indies. Edward Horsey we have mentioned as sending a ship from the Solent. Most likely it was not his only one, for it is known only by the accident that it fell in with Drake on the treasure coast and figures in Drake's narrative. Another venture has rested unknown for centuries in the records of the Admiralty Court. In 1574 one Gilbert Horseley took command of a little ship named the *John*, owned by John Tipkin, a London merchant. With only twenty-five men he worked the Spanish Main and took several prizes worth altogether £3000 ; and then, with fifteen men remaining, he returned to Plymouth. It was not at a favourable moment, for an attempt was being made to end the cold war by a mutual cancellation of damages. Plymouth in a mood of rectitude might have sacrificed his booty. So Horseley gave the Admiralty officer £10 to keep his mouth shut and passed on up Channel to Arundel, where his business could be unobtrusively done. At the quiet little Sussex town, where the houses and the castle still look over the Arun and the broad meadows

---

[1] *Sir Francis Drake Reviv'd*, London, 1626. Some have thought parts of the story incredible, but in all essentials it is corroborated by Spanish documents discovered in recent years by Miss I. A. Wright.

that were once the Arun's spreading estuary, Horseley met his owner from London and got his stuff ashore and away before authority woke up to what was going on.[1]

John Oxenham of Plymouth, one of Drake's men in 1572, sailed with a somewhat larger ship in 1576. He landed on the Isthmus of Panama and crossed to the Pacific side, where he built a pinnace and captured much wealth from Spanish treasure carriers. The Panama Spaniards with aid from Peru turned out large forces and gradually hunted him down, but they took a long time to do it, and he was still at large in the wilds of the Isthmus in the summer of 1577. Finally they got him and sent him to Lima, to the Viceroy of Peru, who hanged him. Twelve of his men were said by the Spaniards to have captured a Spanish coaster and escaped. Whether any of them came home to Plymouth is unknown, for the English records are silent. Not all of the treasure-hunting expeditions were successful, and the penalty of capture was death or the galleys. Most of Oxenham's crew were hanged, but two or three youngsters were made galley-slaves.

Plymouth had thoughts of empire-building on England's account. In 1573 Sir Richard Grenville, William Hawkins, and others planned a voyage to go through the Straits of Magellan and discover Terra Australis Incognita, the unknown southern continent in the South Pacific. They expected to find it stretching through temperate and tropical latitudes, full of civilised people and rich trading possibilities. They bought ships for the purpose, but ultimately the Queen disallowed it because of the new attempt to patch up the quarrel with Spain. Four years later the attempt had broken down and the cold war was as bad as ever. In 1577 Drake sailed out of Plymouth with the purpose that Grenville had laid aside, to find Terra Australis. That at least was the official plan, approved by the Queen and her ministers. But Drake had a secret understanding with the Queen for something else. When a man was to do something important Elizabeth saw him personally. She summoned Drake to an interview and gave him her instructions

---

[1] I have read with sorrow in a book by a descendant of Horseley that his ancestor was ultimately hanged for piracy. But that was afterwards and had nothing to do with the West Indian voyage.

by word of mouth. What they were, no one knows. What Drake did was to raid the treasure coast of Peru instead of looking for Terra Australis. Probably the Queen sanctioned that, but there may have been something more. For neither of them knew that the Spaniards had overcome Oxenham ; and if Drake had arrived off Panama to find Oxenham seated in the Isthmus, it would have been a pretty piece of empire-building to create an English colony there, with Drake's ships as its sea power, right across the narrowest stage of the treasure route from Peru to Spain. But that remained a dream, for Oxenham was a prisoner long before Drake got there.

While Drake was away Plymouth was lively with mysterious ships and squadrons. In 1578, while Oxenham's fate was still unknown, there were five ships fitting out under one Captain Sharpham, and a possibility is that they were to furnish the Atlantic side of co-operation at the Isthmus. Where they went and what they did are unknown. But next year the Portuguese said they saw ten English ships prospecting for a colonial site on the coast of Brazil. There is absolutely no indication of this from the English side unless they were Sharpham's squadron exaggerated by rumour. In the autumn of '78 also Sir Humphrey Gilbert had an expedition assembling, first at Dartmouth and then at Plymouth. Gilbert was in a sense a Dartmouth man, for his family seat was up the river. Walter Ralegh his half-brother was with him. Gilbert had a patent to colonise in North America, but when he left Plymouth in November it was the wrong season for that. One rumour was that he would follow Drake through the Straits of Magellan. He certainly came nowhere near that, for he was back in February, having suffered losses at sea. Both he and Ralegh were uncommunicative about the voyage, which was evidently a failure.

Then Drake came home in the autumn of 1580, with his *Golden Hind* literally full of treasure. As he sailed into the Sound he spoke with some fishermen, asking whether the Queen was alive and well. He had had no news of England for a long time, and if Elizabeth had been supplanted by pro-Spanish Mary Stuart he would have been in a tight place. Most likely he would have put about there and then and sought some other country. All was well and he came into Plymouth, the most momentous arrival of the time. For not only had he captured Spanish gold and a shipload of silver, but he had sailed home through the East Indies and round the Cape. In the Moluccas he had made friendly contact with the Sultan of Ternate and had laded some tons of spices, the first ever brought to England from their place of origin by an English ship.

Although the Queen took the greater part of Drake's treasure —as was right, because she had to risk war with Spain in order to keep it—enough was left to Drake and the investors to make them rich. Drake's men were mostly from Plymouth, and they also did well from their shares of the prize. Plymouth as a town was undoubtedly enriched, as it had been for twenty years past by the equipment of so many expeditions and the profits made by some of them. We have no figures of population, but the place was undoubtedly growing. In 1591 a plan was drawn for a complete and up-to-date fortification, with bastioned walls and a dry ditch.[1] It is almost certain that this was not carried out, although a strong fort was made on the Hoe, its site subsequently covered by the seventeenth-century citadel. The Stonehouse inlet was a subsidiary harbour, and the Hamoaze was a regular anchorage. Both William Hawkins and Drake spent their money on their town, and first one and then the other improved the water supply by bringing a moorland spring into the place.

Until this period Dartmouth and Plymouth had run level in maritime importance, but Elizabethan Dartmouth fell behind. It had no great shipowning family like the Hawkinses and no sea commander in the class of Drake. Its port was better than Plymouth's, although its land communications were worse. Sir Humphrey Gilbert we have seen as a Dartmouth ocean adventurer. His leadership produced dissensions, and he was persistently unlucky with the ordinary risks of the sea. Bad weather delayed his start in 1578 and seems to have been at least a partial cause of the subsequent failure. In his next ocean expedition in 1583 shipwreck on the Nova Scotian coast lost him the men with whom he intended to plant a colony, and then the foundering of the *Squirrel* on the voyage home cost his own life. A Dartmouth man of a different type was John Davis the navigator, justly so called for his scientific attain-

[1] Brit. Museum Map Room : photostats of maps at Hatfield House, I, 35.

ments, and also in achievement the finest seaman of his age. His three north-western voyages added solidly to geographical knowledge. His passage home in a rotten ship through the Straits of Magellan in 1593 was a miracle of seamanship. His knowledge of navigation made the first voyage of the East India Company successful. But he was never a money-maker, and his great career profited Dartmouth nothing in material gain.

While Plymouth enjoyed forty years of booming prosperity with the Hawkins trade, the privateering profits, and the assemblage of great regular expeditions in the Spanish War, Dartmouth had only one moment of financial uplift. In 1592 the captors of the great East Indian carrack, the *Madre de Dios*, brought her into the Dart. She was stuffed with pepper and more costly spices, drugs and perfumes, gold and precious stones. The privateer crews who had taken her grabbed everything they could lay hands on and dispersed over the Devon countryside. The Queen was outraged, for she was left with little but the pepper. She sent down Robert Cecil and Walter Ralegh to save what they could. They met the mariners swarming on the roads, pockets full of jewels, packs full of musk and rare perfumes. Cecil said that he could smell them from afar, and to examine them on oath was but " offence to God." But to Dartmouth's permanent prosperity it added nothing.

Exeter continued its cloth export, but is little heard of in the wars. In 1588 its leading merchants obtained a patent to monopolise the trade of the Senegal and Gambia region on the African coast. Little is known of their proceedings save that they continued for some years, and very possibly into the next century, when the trade was more commonly frequented. Southampton has a curious record in the Elizabethan time, not, as might be expected from its position, one of energy and enterprise, but rather of quiescence. Southampton seemed to have fallen asleep. It had some trade, and the privateers who based themselves on the Solent used it as a mart, but the town produced no prominent captains or notable sea enterprises. The status of all the ports was largely dependent on the characters and personalities of their leading citizens, and after Robert Reneger, Southampton had none of outstanding talent. Its geographical advantages were unchanged, but they alone did not produce greatness. Portsmouth, deserted by the Navy, sank in status. Elizabethan Portsmouth was a somewhat Alsatian place, the haunt of smugglers and pirates and a port of entry or escape for people in whom government was interested, Jesuit missionaries, foreign agents and spies. The poverty of the inhabitants, bereft of the naval expenditure, no doubt accounted for a good deal of delinquency.

Up Channel, Chichester, Arundel and Shoreham were ports of mainly local trade. Elizabethan Hastings—the second Hastings, in the Bourne Valley east of the castle—had a protective harbour arm until it was destroyed by a storm and not replaced. Thenceforward fishing and small trade were limited to such boats as could be hauled up the shingle beach. Rye still had water for vessels engaged in cross-Channel trade. In 1572 it received many Huguenot refugees from the Massacre of St. Bartholomew. The sea route from Rye to the Norman ports was favoured by travellers who could thereby shorten their land journey on the other side, as compared with passing through Dover and Calais. Dover no doubt kept most of the passenger traffic as promising less of the perils of the sea that most travellers dreaded. Sandwich, although becoming obstructed, kept a considerable second-class trade with the Netherlands.

Between all these ports were fishing communities on open beaches and in petty havens, inshore fishermen using open boats and probably more numerous than they are to-day. Many of them in the narrower part of the Channel were also smugglers, although smuggling was not yet what it was to become later, in the days of high protective duties. At this time the Customs were defrauded rather by corrupt dealing between merchants and officials in the ports. Elizabethan coastal smuggling was rather of forbidden than of taxed commodities, of seditious books printed abroad and of the book-runners who brought them, and of the letters of enemies overseas to plotters in England. One notable example was the copy of the Pope's bull of 1570, excommunicating and deposing the Queen, found nailed one morning on the Bishop of London's door. The difficulties are illustrated by the fact that its appearance took place three months after its issue in Rome. It was not safe to send such things through the ports, for incoming passengers were liable to be searched. Ridolfi from the Netherlands sent a batch of letters to his fellow-plotters in England, and the man who carried them was arrested as he stepped ashore at Dover.

From 1573, when Elizabeth attempted her reconciliation with Spain, she genuinely discouraged Channel privateering, and for some years the home waters were quieter. Privateering enterprise shifted to the western Atlantic and, with Drake, to the Pacific. Anglo-Spanish relations again broke down. The Queen's determination not to restore Drake's enormous booty made open war grow probable. Philip in 1580 asserted his claim to the throne of Portugal and forcibly occupied that country. Don Antonio, the defeated Portuguese claimant, came to England and was recognised by Elizabeth as the rightful king. As such, he also began to issue commissions to privateers, and the irregular war blazed up more intensely. In the early eighties there were plans for Drake, with Antonio at his side, to seize the Portuguese colonies and inaugurate a grand oceanic offensive against Spain. At the same time Philip's armies in the Netherlands under the Duke of Parma were making headway against the Dutch rebels, William of Orange was assassinated for a reward publicly offered by Philip, and it grew evident that Elizabeth would have to give military aid to the Dutch. If she did not, the Spanish army would be victorious, and would then turn its attention to the invasion of England.

Plymouth and London were active in these affairs. In 1582 Edward Fenton sailed with a fleet intended for the East Indies. The subscribers included Drake, some of the Queen's ministers, and some merchants of London. But Fenton was no commander, and the expedition broke up in quarrels between himself and his officers. William Hawkins the third (son of the second) was one of them, and Fenton put him under arrest and brought him home in irons. Meanwhile William Hawkins the second, brother of John, was at sea in 1582–3 with a Plymouth expedition of his own. He had with him yet another of the family's third generation, Richard, the only son of John Hawkins. The expedition went to Brazil and the West Indies, and appears to have been very successful. Bernardino de Mendoza, the Spanish ambassador, believed that it had taken a treasure ship, and a Dutchman in London wrote home that the booty was worth 800,000 crowns. But the habitual Hawkins taciturnity prevented any full account from being published, and we have only scattered hints on the proceedings in the West. Young Richard Hawkins has left some statements implying that he had a great respect for his uncle. They were a loyal and united family.

Meanwhile the Jesuit missionaries were seeping into England, and their followers were distributing the books forwarded from a centre at Rouen and landed across lonely beaches. The Pope's secretary wrote to an inquirer that to murder the Queen would be no sin. Plotting became almost continuous. Mendoza was expelled from the country for implication in Throgmorton's conspiracy, and Philip sent no other in his place. A great war was brewing, and at length it began. It is usually dated from Philip's arrest of all English ships and men in Spanish ports in 1585 ; but there was no formal declaration by either side.

CHAPTER TEN

The Spanish War

I. DRAKE IN 1585-7

IN ITS first years it was Drake's war, and Drake's base was always Plymouth. The expeditions which he commanded were not strictly naval, in the narrow sense of being composed of the Queen's ships. He had always the Queen's commission and instructions, and his senior officers were appointed with her approval. But not many of the ships which composed his fleets belonged to the regular Navy. There were only two in his great West Indian raid of 1585-6; four in his campaign on the Spanish coast in 1587; and six in the Portuguese expedition in 1589. In fact Drake never commanded more than six of the Queen's greater ships at any one time. This was primarily because Elizabeth's finances could not afford the full employment of the Navy every year. The whole Navy had to be turned out in 1588 when the great Armada came, and the cost of victory almost broke her. But at other times the money was raised by powerful joint-stock syndicates whose members were the Queen herself, her great officers of state, her courtiers, and the leading merchants of London and the other ports. The Queen had a good idea of what these various people were worth, and they had to contribute or lose her favour. The joint-stock expeditions more commonly made a loss than a profit. The loss was compensated by the Queen's favour in granting trading facilities (the hated "monopolies" among them), and privateering commissions; and the privateer ships all over the Atlantic brought in great gains to their owners. A loyal Parliament granted taxation, but not nearly enough for the war. The armies in the Netherlands, and later in northern France and Ireland, ran away with fantastic sums without hope of compensating booty. The war was largely financed by the Queen's more powerful subjects operating as individuals in sea adventure.

Drake's fleets then, assembling at Plymouth, were chiefly of privately owned vessels, with only a stiffening of the Queen's. They were not all unarmed merchantmen, for private men were building powerful fighting ships for their own ocean purposes. The old 50-ton Channel privateers of 1570 were superseded by something bigger for Atlantic work. Men like the Lord Admiral, Ralegh, Leicester and the Hawkinses are known to have built fighting galleons, and every ship of the Levant Company had to be a ship of war to survive amid the anarchy caused by Turkish power in the Mediterranean. The bulk of the officers were chosen by the owners of the ships, and the captains recruited the crews. Obviously such forces depended greatly on the personal reputation of their commanders ; and it was Drake who supplied the magic name.

In September 1585 Drake was at Plymouth with the fleet gathered for his first expedition as the Queen's admiral. His commission had been issued at midsummer, but he was still awaiting the order to sail. Diplomatic policies were uncertain, and the Queen had not come to a decision. This was the first occasion on which Plymouth had witnessed an assemblage of this sort, and the scene was typical of others in later years. The town was lively with business, the tradesmen selling food and clothing, farmers driving in cattle for slaughter, seamen filling water-casks, soldiers coming in along the roads, the inns pouring out drink for all ranks, a general air of fairing and jollity, very prosperity-making for the citizens, not too good for morality as viewed by the strait-laced. This was how Plymouth grew for the next twenty years. At last came the Queen's orders. Drake knew that a change of purpose might follow, and lost not a moment. Water casks and victuals to make good the current consumption were lying on the quays. The casks were taken off empty, the food tumbled into the nearest ships available, and the fleet crowded out of the Sound, to sort things out as the voyage proceeded. The first point of action was not far off, Vigo in north-west Spain, and there Drake completed his watering before crossing the Atlantic. Plymouth saw no more of that expedition, for after beating up the Spanish colonies and destroying their defences Drake returned to Portsmouth and there paid off in the summer of '86.

In '87 the situation was more serious, for Philip meant business, and the great Armada was slowly getting ready to sail if possible that year. Drake set out to make it impossible. He again gathered his mixed force at Plymouth. He had orders " to impeach the gathering " of the Spanish fleets, but he wanted something more, for his purpose was not limited to action on the high seas. At length his friends at court persuaded the Queen to an additional command " to distress the ships within the havens themselves." The Queen was reluctant, for she still hoped to strike a bargain with Philip and did not wish to enrage him too much. No sooner had she issued that last order than she countermanded it, and sent yet another horseman racing down the Plymouth road. Drake with his flair for reading minds expected just that, and did not wait for it. He got clear in time, with his victualling in more disorder than ever. John Hawkins was in Plymouth and dutifully sent the new order after Drake by a pinnace. The pinnace strangely failed to find the fleet, and came back with a fat prize instead. Drake was unleashed for the most brilliant campaign of his career, the singeing of the King's beard, with a most distressing treatment of his ships in the haven of Cadiz, rounded off by the capture of an East Indian carrack that paid a handsome profit on the whole affair. Drake was back at Plymouth within three months, having indeed impeached the Armada for that year. His men came in hungry and sick, and many were dead, killed not by the Spaniards but by the victuals. These joint-stock managements were very bad in that respect, and thought more of profit than of sailors' lives.

Drake wished to refit and make another stroke at the Spanish ports, but the Queen forbade it. She knew very well why he had cleared off in such a hurry, and regarded it as a breach of her commands. She was genuinely angry, for she hoped, as none of her statesmen did, that the war could be stopped at that stage by negotiation. And so Drake was held at Plymouth while the Armada got itself ready for the invasion of England in 1588.

II. HAWKINS AND THE NAVY

That was the business of the whole Navy with the Lord Admiral in command. And here we must review shortly the progress of the Royal Navy since Henry VIII had died. In the eleven years after his death his fine fleet was diminished by neglect and corruption. Wooden ships laid up required continuous attention, lacking which they decayed. We have no details of what went on, but we have the results. The total tonnage of the fleet diminished by one-third, and many of the ships remaining existed only on paper and were too rotten to be sent to sea. One consequence was the loss of Calais by Queen Mary, due largely to lack of naval force in the Straits of Dover. The disgrace led to a programme of new building, continued in the early years of Elizabeth. Her Navy Board, as it turned out, was also corrupt, but much less flagrantly than that of the previous decade. Its nominal head was its Treasurer Benjamin Gonson, but it was really controlled by the Master of the Ordnance Sir William Winter. Under his rule, in a period of small campaigns, the Navy could turn out a few good ships as required, but those in reserve were neglected, and the total cost was twice as much as it should have been, to the profit of Winter and his associates. Elizabeth and Burghley had keen eyes for financial matters, but they had not the technical knowledge of ships to enable them to penetrate Winter's corruption.

In the seventies John Hawkins grew alarmed at the state of the Navy. He knew from Gonson, his father-in-law, what was going on, and he foresaw a war with Spain, which indeed needed no great foresight. He revealed what he knew to Burghley and wrote at the minister's request a formal indictment specifying in detail all the corrupt practices and clearly stating the amount of money that the Queen was over-spending on a partially rotten fleet. Burghley accepted the accusations, and in 1577 Hawkins was appointed Treasurer of the Navy, Gonson dying in that year. Hawkins made ruthless war on slackness and roguery, and heavily reduced the peace-time cost of the fleet. At the same time he made it a much better fleet. He made sure that all the ships were really fit for action, and he turned out, by new building and rebuilding, the new type of fast-sailing galleon, low-built and heavily armed, which was very much more efficient than the great high-charged ships of Henry VIII's time. They had been designed for service in the Channel. Hawkins made the Navy fit for service on the ocean. He was bitterly denounced by the conservative-minded old hands and by the fraudulent merchants and contractors who had shared in Winter's pickings. They never ceased to declare, right up to the Armada year, that Hawkins had ruined the Navy, and even that he had been paid by Spain to do it. And then the Lord Admiral, taking command of that fleet, reported that the ships were excellent, and fittingly remarked that their condition revealed " certain persons to be notable liars."

III. THE ARMADA IN THE CHANNEL

The Armada year was the great year of crisis on the Channel coast, a greater crisis than that of 1545 ; for, as fate decreed, the fighting took place, not on the ocean waters of Spain, where the seamen desired it, but in sight of the English shore. The entire Navy was mobilised, for the first time in any campaign since 1545. In command was the Lord Admiral, Lord Howard of Effingham, the fourth of his name to hold that office in the Tudor century. In the spring, as the peril drew near, he concentrated three-quarters of the fleet at Plymouth, leaving the remainder to blockade the Flemish ports whence Parma's army was intended to issue in invasion barges and land on the Kentish coast. At Plymouth Howard had with him Drake, Hawkins, Frobisher, Davis, young Richard Hawkins, and most of the notable captains of the age. William Hawkins, John's brother, was Mayor of Plymouth, a man of seventy, making great exertions for the service of the fleet. Sir Walter Ralegh and Sir Richard Grenville did not go to sea. They were employed in mustering and training the militia of the west country. Leicester commanded the eastern land forces, with a central camp at Tilbury on the Thames.

The whole country was tense and ready. Every man was a constable, ready to hale any stranger before the nearest magistrate to give an account of himself. Mendoza, now in Paris, confessed that he could not get a spy into England. Not a man, he said, not even a fly, could approach the naval ports without being seized. A static society, in which all men knew all their neighbours for miles around and so could instantly spot a stranger, had that advantage. The Channel fishermen may have been smugglers of books and priests in easier times, but they were " mere English," like their Queen, in 1588. In the event, the Armada came up to Plymouth without knowing that the greater part of the Navy was there. The beacon fires were ready on the hill tops, a telegraph of flame to summon the militia to fall in, the church bells also as a telegraph of sound. Every port was closed, not a ship to leave save on national service. And in the nerve-centre were the Queen and her Council, level-headed Burghley, the hot Puritan Walsingham, Hatton the Lord Chancellor, Whitgift the Archbishop, and others of knowledge and weight.

The Armada sailed from Lisbon in May, but was delayed so long by contrary winds that it ran short of food and water and had to put into Corunna, where it lay for more than a month. Howard and his captains tried hard to strike it on its own coast, but were delayed by the Queen, their victualling, and westerly gales. It was a stormy summer, and on each of three occasions when the English sailed for Spain they were driven back. Finally they put back to Plymouth on 12th July, short of food and with many sick. But their information was that the Armada was in so bad a state that it could not sail at all. That in fact was what Medina Sidonia represented to the King, but Philip overruled him. In Plymouth all were hard at work refitting, revictualling, taking in new men. If the Armada did not sail, they meant to blockade or destroy it in its own ports and then to intercept the homecoming plate fleets. The ships were foul with the summer's growth of barnacles and weed. They had to be grounded and scrubbed. William Hawkins took charge of it, bringing them in in relays on every tide, keeping his shipwrights working night and day, cleaning the bottoms with brooms and scrapers, finishing with a coat of tallow, the only anti-fouler known. He was cheery and happy, declaring the hulls as stout as if they had been carved from solid blocks.

Next year he died. A good end for an old man, Mayor of Plymouth in '88.

The English were working hard, but they were not expecting to put to sea that week. On the 19th at midday the senior captains were on the Hoe, taking an hour or two of relaxation, and some were playing bowls. And then came the thunderbolt. The Armada, supposed to be in Spain, was coming up the Channel. There were men to be embarked, stores to be completed, rigging to be set up, all the disorder of refitting to be overcome. Few ships were ready to sail that day, but all must go on the next. Howard had orders to give, and called the officers to attend him. And Drake, by some romancer's yarn of the following century, made answer that there was plenty of time to finish the game first. Believe it who will.[1]

The Armada's progress is an oft-told tale, and here we view it from among the people on the coast. On 20th July Plymouth saw the fleet put out to sea, just in time, for that evening they sighted the Spaniards against the sunset beyond the Eddystone. The Spaniards did not see them, and in the night the English worked up past them, and in the morning had the coveted windward position, the wind being light from the west. On the morning of the 21st Plymouth heard a two-hour cannonade, dying away to the eastward, and knew with relief that the invaders were past the Sound. For a week amid calms and gentle breezes the combatants sailed and drifted up Channel, 240 miles from Plymouth to Calais in seven days. " We drummed them up the Channel " has a brisker sound than the reality warranted. Howard did not press the attack, for he was not yet at his full strength, and in real fighting ships was inferior to the Spaniards. Medina Sidonia had many soldiers in his fleet, but he was under Philip's orders not to land anywhere before making junction with Parma's army in the Netherlands. The English did not know this, and were anxious whenever the Armada drew near a good landing place. Medina Sidonia's chief captains

---

[1] The game of bowls itself is quite possible. There is some evidence for it, of the second-rate sort, dating back to 1625. It was a Spanish gibe : " We caught you playing bowls." But in this there is no mention of Drake. His famous reply, and indeed his presence on the scene, rest only on some story from an unnamed source that Bishop Burnet picked up a century later.

thought the order to be wrong, and sought to persuade him to disregard it ; and if there had been a good chance he might have done so. Perhaps for this reason the Armada after passing Portland Bill drew in towards Weymouth. There the shore people had view of a second action, fought for some hours with great expenditure of ammunition but without loss of ships by either side. But Weymouth none the less welcomed a Spanish prize, a galleon abandoned in the previous night, wrecked by the explosion of her magazine. Another slow drift brought the fleets just south of the Isle of Wight, and in a flat calm off St. Catherine's Point the English attacked again, towed into action by their boats. This went on for five hours, with a light wind arising as before. The island cliffs were crowded with watchers, of whom some saw a great chance for the outcome of the day. For the tide was flooding north-eastward towards the Owers shoals, and the crowd, following round to the high ground above Bembridge, hoped to see the Spaniards driven on them. But the wind freshened and they sailed clear, and the English broke off the attack, and the tide turned westward, but so slow was the progress of the fleets against it that another five hours elapsed before all were swallowed in the up-Channel distance. It seems that the Spaniards had some view of entering Spithead and trying a landing, as the French had done forty years before ; and Howard had to expend precious ammunition to shoulder them away.

All the way up Channel the coast was alert and ready, the militia embodied, the defences manned. And everywhere, as the instant peril passed, the English fleet was sending in boats and pinnaces to seek victuals and powder and shot. Every little port did its best, but these things were desperately short. In Sussex they were sending out bunches of plough chains in default of round-shot, but powder could not be improvised : the barrel was scraped bare. Howard had only enough for one day's fighting, and he held it until the Armada sailed up to Calais on the evening of the 27th and anchored off the little harbour.

There was the place of decision. To the eastward stretched Parma's coast, his army blockaded in shallow ports by small Dutch fighting craft that could sail amid the shoals. Away on the English side lay a quarter of the Queen's Navy in the Downs covering the blockade. Howard anchored close to windward of the Spaniards, and the Downs squadron crossed the Channel and joined him. Howard was now at his fullest strength, and Medina Sidonia was perplexed. He had no chance of bringing out Parma's troops without first driving the English off the sea. A deep-water port would have served for the junction, but there was none save the Dutchmen's Flushing, which Elizabeth's councillors had prudently arranged for an English garrison to hold. Howard forced the situation with the famous fireships, blazing in among the Spaniards at midnight on a flowing tide. The Armada made off in confusion from Calais, and the English fought it to the eastward off Gravelines next day. This was intentionally the decisive action, unlike the fights in the Channel. The Armada was thoroughly beaten and fled into the North Sea, never to return. It had been a near thing for the Queen's Navy, with scarcely a round left after Gravelines, hardly any food, and the men falling sick as they always did in these crowded ships.

There was one more chapter in the story, a sad one enacted on the Kentish coast. After seeing the Spaniards past the Forth and committed to their disastrous passage round Scotland and Ireland, Howard returned to demobilise and pay off. There were two reasons for haste. The Treasury was almost empty, and every day increased the claims on it ; and the sick were now numbered in thousands. The fleet anchored in Margate Roads and in the Downs. Hawkins as Navy Treasurer had charge of the work, but he found it slow on account of the weather, which made boat transit from ship to shore very difficult. At length the unfortunates were landed, and the little coast towns were so crammed with them that many had to lie, and die, out in the streets. The fit men gradually got the ships up the Medway to Chatham. Plymouth had seen the beginning of the great victory ; Deal and Sandwich and Margate saw its end.

Thenceforward the war followed a pattern for fourteen years : very little fighting in the Channel, but assemblage of expeditions great and small at Plymouth for distant strokes at Spain and her possessions. Drake and Sir John Norreys took a great force to Portugal in 1589, and came back in failure with less than half of their men. Grenville sailed in the *Revenge* to meet his end at Flores in 1591. Richard Hawkins set forth in his private galleon *Dainty* in 1593, to be overcome and captured by overwhelming force on the Peruvian coast. Drake and John Hawkins left together in '95 on what was to be their last unhappy voyage, from which neither returned. Lord Howard with Ralegh and Essex changed the luck in 1596 with their brilliant capture of Cadiz. And so forward to the war's end in 1603. There was only one Spanish retaliation on the English coast, when on a summer morning in 1595 four Spanish galleys from Brittany appeared in Mount's Bay. They landed 400 soldiers and burnt the villages of Mousehole, Newlyn and Penzance. Then they made off before the militia could concentrate and ships from Plymouth fall upon them. It was the only instance, in the nineteen years of the war, of a raid on the Channel coast such as previous ages had witnessed in an almost regular routine. It shows by contrast the prestige of the Tudor Navy. Meanwhile the privateers were swarming on the ocean, seeking their captures on the Spanish coast, round the Azores, and in the Caribbean. They were owned by all the great men, the Navy officers, the Privy Councillors, the leading merchants of London, and by many more from the minor ports. On the whole they were profitable, and when the war ended a depression not only of the spirit but of the purse fell upon the Channel coast.

We may end this brief survey (which has omitted much) with Richard Hawkins's description of his sailing from Plymouth in 1593 :

> The greater part of my company gathered aboard, I set sail the 12 of June 1593 about three of the clock in the afternoon, and made a board or two off and in, waiting the return of my boat, which I had sent ashore for dispatch of some business : which being come aboard, and all put in order, I luffed near the shore to give my farewell to all the inhabitants of the town, whereof the most part were gathered together upon the Hoe, to shew their grateful correspondency to the love and zeal which I, my father, and predecessors have ever borne to that place, as to our natural and mother town. And first with my noise of trumpets,

after with my waits, and then with my other music, and lastly with the artillery of my ships, I made the best signification I could of a kind farewell. This they answered with the waits of the town, and the ordnance on the shore, and with shouting of voices ; which, with the fair evening and silence of the night, were heard a great distance off.

CHAPTER ELEVEN

The Highway to the Ocean
and the Colonies

I. THE SEVENTEENTH CENTURY
A NEW COMMERCIAL AGE

WITH the end of the Spanish War in 1604 the port of London and the Channel coast entered on a new phase of their history. London's trade and England's trade were still, so far as money values went, predominantly with the continent of Europe ; and with the growth of material civilisation the European business steadily expanded. But the oceanic trades expanded at a much greater rate. In them, the economists believed, lay the future greatness of the country. By a general instinct the enterprise and energy of investors and adventurers flowed into the founding of western colonies and eastern trading citadels. The suddenness of the outburst on the signing of peace is remarkable. It is explained by the fact that the country had been all ready for the movement when the Spanish War began, and that the war had been an interruption rather than a stage in the advance. In 1604 England took up policies which had been laid aside but not forgotten twenty years before. They had in fact not all been laid aside, for the East India Company had received its charter in 1600.

The proportionate share of London in oceanic business increased. We have already seen one main reason for this, that London had the money and the access to government in far greater measure than the outports. The power of London's money was increasing. Fluid capital was growing available in sums incredible in Tudor times. This was not only in London but in Amsterdam, which Dutch independence made the economic capital of the Netherlands. The Dutch on the oceans were a growing power, permeating everywhere ; and for a generation there was much cooperation between them and the English. Some business firms were Anglo-Dutch, their London houses founded by refugees from Spanish tyranny. The Dutch Netherlands were full of Englishmen, soldiers, sailors and merchants, and notably some Puritan exiles. It was only later that these two vigorous peoples concluded that the wide world was not big enough for both, and the period of rivalry and war set in.

There was another reason for London's advance. It lay in the growing availability of the Thames estuary for the larger shipping. Through the past centuries there had been pilots to bring ships through the maze of sands and tortuous channels, but without accurate charts and buoyage the risks were great. Henry VIII refounded the pilot fraternity as the Guild of the Holy Trinity of Deptford Strond, and slowly the work grew more efficient. The banks and the soundings were more accurately known. Beacons and buoys were provided by the Trinity House from the fees levied on shipping. The buoys were not very numerous. They were placed in the channels close to the Kent and Essex shores, and the deeper central channels of the estuary were not much used. Thenceforward, as the seventeenth century progressed, a cumulative body of knowledge bore fruit in broadly trustworthy charts. The improved gear and rig of ships made them more handy in narrow waters. The great tonnage of merchant shipping could use London more confidently, and with less delay than in the past.

The larger south coast ports grew more slowly, but at least they grew. Dover and Rye had their special places in the passenger traffic. Southampton, exceptionally, was stagnant. Exeter, Dartmouth and Plymouth were all bigger places after the Tudor advance, and they did not decline. Portsmouth stagnated until the Dutch wars of the mid-century. Sandwich, Shoreham and Chichester, Poole, Weymouth, Lyme Regis and Falmouth were all of local activity for the service of their hinterlands. But some were almost finished as ports, Hythe, Winchelsea, Hastings, their harbours diminished by geographical changes.

It would be disproportionate in this book to give a detailed survey of the outburst of colonising and trading projects, or even to list all the expeditions. Colonies, closely interlinked with trade in the minds of their promoters, were planted or attempted on various parts of the North American coast, Virginia, Newfoundland, New England, Maryland. Another group sought to create plantations and Indian trade in the mouths of the Guiana rivers and the great delta of the Amazon. A third, somewhat later, took possession of the more promising smaller islands of the West Indies; and probably in number of emigrants this was the largest category of the three. Western trade without colonisation also increased. On the Spanish Main, where Hawkins had once pioneered, English and Dutch merchantmen called at the ports for cargoes of tobacco and laded salt for the fisheries at the great natural salt pan of Punta de Araya. Spanish complaints declared that 200 sail were there in a single year, and suggested that the salt should be poisoned. English merchants returned to Lisbon after the peace and took an increasing part in operating the Brazil trade of Portugal. That country was economically misgoverned by its Spanish masters and badly impoverished, short of ships and men. It asserted its independence in 1640. Both before and after that event it was chartering English ships for Brazil, and English merchants obtained legal recognition in the colonial trade by treaties in 1641 and 1654.

The Mediterranean was settling down and growing less disorderly—although by no means orderly; and the Levant merchants, their fighting ships no longer requisitioned for the Navy's campaigns, increased their business in the Turkish Empire. Out of the Levant Company had grown the East India Company, whose members included many of the Levant men, whilst the same secretary at first acted for both and kept the minutes of both in the same book. Before the East India Company was founded there had been some terrible independent voyages to the East, terrible because they had lost the lives of nearly all the men concerned. The cause was ignorance of the navigation of the Indian Ocean, and the climate of Indonesia. James Lancaster and John Davis suffered and learned by hard experience and survived to lead the company's first expedition to the East, which returned successful in 1604. Thenceforward the company's voyages were continuous, and there were others too, for interlopers were attracted to break in upon the company's monopoly. A by-product of eastern trade was a new intensive push to open the North West Passage as a shorter route to Asia, and Arctic expeditions were numerous until 1631.

Meanwhile Europe, the solid basis of it all, was for a brief period growing tranquil, the French wars of religion ended, England and Spain at peace, Dutch independence assured and virtually acknowledged by a twelve-year truce in 1609, Italy settled under Spanish rule. For England a new chapter began in 1604, the war ended, the Navy laid up, mercantile enterprise wonderfully expanded, capital accumulating as never before. Economically it was a new world. Politically and constitutionally it was still the old one of Tudor England, without the Tudor genius to make it work. The new wine in the old bottle was to produce the traditional result in civil war and revolution before the century was half-way through. But for its first generation early Stuart England seemed a good country to the enterprising and intelligent, although some Puritans were unhappy, and the poor were very numerous.

The Channel coast looked out upon a growing procession of ocean-going shipping, mostly London shipping, although the southern ports prosperously took their shares. The leaders of enterprise were not now all west-countrymen. Their great generation had passed, though Ralegh survived to 1618 and Richard Hawkins, a smaller figure than his father, to 1622. The empire-builders, leaders and followers, were from all parts, many from the eastern half of England. The Channel ports saw them call on their way out, and put in, sometimes in distress, as they came home. The general result for southern England was of growth. The early seventeenth century, less romantic than the sixteenth, has its own charm, the soothing charm of growing well-being and sobering maturity. To us it seems real progress in civilisation.

The Cinque Ports coastline had attained very nearly the outline that it shows to-day, with the reclamation of the tidal lagoons virtually complete and the resulting dry " marshes " defended by sea-walls. In general it may be said that there was now very little maritime trade in this region, although fishing was active, and Rye sent fair-sized boats for the North Sea cod. Local complaints of decay are frequent, but some are evidently exaggerated, for their object was to attract government assistance. Only a few years after the death of Henry VIII Rye was reporting that Camber Castle was tumbling down, with a general implication that its condition was as bad as it now is four centuries later. But the description had a motive, the desire of the townsmen for permission to use the masonry to build a quay; and considerably later we find the castle armed with numerous guns and accounted a good defensive work. By the early seventeenth century, however, it is evident that the deep Camber anchorage had filled up, and access to the town was by the river channels as at present. The position at Hastings is somewhat obscure. The Bourne stream in the valley between the Castle Hill and the East Hill had a miniature estuary where it reached the sea, an outflow almost drained at low water. It had been protected by a jetty or breakwater on the more exposed western side, and the port was available for small vessels taking the ground as tide flowed out. It must always have been a risky place. An Elizabethan gale was stated to have washed away the harbour arm completely, as the account would imply, leaving the port open and defenceless. But in subsequent years it is evident that something was left and that repairs were made, to be " destroyed " again by later storms. But no engineering work of those times, nothing short of the most massive modern construction, was sufficient to withstand the battering that a south-west gale can deliver on this coast, and Hastings never got its problem permanently solved.

The decline of the Cinque Ports as ports does not mean that the towns themselves diminished. A town once established attracts business as a market centre and a place of law and administration, and in this character they flourished in a sober and dignified way. The amount of good house-building still extant and dating from the seventeenth century or late sixteenth in most of the Ports is evidence of this; they were not impoverished places. Dover has little of this interesting building to show. Its passenger traffic, growing with the growth of European business, made it an expanding place, and with a five-fold multiplication of the inhabitants in the course of the nineteenth century almost everything was pulled down and rebuilt.

The little town of Deal, on whose beach our written history

began with Cæsar's landing, looked eastwards over four miles of semi-sheltered water to the Goodwin Sands. The water is the Downs, an anchorage, not a port, and in the sixteenth century it was increasingly frequented with the growth of London's west-bound shipping. For here, under the cover of the Kentish shore, the merchantmen waited for a change of wind to enable them to sail down Channel to the Atlantic. Sometimes they waited long, with much coming and going between ships and shore for victuals and gear and passengers and letters. The Deal fishermen made an increasing share of their living out of this service to the ships, and evolved a class of fast, hard-weather boats for the purpose. How they were rigged in the seventeenth century is not clearly known, for no one troubled to record particulars of such small fry, although the Navy's great ships were now being accurately described. For a long time past a fore-and-aft rig for small vessels had been coming into existence. Drawings of the mid-sixteenth century show minor craft with a spritsail like that of the modern Thames barge, and indicate less certainly the triangular foresail that is its complement. A picture of the siege of Sluys in 1604 preserved at Hatfield House leaves no doubt. It shows numerous small vessels with sprit main-sail and a triangular foresail set on a forestay leading high up the mast. Statements of 1544–5 name John Fletcher, Mayor of Rye, as turning out some notably weatherly little boats, and he has even been hailed as the inventor of the fore-and-aft rig. But it existed before his time, and no one person ever invents such things, which grow by long evolution.

The maritime slumber that had fallen on the east Sussex coast extended westwards to the Solent and Southampton. None of the ports here were relatively so important as they had been a century or two earlier, although as towns they were sharing in the general growth of the country as the population increased and the land was more fully exploited. Brighton had a fishing fleet, Shoreham and Chichester did the small sea trade necessary for their districts. Littlehampton was coming into being at the mouth of the Arun, where Arundel still owned a ship or two higher up.

Portsmouth, as we have seen, lost its naval prominence in Elizabeth's time, and in the period we are now examining it did not regain it. Even the dry dock made by Henry VII was filled in. For a very brief interlude at the opening of Charles I's reign, when Buckingham urged the King to warlike adventures, Portsmouth saw the Navy again, but the stimulus was soon removed, only a few small craft being subsequently kept there. Portsmouth needed the Navy, for its geographical position on Portsea Island did not yield it a sufficient hinterland to flourish as a country town.

Southampton was better placed in this respect, and was also able to carry on a small sea trade for the local needs. But it had lost the big trade it had once enjoyed as an outport of London. The medieval conditions that had made Southampton great had faded out in early Tudor times. Its own shipping declined, and it did not contribute a single vessel to the national turn-out against the Armada in 1588. In the early seventeenth century ships taking emigrants to the new colonies did sometimes call at Southampton to embark their passengers, in order to avoid the expenditure of victuals by the delay for weather in the Downs. The port also sent some ships to the growing Newfoundland fishery. A map in the possession of Southampton University shows the town in the mid-sixteenth century. It is for the most part restricted within the medieval walls and moat, in plan an oblong with its length running north and south from the Bar Gate down the High Street to the Water Gate, and its breadth considerably less, from the western walls and quay to the walls and moat looking eastwards across a marsh. But there is already some small building outside the Bar and East Gates. Standing in the water east of God's House Gate are two gallows, each with a hanging corpse, perhaps pirates. John Speed's map shows essentially the same arrangement, but with more precision, in 1611. The walls and castle look efficient, but in fact the castle was so ruinous that it was sold by the Crown to private hands in 1618 and ceased to be a defence.[1]

Down Channel the ports were more active. With the peace Plymouth indeed lost the continuous naval activities of the past generation, but there were large compensations. West of England

---

[1] The maps are reproduced in the *Southampton Atlas* with commentary by W. H. Rogers, published for the Southampton Record Society, n.d., c. 1905. The 1611 map was copied with the omission of the streets, in a French Atlas of English towns, c. 1650, in B.M. Add. MSS. 11,564, art. 33.

cloth gave a prominent export trade. The Newfoundland fishery was booming as never before, and Dartmouth, as will be shown, was peculiarly suited by it. The Peninsular trades revived, and their imports of wine and fruits were such as did not lend themselves to canalisation through London, but were best distributed from various ports of landing. The south-west as a whole had a denser population than Hampshire and Sussex, and had certainly gained some permanent enrichment from the privateering of the Spanish War.[1] The down-Channel coastline was by no means stagnating. To balance the picture, however, we must bear in mind that Bristol, after London, reaped the best of the harvest from the new colonial trades and had a larger share than the south coast in the solid commerce with Portugal and Spain.

With the peace of 1604 privateering came to an end. James I issued no more licences and did not permit his subjects to take them from the Dutch. Many ex-privateers, having no other occupation, became pirates, and men of substance, previously investors in privateering, became connivers in piracy. Richard Hawkins is an example. He was captured by the Spaniards on the Peruvian coast in 1594, and remained a prisoner until released for a ransom in 1602. He returned to take his place as Plymouth's leading magnate. He was knighted by James I, appointed Vice-Admiral of Devon, and chosen a member for Plymouth in the Parliament of 1604. Yet with all this he was continuously accused of consorting with pirates and receiving their winnings. He explained away the various complaints, but they continued to accumulate until in 1608 even his powerful friends could not prevent his being brought to trial and condemned to a heavy fine and a short imprisonment. His case did not stand alone, and it was several years before the post-war phase of English piracy was abated.

II. THE BARBARY CORSAIRS

Meanwhile piracy of a new sort was producing alarm and indignation. From time long past Moslem pirates had preyed upon trade in the Mediterranean, issuing out of all the North African

[1] See two population maps in Darby's *Historical Geography of England*, pp. 438-9.

ports from the Levant to the Straits of Gibraltar. The growth of the Ottoman Empire encouraged them, and the Italian merchant cities were at first the chief sufferers. Spain also was a Mediterranean as well as an Atlantic power, and Charles V and Philip II had been involved in an endless war with the Turks and the North African potentates. To the Europeans they were all Turks, the word being synonymous with Moslem. Just as the Anglo-Spanish war was ended it became noticeable that the corsairs from the Western Mediterranean were coming out of the Straits and beginning to operate in the Atlantic. The development was natural, in view of the spoils which Christian privateers were gaining round the Spanish coasts, but much has been made of the story of an Englishman named John Ward, a renegade bos'n who deserted from the Navy and " turned Turk." He is said to have taught the Barbary corsairs about ocean sailing and the sort of shipping needed for success. Be that as it may, the corsairs multiplied in the Atlantic and began to use home ports like Sallee, in Barbary without the Straits. In the reigns of James I and Charles I the new pirates became a plague in the Channel approaches and all along the south coast. One is even recorded to have been captured in the estuary of the Thames. They took ships in numbers that seems incredible, seeing that nothing effective was done about it ; and besides the loss of property they inflicted loss of men. For they did not release the crews whom they took. The Mediterranean wars for generations back had been waged by galley fleets whose rowers were slaves. The demand for galley slaves was inexhaustible ; and the men taken on their lawful occasions in the Channel went to Algiers and Tunis and Tripoli to sweat out the short remainder of their lives under the whips of the galley-slave masters. Men of substance could get release for a ransom, for there were always agents in the Moslem ports to effect such business ; but for the fisherman or coasting seaman taken in sight of his own beach it was the end of life. Not only this, but the pirates made landings and captured labourers out of the fields. There were many instances, both in England and southern Ireland. It was the African slave trade in reverse.[1]

The complaints of the Channel coast were loud and long, but

[1] For Ward and the Barbary pirates see J. S. Corbett, *England in the Mediterranean.*

James I was deaf to them. The Elizabethan Navy would have dealt with the matter, for Sir John Hawkins had built for it many fighting pinnaces which would economically have abated the plague. But James in his zest for peace and his reckless court extravagance had permanently laid up the Navy. It decayed rapidly and thoroughly under the Navy Board headed by Sir Robert Mansell, probably the most eminent master of graft in our history. Until 1621 there was not even a show of doing anything against the pirates. Then Mansell and Sir Richard Hawkins were sent with a feeble squadron into the Mediterranean. Their supposed mission was to attack one source of piracy at Algiers, but James's real motive was to make a demonstration in support of his European diplomacy. The expedition was ill-found and ill-supported, and achieved nothing. Mansell was nothing but a rogue, and Hawkins was over sixty and near his end. They came back unsuccessful. Early next year Hawkins was complaining that his men were unpaid, and the worry killed him. He fell dead, some said at the very council table where he was urging the case of his seamen.

Charles I made a show of naval action, but he never really tackled the deep-seated graft and corruption. His later ship-money fleets spasmodically patrolled the Channel, but not by any means to the satisfaction of the inhabitants of its coastline. Their minds retained the Tudor tradition and saw it sadly tarnished. Not until new men and a new spirit came into the Navy with the Commonwealth did the epoch of the Barbary corsairs in English waters come to an end.

III. THE BUCKINGHAM WARS

In his first three years Charles I was completely under the influence of the Duke of Buckingham, the favourite whom his father had promoted from obscurity to the highest rank in the peerage. Buckingham, to his credit, had done something towards rescuing the Navy from the condition into which it had sunk under Mansell's control. But he had not done nearly enough, and the fleet was quite unequal to the moderate efforts required of it when Buckingham urged Charles into war, first with Spain and then with France. These undertakings were parts of a complicated European diplomacy centred in the religious war which had begun in Germany in 1618, the Thirty Years War. Buckingham handled matters with reckless violence, although England had at that time little real interest to justify fighting. In 1625 he collected an expedition to attack Cadiz. It assembled at Plymouth, with altogether ninety ships to carry 10,000 troops. The King's ships were in an unfit condition, with worn-out gear—some of the sails were forty years old. The impressed soldiers and sailors were unpaid and mutinous. The leadership was incompetent and the victualling deplorable. It was not a brisk and cheerful preparation like those of Drake's time, and the people of Plymouth were resentful as the penniless and disorderly mob was billeted upon them. Under Edward Cecil, Lord Wimbledon, the expedition sailed in the autumn, reached Cadiz, stayed little more than a week before giving up the attempt on the town, and returned to Plymouth without essaying any other enterprise. The lives of the men might as well have been thrown into the sea.

For the expedition had been terribly costly in life. It set out hungry and returned starving, with the usual typhus and dysentery raging through the ships. Hundreds died on the voyage, and hundreds more at anchor in the Sound after the return, and more still in Plymouth itself; and the warlike achievement had been nil. There had been disease and hunger in almost every Elizabethan fleet, and the greatest of all in 1588 had come back to port in very bad shape. But men noted the difference. The Elizabethan government, poor though it was, always paid its men, down to the humblest. After the Armada was beaten, the Lord Admiral, though summoned to court to tell his story, got back to his fleet as soon as he could, and took his part with Hawkins in relieving the sick and paying off the survivors. " I must see them paid, and will," he wrote. Very different was it under Buckingham and his King. They had both gone down to see the expedition start, but on its return they recognised no humane obligation to the wretches whose lives their incompetence had thrown away. It was their terrible incomprehension that exasperated : Charles honestly did not see that he and his favourite had a duty, and were failing in it. A principal offender was Buckingham's adherent Sir James Bagg, who was responsible for the victualling and much else. He undoubtedly made dishonest gains, and the gang of minor rascals accumulated through twenty years of corruption also took their pickings. Sir John Elyot, a Cornish Member of Parliament, saw the sufferings at Plymouth and spoke forcefully to the Commons, who on other grounds were hostile enough towards the favourite.[1] English patriotism took an ominous turn. Its enemy became not Spain but Buckingham.

Not content with failure against a Spain that itself was feeble at sea, Buckingham forced a quarrel on France, where Richelieu was strengthening the royal power against all dissidents. The Huguenots were among them, and La Rochelle was required to resign its autonomy. This should have been a popular cause to English Puritans, but Buckingham could make nothing popular. In 1627 he gave Portsmouth a turn as a naval base, and there gathered an expedition which he personally led for the relief of La Rochelle. It was the same story of improvidence and incompetence, of unwilling men bound for death under a leadership they despised. Portsmouth was at that time less suitable as a base than Plymouth. The crews of those days were supposed to provide their own simple outfits out of their advance pay, if they had any, and the place was so poor that neither clothing nor bedding could be had. When Buckingham returned defeated from his attempt to seize the Isle of Rhé, outside Rochelle, his men were in a dreadful state of hunger, nakedness and typhus. Of the 8000 men who had set out only 3000 came back, nearly all sick. The townspeople objected to their being landed to spread the infection, but it ravaged the town nevertheless. In 1628 Buckingham was there again preparing another of his ghastly expeditions, and at Captain Mason's house in the High Street, John Felton, a junior officer, plunged a knife into his heart. The murderer conceived that he had done England a service, and many agreed with him. Expecting to be lynched, he had placed a written statement inside his hat : " He is unworthy of the name of a gentleman or soldier that is afraid to sacrifice his life for the honour of God, his King, and his country. John Felton." A half-hearted expedition sailed, and failed again, and thereafter Portsmouth relapsed into peace and poverty.

[1] In a later debate on corruption Sir Francis Seymour denounced " the bottomless Bagg."

IV. THE NEWFOUNDLAND FISHERY

The Buckingham wars were terrible and shameful, but they covered only four years out of forty that witnessed a growing prosperity. The Newfoundland fishery bore a great part in it. We have already mentioned its beginnings in the sixteenth century, and the method of curing the stockfish on stages set up on the shore. In the closing years of Elizabeth's reign the number of English ships in the fishing increased, and in the peace period that followed they increased more rapidly. The fishery became a constituent part of the magnified commercial complex that made the seventeenth-century world so much more intricately capitalistic than anything that had been seen before. The fishery was the industry of the western Channel from the Isle of Wight to Cornwall. Its rapid increase gave the ports not only a new occupation but a means of strengthening their commerce with the Peninsula and the Mediterranean. When in 1634 the Crown issued orders for the regulation of the fishery, it vested authority in the mayors of Southampton, Weymouth, Lyme Regis, Dartmouth, Plymouth, East Looe, Fowey and Barnstaple, the last named being the only non-Channel port. Poole for some reason was not in the list, but is otherwise known to have taken part in the fishing. Exeter is also omitted, and its share was probably small, although its port at Topsham did send out ships to Newfoundland.

The fishing ships were growing larger. A writer of 1615 spoke of a 100-ton ship with 40 men as the standard size. Of the crew, 24 would do the actual fishing, and the remainder the curing on-shore. The expenditure was on the capital cost of the ship, the fitting out and victualling, and the purchase of salt. The crews were not paid wages, but divided a share of the gross receipts for the season's catch. When all went well it was a profitable trade for all concerned, but the risks were great, from shipwreck, piracy and the King's enemies. Great mercantile skill was needed, for the prices of salt and of the marketable fish varied from season to season, and the various European markets themselves offered differing profits in the same season. The statistics of total numbers engaged are scanty, and yield no firm over-all statement, for the industry fluctuated greatly within brief periods. In 1634–7, a peak period, there were said to be 500 English ships and 18,000 men regularly engaged,[1] but by 1640 the numbers had fallen, and in the Civil War they fell still more. The figures show the enormous increase of maritime activity during the seventeenth century ; for at the time of the Armada they would have represented or even exceeded the entire marine strength of the country, while in the 1630's they stood for one trade among many.

The Newfoundland fishery had a greater effect on the Channel coast than even the above figures indicate, for it gave employment to numbers of shipwrights and labourers, dealers in timber and marine stores, and providers of victuals, while the seamen were mostly in their home ports spending their money in the winter. It was what the mercantile economists called a gaining trade, for the outlay was all (save for the salt) in England, while the receipts were in foreigners' money obtained in the European market. By far the greater part of the fish was sold abroad. The English of the period were a well-fed people by comparison with the continent, and they had no great taste for dried cod ; neither were they compelled by their religion to eat nothing but fish in Lent. The English demand was chiefly for the victualling of ships, particularly for tropical voyages ; for stockfish was the only foodstuff which would keep uncorrupted in a hot climate while salted meat went putrid. The fishermen sometimes brought their catch to an English port, from which it was re-exported. Frequently they sailed direct from Newfoundland to Southern France, Spain or the Mediterranean, where they sold the cod and picked up a wine cargo for England. But the merchant capitalists of London saw better ways of marketing. The fishing ships carried twice as many men as were necessary to sail them across the ocean, and it was uneconomical to pay and victual the extra hands for the passage to a European market. It was also wasteful for a ship to leave Newfoundland merely because she had a full hold, while part of the season remained. The merchants therefore sent out the so-called " sack ships " to collect the

[1] H. A. Innis, *The Cod Fisheries*, Yale U. Press, 1940, p. 70. This is the best detailed work on the subject, and is the authority used for this chapter.

catch from the fishermen and carry it where required. This differentiated the actual fishing from the trade in fish.

The seasonal fishermen behaved very wastefully on the Newfoundland coast. They made their store sheds and drying stages out of timber cut near the shore, roofed the sheds with bark stripped from living trees, and burnt a good deal of the timber which they abandoned in any case on leaving. The result at the best harbours was a shortage of timber. Merchant syndicates therefore sought to plant little colonies of permanent residents, to stay through the winter and look after the property, and to save fishing time by having things ready for the fishermen on their arrival. Thus arose the colonisation of Newfoundland, begun on a tiny scale by John Guy, acting for a London and Bristol company in 1610.[1] It was then an easy development for the colonists to become fishermen themselves, using boats from the shore, and to gather cargoes for the merchants' sack ships to take away. This aroused violent opposition in the Channel ports, which saw in a permanent colony a threat of extinction to their seasonal business. The war of propaganda, lobbying, and sometimes physical violence between the rival interests continued for more than a century—ship fishermen (Channel men) versus boat fishermen (colonists). In the outcome both survived side by side, but the colony was certainly discouraged and retarded. At one juncture in the late seventeenth century the Channel interest even secured a government decision to end the colony and deport the colonists. But the naval officer sent out to do it protested that it was unjust and pointed out that if persecuted the colonists would join the French, who were also forming small settlements; and this caused the Newfoundland colony to be reprieved.

V. EMPIRE-BUILDING AND THE INCREASE OF SHIPPING

The stream of emigration that founded the colonies of the old Colonial Empire flowed for the most part in the first forty years of the seventeenth century. It was caused by growth of population,

---

[1] Sir Humphrey Gilbert proclaimed the annexation of Newfoundland in the Queen's name in 1583, but no colonisation followed.

both in the towns and the countryside of England; by a quest for new forms of adventure after the peace with Spain; and by the determination among a minority of the Puritans to found communities in which the religious jurisdiction should be of their own fashioning. The growth of capital seeking profitable employment and of ocean shipping for transport gave these aspirations their opportunity. The intangible floating idea of the age, that it was a time of opportunity, called forth the landless men of England in their tens and even hundreds of thousands to the goal of becoming small freeholders in the colonies instead of working for wages at home. Except for the Puritan part of the movement, London was the organising headquarters. Some of the emigration proceeded from Bristol, but most of it passed down-Channel and had contacts with the Channel ports. Most of the Puritans chose New England, and there after much hardship and mortality they established five distinct settlement colonies practising agriculture in the English style for the subsistence of communities as much like English villages as they could make them. Most of the more secularly minded emigrants went farther south, to Virginia and Maryland, the Guiana river mouths and the Amazon delta, and the lesser West Indian islands unoccupied by Spain. In these regions they did not reconstitute the English way of life, but devoted themselves to growing and exporting plantation crops, tobacco, and later sugar, using servile labour and importing their foodstuffs from New England and the fishery, and their manufactures from Old England. As the colonies grew, a network of trade routes covered the Atlantic. Its centre lay not in London alone, for Amsterdam took its share. Much of the capital, the mercantile profit and the shipping were Dutch, or mixed Anglo-Dutch, although most of the colonists and nearly all the political sovereignty were English. This held good broadly until the middle of the century.

The call of the new enterprises for shipping and seamen was enormous, and it was easier to build the ships than to find men to sail them. There were more English seamen than there had ever been before, and yet there were not enough. Shipmasters competed for hands. Wages in merchantmen increased. Prudent seamen took little cargo ventures of their own with them—a roll of calico purchased in Holland and sold for twice its cost in the Mediterranean, and the money laid out in a chest of dates or raisins to make a similar gain home in England. The mercantile marine offered advancement to a young man of courage, enterprise and luck. The luck was needed, for the risks were great—foundering of rotten ships, wreck on unlighted coasts, capture by pirates. The merchant skipper who saw a distant sail did not attempt to close and communicate, but made off for all he was worth. If a strange ship appeared anxious to speak with him, she was most likely a wrong 'un. All merchant ships carried guns, and the master gunner was as important a man as in the Navy. A Dover sailor, Edward Coxere, who was converted by the Quakers when he was thirty, found sea employment hard to get by one who would handle no weapon. He could sail only in a hoy on short coasting passages. A Quaker shipowner built a new vessel without guns and, although she was not lost, found his anxiety so great that he armed her for the next voyage in the usual way.[1]

The most celebrated of all the emigrant voyages was that of the Pilgrim Fathers in the *Mayflower*. They were a small church of English Puritans who had settled in the Netherlands at Leyden. After a dozen years their younger members decided to emigrate to North America, and it was they who began the colonisation of New England. They did not call themselves the Pilgrim Fathers, being plain sober people whose ideas did not run to a fancy title. The term was coined long afterwards, a product of the romantic period, and first used in 1799. Thirty-five of these people set out from Holland in 1620 and sailed to Southampton in the small ship *Speedwell*. There they were joined by sixty-seven others from various parts of England, and a merchantman of 180 tons, the *Mayflower*, chartered in the Thames, came round to Southampton to receive them. The numbers given above are of those who were destined to cross the Atlantic, and there were about forty more who embarked at Southampton but were left behind at Plymouth. For, after sailing, the *Speedwell* developed a leak, and the expedition put

[1] *The Adventures by Sea of Edward Coxere*, Oxford, 1945, is a vivid account of life and dangers at sea in the middle of the century written in a racy, carefree style up to the point where the author became a Quaker. Thereafter the manner is that of the more sober spiritual writings of the period.

in to Dartmouth to have it stopped. After a week they sailed again and got beyond the Land's End, when the leaks grew worse than before, and they put back to Plymouth. There it was apparent that the *Speedwell* was unseaworthy and must be abandoned, and it was there that the weeding-out of the emigrants took place. Thence the hundred and two, men, women, and a few children, sailed in the *Mayflower* to their destiny as the founders of New England. A stone on the Plymouth landing-stage near Sutton Pool commemorates the departure. No details of the *Mayflower* are known save her tonnage. She was an old ship, and some have surmised that she may have been the *Mayflower* that served in the Armada campaign of 1588. But the stock of ships' names was limited, and repetitions were frequent. The *Mayflower II* of 1957 can hardly be considered a replica, for lack of original details ; but she was constructed after keen research into the building of merchantmen in general at the period.[1]

Dartmouth's great seaman John Davis entered the port in the spring of 1601 with the first expedition of the East India Company, of which he was chief pilot. The four ships, having suffered delay by adverse winds since leaving London, came into Dartmouth to top up their victuals and water casks. They made a long and successful voyage which founded the fortunes of the company. On returning in 1604 Davis seems to have had some disagreement with the Company, for he transferred his services to an interloping expedition commanded by Sir Edward Michelbourne. He was with them in the *Tiger* early in 1606 when they were trading on the coasts of Malaya. They had friendly communications with a Japanese ship, and a number of polite little men came on board the *Tiger*. Then in a flash the guests drew their weapons on the English crew. They killed many before they were chased overboard, and among the slain was John Davis, cut down as he rushed on deck at the first alarm.

[1] See *Mariner's Mirror*, Vol. 12, No. 8, July 1926, *A " Mayflower " Model*, by R. C. Anderson, who, after pointing out that a real model is impossible, described the building of a model of a typical merchantman of the *Mayflower's* tonnage from dimensions preserved of the *Adventure* of Ipswich, 1627. See also a report of a lecture by Allan Villiers, commander of the *Mayflower II*, in *Mariner's Mirror*, Vol. 44, No. 22, May 1958.

The Newfoundland fishery gave Dartmouth half a century of booming prosperity. It was an entrepôt trade peculiarly suited to the port, not greatly depending on inland communications. Many new people settled in the town, and the money they made is expressed in some beautiful domestic buildings in the Jacobean style, a new quay, and rebuilt churches. The famous Butterwalk, " adjudged by competent critics to be the finest example of the seventeenth century Devonian style in domestic architecture,"[1] dates from 1640. It was severely damaged but not destroyed by bombing in 1943.

The fishery provided winter work, when the ships were fitted out. None was allowed to sail before March 1st, for the outward passage was a race, and the master of the first ship to arrive in any Newfoundland cove was admiral of the port for the season, with power to regulate the occupancy of the curing places, and the best of course for himself. Dartmouth sack ships followed the fishermen, taking out the salt, taking away the fish to exchange for tobacco in the West Indies plantations, or for wine in Portugal and Spain. All this inflow of overseas products was absorbed into the growing prosperity of English life. The period before the Civil War was seen by contemporaries—and notably by Clarendon the historian— as a sunny time. The revolution was caused not by economic misery but by politics and religion, ultimately by the personalities of Charles I and his advisers and of John Pym and the Puritan reformers.

The poor figure cut by the Stuart Navy under Buckingham, and the continued depredations of the pirates in sight of the English coast, inspired Charles I to attempt to assert his sea power. His ship-money fleets of the 1630's had the duty of putting down piracy, guarding English neutrality in the renewed war between Spain and the Dutch, and regulating the colonial trade. They were not very successful, for the money was never enough for the effort, and administration was bad. The officers were not of the Elizabethan quality, and the men were chronically discontented and ready to desert. At a time when merchant seamen were well paid and enjoyed perquisites it seemed intolerable to them to be pressed for

[1] Percy Russell, *Dartmouth*, p. 98.

the King's ships at wages which were half the merchant rates and were often unpaid. These wages were not pocket-money, for the men had wives and families ashore. Discipline deteriorated, and the new sort of officers relied less on leadership than on brutality. Piracy was not effectively dealt with, neither was neutrality preserved, as was seen in 1639 when Dutch and Spanish fleets fought a pitched battle in the Downs, close to the English shore, with an English squadron looking helplessly on. In the following year sixty sail of Turkish rovers were reported to be cruising off the Lizard.[1] The colonial trade was concerned because in the interest of customs collection all English plantations were ordered to ship their tobacco exclusively to English ports. Much of it went on to central European consumers, but the English government wanted its duty first. Colonial shippers obviously desired to send their stuff direct to the Netherland ports. The Channel patrol had orders to intercept homeward-bound ships and place men on board to ensure that they were taken to London. But many slipped through, and the merchants regarded it as one more arbitrary hazard to their trade.

VI. THE CHANNEL IN THE CIVIL WAR

All these things considered it is not surprising that when war did break out between King and Parliament in 1642, not only London, but almost the whole Channel coast, merchants, seamen and people, were against the King. His own Royal Navy also sided against him, moved not only by the grievances of the lower deck but by the shame of the higher ranks at the record since Elizabeth had died. The Navy in effect had the decision of the war. The wealth of London was the main support of the Parliament's cause. If the Navy had served the King and blockaded the Thames the war would have been quickly finished in his favour. Few historians have recognised that what the Navy could have done and did not do, like Sherlock Holmes's dog that did not bark, was the decisive factor of the story. The natural loyalty of seamen throughout our history has been to the Crown. Charles I alone among our sovereigns had the perverted talent to place it at the disposal of his enemies.

[1] Mary Coate, *Cornwall in the Great Civil War*, Oxford 1933, p. 8.

The only exceptional part of the Channel coast was that of Cornwall. There the majority of the gentry were Royalists, and they carried the ports with them. Fowey and Falmouth became the King's means of communication with the continent, and through them he obtained munitions which helped to prolong the struggle, paying for them with Cornish tin. All the other ports from Plymouth eastward were for Parliament, although many of the inland gentry of the southern counties were for the King. The Channel Islands were Royalist, and so also were the Scillies, their control depending on the possession of a couple of small castles. The islands and the Cornish ports afforded bases for Royalist privateers, which operated against the commerce of London and the south. Their captures were not proportionately great, but they had a nuisance value as a diversion.

In 1643 the small army of Cornish Royalists, led by Sir Ralph Hopton and some officers of exceptional talent, crossed the Tamar, threatened Plymouth, and marched on through Devon. They joined hands with an army from Oxford under the King's nephews Rupert and Maurice, and stormed Bristol, another Parliamentary port. In the storming of Bristol the Cornishmen suffered heavily and lost all their best officers. Thereafter they returned to their own soil west of the Tamar. Meanwhile the Royalists under Prince Maurice pushed for control of the south coast. Early in September he captured Exeter after a siege in which the citizens made a stout defence for Parliament. He had then the choice of attacking Dartmouth or Plymouth. He chose Dartmouth, thought to be an easier prey owing to its topography, and offering a good harbour for Royalist traffic with the continent. There was no force in Dartmouth able to hold the surrounding heights, and the Royalists looked into the town ; but it was defended so well by its own people that Maurice was a month in taking it. His men, in bivouac in the equinoctial weather, lost heavily by sickness, and he had to leave a garrison in Dartmouth. It was with diminished force that the Royalists turned towards Plymouth.[1]

From 1642 to the opening of 1646 Plymouth was threatened with siege, and for part of the time closely besieged ; and on its

[1] For the siege of Dartmouth, see Russell's *Dartmouth*.

fate much turned, for after Dartmouth was lost it was the only port west of the Solent capable of serving the Parliamentary Navy. Of the smaller places, the Royalists took Weymouth and Portland, but Poole and Lyme Regis were stubbornly held for the Parliament. At Lyme the Parliamentary commander was Robert Blake, a colonel destined to yet greater achievement as an admiral. With supplies from the sea he made a brilliant defence of a little unwalled town against heavy odds ; but the harbour of Lyme was insignificant, and the issue was small as compared with that of Plymouth. The first move against Plymouth was made by Hopton at the end of 1642, and he captured Saltash in January 1643 ; but he passed on to the campaign against Bristol already noted. Later in the year, as we have seen, Prince Maurice came westwards with another Royalist army and took Exeter and Dartmouth.· Plymouth was next on his list.

Here we come to the somewhat unclear question of the fortifications of Plymouth. According to the plan of 1591 they should have been excellent,[1] but in 1643 it would seem that they did not exist, for the Corporation made order that a wall should be erected round the town.[2] It thus seems likely that the defences of 1591 were on paper only, and never did exist. A sketch-map of 1643 [3] shows a line of what may have been mainly earthworks surrounding the town, probably those thrown up by the Corporation for the emergency. Outside the town to the northwards the map shows a separate line of forts and trenches, up-hill from the present city centre and well clear of the old town as it was then. It was on this line that most of the fighting took place. For manpower the Parliament sent 500 soldiers by sea from Portsmouth, and the rest of the defenders were from Plymouth's own population of six to seven thousand, the number estimated by R. N. Worth.

In October Maurice came on from Dartmouth and began a close siege that lasted well into the next year. The crucial day was 3rd December, 1643, when the defenders won a great fight up the

[1] See above, p. 200.
[2] *The Siege of Plymouth*, by R. N. Worth, in *Trans. of the Plymouth Institution*, Vol V, Plymouth 1876.
[3] In Plymouth Public Library. For advice of it I have to thank the City Librarian, Mr. W. Best Harris.

northern slope at Freedom Fields. Maurice gave place to Sir Richard Grenville as the King's commander, and the siege went on. Lord Robartes, a Puritan Cornish peer, was made governor for Parliament. He urged that a Parliamentary army should move into the south-west and secure all the ports. The Earl of Essex accordingly marched down in 1644, raised the siege of Plymouth, and went on into Cornwall. From Oxford the King in person pursued him and rounded him up at Lostwithiel, up the Fowey river. Essex escaped by boat to Plymouth, but his infantry had to surrender (1st September), while his horse cut their way out. The King then turned on Plymouth with a force 15,000 strong. He hoped that his numbers and prestige would ensure surrender. But Plymouth did not surrender, and Charles could not stay, for this was the summer of Marston Moor and things were going ill elsewhere. Grenville remained to continue a blockade, while 1645 witnessed Naseby, and 1646 the end of the war. The Royalists withdrew from Plymouth in January of that year.

Plymouth was held by the resolution of its own people, their forces nourished from the sea. Its fall would have been a first-class gain to the King in two ways. The whole trade of the south-west would have come under his control, with a consequent access of revenue; and the prestige success would have convinced waverers that his was the winning side. Money, even in small amounts, meant everything to both combatants, who had almost literally to count it by sixpences. Parliamentary waverers grew more numerous as the war dragged on. It was not until 1645 that Cromwell gained substantial control and his New Model army gave the war a new aspect. Cornish resistance to Parliament ceased at the end of that year, except that John Arundell in Henry VIII's Pendennis Castle at Falmouth held out until the following August.

In the Civil War sea power was the determinant, although all the battles were between armies. Charles lost the war in its fourth year because Cromwell and Fairfax were better soldiers than he. But it had taken them all that time to work their way up to command; and there would have been no fourth year, or third, or New Model army, if the fleet and the merchant shipping had supported the King.

A Channel pendant to the civil wars is the story of Charles II's escape after his incursion from Scotland in 1651. After the battle of Worcester on 3rd September Charles was on the run for nearly six weeks before he got out of the country. The last phase of his wanderings brought him to the Channel coast. After failing to get a ship at Lyme Regis and at Bridport he struck inland again and came by Salisbury and Winchester to the Hampshire-Sussex border at Hambledon. Here he made contact with Colonel George Gounter, a Royalist ex-officer who lived at Racton, four miles from Chichester. All this time there was a hot search for the fugitive, the country placarded with offers of £1000 for the arrest of " a black young man above two yards high." A number of people recognised him but none betrayed him. Gounter heard in Chichester of a small coaster, the *Surprise*, lading at Shoreham, whose master might take the King to France. Gounter and Lord Wilmot and another set out with Charles from Hambledon and rode eastwards along the line of the Downs. They could not use the coast road because there were soldiers in Chichester. The King, with his hair cropped and a puritanical scowl disfiguring his handsome countenance, was taken for a servant of the party. A Royalist who was not in the secret twitted them with having a Roundhead dog with them, and swore profanely in order to annoy the fellow : to which Charles answered meekly, " Brother, do not swear ! " So they went along the Downs north of Chichester and on by Goodwood to Arundel, where they came face to face with the major commanding the Parliamentary soldiers, who suspected nothing and passed them by. They came down from inland to Brighton and thence with great caution to Shoreham. The shipmaster, Nicholas Tattersall, demanded payment of a good round sum, for which he carried Charles and Wilmot to sea and landed them at Fécamp next day. After the Restoration in 1660, Tattersall reminded the King of the service by sailing the *Surprise* up the Thames and anchoring her off Whitehall. Charles was no doubt amused, and took the vessel into the Navy as a royal yacht, and the owner as her captain. She was renamed the *Royal Escape*.[1]

[1] For the escape in general see Sir Arthur Bryant's *King Charles II*, London, 1931. Colonel Gounter wrote an account of the Sussex part, which was printed in J. D. Parry's *Coast of Sussex*, London, 1833. There is a painting of the *Royal Escape* by Van de Velde in the National Maritime Museum. It is here reproduced.

CHAPTER TWELVE

The Anglo-Dutch Wars
and the Invasion of 1688

I. THE COMMONWEALTH AND
THE FIRST DUTCH WAR

THE Anglo-Dutch connection, which had been allied and co-operative at the opening of the seventeenth century, broke down into jealousy as the overseas commerce of both countries expanded and either began to view the other as a rival for oceanic supremacy. The Anglo-Dutch war which began in 1652 was partly occasioned by English and European politics, the difficulties and fears of the new Commonwealth proclaimed on the execution of Charles I. But in the main its cause was grievance in the Far East, and still more the intrusion of Dutch commerce into the colonial empire founded by the English in the North Atlantic. Charles I had tried somewhat ineffectively to restrict the trade of the colonies to the English mother country. During the Civil War control entirely broke down, and the Dutch freely traded with Barbados and St. Kitts, Virginia and Maryland. The new sugar culture (from about 1640) in the English West Indies needed capital equipment in the shape of crushing mills and boiling plant and negro slaves for gang labour. London's mercantile ability was disorganised by the Civil War, and Amsterdam supplied the want, giving credit to the planters and acquiring economic control of the plantations. It seemed that the English had founded the colonies only for the Dutch to enjoy the profit of them. In the East the Dutch Company had evicted the English from the Spice Islands and were competing vigorously in the remaining sphere of continental India. In the North Sea herring fishery, a source of enormous wealth, the Dutch had grown preponderant. Everywhere the London merchant saw himself beset and defeated.

Here were the elements of a rancorous conflict, and there was, of course, a good deal of war-hatred once the fighting had begun. But it never in the three Dutch wars reached the intensity that we have regarded as normal in our time. The dispute was economic rather than emotional. Protestantism was a common bond in face of Catholic France and Spain. Large numbers of Dutchmen were settled and married in England, and Englishmen in the Netherlands. Communication between these individuals and their homelands continued, and there was little internment of enemy civilians. Edward Coxere, returning to see his mother at Dover while the war was in progress, tells us that he he found it expedient to pose as a Dutchman in order to avoid impressment for the English Navy. He had served in a Dutch ship and became a personal friend of its captain, who was himself an Irishman of Amsterdam. Merchant crews were cosmopolitan.

In the three years before the war broke out the Commonwealth leaders were hard at work to strengthen the Navy. They put in good order the ships taken over from Charles I, and by new construction they doubled the total number. They also placed in the higher commands some energetic soldiers out of the New Model army, a remarkable experiment which turned out to be highly successful. Among these officers was Robert Blake, the defender of Lyme Regis in the Civil War.

His early career is somewhat obscure. He had been a merchant and had travelled overseas, but whether he had any actual experience as a seaman is not established. The manning of the expanded Navy was the chief difficulty. English seamen did not volunteer in sufficient numbers, chiefly owing to the inadequacy of the pay. They were pressed whenever found on shore and were taken out of homeward bound merchantmen. Even so, the fleet was undermanned. War in the Channel had begun shortly before the execution of Charles I. In 1648 some of the officers of the Navy, seeing the tendency of Cromwell and the extreme leaders to abolish the monarchy and proclaim a republic, had revolted and carried a few ships over to the Dutch coast. Prince Rupert, with his brother

Maurice, took command of them and others obtained from the Dutch, and went to sea on a campaign of commerce destruction. There were already Royalist bases and cruisers in the Scilly and Channel Islands. As soon as the King was beheaded, in January 1649, his exiled son assumed the title of Charles II, and issued letters of marque to numerous French and Dutch privateers. The new Commonwealth Navy had its work cut out even as it came into being. A state of active though undeclared war with France existed, and mercantile losses on both sides were heavy. The existence of the Commonwealth depended on sea power and on whether the Navy could keep the Channel sufficiently open to permit the trade of London to continue. In addition, the year 1650 saw the revolt of four plantation colonies, Barbados and Antigua, Virginia and Maryland. They proclaimed Charles II as their King, defied the Commonwealth, and welcomed Dutch traders as their friends.

Rupert sailed early in 1649 for the coast of Ireland, where a complex of factions was combining to resist the Commonwealth. On his way he captured so many prizes that he was able to finance his further operations. If he could have remained at large he could have prevented Cromwell and his army from crossing the Irish Sea later in the year to carry out the reduction of Ireland to obedience. But the Commonwealth dispatched Blake to look after him, and Blake blockaded Rupert in Kinsale while Cromwell got his army to work. In October, two months after Cromwell had landed in Ireland, Rupert got out of Kinsale while the blockaders were driven off by bad weather, and sailed southwards. He was not really free, for Blake pursued him. Rupert went into Lisbon. The Portuguese befriended him, but had to withdraw their support when Blake included their commerce in his blockade and captured several ships homeward bound from Brazil. In October 1650 Rupert had to quit Lisbon. He made for the Mediterranean, where he got no aid in Spanish ports. He lost one ship to Blake in action and several by shipwreck, and ended his long flight with only two remaining ships at Toulon, where the French received him. They aided him to increase his force to five ships, with which he sailed in 1651, intending to support the Royalist revolt in the West Indies. Lack of money compelled him to stay in the eastern Atlantic cruising for prizes until the Royalists in the West were overthrown. Only after that event, in the summer of 1652, did he reach the Caribbean, there to meet final ruin from a hurricane which drowned his brother Maurice and left Rupert himself with only one ship. In her he returned to France and the Royalist campaign at sea was over.

In the Channel meanwhile another naval squadron under Sir George Ayscue reduced the Royalist privateer bases in Scilly and the Channel Islands, which had been a nuisance to Parliament since the Civil War began. Ayscue was then free to sail to the colonies. He reached Barbados in October 1651 and established a strict blockade. The planters were faced with ruin and capitulated in the following January. Antigua conformed without a shot fired. The other islands had not actually proclaimed rebellion. While dealing with Barbados, Ayscue sent a single cruiser to Chesapeake Bay. Her presence there paralysed the trade of Virginia and Maryland, and they also submitted to the Commonwealth. This was the first application of the Navy to the problems of the colonial empire, its first appearance in western waters since the colonies had been founded. Neither James I nor Charles I had ever sent a ship across the Atlantic. It was not that there had been no need. Very slender naval support would have preserved the English plantations in the Amazon delta from their fate of being overrun by the Portuguese of Brazil; and in the conditions of the time the Amazon was a valuable trading and producing area.

The first Dutch War (1652-4) was for the most part located in the Channel and the Narrow Seas between the Thames estuary and the Netherlands. As we have noted, there were no differences of religion or political ideology in its causation, no moral indignation or racial hatred; and there was no ambition in either country to invade and conquer the other. But it was a very determined effort of either side to get its own way in the control of maritime trade, and it produced much more continuous and sanguinary fighting than did the Anglo-Spanish conflict of the previous century. The English grievance was that the Dutch were engrossing the trade of the English colonies and encroaching on the English fisheries. The Dutch were indignant at English measures to conserve the colonial trade, and at the usual offences to neutral commerce involved in the Anglo-French contest on the seas after the execution of Charles I. Two English Navigation Acts in 1650 and 1651 expressed the English view on oceanic trade and some aspects of the home trades. The Dutch disregarded the first, which prohibited foreign ships from trading with English colonies ; and Ayscue on arriving in the West Indies seized a number of Dutch merchantmen in the anchorage of Barbados. In London the decisions of the Admiralty Court recognised the claim of English cruisers to take French merchandise out of Dutch ships, and this was probably the most important cause of war. Negotiations grew acrimonious, but neither government was committed to fighting. It began, almost spontaneously, with an undesigned encounter between squadrons under Blake and Tromp off the coast between Folkestone and Dover. Either side had sent out armed forces to protect its commerce ; and the forces met. That was sufficient, although ambassadors were not withdrawn until more than a month afterwards. The actual fight off Folkestone was due to a misunderstanding of intentions between the admirals.

The contending fleets in this war contained larger numbers of ships than were common in the great Anglo-French wars of the next century, but the ships themselves were smaller. Either side used armed merchantmen in addition to its regular navy. In England all merchant ships above 200 tons were made liable to be requisitioned. Blake reported that the armed merchantmen were backward in action. This was generally because their captains were either part-owners or devoted more to the interests of the owners than to those of the service, and their prime motive was to avoid damage and loss. There was another reason, which affected the Navy also, and that was undermanning. Many captains complained that they had not enough hands to work the ships and serve the guns. The men could not be obtained. In peace the merchant service had been working in conditions of full employment, and the Navy had been out of commission. The Navy's mobilisation created an impossible demand. The press was unsparingly used to gather in every available man on the coasts and in the ports, and for this job the soldiers of the Commonwealth's army were employed. There was no conscription of landsmen in general, and only those having some acquaintance with the sea were considered serviceable. This was the ingrained common law going back to Saxon times, that the seamen were a distinct category with distinct obligations, and it applied to the shipowners also. In this view " the Navy " meant not merely the state's ships, but every vessel owned in the country and every man who made his living by using them. The Commonwealth had at its service some good administrators with much higher standards of industry and integrity than had prevailed under the Stuarts. They did good work in coping with the confusion of war. Among the Puritan leaders also there were some men of humanity and an ethical outlook not noticeable in Charles I and his courtiers. They took action for the care of the sick and wounded who had been callously abandoned in the past. After the Channel fights of 1653, when Portsmouth was full of wounded men, a lady named Elizabeth Alkin, whom the men called " Parliament Joan," was sent down to organise the nursing. She had a government grant, and spent all her own money as well.[1] The officials tried honestly to get the men paid ; but money was short and the costs of the war enormous, and towards the end there was some rioting by unpaid seamen.

The principal English anchorage was in the Downs, where land batteries were established to command the inshore water. There a battle-damaged fleet could retire to refit its spars and rigging. England had the advantage that she was still in the main an agricultural country not so hard hit by the interruption of trade as the highly commercialised Dutch Netherlands. For them it was essential to keep huge merchant convoys moving, and this was the chief preoccupation of the Dutch admirals. England moreover had the better geographical position, for the Dutch routes to the Atlantic passed her eastern and southern coasts.

In August 1652 Ayscue and de Ruyter, both convoying merchant fleets, converged half over between Plymouth and France and fought a battle from which Ayscue had to retire to Plymouth to refit. In September de Witt and a large Dutch fleet approached the Thames estuary, and Blake went out from the Downs to fight him off the

[1] *Vict. County Hist., Hampshire*, V, p. 380.

out-lying sand called the Kentish Knock. After a very fierce battle the Dutch retreated to their own coast. In November the Dutch, having refitted, came out in great strength under Tromp, who was charged with escorting a huge convoy down Channel. Blake from the Downs followed, with only half of the Dutch strength in fighting ships. They fought off Dungeness, and Blake was badly mauled and driven back to the Downs, while Tromp was left in command of the Channel, to see his convoy of 450 merchant ships safely off to the markets of the world, and to round up incoming English trade at will. This was the occasion of the broom-at-the-masthead story, an invention like some others of its kind. A naval historian remarks : " There is of course no good authority for crediting so steady and sober-minded a seaman as Tromp with any such melodramatic proceeding." [1] But without the aid of the broom Tromp had certainly swept the Channel. It was not until three months later, in February 1653, that Blake could go to sea with a force equal to that of his opponent. They met off Portland, Tromp returning with another great convoy of incoming trade. The Dutch lost nine fighting ships and the English two, and Tromp saved most of the convoy. But thereafter the Dutch had to give up the Channel route for their commerce, and to direct it north-about round Scotland. The great fighting was thenceforth in the North Sea, and from economic causes the Dutch weakened faster than the English. Tromp lost twenty ships in a great battle off Harwich in June, and was killed in another on his own coast in July. The Dutch made a last revival, turning out sufficient force to contemplate an entry into the Thames and a blockage of the river by sunken vessels. This time a gale defeated them and cost them many ships. Thenceforward they were virtually blockaded and were glad to sign a peace in the spring of 1654. The peace contained provisions satisfactory to the English, but it was really the war that had given them what they wanted, a first-class Navy to ensure the control of their own colonial trade and the protection of their European business. Without it the Navigation Acts would have been waste paper.

With the presence of large fighting fleets in the Channel, the

[1] J. R. Tanner, in *Cambridge Modern History*, IV, p. 474.

depredations of the Barbary pirates in England's home waters came substantially to an end, although there were sporadic revivals. The Mediterranean trade, however, still needed protection within the Straits of Gibraltar. In 1654-55 and in 1658 Cromwell sent English fleets to the Mediterranean, the first one under Blake, to visit the Bey of Algiers, the Bey of Tunis, and other proprietors of pirate ports on the North African coast. At Tunis Blake destroyed nine ships, but elsewhere persuasion sufficed, and the rulers agreed to leave English shipping alone and restore all English prisoners. It was only a temporary improvement, and the remedy needed to be continuously applied.

In 1654 Cromwell embarked on war with Spain by sending an expedition to attack the Spanish colonies in the West Indies. As compared with the great results anticipated it was a failure, resulting only in the capture of Jamaica, an island of small estimation. It was only towards its end that this Spanish war had any great contact with Channel history. In pursuit of it, Cromwell ended the long maritime hostilities with France by a treaty with Cardinal Mazarin in 1655, and two years later allied himself with Mazarin to achieve conquests in the Spanish Netherlands. The result was the siege and capture of Dunkirk in 1658, and the overrunning of the provinces nearest to the French border. An English fleet covered the siege of Dunkirk, and an English army took the principal part in its capture after winning the battle of the Dunes against a relieving force. In one aspect it was the last battle of the Civil War, for on one side were the redcoats of the New Model army, and on the other Charles II's exiled Royalists commanded by his brother the Duke of York, afterwards James II. The redcoats routed the Royalists while, almost as a sideshow, the French routed the Spaniards. At the peace of the Pyrenees in 1659 England received Dunkirk, and the French the three Flemish provinces which gave them substantially their modern frontier with Belgium. Soon after the Restoration of 1660 Charles II sold Dunkirk to Louis XIV, for lack of money to maintain its garrison. Before and long after this event Dunkirk was of sinister importance to English commerce as the home port of numerous fast-sailing privateers and pirates. In the following century their depredations were sufficiently notable for Pope to include them as representative bad characters in his line on " thieves, supercargoes and Dunkirkers."

The decade of the Commonwealth and the Protectorate, with its wars and heavy taxation, was a period of depression in English trade. Even the great business interests of London, the most anti-Stuart community of the country, grew weary of the losses, un-settlement and uncertainty, and it was by general consent that the Interregnum was ended by the restoration of Charles II in the spring of 1660. Maritime losses had been great. Yet there were three solid gains, two of them calculated to ensure future prosperity. They were the establishment of the Navy as a great fighting force, equal to that of the Dutch, and the consolidation of England's economic hold upon the colonial trades of the North Atlantic. The third material gain was that of a capital asset, a mass of Dutch merchant shipping captured in the war and amounting to twice the tonnage of the pre-existing English mercantile marine. With these advantages and a return to the traditional government that Englishmen in their hearts preferred, the sea-trading interests were ready for a great advance.

II. THE RESTORATION AND THE SECOND DUTCH WAR

The restoration of Charles II was achieved with immense enthusiasm. A naval squadron went over to the Dutch coast to escort him home, Breda in Holland having been his last place of exile. There was festivity and firing of salutes. Samuel Pepys, secretary to Admiral Montagu, personally fired a gun, and nearly " spoilt " his right eye by leaning over the touch-hole, which spurted flame in his face. One can imagine the professionals stolidly watching the office gentleman's performance. Charles landed at Dover, where he received a Bible from the Mayor and the loyal congratulations of a distinguished assemblage. His brief interview with the Mayor, as described by Dr. Trevelyan, is one of the choice passages of historical humour.[1]

One of the King's possessions was a yacht, the gift of the Dutch government. Charles and his brother the Duke of York became

[1] G. M. Trevelyan, *England under the Stuarts*, p. 000.

enthusiastic yachtsmen, and in the Restoration period they and some of the courtiers owned a little fleet of yachts with which they cruised in the Thames estuary and on the south coast. The Restoration introduced many new things into English life, and one of the least exceptionable was the passion for amateur sailing which never quite died out thereafter. It seems not to have occurred to anyone before that time to go to sea for pleasure. In 1671 the royal brothers made a cruise down Channel to inspect the new citadel at Plymouth. They joined a newly built yacht, the *Cleveland*, at Portsmouth. She was cutter rigged, with a loose-footed mainsail and a square topsail, and by modern Thames measurement was of about 75 tons, with a broad-beamed hull designed rather for comfort than speed. She had a crew of twenty and even a few little guns, necessary perhaps in the Channel of that day, although in open water the royal yacht was always well escorted. They left the St. Helens anchorage on 17th July and ran westwards with a fresh east wind, reaching Plymouth next day. Charles wasted no time, and made his inspection and received the loyal welcome of Plymouth that evening. Next day he went over to Mount Edgcumbe, and sailed the same afternoon eastward bound up Channel. But the east wind continued, and this passage was no quick affair. After anchoring for a night in Torbay they spent a whole day beating to windward until they came nearly up to Portland. The King enjoyed it, but there was business in London ; and so the *Cleveland* bore away westward for a quick run to Dartmouth, where Charles landed and journeyed home by road. There was no cooking on board the royal yacht. She was accompanied by a cook-boat which delivered hot meals as occasion offered. One may suppose that there must sometimes have been disappointments.

The second Dutch war began four years after the Restoration, when in 1664 English and Dutch seized and counter-seized slaving stations on the West African coast, and the Duke of York dispatched an expedition to conquer the Dutch colony of New Amsterdam on the North American coast, which he then renamed New York. The Dutch did not want this war, and neither did Charles II, although he made no great stand against it. It was caused by the bellicose element in English commerce and the large party in the

House of Commons that voiced its views. The first war had left the combatants on an equality of naval power and oceanic opportunity, although the Dutch retained a great preponderance in actual trade. In the second the English mercantilists sought the obliteration of their rivals. Pepys recorded a sea captain as saying : " The trade of the world is not enough for us two, therefore one must down."

The Channel did not see much of the fighting, which was nearly all in the southern end of the North Sea, between the Thames and the Dutch coast. The fleets were about equal in strength and the seamen in dogged valour. Both sides had a variety of good commanders, with Michael de Ruyter the Dutchman in a class by himself above the rest. The Duke of York was Lord Admiral and commanded the English fleet in the first battle, a close and deadly action off Lowestoft, which ended in an indecisive Dutch defeat. The Duke had been as much exposed to death as any seaman, and he was the heir to the throne. Charles therefore withdrew him to land service, and entrusted the command to George Monck, Duke of Albemarle, one of the Commonwealth's " generals at sea," and to Prince Rupert, whose sea services have already been related. In 1666, while Rupert was detached from the main fleet by ill-conceived orders from London, Monck, heavily outnumbered, fought the Four Days Battle with de Ruyter. At its end, with the loss of many ships and 8000 human casualties, Monck had to retire into the Estuary, while the Dutch also were glad to break off and repair their hurts. Within three weeks both were at sea again and fought another terrific battle nearer to the outlying sands of the Estuary. This time the Dutch suffered the heavy losses, while those of the English were light.

It was evident that the mercantilists' war was not going to end in an extermination of the rival mercantile state. The Plague ravaged London in 1665 and the Great Fire destroyed most of it in '66, two months after the Four Days Battle. Administration was going to pieces in spite of the efforts of able administrators like the Duke of York and his henchman Samuel Pepys. For the court was rotten, and " the court " embodied the government of England, reverting to Stuart type. Great sums voted by Parliament for the war were vanishing in corruption and incompetence, the seamen unpaid, the dockyards devoid of stores, their defences devoid of guns and powder. Charles II's personal expenditure was not relatively heavy, but he did not diminish it, and the court butterflies continued their costly life as in times of peace. If it could be considered a choice between maintaining a mistress or fitting out a first-rate ship, it was the woman who was kept in commission and the ship laid up. The shortage of seamen was even greater than in the former war, and the press was taking landsmen as it had not done in the past. In the Four Days Battle many of the floating corpses were seen to be in black clothes, villagers and townsmen taken at the church doors and hurried off to sea in their Sunday blacks. Among the fighting men there was far less animosity than in the days of the Armada, for religion and freedom were not at stake. These men did their duty to the end, at a much greater cost to themselves than ever before, but they did not really hate the enemy.

As '66 merged into '67 it was time on all counts to end it. The Dutch were ready enough for peace, and negotiations began. They were far advanced although nothing was signed when the last action of the war took place. The government, with the King responsible, decided not to fit out the main fleet. The great ships lay unrigged and unmanned in the dockyards while the diplomats passed to and fro. The Dutch on the other hand sent a fleet to sea in the spring of 1667. At midsummer they entered the Thames estuary and hovered for some days awaiting the right wind and tide for the design concerted between de Ruyter and his government. Monck guessed that Chatham was threatened and, having no fleet to command, went down by land to see what could be done. He found the forts and batteries almost incapable of firing a shot, the thick oak planks for the gun platforms having been stolen, ball of the wrong sizes for the guns, sham gunpowder so feeble that it would hardly explode. A few Dutch ships passed these defences with ease, fired three large English ships, and towed away two others, including the *Royal Charles*, the pride of the Navy. Considering the narrowness of the channel it was a great feat of seamanship, and of daring based upon accurate information. The Dutch knew more about the defences of Chatham than did the English government.

It was a sore blow to pride and prestige, but it made little difference to the terms of peace signed shortly afterwards. The mercantilists of both sides (for those of Holland had also been aggressive enough) had expended an ocean of blood to no purpose, and the Treaty of Breda embodied no fundamental gains for either.

In this war there was a Commission of sick and wounded and prisoners. The commissioners, including John Evelyn, were good men, but they could not get the money supposed to be allowed. Sufferings were very great, and some died from sheer lack of clothing and food.[1]

III. THE THIRD DUTCH WAR: THE GROWTH OF TRADE

The terrible slogging in the Narrow Seas had produced a mutual respect between the combatants, which had the elements of a slow growth into friendship. But a third Dutch war intervened. It was not caused by bellicose elements in Parliament and commerce, but by the King himself. For all his easy good nature and addiction to pleasure, Charles had the Stuart hankering after absolute power. His temperament was not religious, but he held that if one must have a religion the Catholic was the best for a king. For in seventeenth-century Christendom the Catholic Church was associated with absolute monarchy, and Protestantism with those awkward political upstarts who would question and criticise the doings of kings. The Commons were verging on insolence to the King in their inquiries into the conduct of the late war. The Presbyterians of Scotland had treated him as an inferior reprobate in the days of Dunbar and Worcester. The Calvinists of New England were frankly contemptuous of his authority. And across the Channel his cousin Louis XIV reigned in mighty splendour, *Le Roi Soleil*, with not a dog to bark at him : to that glamour of majesty Charles was a devotee. In 1670 he made a secret treaty

[1] See an article on the subject by J. J. S. Shaw in *Mariner's Mirror*, XXV, No. 3, July 1934.

with Louis, whereby Charles was to declare himself a Catholic and establish Catholicism as a fully tolerated religion, and Louis was to assist with French troops in case of resistance; and Louis's price was that the English Navy should combine with the French army in a conquest of the Netherlands, the major part of the spoil to go to France. Elizabeth I and her subjects had recognised that a strong military power in the Low Countries was a threat to England's freedom, and every statesman from her day to ours has agreed. Charles knew it well enough, and his design was substantial treason to his country.

In 1672, when the plan went into action, there was much whipping-up of indignation against Dutch commercial offences, but it did not excite the same enthusiasm as in 1664. The country was from the outset suspicious of the reasons for this war, although it had no exact knowledge of what they really were. Just as war was declared Charles issued a Declaration of Indulgence for the Catholics, but did not announce his own change of religion. Louis preferred that it should be postponed until victory was secured, in case it should cause dissension in England. The fleet went to sea under the Duke of York, who was now an openly avowed Catholic. Off Southwold Bay in Suffolk he fought one of the terrible indecisive battles which cost so much blood for no result. He was a brave man but not an inspired commander. In this fight he had two successive flagships shot to ruin under him and finished the day in a third. The French allies had a squadron present, which took a less serious part in the fighting. Meanwhile the French armies sought to overrun the Dutch by land and were stopped only by the desperate energy of the young Stadholder William III of Orange. So hard pressed were the Dutch that they had to land several thousand of their seamen to serve with their army, and de Ruyter was reduced to a brilliant defensive with an inferior fleet.

The country was alarmed by the Declaration of Indulgence, which, however liberal it may look now, was then read as an attack on English liberty for the reason given above. Parliament in 1673 insisted on its withdrawal and passed the Test Act excluding Roman Catholics from office. This removed the Duke of York from his command, and Prince Rupert took his place. In August, close to the Dutch coast, Rupert fought a battle with de Ruyter's weakened fleet and might have destroyed it if the French had played their part. But the French commander remained inactive, explaining afterwards that he did not understand the signals, to which Rupert retorted that any man seeing the position of the fleets required no signals to tell him what to do. The English Navy and the nation were now more thoroughly incensed against the French than against the Dutch, guessing correctly that it was Louis XIV's policy to allow the English and Dutch to destroy one another while France took their place as the senior naval power. Rising indignation compelled Charles II to make a separate peace early in 1674, and the Anglo-Dutch wars were over. The last of them had been forced on the two peoples by secret and discreditable politics. While it was actually in progress organised parties of Dutch weavers came over to settle in England, and many Englishmen were serving in the Dutch fleet. The long period of Franco-British hostility that extended to the fall of Napoleon may be dated from this unfortunate war.

Portsmouth, as we have seen, became an important naval base during the Dutch wars, and it never afterwards lost that position. Large ships for the fleet were built there, and a new dry dock was ordered in 1655. Ships damaged in battle came in for repair, and 4000 men were victualled from Portsmouth in 1653. All these activities rescued the place from its long period of poverty and set it forward on its course of modern growth. Nevertheless it suffered badly under Stuart administration. In 1664-5 great energy was required for the new Dutch war, but no money was forthcoming to pay the dockyard hands, who were being evicted from their lodgings and were dying of want. The Comptroller vainly wrote for money to still the " bawlings and impatience of these people, especially of their wives, whose tongues are as foul as the daughters of Billingsgate." [1] The poor creatures had something to be foul about. Billingsgate " language " had by then an established reputation. There is another reference at that time to the " idiom of Billingsgate " in a quite different connection. At the beginning of the third Dutch war in 1672 Portsmouth dockyard reported a

[1] *V. C. H., Hampshire,* V, p. 380.

lack of all the necessary stores. In that year a French fleet came to Spithead to join forces with the English Navy.

Southampton did not benefit from warlike activities and was still in quiet decay. After the great London fire Southampton offered to receive London business men, saying that it had good houses with cellars and warehouses vacant, but there seems to have been no migration.

Plymouth seems on the whole to have been more prosperous than Portsmouth, having secured its position in the growing western trades of the century. There was considerable naval activity in the Hamoaze, in fitting-out and repairing, although the location of the fighting in the Dutch wars did not give Plymouth the importance it had possessed in the Armada time and was to regain permanently in the subsequent long wars with France. The Citadel on the Hoe, which we have seen Charles II inspecting in 1671, had been under construction since 1665. The town at that time had perhaps 12,000 people, a growth of about 50 per cent from its Elizabethan population. Dartmouth, which had been the premier port in the New-foundland fishery, suffered decline during the Stuart wars. The fishermen, coming home in the winter from their round voyage to the fishery and southern Europe, were then available for the Navy, and impressment did not spare them. The Newfoundland fishery was of course consciously promoted for this very reason, and the Channel ports' " ship fishermen " were favoured as against the colonial " boat fishermen " because of their value to the national defence. But the continuance of the wars and the desperate need for pressed men disorganised the fishery. The colonists of the New England ports, Boston and its neighbours, gained a permanent hold on the ship fishery and sent the cod to its European markets to the profit of the colonies, while the share of the Channel ports per-manently declined. In the later seventeenth century it seems to have run at about half its strength in the earlier. Dartmouth was especially unlucky in its losses to Dutch privateers.

In spite of the wars the whole trade of England increased, absolutely and relatively, in the reign of Charles II. It was com-monly estimated that foreign trade doubled between 1660 and 1685. The customs receipts very nearly confirm this, showing a rise from about £300,000 a year at the beginning of the reign to something between £500,000 and £600,000 at its close.[1] London absorbed the largest share in the expansion, which was greater in the down-Channel than the North Sea trades. The ocean-going companies, the East India in particular, experienced a boom. The original East India Company had its most profitable time under Charles II, with assured royal favour and the Duke of York for many years as its governor. The Hudson's Bay Company, under the lead of Prince Rupert, was chartered in 1670, and also did well. So, in its early years, did the Royal African Company of 1672, whose main business was the supply of slaves to Virginia and the West Indian sugar planters. The commodity trades with all the colonies were in the hands of independent merchants, the majority Londoners. The colonies were increasing in numbers—Jamaica, the Carolinas, New York, New Jersey, Pennsylvania—and growing in population, to " take off " ever-multiplying cargoes of English manufactures and swell the fleets of long-distance merchant shipping that carried them. An Elizabethan propagandist of empire, like Richard Hakluyt, or a Plymouth merchant, such as John Hawkins, could he have seen the stream of Channel shipping a hundred years after his time, would have been satisfied that he had been among the beginners of a mighty work. The greatest increase of Restoration trade came after the last Dutch peace in 1674. Between the French and the Dutch the war continued for another four years, and England in the unusual role of a neutral cut into the Dutch carrying trades with permanent effect. Louis XIV in his lust for aggrandisement unwittingly contributed to the growth of England's wealth and sea power. Anti-French sentiment increased, with Louis held up as the tyrant of Europe, as Philip II had been a century earlier. By 1678 a strong demand for war against France in alliance with the Dutch was stilled only by the conclusion of a general peace. Parliament enacted measures virtually prohibiting imports from northern France, and this inaugurated a long phase of Channel smuggling of brandy, silks and fine linens, which endured until the nineteenth century.

[1] David Ogg, *England in the Reign of Charles II*, Oxford, 1934, p. 421.

IV. WILLIAM III'S INVASION

Charles's reign ended in 1685 amid growing prosperity and growing political tension, with the King suspected as a dependant of the hated French. His brother James succeeded him and pursued policies that in three years produced a revolution. They do not concern us here, but the revolutionary actions do, for in 1688 they involved a successful invasion, landing an army on the Channel coast and carrying its leader to the throne.

First, however, there was an invasion that failed. In 1685 the Duke of Monmouth, illegitimate son of Charles II, was living in exile in Holland. He was popular in England among the ardent Protestants who resented the Catholic attitude of the new king, James II. Many ill-informed people half believed that Monmouth's mother Lucy Walter had been legally married to Charles II and that Monmouth was the rightful heir to the throne. There were numbers of English and Scottish exiles in the Netherlands, men who had fled because their opposition to the later Stuart policies had endangered their lives. They persuaded Monmouth to attempt a revolution, he himself to land in the west country while the Earl of Argyll was to start a revolt in western Scotland. Argyll's effort was already failing when Monmouth got into action with the English attempt. His preparations had long been reported to the English government, and there was no element of surprise. He nevertheless sailed from the Texel and made a slow voyage against strong winds through the Straits and down the Channel without being intercepted. He arrived off Lyme Regis on 11th June. Macaulay's description of the port as it then was may be quoted : " That town is a small knot of steep and narrow valleys, lying on a coast, wild, rocky, and beaten by a stormy sea. The place was then chiefly remarkable for a pier which, in the days of the Plantagenets, had been constructed of stones, unhewn and uncemented. This ancient work, known by the name of the Cob, enclosed the only haven where, in a space of many miles, the fishermen could take refuge from the tempests of the Channel."

From three minor Dutch vessels Monmouth landed about eighty

persons, mostly officers for the army he hoped to raise in the south-west. The defect of his plan was that he brought hardly any equipment of arms and ammunition. In Dorset, Devon and Somerset numbers of the people came to join him, but since they were mostly unarmed he had to turn many away. The gentry stood aloof. One peer, Lord Grey of Wark, landed with him, but no other came forward to join. The upper class knew two things: that Monmouth was certainly illegitimate and the sense of England would not tolerate him on the throne; and that however many thousands of unarmed civilians might join him, their extinction was inevitable by the regular forces and machinery of government that the unpopular James II could dispose of. That indeed was the outcome. Three weeks after his landing Monmouth found himself facing a small professional army of trained and well armed regiments on Sedgemoor, outside Bridgwater. He took his only chance with a night attack in which scythes and pitchforks might do execution against firearms in the darkness. But everything went wrong, and dawn revealed a gallant remnant of peasants being shot down by the regulars. Monmouth himself fled before the end, to be taken and executed after grovelling appeals for mercy, which showed that all his thoughts were for himself and none for the unfortunates who had trusted him. They were being hanged by the hundred or enslaved to the West Indian plantations.

Support for Monmouth had been due to indignation at what James II was expected to do. Three years later it was a question of what James had done and was doing—a general violation of the constitution and the law with the purpose of setting up an absolutist Catholic government. This made the true leaders of the nation ready to oppose him in arms, and they knew that they would need considerable trained forces for success. Seven leading men, representing a majority of the ruling class, signed an invitation to William III, Prince of Orange and Stadholder of the Dutch Netherlands, to come to England and aid them to restore their liberties. William was a strongly interested party, for he was the recognised champion of the liberties of Europe against the encroachments of Louis XIV, and he was also in two ways connected with the English throne, for he was James II's nephew, and his wife was James II's daughter.

This was in the summer of 1688, and William took his time to prepare a powerful expeditionary force, very different from Monmouth's amateur undertaking.

The outcome was the invasion and revolution of 1688, the only successful invasion of England from the Tudor venture of 1485 to the present day. It was in one aspect a civil war, for an undoubted majority of the English people wished it to succeed, and it was only on their invitation that William moved. James's army proved disaffected and refused to fight for him, but his Navy was apparently ready to serve him, remembering how he had led it in battle and had always been devoted to its interests. There were indeed some officers who put their Protestantism before their allegiance and were uncertain how to act, but it looks as though their professional honour would have caused them to fight for the King if the occasion had arisen. That it did not do so is the subject of a remarkable story of luck, weather and manœuvres. Lord Dartmouth, James's admiral, although a Protestant, was completely loyal.

The geography and the weather of the Narrow Seas and the Channel dominated the outcome. William was ready towards the middle of October, with his army in more than two hundred transports guarded by a fleet of fifty sail, middling and small. Neither side turned out its first-rate ships, which the seamen thought unfit for a campaign late in the year in shoal waters, long nights and strong winds. Even in summer conditions it was easy to strand the deep-draught ships on the outlying shoals of the Thames estuary and the Dutch coast, and in the autumn of 1688 there were several strandings of the smaller ones. William sailed on 17th October, and immediately ran into a north-westerly gale that drove him back with considerable damage into his own ports.

Meanwhile Dartmouth's position was not an easy one. His fighting force was a little inferior to the Dutch, although the great convoy was a liability against them and in his favour. His main difficulty was that he did not know whither the invading expedition was bound, for the east coast of England or for the south. He was not strong enough to blockade it in its own ports, since the wild weather might have driven him disastrously upon the enemy coast. He had no reserve against such a misfortune, for the Navy was not out in its full strength even of the middle-sized ships. James II had not taken the invasion threat seriously until too late. Like his father Charles I he was a man of fixed judgments based too often on wrongly assessed evidence. His whole predicament resulted from a wrong assessment of the feelings of his subjects and of how much misgovernment they would endure. Dartmouth thus felt obliged to keep his fleet in the Thames estuary, to strike north or south as the occasion might demand, and the defect of the position was that in certain conditions it precluded him from striking at all. He could not cruise clear of all the outer sands, but had to remain within the shelter that they yielded.

In England there was extreme excitement. All knew that the invading expedition was ready, but none could move against the King until it came. His army was too strong, and Monmouth's fate was a warning. That autumn men looked anxiously at the skies, for signs of the " Protestant wind " that would bring the deliverer. The false start in October was a dreadful disappointment. Some feared that it was already too late in the year for any success.

And then, on 1st November, William sailed for the second time, with an easterly wind that promised fair. Until after the anchors were raised and the great concourse of ships was under way, he did not know the direction he would take. For political reasons he favoured the Yorkshire coast. His seamen disliked the prospect of a lee shore and persuaded him to go for the Straits of Dover and down Channel, and so on the 2nd it was decided. On the 3rd at noon the great fleet filled the narrow twenty miles between Dover and Calais, its flanking ships on either side coming close to the shores of England and France, with braying of trumpets and beating of drums, watched by crowds of English and French spectators. And still no one knew where they would come to land. James believed it would be near Portsmouth, and Dartmouth thought so too. But William took his seamen's advice and agreed to go on to Torbay in East Devon, where there would be open water for the fighting ships to force an action well out from the land while the army disembarked behind them. A Torbay landing would quickly give him Exeter, with reasonably good country for a winter march towards London. Beyond Torbay he would not go, not to Plymouth, with its strong citadel and garrison to dispute a landing, and the whole breadth of Dartmoor and the deep muddy lanes of South Devon as a winter obstacle to the quick solution that politics required. If he had landed on the wrong side of Dartmoor he would have found James's army at Exeter before him.

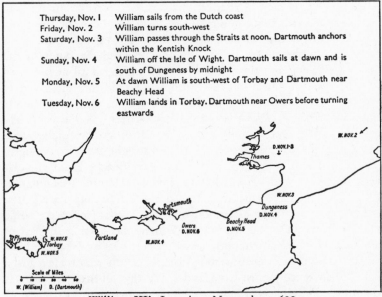

Thursday, Nov. 1	William sails from the Dutch coast
Friday, Nov. 2	William turns south-west
Saturday, Nov. 3	William passes through the Straits at noon. Dartmouth anchors within the Kentish Knock
Sunday, Nov. 4	William off the Isle of Wight. Dartmouth sails at dawn and is south of Dungeness by midnight
Monday, Nov. 5	At dawn William is south-west of Torbay and Dartmouth near Beachy Head
Tuesday, Nov. 6	William lands in Torbay. Dartmouth near Owers before turning eastwards

William III's Invasion, November 1688

On the morning of the 4th November the expedition was west of the Isle of Wight with the fair wind continuing. Dawn of the 5th presaged disaster. The chief pilot had miscalculated, and in the night the whole force had overshot its mark and was down beyond Berry Head, the southern arm of Torbay. It meant either going on to Plymouth or slowly beating back up wind to Torbay, with James's fleet presumably coming on with the wind in hot pursuit. Edward Russell, an English sea officer on board the Prince's ship, told Gilbert Burnet the clergyman (afterwards Bishop of Salisbury) that all was lost and he had better get to his prayers. And then the wind, faithfully Protestant, veered round to the south-west, and the expedition sailed comfortably into Torbay by midday. The Calvinist William, landing at Brixham, grasped Burnet by the hand and asked him if he did not believe in predestination now.[1] The disembarkation took two full days and was entirely uninterrupted.

Meanwhile Lord Dartmouth had had a terrible time. On Saturday the 3rd his scouting vessels brought news of the great armament streaming through the Straits of Dover. But the wind that drove it through kept him pinned between the sands of the Thames estuary, and the whole day was wasted until at last with a fair tide he got away on the morning of the 4th. He sailed in pursuit, a day behind. He might still catch the enemy in the act of disembarkation. By various accidents his fleet was now decidedly inferior to the Dutch, and some of his Protestant captains were showing signs of disaffection; but he thought they would fight. On the morning of the 5th, when he was off Beachy Head, the east wind died out, and he was left becalmed. He still thought that William would have entered Spithead and be landing near Portsmouth. Not until the afternoon of the 6th could he make some slow progress. On the 7th (when William was getting the last of his troops ashore) Dartmouth was between Beachy Head and the Owers when the wind came strong from the south-west. He realised that William's army must have landed and that all that was left was to fight the Dutch fleet, a fight for which the main purpose was now eliminated. With disloyalty growing in his fleet, he turned back for the Downs, retiring on his reinforcements. The Dutch fleet did not go back up Channel, but made its way round to Plymouth Sound.

After that all was really over, for James's army would not fight. William occupied Exeter and pushed on eastwards to Salisbury Plain. James marched from London and made contact with him. Then wholesale desertion left James without an army, and he returned to London as a fugitive. The rest of the story is political, the history of the revolution of 1688-9. The apparently easy

[1] The statue of William on Brixham Quay was erected in 1889.

success has tended to obscure the fact that William had committed himself to a desperate gamble. He could not expect, and none of his seamen expected, to get through the Channel without meeting the English fleet. He had supporters among its officers, but he had no undertaking from them that they would desert from their duty to James. If the fleets had closed, a single broadside would have altered the whole course of the venture. The old Anglo-Dutch fighting spirit would have flamed up. If William had lost the battle he would never have landed. If he had won, he would have landed with English blood on his hands, and would not have been whole-heartedly received by the people and the army. There might well have been a revulsion of sentiment to James II, and a long war with a doubtful issue, and probably French intervention the decisive factor. William was a man of calculation, wary and not swayed by enthusiasm. Why did he gamble so flagrantly ? Because, at the crisis of his career, he was a Calvinist and believed in destiny.[1]

[1] The conclusion of E. B. Powley, whose *English Navy in the Revolution of 1688*, Cambridge, 1928, is the only full analysis of the events by sea. The present author acknowledges his debt to it in writing the foregoing paragraphs.

CHAPTER THIRTEEN

The Eighteenth Century

I. SOCIAL ASPECTS OF THE NAVY

THE eighteenth century, stretched at either end to cover the reign of William III from 1689 and the empire of Napoleon to 1815, is the period of the great French wars, the expansion of the Old Colonial Empire, and the transformation of the thirteen colonies into the United States. It is not in proportion to our subject to give even a sketch of these complicated events, and such fighting as took place in the Channel will be discussed in the next chapter. The wars had their effect on the people of the coast, who on their side played a prominent part in the conflict. But they were not " total wars " in the sense that we have learnt to use the phrase, and there were peaceful intervals. Civil life changed greatly for purely economic reasons. The growth of trade and invested capital, so noticeable in the seventeenth century, proceeded at an ever greater rate, and the social order and way of life made the southern England of 1815 very different from that of 1689. In all this the coast and its people were involved.

When that has been said, the Navy still stands forth as a great factor in the Channel history of the time. Its dockyards and habitual anchorages were all in the Thames estuary or on the south coast, from Harwich round to Falmouth. Its officers were perhaps mainly drawn from that coast and its hinterland, and its men markedly so. Experience of Cromwell's dictatorship and James II's intention to use his regular troops to establish an absolutism had left the country suspicious and distrustful of what it called a standing army, and the unpopularity of the army was maintained by the fact that it had to be used to cope with civil disturbances in the absence of any capable police force. The Navy never incurred the suspicion of being an instrument of arbitrary rule. This is remarkable in view of the fact that its press-gangs did very cruel and arbitrary things, to the suffering of a multitude of individuals. Yet so it was : the Navy was always popular, the subject of patriotic songs and hymns of praise, the idol of the public ; while at the same time its seamen were badly treated and in great numbers lost their lives by hardships and diseases which were preventible even by the medical knowledge of that time. Love of the Navy and callousness towards its men co-existed in the same high degree.

The roots of the matter lay in a tight little dockyard bureaucracy that was both corrupt and incompetent, and in the inadequate sums voted by Parliament and accepted by the King's ministers for the pay and feeding of the seamen. Not enough men would volunteer to serve for lower pay, generally long deferred, than they could earn in merchantmen, and for food devised on a low scale and hardly ever reaching that scale in practice. Men had thus to be pressed into the service. The pressed man was not trusted and was in effect a prisoner, allowed no shore leave, not even when his ship came into dockyard hands for prolonged repair, but turned over at once to some other ship on the point of going to sea. Admiral Vernon declared that the fleet was " manned by violence and maintained by cruelty," and that the seaman taken by the press-gang was in effect condemned to death. The cruelty was an outcome of the initial violence, for its victims were in no mood to yield cheerful obedience and had to be flogged into shape. Still greater was the mass-cruelty of recruiting unfit men and making no provision of food, clothing or quarters adequate to even the roughest standards of a healthy life. Fighting with the French was not so bloody as the fighting with the Dutch had been in the previous century. In the whole Seven Years War the Navy lost 1,512 men killed in action—and 133,708 deserted or dead of disease. Some of this disease was in tropical fevers beyond the control of existing medicine, but a great deal of it resulted from stupidity. When James Cook joined the Navy as the Seven Years War broke out and served as boatswain of a ship-of-the-line, she buried 22 men in a month on a short summer cruise in European waters, and had to send 130 into hospital on coming into port. Sir Edward Hawke reported that the men sent to his ship were " poor little sickly fellows," who broke down in large numbers on the passage from Portsmouth to the Mediterranean. Long voyages were much worse. Anson returned from his circumnavigation in 1740–4 with one-fifth of the men with whom he had set out. They included what his chaplain called " a decrepit detachment " of old army pensioners, who were quite literally condemned to death, for none survived. The smug administrator who arranged that piece of recruitment probably never noticed its result. Before the expedition was through the tropics on its voyage south to Cape Horn, the officers were taking measures " for correcting the noisome stench on board and destroying the vermin ; for, from the number of our men and the heat of the climate, both these nuisances had increased upon us to a very loathsome degree, and besides being most intolerably offensive, they were, doubtless, in some sort productive of the sickness we had laboured under." The " doubtless, in some sort " is rich, like the stench.

The officers of the eighteenth-century Navy have often been represented as tyrants and bullies. Some of them were, captains for the most part promoted by political influence when far too young for their responsibility. But most were not. They were good sound men, many of them from the professional middle class rather than from the land-owning families who officered the army. They had to be severe in an age when all punishment tended to be corporal, but they did their best for their men, not conniving at the evils under which they suffered, but remonstrating, though with little effect, against the poisonous beer, the putrid meat, the maggoty biscuit, which the scamps ashore were allowed to pass off upon the fleet. Cook flogged in moderation and for just cause, but he was a humane man who brought his crews home alive and found them willing to serve with him again. Captain Pasley wrote a private journal which shows that he had the men's welfare at heart, and expressed great concern when one was accidentally killed at gun training.

The administration was to blame for the evils of naval life, and the administration was part of the whole system of eighteenth-century government as approved by the eighteenth-century nation. One cannot get beyond that. The British were a free people, and that was how they chose, in one direction, to express their freedom. And so, at Plymouth, Portsmouth, Chatham and the riverside of London, and at all the ports between and beyond, the armed gangs went ashore from the King's ships and raked men out of their inns and their houses, knocked them senseless and left their wives penniless, in order that ship's companies should be made up to withstand the assaults of enemies far more deadly than the French. Proportion must be observed in presenting general statements. It is obvious that the crews could not have consisted entirely of pressed men, since there would have been no one to impress them or to stop them from deserting. It seems that at some times little more than half of the men were pressed and the proportion tended to grow smaller in Nelson's time than it had been earlier. And not all the pressed men were of the unfit landsman kind. Many were merchant seamen, taken out of homecoming ships as they neared port, hoping to go home with their pay for a long voyage, and perhaps losing it when carried off without a moment's respite for the duration of a long war. As the backbone of all, many men were volunteers, of character and strong physique, who backed their chance of rising in the service which they deliberately made their profession. James Cook was one of those. As mate of a merchant-man he joined the Navy as an able seaman, and in a month was a petty officer. Nor was he exceptional in rising to commissioned rank. Numerous warrant officers were commissioned, although few rose higher than lieutenant. The Navy of the eighteenth century was a rough school in which the weak suffered terribly and the strong might thrive.

II. THE PORTS AND MERCHANT SHIPPING

Apart from its being the capital, London was more than ever the greatest port. From the Pool below London Bridge its anchorages stretched down miles of the winding tideway, bordered on either hand by shipbuilding yards turning out merchantmen great and small, and by villages in process of conurbation, with a population of seamen, shipwrights, watermen, lightermen, storekeepers, and the criminal fringe always attached to marine activities in an age devoid of police. The estuary was now being scientifically charted and the pilot service was adequate, and the shipping of all the world passed up and down. In the late eighteenth century it was estimated that on one average day there were 1,400 vessels large and small lying in the port of London. Defoe fifty years earlier put the number at over 2000, counting in the river craft that did not go out to sea. Small and middling merchantmen swarmed in with the " home trades " of northern and western Europe. Hundreds of colliers brought coal from the Northumberland coast. The coal trade was a nursery of seamen as great as the more publicised Newfoundland fishery. Fishermen from the North Sea and the Estuary brought their catch up to Billingsgate Market. There was some passenger traffic, but most travellers for France went from Dover, and for the Netherlands and Germany from Harwich.

All this was steady growth. But the most phenomenal increase was in the shipping of the ocean trades, West Indiamen, North Americans, the seasonal fleet from Hudson's Bay. Many ships of the eighteenth century were New England built, from the abounding timber there available, launched from little harbours and creeks on the rugged coast, and sent off to be sold at once to London shipowners at the end of their first voyage. By the law of the Navigation Acts British shipping had to be British built, and the qualification covered the colonies of the Old Empire. The greatest of London's ships were the East Indiamen, armed like ships of war ; and their numbers were growing too. In the century after the Restoration the company's trade multiplied four-fold, and after that there was a runaway increase, with China and all the tropic East added to India as the field of business. In the sixteenth century Antwerp had been Europe's greatest port, in the seventeenth Amsterdam ; but in the eighteenth it was London. In consequence there was a new social class arising in London and southern England, men not actively working as merchants or administering estates as landowners ; but the sons and grandsons of the makers of mercantile fortunes, and all the family connections among whom the wealth was spread, a moneyed class without well-marked functions save that of being merely " the rich," a considerable factor in the life of the century to follow.

South of the Estuary the Downs was a busier anchorage than ever, and Dover a growing town. From there on to Portsmouth there was no considerable port and, as we have seen, geographical changes had reduced the earlier harbour facilities. William III's French war brought the Navy again into the Channel, and in 1698 the Government ordered a survey of the whole south coast. It was carried out by the Surveyor-General Edward Dummer and Captain Thomas Wiltshaw. They produced factual accounts of the various ports, illustrated by beautiful little coloured sketches of the topography.[1] The first river-mouth, going westward, was that of the Rother at Rye. The report shows that Rye had by this time very little port business, since the entrance had become more difficult even than it is now. The shoreline ran close to where the village of Rye Harbour now exists, or nearly a mile inland from its present position. But outside there was a broad sand bar which made it impossible for vessels to enter or leave save at high tide and in fine weather. The surveyors blame the inning of the marshes and the consequent diminution of the tidal scour for the accumulation of the bar. At Arundel it can be seen that the Arun was embanked from its mouth up to the town, and that the marshes of the estuary had been reclaimed. The river-mouth at Littlehampton was a miniature delta of channels running between sands, and there were no jetties to control it as at present. Southampton is shown still confined to little more than its medieval site, but the report states that it had built ships of 50 to 80 guns for the Navy during the late war. These were ships of the line, yet the surveyors make no recommendation that Southampton should be developed as a naval dockyard, probably because Portsmouth was sufficient for that area. The drawings of the little Solent ports are interesting, and one small detail is worth mention. Present-day yachtsmen are familiar with the beacon called Jack-in-the-Basket at the entrance of the Lymington river. The sketch reveals that Jack-in-the-Basket was there, under that name,

---

[1] Several MS. copies of the report exist. The one consulted for this account is in Sloane MSS. 3,233. I have to thank Mr. R. A. Skelton, Superintendent of the Map Room, British Museum, for telling me of it.

and looking much as at present, in 1698. It is not the same Jack, of course, for his timber post and cage-work are perishable—a few years ago, in fact, some miscreant vessel knocked him down and carried him completely away—but his name has persisted through the centuries.

Another collection [1] of the same year 1698 gives full details of existing dockyards, with architect's elevations of their buildings, together with views of their surroundings. The Plymouth drawings are of interest, as showing that Plymouth itself was now an open town, with no sign of the walls of the Civil War. It had grown considerably in population, and the built area had extended beyond the earlier line. The Citadel, however, had expanded to cover the eastern end of the Hoe, and this was the main military defence. There were also fortifications on Drake's Island and at other outlying points. There had long been naval activity in the Hamoaze. In 1691 the government decided to make it a properly equipped dockyard. The 1698 survey shows that a beginning had been made. It includes a view from Mount Edgcumbe of " the King's Dock," indicating some substantial dockyard buildings and a few dwelling-houses. In another hundred years the population of Dock—simply so called—was to exceed that of Plymouth itself.

Although the up-Channel ports in the eighteenth century were doing very little trade and employing only fishing-boats and small coasters, some of them were building ships of a size much greater than could be habitually used from the ports themselves. The shipbuilding industry was widely spread along the coast. Supplies of oak timber were well distributed in Kent, Sussex and Hampshire, and since the transport of great logs was expensive it was advantageous to build at places where they could be had near at hand. A more decisive factor was probably the availability of shipwrights habitually employed on the coastal fishing fleets. Demand and supply were alike flexible. The French wars produced employment for privateers, and the coast built them. Dover launched many. Records of Folkestone in the war of 1778–83 show that very secondary port as turning out numbers of armed ships up to 400 tons, although mostly much smaller. They were launched at high water

[1] King's MSS. 43, 3.

in the shallow little harbour, and got away in fine weather. One vessel of this type was launched off the open beach at Sandgate. Rye also never lost its shipbuilding. In picked weather on a spring tide a large hull could be taken out over the bar. Hastings by now had only a beach, up which its fishing-boats were hauled ; but it had craftsmen who could build much larger than fishing-boats. It produced privateers in the eighteenth century, and it is on record that in the early nineteenth Hastings built a series of brigs and schooners for coasting trade and a vessel of 220 tons as a rich man's yacht, all of them being launched down the beach. In the eighteenth century the demand was not only for privateers and coasters but for fast vessels, larger than fishing-boats, for smuggling. The ketch was a rig much in vogue. It was not the same as the present ketch, but was a combination of square and fore-and-aft sails. In the late eighteenth century the lugger rig came in, probably first developed [1] by the French, and large three-masted luggers were used for smuggling and fishing. The dipping lug sail could hold a better wind than any other, and the smuggling skipper, when chased by the revenue cutter, turned close to windward and was unapproachable.

Farther west, the small places did even more ambitious building. Most East Indiamen were built on the Thames, but about 1786 two, of 938 and 987 tons, were launched at the village of Itchenor on Chichester harbour ; and others were built at Bursledon, up the Hamble river, and at Topsham on the Exe.[2] Lymington, and Buckler's Hard on the Beaulieu river, also produced large ships. At Buckler's Hard, well up in the New Forest, were built not only Indiamen but ships for the Navy. Nelson's *Agamemnon* was one of them. In all these little river ports the maximum draught of water was not much over fifteen feet, and the great hulls were floated out unrigged and unballasted, to be towed away to some place where they could be equipped for sea. Buckler's Hard still consists of two rows of cottages facing one another across a broad space

[1] The sail itself was much older, a simple development of the square sail, but its virtues dependent on its proportions and method of setting did not become evident until this period.

[2] C. N. Parkinson, *Trade in the Eastern Seas*, Cambridge, 1937, pp. 125, 167.

sloping down to the river, and this was the location of the building berths and the slipways for launching.

III. SMUGGLING AND WRECKING

The period of the French wars was the great age of Channel smuggling. In wartime the trade with France was supposed to be stopped, and in the intervals of peace it was subject to high protective duties. Both in war and in peace there were plenty of customers for smuggled goods of high value as compared with their bulk, such as brandy, silks, lace and fine linen, and tea also was so highly taxed as to enter the list, together with other choice wares from the East. The smuggling in fact was not all of French-produced goods, nor were they all brought in from France.

Walpole's well-known Excise Bill of 1733, which he had to withdraw owing to the opposition it excited, was primarily intended to check frauds on the revenue in the importation of tobacco. These were on a greater scale than mere coastal smuggling and were effected by misdescription and collusion between big operators and the customs officials at the regular ports of trade. Tobacco on import paid the whole duty, but if re-exported could claim a drawback or repayment of it. The fraud consisted in obtaining the drawback without re-exporting the tobacco. A dummy cargo was made up of dirt and tobacco stalks and passed as genuine through the customs, to be dumped overboard at sea after earning the repayment. Walpole proposed that there should be no custom and therefore no repayment, but that all incoming tobacco should be stored in bond in warehouses and issued to home traders on payment of an excise. Any vendor of tobacco could be challenged to show his receipts, and his premises were to be liable to search by the excise officers. It was this that caused the public outcry against tyranny, a host of government agents violating the sanctity of the Englishman's castle ; and the sentiment was skilfully utilised by the corrupt interests that desired to keep things as they were.

In spite of Walpole's failure the system was gradually introduced for various goods in the course of the century. But it did not greatly affect the sort of trade done by the Channel smugglers, who sold their stuff clandestinely to small middlemen in personal touch with groups of consumers—a black market trade, in fact, which could defraud the excise as well as the customs. The smugglers conducted a large number of comparatively petty transactions. In its relation to the whole national business the smuggling has sometimes been exaggerated, for it is obvious that no high proportion of the trade of a great commercial country could have been conducted by furtive landings at night across open beaches. But in the small luxury articles already mentioned it did account for a large proportion of the import, and it occasioned not only a serious loss of revenue but some yet uglier consequences.

The smugglers in war-time went over to the French ports. They were accused of giving information to the enemy and of introducing French spies into England, and for this reason the French authorities allowed them in. Having got his cargo the smuggler anchored close to the English beach on a fine night. His confederates ashore were looking out for his signals and were ready with a gang of men to receive the packages and brandy casks and run them by packhorse well inland before morning. The land gangs were recruited from the farm labourers, who were paid as much for the night's work as they could ordinarily earn in a week. In some places agricultural wages were forced up because the men took to refusing work and living wholly on smuggling. The horses too were normally blameless animals belonging to the farmers, who were also in the business. The goods would be hidden in some lonely inn or farmhouse on Romney Marsh or the Selsey plain or the upland coast of the western counties, and dispersed piecemeal to known receivers or private buyers. And so respectable citizens drank uncustomed tea and brandy, and ladies and gentlemen wore fine cambrics and silks whose importation might be altogether prohibited. All ranks of society were implicated in a business whose ramifications were not confined to the coast, but spread far inland. Its methods were infinitely various. Smuggled goods were passed to boatmen from the regular merchantmen in the large ports. Captains and officers of the East Indiamen had a privilege of private trade to specified amounts on each voyage, and if the great ship anchored in the Downs to land passengers, the Deal luggers which came off to render their services could unobtrusively receive a few tea-chests for a fee much lower than the duty that would be payable in London.[1] A case is recorded of an East Indiaman met off the Lizard in 1770 by a large smuggling craft whose skipper received the whole of the captain's private trade investment and paid for it by a bill. The East India captain, asked if he could trust the bill, replied that the smugglers always dealt with the strictest honour.[2]

There was a preventive service of customs and excise men, but its cost precluded its numbers from being adequate to cope with a coast population wholly in sympathy with smuggling. At sea there were the revenue cutters, fast craft with a broadside of small guns, and a spread of canvas that could be handled only by a large crew of good seamen. Off the wind the cutters could catch almost anything they chased, but close-hauled the luggers could keep ahead until darkness saved them. It did not always work out so, for the cutter might appear from the windward, and then she could win the race. As King's ships the cutters could lawfully board and search any British vessel without special formality. On land it was different. Eighteenth-century England was sensitive to the liberty of the subject, and all men rose in wrath against any symptom of arbitrary rule such as those slaves the French put up with across the Channel. A domiciliary visit without due warrant from a magistrate would have been an outrage to stir high heaven. Thus the revenue officer had to go to the magistrate before searching premises, and he had to produce facts to justify a search. There were no fact-finding police to aid him, and the countryside was solidly against him, the magistrate possibly unsympathetic. Evidence against smugglers was hard to get, for people were terrorised. There were too many involved, and they were organised by ruthless men. Anyone suspected of betraying or even blabbing was likely to be beaten to the danger of his life, if not murdered outright. The

---

[1] The high duties on tea were reduced by Pitt to 12½ per cent in 1784, and tea smuggling became unprofitable ; but the renewed French wars soon increased the duty, which was up to 100 per cent at the fall of Napoleon. With the good qualities of tea selling at 10s. to 16s. a pound, half of which was tax, this gave a handsome premium to the smugglers.

[2] Sir Evan Cotton, *East Indiamen*, London, 1949, p. 38.

best chance of the preventive men was to surprise the smugglers in the act of landing their cargo, which often led to a running fight in the darkness. It sounds romantic and high-spirited, but in reality it was a dirty business that demoralised the whole countryside. *Ingoldsby* gives the romantic aspect in the legend of The Smuggler's Leap. " Smuggler Bill was six feet high, with curling locks and a roving eye," and so forth, and he led a rattling, galloping, pistol-firing race across country with Exciseman Gill in pursuit ; but the poem does not add that, if a typical smuggler, he was also a rascal who would commit violent crime against any person who failed to connive at his doings.

Wrecking was due to the same root causes as the implication of the whole coast population in smuggling : the administration was feeble, and the people were poor, their livelihoods at the mercy of sea calamities against which fisherfolk had not yet reached the stage of insurance, while the field labourers were, if anything, declining rather than rising in economic status as the century advanced. Wrecking did not primarily mean the luring of ships to disaster by showing false lights, for the ordinary effect of seeing lights on shore would have been to warn the seaman to keep off. Wrecking usually meant the plundering of a wreck which had occurred from natural causes. The people, particularly of the western Channel, were accused of callous inhumanity in salving goods while neglecting to save life. Wrecked goods, like smuggled goods, were hidden away, and intimidation was used to suppress the evidence and defraud the rightful owners. The evil was older than smuggling and went back to prehistoric time. The coast dwellers regarded a wreck simply as a gift of God and had no sentiment for the survivors. In the Middle Ages there was some attempt to regulate the plunder of wrecks in an international sea code called the Laws of Oleron, traditionally recognised by the maritime interests of western Europe and in part adopted in English law. A thirteenth-century English regulation enacted that there was no true wreck in the legal sense (with legitimate plunder) if any creature, even the ship's cat, came ashore alive. Poor pussy was merely a piece of lawyer's rhetoric, but the embodied legal principle did put a premium on the murder of survivors, which in earlier times undoubtedly took place. The eighteenth century was not as bad as that, but the Cornish wreckers were accused of brutal treatment of witnesses.[1] It was a matter of the ethical climate of the age, which changed rapidly as the eighteenth century merged into the nineteenth. The descendants of the wreckers have now become through several generations the lifeboat crews ready to give their own lives to save others without thought of gain.

IV. CHANNEL SAILING

In 1703 there occurred the greatest storm of which details have been preserved in English history. On the evening of 26th November a gale set in from the south-west, and through the night it raged up the Channel and across southern England. The wind must have reached true hurricane force, a thing hardly ever known in our country. Houses were overthrown in hundreds and unroofed in thousands, people were killed in their beds by falling masonry—the Bishop of Bath and Wells was one of them—and town and country littered with destruction, a great air raid before its time. In the Channel the nearly new Eddystone lighthouse was swept away with its crew, and the shipping suffered terribly, although the full toll was never recorded. The casualties of the Navy, with its strongly manned ships, may serve to indicate what happened to the merchantmen. Four ships of the line were driven ashore or foundered on the south coast with most of their men. One of them was the *Resolution*, which dragged her anchors off St. Helens in the Isle of Wight, was thrown across the Owers, on which she struck five times, and finally wrecked on the coast between Beachy Head and Hastings. A squadron was anchored in the Downs in what should have been smooth water under a weather shore. Of this squadron four 60- and 70-gun ships, with others smaller, were torn from their anchors and driven across upon the Goodwin. Of two of the great ships there were no survivors, of a third three only, and of the fourth 70 out of 276. In the Medway a 90-gun ship out of commission was sunk. In the port of London, far up from the open sea, many vessels were sunk or shattered in collision. Defoe

[1] See Cotton's *East Indiamen*, pp. 129–30, for a wreck near Polperro in 1708.

wrote a vivid description of the damage in the city and the port, purporting to be that of an eye-witness, although in fact he was in prison at the time.

The lighting of the coast began early in the seventeenth century. A private projector established a lighthouse on Dungeness in 1615, having secured the right to charge passing ships a penny per ton, which must have been a levy difficult to collect. Many lives had been lost by wreck upon Dungeness, and it was said that the light, feeble as it was, greatly diminished the casualties. In 1637 the North and South Forelands were also lighted. The idea of lightships for the outlying sands was not yet practicable, but on the South Foreland two lights were placed in line leading clear of the South Sand Head of the Goodwin, so as to give the mariner some indication of the danger area. These early lights were very dim and ineffective, and the element of private profit in their upkeep led to parsimony in fuel.

The Eddystone Rocks off Plymouth were the first outlying shoal to be tackled. The highest of the rocks are at or slightly above the level of high water. In 1691 it was suggested that a lighthouse could be built on them. Henry Winstanley, an Essex gentleman, designed and erected the work, mostly in timber, and the light was first shown in 1698. Winstanley devoted himself to improving the construction, and raised the height of the tower while strengthening its basis. He was out on the work in November 1703 when the great storm overwhelmed the lighthouse and all in it. Soon another philanthropist came forward, John Rudyerd, a London silk mercer. He built a granite base, and on it a strong tower of oak timbers. His light was first in use in 1708, and lasted to 1755, when the timber tower caught fire and was destroyed. The light itself was given by twenty-four large candles, whose fat had no doubt impregnated the woodwork. John Smeaton, a professional engineer, built the next Eddystone entirely of masonry. Its light shone for over a century, from 1759 to 1884. It had then to be condemned, not for any unsoundness in the work itself but because the rock on which it stood was disintegrating. Its upper part was re-erected on Plymouth Hoe. Its base is still visible on the original rock. It was replaced by the present lighthouse (from 1884) built by Sir J.

Douglass on another of the rocks. The Douglass light is nearly twice as high above water (133 ft.) as its predecessors, which were all between 70 and 80 feet.

Portland Bill had a lighthouse early in the eighteenth century, a squat, thick building, hardly a tower, with a light which seems to have consisted of a fire in a brazier, like the old beacon warnings of invasion. By 1790 it had been superseded by a new tall lighthouse of the more modern sort.[1] The Lizard was another early light, visible at twelve miles in clear weather. The first floating light-vessel appears to have been moored at the Nore in the Thames estuary in 1732. Even with these safeguards, which seem so pitifully inadequate on the scale of our time, the risks of Channel sailing were very great, and thick weather which dulls powerful modern lights must have rendered their predecessors totally inoperative. The Channel seaman of those days had to trust his life to the sounding lead, which warned him of the shoaling of the water. Even so, familiarity with danger begot carelessness. Sir Richard Hawkins, writing in 1602 of a ship which found herself out of her course, said : " which error often happeneth to those that make the land in foggy weather and use not good diligence by sounding . . . to search the truth ; and is cause of the loss of many a ship and the sweet lives of multitudes of men."

Compass and lead were the navigating instruments of the seamen who worked the coasting trade. But still greater we must account the mass of detailed knowledge that they carried in their brains. They knew the direction and speed of the tidal streams at any state of the moon, the eddies and counter-currents caused by shoals and obstructions, the tidal modifications due to wind-force, the indications of position yielded by ripples and overfalls, the depth at any given place under all these varying conditions, the nature of the sea-bed as revealed by the samples adhering to the tallowed base of the sounding lead. The skilled man could assess all these indications and give the answer, his position at the moment, by what it is superficial to call an instinct ; for it was really a rational process resulting from personal and traditional knowledge. The same sort of

[1] Both are delineated in Add. MSS. 15,537, 155 and 159, a collection of sketches by S. H. Grimm, 1790.

knowledge gave them their weather-wisdom, towards which there was little other aid : we do not hear of barometers carried in the small coasting craft, although they were now common in ocean-going ships. With all the skill the dangers were great. The skippers of that time had their failings as well as their virtues. They were sometimes drunken and often reckless ; and advancing age which matures some men's wits dulls others'. There were risks which they could not avoid, the thick fog or the storm wind and sea which left no choice of course ; and others which they had to take because they were earning a competitive living. The weather signs might be evil, but the coasting man had to sail. He might know that his canvas was worn out or his hull far gone in decay, but he could afford no better. He had to deliver his cargo at places without sheltered harbourage, but only a beach or an open roadstead. He had to take a chance in entering harbours where a rough sea broke dangerously on a bar. The coasting seamen, more numerous than the deep-water men, were the school, the nursery, the parentage, from which maritime England spread over the globe.

James Cook is the outstanding example. For he was coast-bred, in the Newcastle coal trade ; and he became not only an ocean seaman of surpassing competence but an explorer and surveyor of a genius never equalled in the recording of vast new coastlines. The ships he used were all coasters, collier barks specially bought into the Navy, strongly built to take a hammering if they went aground, roomy of stowage for the supplies to maintain his men for two or three years beyond civilisation's ken. Cook was the first explorer to practise the doctrine that if one wants to come to grips with a new coastline and stick to it close enough to record full detail, a coasting vessel is the best for the purpose.

Although Cook was not a Channel man, each of his three great voyages had a Channel departure. Of the first, in August 1768, in the *Endeavour* of 368 tons, built at Whitby four years previously, we may give some particulars from Cook's Journal, as indicating the incidents of a summer passage down Channel. The ship was fitted out at Deptford, and the Thames pilot took her to the Downs whence Cook returned to London for final business : " on Sunday the 7th I joined the ship, discharged the pilot, and the next day

279

sailed for Plymouth." Monday 8th: "fresh breeze at NW and cloudy weather the most part of these 24 hours. At 10 a.m. weighed and came to sail. At noon the South Foreland bore NE½N distant 6 or 7 miles." Tuesday, 9th: "Gentle breezes northerly and cloudy weather. At 7 p.m. the tide being against us, anchored in 13 fathoms water, Dungeness SWBW. At 11 weighed and made sail down Channel, at noon [1] Beachy Head NBE½E distant 6 leagues." The anchoring over a foul tide will be noted, part of the technique of Channel sailing, as it was in the Thames estuary. Wednesday, 10th: "Variable light airs and clear weather. At 8 p.m. Beachy Head NEBE distant 4 leagues, and at 8 (next morning) it bore NEBN, 9 leagues." This shows that the *Endeavour* lost ground during the night. "At noon the Isle of Wight NWBW." Thursday, 11th: "Light airs and clear weather. At 8 p.m. Dunnose NBW 5 leagues and 4 a.m. it bore NNE, distance 5 leagues." Friday, 12th: "Light airs easterly or calms all these 24 hours. At noon the Bill of Portland bore NW½N distant 3 leagues." Saturday, 13th: "Winds variable, ditto weather. At noon the Start Point west 7 or 8 miles." Sunday, 14th: "Fine breezes at NE and clear weather. At ½ past 8 p.m. anchored in the entrance of Plymouth Sound in 9 fathom water. At 4 a.m. weighed and worked into proper anchoring ground and anchored in 6 fathom, the Mewstone SE, Mount Batten NNE½E and Drake's Island NBW. Dispatched an express to London for Mr. Banks and Dr. Solander to join the ship, their servants and baggage being already on board."

So the *Endeavour* made her passage down Channel, before going on some way farther for the discovery, among other things, of the whole coast of New Zealand and of eastern Australia. She remained a fortnight at Plymouth, making preparations, and receiving stores and her final complement of men. On Friday, 26th August she sailed at 2 p.m. with a north-west wind. Her last sight of England was the Lizard at 23 miles distance. Three years later the Journal reads in July 1771, Wednesday, 10th: "Pleasant breezes and clear weather. At 6 o'clock in the morning sounded and struck ground in 60 fathom, shells and stones, by which I judged we were the length of Scilly Isles. At noon we saw land from the mast head

[1] Next day by the land calendar, but the ship's day was from noon to noon.

bearing north, which we judged to be about the Land's End. Soundings 54 fathom coarse grey sand." On this cool professional note ended the greatest voyage of exploration yet accomplished. " Saturday, 13th: At three o'clock in the PM anchored in the Downs, and soon after I landed in order to repair to London." [1]

V. PRIVATEERING

The naval wars against France, and often against Spain as well, grew more intense as this long period progressed. From 1739 to 1815, a stretch of seventy-six years, there was war with one or both of the rival powers during forty-two years ; and in the final struggle with the French Revolution and Napoleon there was continuous war for twenty-one years broken only by the fifteen months of the Peace of Amiens in 1802–3. In the Maritime War of 1778–83, which grew out of the War of American Independence, the British Navy did not possess a general command of the sea, although it attained it in the final months. During the other long wars of the period there was usually a British command of the sea. It meant that French fleets issuing from port would be brought to action, French colonial expeditions followed and frustrated, and British colonial expeditions successfully carried out. It did not mean that British commerce was safe from attack, but far the contrary. The *guerre de course* or war of commerce-destruction was the French compensation for inferiority in battle fleets. Fast frigates ranged the oceans, capturing merchantmen and sending them under prize-crews into the French and Spanish colonial ports available to receive them in many parts of the world. In the last long struggle Holland became a satellite state of the French, and her widespread colonial possessions, especially in the East, were of immense assistance to the war on British trade. In addition to the regular French cruisers, swarms of privateers issued from the European ports of France and Spain and from their colonies the world over. French trade on the great scale was fairly well blockaded, and its seamen were available for privateering. They practised it with energy and success. In

[1] The extracts are from *The Journals of Captain James Cook: The Voyage of the Endeavour*, 1768–1771, Hakluyt Society, 1955, edited by J. C. Beaglehole.

the long run or the short the privateer generally came in the end to his unlucky day and was overcome by something stronger than himself ; but on the average he had a very good time first, and his captures showed a profit on his running-costs and eventual over-throw.

The fact that privateering was for private profit caused it to be viewed as something not respectable in civilised warfare, and this view bore its part in the decision of the maritime powers to abolish it in the next century, by the Treaty of Paris in 1856. But there was another aspect of the business not realised then. Commerce-destruction is a legitimate object of warfare, and the privateers were serving their country as well as themselves. They had a material incentive not to destroy the ships and goods that they took, and with them they preserved the lives of their prisoners, in accordance with the steadily growing civilised outlook of European society. Centuries back, in the Middle Ages, they would not have done so, but would have killed them as a matter of routine. We can say now, strange as it would have sounded in the eighteenth century, that privateering was a humane form of warfare. For we know what has been done in our time by the German U-boats, killing merchant seamen as a cold-blooded act of state. Western civilisation is not ill seen in the warlike eighteenth century.

The insecurity co-existing with the command of the sea on the battle-fleet level caused the big ocean trades to sail in convoy. The richest British ocean trades were with the West Indies and the East Indies. Of these the West Indian business was the more valuable until about 1770, after which, with the growth of the China trade, the East Indies drew ahead. By the time of the Napoleonic War the great eastern commerce was essential to British survival, for without it British finances and industry would have collapsed, and a population already suffering heavily from war privations might well have broken into revolution. The swarms of London mer-chantmen made their way through the narrow sea to assemble at Spithead, and thence to issue to the ocean under protection of ships of war. In any year there were more than a hundred East Indiamen afloat, going or returning, or lading and discharging in their ports. The naval convoy did not as a rule see them all the way south through the Atlantic, but they were themselves armed like strong frigates although not manned on the naval scale. They kept in company into the Indian Ocean, where the Navy had a squadron in service. But there they had to part for different destinations, and bad weather often scattered them. The *guerre de course* was very active in the Indian Ocean, right up to the capture of Mauritius from the French as late as 1810, and of Batavia from the Dutch in 1811. Earlier the successive captures of the Cape of Good Hope in 1795 (returned at the Peace of Amiens), and again in 1806, were steps for the preservation of the eastern trade. Not until all these bases were in British hands was it secure. The West Indiamen were much more numerous, but smaller. Their convoy often took them all the way to the Caribbean, but there were many stragglers who failed to keep up, and thrusting skippers who pushed ahead ; and the privateers took their toll.

In the Channel and the North Sea worked the swarm of home-trade and coasting shipping, vulnerable to the smaller privateers of the ketch and lugger type coming out of the northern ports of France. Here there was little convoy possible, and fights and captures and escapes were of almost daily occurrence. The total losses were enormous. In the Napoleonic War, after the breakdown of the Peace of Amiens, over 5000 British merchantmen were captured, and over 400 French privateers ; so that on the average the privateer did pretty well. But building in all the little ports kept pace with the losses, and trade increased. It did so only at a price. The delays and the risks made transport very expensive. On exports this had to be compensated by low wages for production, and on imports by high selling prices ; and living grew extra-ordinarily hard for the mass of the people. Yet at the same time mercantile fortunes were rising and war profits multiplying. There was an enormous vigour in the country as a whole, though its rewards were ill distributed. The rich and the middling people grew richer and the poor poorer, and the " two nations " of Disraeli's later definition were drawing apart.

VI. BEGINNING OF THE PLEASURE RESORTS

In the second half of the eighteenth century a change of social habit set in which was destined to have a revolutionary effect upon the Channel coast: the more prosperous people in town and country began to take holidays by the sea, and some to reside there permanently. They had never thought of doing so, to any noticeable extent, in previous times. The people of the coast had been traditionally thought of as poor, disorderly and untrustworthy, a somewhat discreditable fringe to the solid society of England, based as it was on the ownership of land and the complex obligations of labour, tenancy and proprietorship. The neighbourhood of the sea had been considered unhealthy, possibly from the notion that it was sea air and sea water rather than ship's victuals that caused scurvy.[1] The fashionable resorts were inland places where medicinal waters existed. The pioneer of the change was in the north, where Scarborough early in the century became a pleasure resort for the well-to-do people of Yorkshire. In the reign of George III the movement became active in the south.

The middle-class people of London formed a taste for sea trips down the Thames estuary to Margate, taking passage in the hoys, which were now cutter-rigged coasting craft able to work to windward. With any luck a summer day's sailing would bring them to Margate, and another would bring them back. At least one night's stay was inevitable, and inns and lodgings supplied the accommodation. Deal had long had business visitors in contact with the Downs, and the pleasure-seeking element began to join them. Dover, as the chief port for France, had provision for travellers awaiting shipping or recovering from the prostration of a rough passage, and holiday visitors began to make use of it. Hastings too began to develop. As early as 1744 it had some street lighting presented by its M.P., Colonel Pelham. Thirty years later it had become a fashionable resort.[2] It was so only on a small scale, for

[1] Sir Richard Hawkins in his remarks on scurvy in 1602 considers the victuals a principal cause, but adds, " the water of the sea to man's body is very unwholesome " —*Observations*, 1933 ed., p. 41.
[2] J. Manwaring Baines, *Historic Hastings*, p. 145.

the houses were mostly in the two long streets running down to the sea on either side of the Bourne stream in the valley between the Castle Hill and the East Hill, and the sea front was occupied by the dwellings of the fishermen who drew their boats up the beach, and the shipwrights who, as already noted, built not only the boats but considerably larger vessels. There was as yet no occupation, save by farm buildings, of the land west of the castle, although a street had begun to extend westward from the Bourne mouth round the foot of the hill beneath the cliff. Here at the top of the beach the very short Marine Parade was established in 1797 as an amenity for visitors.

Brighton also was beginning to grow in the same generation, well before the great days of the Prince of Wales and the Regency. The place had always been an active fishing station of the beach variety, and as the Tudor picture shows, had been something better than an ordinary village in 1514. In the early seventeenth century it was said to house 600 families, or about 3000 total population. The location of most of their dwellings is now under the sea. Towards the close of that century, and at the opening of the eighteenth, Brighton fell on evil days. It suffered loss of its coasters and fishing-boats by enemy action. The sea encroached rapidly, pushing back the whole shoreline; the great storm of 1703 and another in 1705 occasioned destruction resembling the effects of a bombardment. The population diminished, and it was feared that the town would be altogether deserted. Defoe, on his *Tour through Great Britain*, visited Brighton about 1724. Its name was still Brighthelmstone, which he says was pronounced Bredhemston, "a poor fishing town, old built, on the very edge of the sea." The fishermen made their living not only in the local waters but by going to Yarmouth in the North Sea herring season and selling their catch to the fish merchants there. "The sea," he continues, "is very unkind to this town, and has by its continued encroachments so gained upon them that in a little time more they might reasonably expect it would eat up the whole town, above one hundred houses having been devoured by the water in a few years past."

Better times were about to set in. Brighton got permission to raise money, apparently by charitable contributions, from the county and even farther afield, for the construction of groynes to retain the beach as a defence. On the whole the policy was successful, although there are later records of damage from gales and high tides. A letter written by a visitor in 1736 betokens the dawn of a new age :

"We are now sunning ourselves upon the beach at Brighthelmstone. . . . The place is really pleasant ; I have seen nothing in its way out-does it ; such tract of sea, such regions of corn, and such an extent of fine carpet, that give your eye command of it all. But then the mischief is that we have little conversation beside the *clamor nauticus*, which is here a sort of treble to the plashing of the waves against the cliffs. My morning business is bathing in the sea, and then buying fish ; the evening in riding out for air, viewing the remains of old Saxon camps, and counting the ships in the road and the boats that are trawling. . . . The lodgings are cheap : we have two parlours, two bed chambers, pantry, etc., for 5s. per week." [1]

This attitude belongs to the century ahead, and the visitors were evidently pioneers, for they found no " conversation " in the sense in which Johnsonian England understood the term. Towards the end of the century the growth of Brighton was very rapid. Dr. Richard Russell inaugurated prosperity by " his fortunate and philanthropic advocacy and confirmation of the grand practice of sea bathing," to which he added drinking regular draughts of sea water. In 1780 the resident population was 3600, but fourteen years later it was 5600. This expansion resulted largely from the fact that the Prince of Wales began his patronage of the place, which he first visited in 1782 ; but the nobility had already been coming for some years.

Along all the Kent and Sussex coasts there was similar although less intense development. The roads were improving. Those of Kent had always been comparatively good, those through the weald of Sussex remarkably bad ; but now they were all becoming fit for

---

[1] Letter of Rev. W. Clarke, printed in full in J. D. Parry's *Coast of Sussex*, London, 1833.

faster traffic. The richest of the new rich class began to seek landed estates within easy reach of London. The moderately rich took houses in which they lived all the summer on the coast. The French Revolution sent a wave of genteel and impoverished exiles across the Channel, and many found a living in the coastal towns, where teachers of the social accomplishments were in demand. The threat of French invasion caused the quartering of troops along the coast, and officers brought their families to live there. Brighton was a military centre in the Napoleonic period, and the important training camp at Shorncliffe brought Folkestone into the social advance.

Farther west it was the same. Portsmouth was a greater naval base than ever before, with a greater fleet to serve. For service purposes it was linked with London by a telegraph line, consisting first of moving shutters (1797) and afterwards of semaphores visible from hill to hill, and messages could be quickly transmitted. With important persons hastening to and fro, the Portsmouth road had to be made first-class. The new custom of mobility brought the Navy's wives and families to Portsmouth, and retired officers and seamen tended to settle there. After the mid-century Portsmouth expanded rapidly outside the circuit of its ramparts, and soon there was a larger population outside the walls than within. South-ampton, commercially still in its long eclipse, was also from the mid-eighteenth century a residential focus for the new *rentier* and pensioned class, and it began to grow substantially beyond its old fixed limits. And so westward to the pleasant Dorset coast, where from 1789 George III made Weymouth a social magnet as his son did Brighton : George III, guarded by the Navy in Portland road, royally taking his sea bath while the band played patriotic airs and the populace looked reverentially on. Dartmouth was compara-tively untouched by the new social movement. The taste of visitors and idle settlers was for bathing beaches and views of the open sea, which it lacked, and its steep surroundings were a barrier to land communication. It retained a diminished interest in the Newfound-land fishery and developed a lucrative share in the new eighteenth-century wine trade with Portugal, whose imports it distributed by coastal shipping. It built ships, as did every south coast port, and there was occasional talk of making it a naval dockyard, which it never became. From Totnes there was a coastwise export of Dartmoor granite; but the Dart, though a perfect harbour, was fatally constricted by its land surroundings, and the supremacy of the west had passed permanently to Plymouth Sound.

Plymouth was a growing town, and its dock on the Hamoaze was growing still faster. By the end of the wars Plymouth had about 20,000 people and Dock 30,000. The latter place had the new name of Devonport conferred on it in 1824. Nearly all the growth was due to the Navy, for that of commerce was moderate. Long-distance shipping outward or homeward bound put in for various reasons, but did not handle much cargo there. The Sound was not at all times a safe anchorage. In 1796 the *Dutton* Indiaman was driven on the rocks under the Citadel and wrecked with loss of life. There was confusion on board, with the seas breaking over the wreck. Edward Pellew, a Cornish naval officer, got lines out from the shore and himself went on board, where he restored order and saved most of the people. Some years later the idea took shape of a breakwater to lessen the violence of the sea running in with a southerly gale. Sir John Rennie the civil engineer planned it, and work began in 1812; but it was a big job which took thirty years to finish.

The small places on the Dorset and Devon coasts began like those up Channel to receive holiday visitors, chiefly no doubt from their own hinterlands rather than from London. Prints of 1815 [1] show the beginnings of a resort at Sidmouth, a library, a sea-front inn, lodgings, promenading visitors. Exmouth and Torquay were also moving with the time. Cornwall experienced the change much later. Its interior was poor, its fishing villages very primitive, and its roads very bad. To travel freely by land in Cornwall entailed riding, for coaches made heavy weather of the narrow tracks among the hills. Yet there was some attempt at a road near the coast from Plymouth westward. Looe had had a bridge across its river for centuries, although the ascent after passing it was daunting. Fowey had been well placed and well shaped as a harbour in the days of small ships and small trade and large gains from piracy. The late

[1] Royal MSS. xi, p. 93b.

eighteenth-century demand for china clay gave it new life. Falmouth, one of the finest natural harbours of the coast, never realised its possibilities before the days of the larger ocean shipping and the exigencies of the great wars with France. The country served by Falmouth offered little trade of its own, and London was more than ever the focus of all the big trade of the Channel. The town of Falmouth came into existence only in the late seventeenth century, Penrhyn, farther within the harbour, having been the original small port. Edward Dummer, whom we have already seen in 1698 as Surveyor-General of the Navy, proposed early in the Spanish Succession War to run a service of packet-vessels for conveying mails to the West Indian colonies. Falmouth was the port designated as giving the nearest access to the ocean and the best immunity from the enemy privateers who haunted the Channel. But in fact the packets sometimes started from Portsmouth or Plymouth, and were apt to return to almost any home port. They were fast vessels, but were nevertheless sometimes captured by privateers—about one a year in the course of this war—and Dummer, who had resigned his official post in order to conduct the service on a contract, was financially hard hit. The Falmouth packet service continued to operate in one form or another until the days of steam.

CHAPTER FOURTEEN

The Great French Wars

I. GEOGRAPHICAL CONDITIONS

WE SPEAK somewhat arrogantly of the English Channel, although only one shore of it is English. But it is true that historically the Channel has been more English than French, and this is due to its geographical characteristics. Amid all changes in shipping the English coast has been easier to navigate than the French. It has few outlying dangers, and its tides are comparatively simple to work, whereas the French coast abounds in reefs and sands lying well out, and its tides are both fiercer than the English and subject to more marked local variations from the general east-and-west alternation. Before the days of coast lighting the French side was much more dangerous at night than the English. So it has been that at all times through shipping has tended to follow the English shore. As late as 1878 an experienced yachtsman remarked that one saw fifteen ships north of the Channel's centre line for every one south of it. The Armada in 1588 must have had good reason for avoiding English observation as it sailed up Channel. Yet the physical conditions were overriding, and its pilots followed the English coast until it neared Calais roads.

There is another big difference between the two coasts which had an enormous influence on the long wars between Great Britain and France. It is that before the days of great artificial works the French coast was deficient in harbours for the greater ships of war. From Cape Ushant east to the Netherlands there was no port affording secure anchorage to the ships-of-the-line or the larger frigates of the eighteenth century. There were plenty of small ports fit for privateers and small cruisers, but not one in which battleships would not take the ground at low water, a process which, with all their heavy guns on board, would quickly have been fatal to their structure. The only base for a French Channel fleet was at Brest, round the corner in the Bay of Biscay. Added to this, the prevailing winds were from the west, and a French fleet, having committed itself to the Channel, might look to being driven eastwards by bad weather through narrowing waters towards a region where no suitable port was under French control. The French did occasionally risk it, but their admirals were always unhappy about it, and the odds on a disaster from weather were much greater than for their British enemy. The English coast, with its naval bases at Plymouth and Portsmouth and Chatham, and its anchorages at Torbay, Portland, the Downs, and the Nore, was in evidently favourable contrast. These were permanent factors in the Channel story of the great French wars.

II. THE BOURBON WARS

In 1688-9, when William III acquired the English throne, Louis XIV, having miscalculated the outcome of William's enterprise, had not fully mobilised the French fleet. The English fleet had been neglected after the close of the Dutch wars and the dismissal of the Duke of York for reasons of religion. When the Duke became King in 1685 he took steps to strengthen it, but enough had not been done when William supplanted him, and the French Navy was potentially stronger when the great war started with the English and Dutch in alliance against France. The Dutch themselves had also weakened at sea under stress of their long land war with France in 1672-8. Thus in 1690, with William absent in Ireland fighting James II there, and England in a disorganised state and not altogether loyal to its new king, Louis sent his fleet into the Channel with the prospect of obtaining command and landing an army on England's southern coast. Part of the English fleet had been detached to serve William's Irish operations. Louis had brought round his Mediterranean fleet from Toulon to join his northern fleet at Brest. The result was that at midsummer the French in the Channel were in a substantial preponderance of numbers over the English and Dutch combined.

The allies under Lord Torrington learned of the French approach while off the Isle of Wight. Torrington, with 56 ships against 68, did not think it wise to fight at once, being convinced that as long as his fleet held off and watched—" in being," as he put it—no French army would be embarked. He retired fifty miles up-Channel and then received positive orders from London to engage the French. These orders were dictated by political alarm, a public outcry against " nothing being done " to avert invasion, and a revival of Jacobite hopes of undoing the revolution. Torrington accordingly fought the French off Beachy Head on 30th June and was defeated. The French suffered no loss of ships, and the allies lost five, of which four were Dutch. It was at first said that Torrington had sacrificed the Dutch in order to preserve the English, but it appeared that the Dutch had disobeyed his orders by attacking the wrong part of the enemy's line, and so occasioned their own losses and the loss of the battle. But it was not a decisive defeat. The allies retreated to the Thames, still substantially " in being," and the French made nothing out of their success. They had no troops or transports ready for an immediate invasion, and the Anglo-Dutch concentrated their forces, turned out new ships, and were in strength in the Channel in the following year. Two days after Beachy Head William III in Ireland defeated James II at the Battle of the Boyne and drove him out of the country. This relieved the political despondency and enabled William to get back to the centre of government. Louis XIV was a great king and a brilliant political strategist, but in 1688–92 he allowed his strength to be divided between too many objectives, Ireland, England and the attack on the Low Countries and Germany ; and so he lost his chance of effecting a counter-revolution in England. The only landing was that of a few men at Teignmouth, to raid the village and then withdraw.

Invasion after Beachy Head would have needed a snap decision and a quick improvisation foreign to the character of Louis XIV. He was a man of stately deliberation and ponderous action. He revolved the idea of invading England and decided to attempt it in 1692. This time he had an army ready round La Hogue on the Norman coast, but the naval chance was gone. The Anglo-Dutch turned out a Channel fleet twice as strong as the French. The allies attacked, and in a disorderly battle, unusual for those times since it went on for nearly a week, ruined the French on the coast of La Hogue, Barfleur and Cherbourg. James II, ready to head the invasion, looked on from the cliffs with mixed feelings. His hope of restoration was being blasted, but he could not repress his admiration for the men whom in happier days he had commanded. " None but they could have done it," he muttered as he watched the English seamen cutting out beaten French ships under the fire of the shore batteries.

After La Hogue there was no more thought of invasion during this war or the next under Queen Anne, which lasted to 1713. Louis XIV concentrated the state's effort on his continental campaigns and laid up most of his battleships. For that very reason the French attacks on commerce were the more destructive, since there was a pool of seamen available for manning privateers and the smaller ships of the French navy. British command of the sea on the higher plane could not prevent crowds of privateers from coming out of the French Channel ports. Some of them worked on the ocean, others in the narrow seas, and they took a great toll of prizes from East and West Indiamen down to coasters and fishermen. The advantage to the French was that the *guerre de course* was self-supporting and cost the state nothing, that it damaged English finances and diminished the war effort, and that it caused discontent and fostered Jacobite hopes. Never afterwards was French privateering relatively so serious. And yet it did not affect the decisions gained in the wars. The losses were marginal, and British commerce took them in its stride. With Marlborough's victories in the Low Countries British trade in northern Europe noticeably increased. While a few British Indiamen were lost, the French East India Company fell into actual abeyance, and their West India trade suffered more than that of the British. After the Peace of Utrecht it was acknowledged that Great Britain, so named from the Union with Scotland in 1707, was the chief sea power.

Twenty-five years of comparative peace ensued, during which France made a great maritime recovery, and Spain, now also under a Bourbon king, emerged from the depths of her previous decrepitude. In 1739 there was a new war, against Spain on account of trade disputes in the Caribbean. The Bourbon family alliance took its time to operate, but war with France was active in 1743 although not declared until the following year. Again there was a plan to invade England across the Channel. Marshal Saxe collected 10,000 troops and sufficient transport at Dunkirk at the opening of 1744, and Charles Edward the Young Pretender was ready to sail with them. Louis XV ordered the Brest fleet into the Channel to secure the crossing of the army. It was something like the old Armada plan again. The British fleet out of Portsmouth blockaded Dunkirk and turned towards the French as they came up-Channel. They got as far as Dungeness, but there was no battle. A February gale damaged the transport flotilla, and the Brest fleet, knowing how precarious was its existence without a Channel harbour—Dunkirk being useless to big ships—made its way westward to safety.

So much for the invasion of 1744. But in 1745 an invasion of a surprising sort did take place, by Charles Edward and seven men, who landed in western Scotland and called out the Highland clans. The Stuart prince came from France in a minor vessel, but otherwise the French at that stage did nothing for him. Louis XV was " pursuing his conquests in Flanders," he and his court being carted thither like some enormous travelling circus, in spite of which handicap his army defeated the British and their allies at Fontenoy and looked like conquering all the Low Countries. Charles Edward, by his own appeal and leadership, gained all Scotland and advanced into England. The French then began to take notice, especially as it was now autumn and the regular campaigning season on the Continent was over. The invasion craft were reassembled and 15,000 troops brought to Dunkirk. If they could have crossed in early December, when the victorious Highlanders were not much more than a hundred miles from London, the Jacobite revolution might have been achieved. It might have been, but probably it would not. For in sober likelihood it would have needed more than 15,000 French and 4000 Scots to conquer England, which was by this time fairly solid against the Stuart cause. But that is the unanswered question of all these invasion projects, unanswered because the invaders never got so far as to put it. The French invaders were ready at the crucial moment, but they could not cross. Admiral Vernon kept a strong squadron out to the westward, and the Brest fleet would not enter the narrowing bottleneck of the Channel with that squadron ready to fall on it from behind. Meanwhile adequate small forces were in the Channel and the North Sea to prevent the invaders from coming out of their ports. There was much excitement on the coast, a day or two of financial panic in London, a rumour that George II was about to bolt to Hanover— probably untrue, for that unlovable man was no coward ; and then the Highlanders began their retreat from Derby and the French threat wilted and died. If the French had had a Portsmouth they might have done something.

In the eighteenth century it was generally observable that the British fleet deteriorated in peace and strengthened in war, while the French fleet was worn down to impotence at the end of a war and was reorganised and made formidable in the ensuing peace. Either process was a function of the respective constitutions of the two countries. In England the Commons voted taxation and would not vote enough for the forces unless there was imminent peril : as soon as peace was signed down came the military and naval estimates to well below danger point. The King's ministers, absorbed in maintaining their positions amid unchecked rivalry and intrigue, had no interest to spare for naval efficiency, and used dock-yard appointments as a means of paying for political services to themselves. The outbreaks of war in 1739, 1756, and 1778 each found the Navy in a bad state, the ships out of repair, the dockyards devoid of stores, the men dispersed, the officers with no recent experience at sea. Then, as each war proceeded, the Navy took the up grade, good officers from below supplanted bad ones above them, and the national talent for rough-and-ready as contrasted with theoretically perfect administration at length got done the things that needed doing. The manning of the fleet was in accord with this vagueness of system. In peace very few seamen were retained, perhaps an eighth of the numbers required in war. The Navigation Acts required that three-quarters of the crew of every British merchantman should be British subjects. When war began this rule was suspended to allow of more foreigners being employed in the mercantile marine while the press took the British seamen into the fleet. But the press was haphazard and unfair to individuals, a rough-and-ready expedient of the most objectionable kind. In Bourbon France the constitutional practices were different. At the close of war in 1748 and 1763 the French navy was virtually knocked out, and in 1783 it was clearly beginning to go down after years of success. Then, with the peace, and especially is this true after that of 1763, able ministers not subject to parliamentary faction got to work and revived it by thorough measures of reform, paying attention to good dockyard work and design of ships, keeping muster rolls of available seamen and giving them gunnery training, seeing that the officers had what instruction was practicable. So in each new war the French had a period of success, and it was fortunate for England that the *tempo* of these wars was slow, giving time to redress the balance. In the end the authoritarian system proved inflexible and brittle and its fleets were overcome by those of the wrangling, jangling parliamentary system wherein men forcibly spoke their minds and were free to act according to their judgments.

Such was the course of the Seven Years War from 1756 to 1763. On land it was a war principally in Germany and on the sea principally oceanic, with objectives in Asia and America. In the Channel there were the familiar features of privateering and alarms of invasion. On the latter head there was great despondency in the bad opening year of 1756, for in the preceding peace the ministry had let down the army as well as the fleet, and the country was denuded of troops ; so that the delinquent minister, the Duke of Newcastle, was seeking in a panic to obtain German mercenaries for the defence of English soil. But in that year there was no real invasion threat, for the French were devoting themselves to the conquests of Minorca and Hanover. Then the disorderly constitution showed its merit by compelling George II, on the national demand, to accept Pitt in place of Newcastle, and by 1758 Pitt's genius had brought the forces into form. Victory on the Atlantic took shape, to be completed everywhere in the succeeding years, in Canada, the West Indies, West Africa—Pitt made it an imperial war.

Pitt's opposite number in France, the Duc de Choiseul, retaliated

by devising a blow at the heart, an invasion of Great Britain—
Scotland as well as England—for the autumn of 1759. This time
the French army was not to issue from the Channel ports but was
gathered on the Biscay coastline south of Brest, to be convoyed by
the French fleet direct from its base to a landing in western Scotland.
The attempt was made in November, and was ruined at once by
Sir Edward Hawke's victory in Quiberon Bay, where the Brest fleet
was put out of action before a soldier had embarked. There was
anxiety in England before the result was known, and some excited
denunciation of Hawke for his supposed lack of competence, but
nothing like the gloom of 1756. For Pitt had created new regular
regiments, the Highlanders among them, and had made the ancient
county militia into a well-trained force. At heart the country was
not despondent of the outcome. In the Channel war Pitt revived
the ancient practice of raids on the French coast, not for the medieval
motive of plunder but for the strategical object of pinning down
French troops to the defensive. He kept a small amphibious force
of soldiers on board ships, to appear unexpectedly and deliver jabs
at the ports. They were not all successful but, win or lose, they
kept the French busy, and Pitt claimed that his little force of soldiers
diverted three times their numbers of Frenchmen from the general
war. His critics scornfully called it mere window-breaking at
excessive cost—" breaking windows with guineas." The plan has
been pursued in our days.

Immediately on the peace of 1763 Choiseul began his rehabilitation of the French navy. He had something to work upon, for
though the French battle fleets had been driven off the sea they
existed in port, and the mere signing of peace reduced the disparity
with the British. In England the ministries of George III reduced
the Navy expenditure and neglected the ships, which deteriorated
rapidly for lack of care when laid up. In 1770, when the Falkland
Islands crisis threatened a new war with France and Spain, the
British government showed a firm front and its adversaries backed
down. But it was a bluff, and Lord Sandwich, the First Lord of the
Admiralty, afterwards averred that he could not have sent fifteen
ships to sea. Two years afterwards a leading minister declared that
never had the international situation been so serene, and that there

was no prospect of war anywhere. Three years after that, and not without prolonged warning, the American revolution broke out. Early in 1778 France declared war in support of the Americans, and in 1779 Spain also joined in for the recovery of past losses, Jamaica, Gibraltar, Minorca, Florida.

Sandwich was blamed until our own times for the decay of the Navy, accused of corruption and complete neglect of his duty. In fact he did work for the Navy, and up to a point was zealous for its welfare. But his point fell short of the sacrifice of his job. He protested to Lord North that the money was inadequate, and when refused more he did not resign and tell the country the truth, but continued. Moreover, what money the Navy was supposed to get was never properly accounted for, and there certainly was more than the normal corruption. War showed the work of the dockyards to be rotten. The *Royal George* sank in a calm sea in the Spithead anchorage by the collapse of the structure of her hull, which was due to prolonged neglect.

In the first years of the new Bourbon war the Channel was an important scene of action. In 1778 Admiral Keppel led the fleet to an action with the new French navy off Cape Ushant. His ships were in poor condition, his men green and untrained, his officers not at the point of efficiency. It was more than suspected that the vile and vicious politics of the time blunted the loyalty of his second-in-command on the day of battle. It was an indecisive encounter with no loss of ships on either side, not a defeat and not a victory. And the situation was such that a victory could have altered for good or ill the course of history. For Spain had not yet come in, and might have been deterred ; and Bourbon sea power nourished American independence, and indeed gave the decisive stroke at Yorktown three years later. Pitt's Navy by all probability would have won the battle of Ushant and established a blockade of Brest.

In 1779 the French and Spanish fleets combined to cover the invasion of England and dictate a peace that would yield full revenge for the Seven Years War by the destruction of the British Empire. It was not only possessions that were at stake but the whole oceanic commerce of the country with East and West, and on that com-

merce now rested the domestic livelihood of the British people.
Their numbers had increased, and industry employed most of the
surplus. Industry was capitalized by the profits of Asiatic trade and
African slaves and Caribbean plantations. It drew its raw materials
and found its markets the world over, and without its distant territories it would have lost them. All this was the prize for which
the Bourbon fleets approached the Channel in the late summer of
1779. Such was the state of the administration and the dockyards
that the British fleet could not fight a battle on its own coast. In '78
Sandwich had told Keppel that his new command at Portsmouth
comprised thirty-five ships manned and fit to go to sea. Keppel
went there, and found six that merited the description. The remainder made up the scratch force with which he failed to win the
battle of Ushant. Now in '79 there was little improvement. The
Bourbons entered the Channel with 66 ships of the line. Sir Charles
Hardy had 39 with which to oppose them. He followed the old
policy of keeping to the westward, to the windward, and watching ;
and while cruising off Scilly he was able to warn the incoming trade
not to enter the Channel. A convoy of eight East Indiamen took
refuge in the Irish ports.

The invasion was planned on the old lines, not those of 1759.
Fifty thousand French troops with 400 transports were ready at
Havre and St. Malo, to cross when the way was open and occupy
the Isle of Wight, and thence to capture Portsmouth—Francis I had
had the same design in 1545. The French fleet left Brest at the
beginning of June and went to the coast of Spain to join the Spaniards. So slow were they that it was not until 30th July that the
allies could get to sea as one fleet under the Comte d'Orvilliers. A
slow passage made it the middle of August before they entered the
Channel and anchored south of the Eddystone on the 16th. It was
as far as they got. At first they had not located Hardy, then they
heard he was to the westward, food and water were running short,
and there were nearly 5000 sick. The commanders deliberated, and
an easterly gale cut short the argument by driving them out of the
Channel. A rarity at that season, it was a godsend to men who did
not really want to go in. Meanwhile authority in Paris had changed
the plan of invasion to a landing at Falmouth, which those who

were to execute it thought foolish. On 25th August they decided that it was too late in the year, and a French officer wrote " it was impossible to re-enter the Channel, from which one might never escape." [1] Escape is a curious word for sixty-six to use in reference to thirty-nine, and it was the geography of the Channel that dictated it : not a port to shelter a battleship, only a fortnight's water left, and westerly winds to be expected. After sighting Hardy and vainly attempting to close with him the great fleet went into Brest in mid-September. For England it was an escape, with no credit due to the British government.

Plymouth had had an exciting time with the Bourbon armada in sight. There were measures to drive off all cattle from the country-side, evacuate civilians, sink blockships in the approach channels, and draw booms across the Hamoaze. But so short-lived was the threat that they were not put in execution. Plymouth had strong-looking fortifications, but possibly under Lord North and the Earl of Sandwich they might have been found to resemble those of Chatham under Charles II.

The Maritime War had no further big events in the Channel. It was an oceanic war ranging from Minorca and Gibraltar to North America and the West Indies, and round the Cape to India. The Dutch joined the Bourbon allies, and the Baltic powers sought to cut off the British supply of naval stores by forming the Armed Neutrality. The Navy slowly gained strength, and in the last two years was dealing its enemies heavy blows in the Atlantic area and succeeding by a narrow margin in averting a French con-quest of India. The French gained one of their objects—it was never a Spanish object—in promoting American independence. Everywhere else they substantially lost the war. They had nothing to show for it in India, hardly anything in the West Indies, those two great fields of European wealth-making. Spain regained Minorca and Florida, but not Gibraltar and Jamaica. The Dutch yielded free passage to British ships through the waters of Indonesia. For Great Britain it was a defensive war, and the defence succeeded in the theatres where the need was greatest. The future of trade

[1] *Mariner's Mirror*, Vol. XXIV, No. 3, July 1938: *The French Fleet in the Channel*, by Rear-Admiral A. H. Taylor.

and industry and the growing population was preserved. Two other outcomes are worth noting. The most shameful period of British politics, the faction fights of North, Sandwich and the unscrupulous King's Friends against Fox and Burke and the equally unscrupulous neo-Whigs, ended with the emergence of the younger William Pitt as the post-war prime minister. The younger Pitt had a talent for finance and sound economy as great as his dead father's talent for war. He pulled the country out of the mess and had it prosperous and expanding after a surprisingly brief interval. On the other hand, Bourbon France, equally hard hit, found no such restorer, but only a succession of ineffectives who allowed the economy to go spinning out of control to the revolutionary crash of 1789.

III. THE REVOLUTION AND NAPOLEON: THE GREAT INVASION THREAT

Pitt fully realised that prosperity depended on sea power, and he did not allow the Navy to run down as previous peace-time governments had done. He reformed the dockyards, built new ships for old, and retained a larger nucleus of officers and men in service. Critics cried extravagance, but he knew that it was economy. He did not allow Chatham and Portsmouth and Plymouth Dock to relapse into dens of corruption derelict of real work. On the other hand he entirely misread the meaning of the early stage of the French Revolution. For him France was Bourbon France, and it was being weakened. In February 1792 he said in Parliament that he looked confidently to fifteen years of peace, and he thought it safe to reduce the naval estimates. Within twelve months he was beginning a twenty-year war. No modern can justly condemn him, for the modern cannot divest his mind of the knowledge of what Pitt did not know—the outcome of the Sovereign People and the Rights of Man, the real meaning of the *Marseillaise*. It is like a jury framing its decision on evidence not given in court.

For its first years the Revolutionary War was a Channel affair only in its dockyard activities in fitting out fleets and its outburst of privateering and the war-time phase of smuggling : the great events were on the oceans and in the Mediterranean. On the

Channel coast the new well-to-do populations witnessed an occasional sea skirmish, training of regiments, and a general watchfulness, as when the Brighton fashionables turned out on an August day in 1793 to watch a great sham-fight of 7000 troops on the Downs, featuring the Prince of Wales taking salutes and various jolly incidents like the arrest of an officer (militia) for sitting on a drum. But somewhat later we hear that the conduct of the French privateers was most audacious, and that at Newhaven they even ran in close enough to take sportive shots at people on the beach.

Then the war came home in unpleasant fashion in 1797, a year in which the outlook abroad was very bad. In April the men of the Channel fleet at Spithead mutinied and refused to put to sea. Their list of grievances is instructive, partly for one that it does not contain. They said little about the cat, on which humanitarian sentiment has shed much ink. To the simple sailor it was evident that a ship needs discipline, or all on board will drown together; and that if a man got drunk or raised his hand against authority it was in order for his skin to feel the smart. By this date flogging had been amended so that it was in a captain's power to award no more than two dozen: anything above that must be by sentence of a court-martial. They complained of the conduct of certain officers, not many; and they were generally incensed by that of the pursers, who made illicit gains by issuing short rations. But the overriding grievance was on pay. The pay had not been raised since the reign of Charles II, while the value of money had decreased as it perpetually does. The soldiers' pay had recently been raised, but the Navy had been left out. Low pay had ever been the standing grievance, for on it starved the wives and families ashore. Sir John Hawkins had induced his careful Queen to raise it in the Armada days: "the wages," he said, "being so small causeth the best men to run away, to bribe, and make means to be cleared from the service." And in 1797 a rise was long overdue.

At this date, it should be noticed, there was an extensive trade union movement in the country producing a series of strikes. One set of craftsmen whose doings would be known to seamen in the fleet were the Thames-side shipwrights. They were notoriously turbulent trade unionists, enforcing their claims with sometimes a good deal of intimidation. Strike action was in the air of the 1790's. And that is what the Spithead men intended. They asked redress of grievances, were respectful to most of the officers, whom none the less they set on shore, and meanwhile refused to go to sea. But that last was conditional. If the French appeared, they would sail against them at once, and postpone the mutiny until after dealing with them. The mutiny, whatever its cause and however it was conducted, was contrary to all the laws and moral obligations of a fighting service. It is evident that many of those who led it were uneasy on this score. No less so were some of those who handled the matter for the Government and who were made by senior officers to recognise that there were violated moral obligations on their side. The Admiralty was at first bewildered by the suddenness of the storm, and then took the sensible view that grievances must be remedied and order restored without vindictive punishment. No doubt the highly critical situation of the country in that year contributed to the decision. The pay was increased and other reforms conceded, and the Channel fleet returned to its duty.

Next month, after these decisions were known, something different took place in the North Sea squadron whose task was to blockade the Dutch fleet then at the disposal of France. The British squadron was based on the Nore anchorage in the Thames, and among its men were a few who held revolutionary views such as had been absent at Spithead. Richard Parker, an educated man soured by personal failure in life, took the lead in a nucleus of conspirators who won over the bulk of the fleet to follow them. The crews of thirteen ships of the line expelled their officers with violence and humiliation, anchored in the Estuary, and blockaded London's trade. Only two ships remained faithful to duty, and with them Admiral Duncan sublimely continued his blockade of the whole Dutch fleet, whose commanders did not know what was going on. This time there were no government concessions. Parker and his associates grew desperate and talked of handing the ships over to the French. The mass of the men were loyal Englishmen who had behaved like traitors and began to realise it. Ship by ship they fell away from the " delegates " and returned to duty. Parker and half a dozen others were hanged. The squadron defeated the Dutch in October at the hard-fought battle of Camperdown.

In the last years of the Revolutionary War General Bonaparte made himself First Consul of France and studied the question of invading England across the Channel. Preoccupations elsewhere prevented him from proceeding with the matter, and a peace was patched up at Amiens in 1802. The First Consul violated its conditions from the outset and intended a new war so soon as he should have reconditioned his navy and replenished his stocks of naval and military material. The British government understood this and forestalled him by itself declaring war in May 1803. Bonaparte assumed the title of Emperor Napoleon in 1804. The French navy was unready and its owner very indignant that he had not been allowed the time he wanted to bring it into form. He announced that his immediate intention was to invade England and dictate a peace of conquest in London. There was no secrecy, and all the world knew his purpose. He calculated that his loud threats would unnerve the defence. They were also useful in establishing his position among the people of France, who had not been monarchically minded in the previous decade.

Napoleon gathered on the coast of north-eastern France and the Low Countries an army of 120,000 of the seasoned troops against whom no force in Europe had hitherto been able to make a stand. Boulogne was the central point, but the embarkation was to be made also from the small ports on either side of it, all subject to the same disability that they could not harbour big ships. Napoleon gave orders for the construction not only of a fleet of barges for conveying the troops but of a flotilla of small armed vessels for attacking the British blockaders. Altogether there were to be 2000 small craft, but the number was never actually attained. He persisted in the flotilla project against the advice of his sea officers, who told him that, whatever their numbers, these little vessels would stand no chance against the heavier sloops and frigates that the British kept close to his coast. He relied also on evasion during fog or a long dark winter night, and seems to have persuaded himself that once the army was embarked he would find some means or other of getting it across. The embarkation itself proved not so easy as he had first thought. Practices showed that instead of the few hours of the earlier estimates it would need a week or even a fortnight for horse, foot and guns to cross the Channel even without enemy resistance or weather interruptions. Low water in these tidal ports entailed suspension of movement, for the boats were aground. Anchoring outside meant exposure to bad weather. This was the state of the project in 1803–4. It was only in 1804–5 that the idea of breaking the blockade by a surprise concentration of all the French battle fleets was entertained. That was a last resort when Napoleon's earlier confidence had weakened. How strong it was may be judged from his production of a medal celebrating the conquest of England and inscribed *Frappé à Londres en* 1804. Even Hitler was never such a fool as that.

In England there were 52,000 regular troops, not all of whom could take the field, since the defences of the dockyards had to be manned. The county militias were called out for training. They were a home-defence force in which service was compulsory for a proportion of men chosen by lot, the drawing of numbers in the so-called militia ballot. In addition, some 350,000 men of all classes and ages enrolled themselves in volunteer regiments for whom there were insufficient arms and instructors, and who were to carry on their ordinary civilian employments until the enemy actually appeared. In the eyes of the regular officers the volunteers had little or no value as soldiers. There was little chance of giving them orthodox teaching in battle formations, but one colonel made an enlightening remark when he said that they should be trained not by drill-sergeants but by poachers and gamekeepers. The martello towers, modelled on a small fort which had made a great resistance against a British landing on the coast of Corsica, were built along all the low-lying shores of south-eastern England. Each tower, of brick in great thickness, carried on its top a single big gun with an all-round traverse, designed to inflict loss on the enemy in the act of landing on the beach. The towers were not all finished before the threat receded, but they were thought so permanently useful that the programme was completed.

It is quite evident that the country as a whole had no conception of submitting to the French. Its people had some moral or immoral elements in their make-up which were lacking in the German and Italian regions that had hitherto been the scenes of French conquest. There, under despotic rule, when invaders had seized the administrative mechanism the people obeyed orders from above by the habit of centuries. In the British Isles on the other hand there was an equally long-seated habit of defying authority. It manifested itself in many forms, disorderly political factions, industrial rioting, illegal trade unions, smuggling, and the socially frowned-upon sects of the religious nonconformists. The aristocracy and gentry would certainly have died before submitting, and they were the natural leaders of the country folk. The old King was determined not to treat even with Napoleon in London. He meant to retire to the Midlands and fight it out.

In reading the details of the volunteer movement one is struck by the fact that these patriotic civilians knew absolutely nothing of war, in spite of the ten years of warfare that lay immediately behind them. They formed their regiments like clubs, each subject to its own particular rules and oblivious of common military discipline. They gave much thought to the extravagances of military tailoring. Those who were offered pikes because there were not enough muskets could not be made to realise the over-all situation, and fractiously complained that their efforts were not appreciated. It is all evidence of the immunity which civil life had enjoyed behind the shield of the Navy. Yet the volunteers meant business. They worked hard, portly middle-aged men endured long hours of drill and dashed about lustily on field days. They really expected to fight.

The Navy viewed all this fever with a tolerant eye. There was no harm in it, and not much good, for the occasion would not arise. St. Vincent, who took his title from his victory of that name, spoke briefly in the Lords to the effect that the invaders would not come. He had no wish to talk of it save, as he said on another occasion, that there were some old ladies who needed comforting. Nelson, chasing Villeneuve in 1805, wrote no word to show that he was worried about invasion. His mind was on far other things, barring the Levant route to India, preserving the Caribbean sugar plantations, obliterating the French wherever he could find them. The

Navy, with a squadron in the Downs and its lighter ships patrolling every mile of the French coast, knew that the *Grande Armée* could issue forth only to be massacred. As for the French battleships based outside the Channel, the western squadron watching Brest was ready to receive them, and knew too well that no French admiral would be willing to sail past into the narrowing trap. The " twenty-four hours command of the Channel " which Napoleon theatrically demanded of his navy might as well have been twenty-four hours command of the moon.

In 1804 the Emperor gave up the idea of the stealthy crossing by virtue of the flotilla alone, the plan of invasion by evasion, and turned to that of concentrating the French and Spanish fleets in the Channel by a combination of surprise movements designed to draw the British away from the decisive area. The details of the plan were frequently varied, but the general idea was that the different fleets should sail in different directions, threatening Egypt, the Caribbean and Ireland, should make a surprise concentration in the West, and should then dash for the Channel, whence the main British forces would have been ordered away in pursuit. The threat to capture the British West Indies was serious enough to cause consternation in London. Napoleon calculated that mercantile alarm and public clamour would compel the Government to send the main force of the Navy to the rescue, by which time his own united fleet would be recrossing the Atlantic to cover the invasion. What he did not calculate was that the British Admiralty was in the habit of weighing up all possible moves, including this one. It had its answer. Nelson might pursue Villeneuve from Toulon wherever he went, but the great fleet in the western approaches of the Channel was not to leave them ; and on that rock the Napoleonic scheme foundered. It did so in the summer of 1805, when in August Napoleon learned that Villeneuve, returning from the west, had not attempted the Channel but had gone south to Cadiz instead. Napoleon expressed furious anger with his admiral, broke up the camp at Boulogne and set the army in motion against Austria, which Pitt had drawn with Russia into coalition against France.

All this was the ostensible. But many have thought that Napoleon had seen invasion to be impossible before the naval moves of the summer and that he was bent only on getting out of it while saving his face. On this interpretation the West Indian conquest was the real objective, with the Boulogne army as the feint to cover it. And when that failed Napoleon was secretly glad that Villeneuve had evaded a smash-up in the western approaches, since his fleet would be available to assist in new conquests in the Mediterranean—a hope that was destroyed at Trafalgar in October. On the surface Napoleon saved his face, abandoning the invasion with loud complaints of the incompetence and timidity of his admirals, riding off to brilliant victories by land over the coalition. Villeneuve was taken prisoner at Trafalgar, to be liberated on exchange in the following year. He was found dead by a knife wound in the prison to which Napoleon consigned him. Suicide, it was officially said. But if he had been brought to trial and had defended himself he would have had some awkward things to say about the dictator and his plans of invasion.

Ten years afterwards the Channel coast saw Napoleon in the flesh. After Waterloo he fled to Rochefort and surrendered to Captain Maitland of the *Bellerophon*, blockading that port. The *Bellerophon* brought him to Torbay and then to Plymouth. He was not allowed to land, but great numbers of people crowded to the Sound and saw him from boats as he showed himself on deck. Thence to St. Helena.

CHAPTER FIFTEEN

Sailing Ships

I. THE LARGER SHIPS

In TWO respects the sailing ship-of-war had reached its final form by the end of the sixteenth century. It had become a purely sailing vessel without auxiliary oars and with a hull form designed, below water, for speed and readiness of manœuvre ; and its chief armament consisted of muzzle-loading guns as heavy as it could carry, ranged along the broadside and firing solid shot through ports opening with hinged lids. Broadly speaking, these two characteristics continued unchanged until the early nineteenth century, and development was rather by increase of size than by the introduction of any new principle. It is remarkable how, from the earliest constructional drawings preserved in England—some designs by the Elizabethan master-shipwright Matthew Baker—right on for more than two hundred years, the shape of the midship section of a large vessel, below water, altered very little. For a long time the proportion of beam to length also changed little, although towards the end length began to increase. With the growing size of ships the guns became more numerous and heavier, and the one or two tiers of the Elizabethans became three in the largest ships-of-the-line in Nelson's time. But still they remained broadside guns firing solid shot with powder producing clouds of smoke.

Above water, apart from the guns, the ships altered greatly. The early upstanding forecastle, quarterdeck and poop sank progressively into the hull, while the low waist was built up higher to meet them, until the ship of the early nineteenth century tended to be flush from stem to stern. This was partly an effect of the growth of the whole ship. The space from one deck to the next above was determined by the average height of a man. As ships grew larger this constant was proportionately smaller, and the height of the superstructures less noticeable. In the Armada time a ship of 700 or 800 tons was very large, and the English seamen found most use for those of the *Revenge* type, about 500 tons. In the Trafalgar period the three-deckers were of well over 2000 tons. The above statements are intended to be broad and general. There were many small variations of proportion within the general type, and innumerable improvements of details ; but the essential differences at successive periods were not as great as would be implied by the numerous pictures showing only the above-water aspect of the ships.

In the rig of the ships the changes were more apparent, although, with one or two exceptions, they were developments rather than the introduction of new principles. The middle-sized Tudor ship-of-war had typically three masts and a steeved-up bowsprit. The fore and mainmasts each carried a large lower square sail [1] and a much smaller topsail. The bowsprit served for leading forward the stays of the foremast and the bowlines of its sails, and also supported a square spritsail on a yard slung beneath it. The mizen mast had a single triangular lateen sail, and the lateen yard hung at the side of the mast away from the wind. If the ship was put on the other tack, the lateen yard had to be eased into a perpendicular position and its forward or lower end dipped round the mast, and it was then rehoisted to its proper angle ; all of which necessitated control by complicated gear. Thus what we may regard as the standard ship was three-masted and six-sailed. The principal driving force was given by the large square foresail and mainsail. The two topsails were an additional driving area in easy weather. The lateen mizen was chiefly useful when working to windward or with the wind abeam. The spritsail under the bowsprit helped in this, and it may also have been an aid when the ship was brought head to wind to be put about on the other tack : a timely backing of this piece of canvas could have made the difference between the ship's getting round or refusing to get round on the new tack. The sails were

---

[1] So-called square sails were not all geometrically square, but were quadrilateral. Their essential was that they were set on yards slung in front of and at right angles to the mast.

evidently used to aid steering, for the mechanism actuating the rudder was not very effective. It consisted of a whipstaff or vertical lever similar in principle to those in a railway signal-box. The helmsman swung the top end of the lever from side to side and it was connected lower down to the tiller running into the rudder head. But the arc in which the tiller could thus be swung was very restricted, and sail-adjustment had to help. The *Mayflower II* in 1957 was steered across the Atlantic with a wheel and not a whipstaff, which would have been the strictly characteristic instrument. Wheel steering was not invented until the eighteenth century.

Larger ships had early a more complicated rig. From the first *Great Harry* onwards they were given two mizen masts, each with its lateen sail. Pictures show also lateen topsails on some of these masts, but realists have found it difficult to see how such topsails could have been efficiently handled. In the large ships also the fore and mainmasts carried little square topgallant sails above the topsails. The masts themselves presented problems. The early ones were each a single pole from heel to truck. But there was a limit to the size of the trees obtainable, and high masts were also a danger in bad weather. In the later Elizabethan period, under Hawkins's administration of the Navy, a method was achieved of making the topmasts separate from the lower masts and strikeable at sea, so that they could be sent down to ease the ship. These separate topmasts, and topgallant masts, are shown in Baker's working drawings of c. 1586, which also do not show lateen topsails. The total mast height was thus less restricted and was reducible at need. It then became possible to obtain greater sail area by higher masts, and in the following half-century the second mizen mast began to die out; and from about 1640 the three-masted ship became standard even in the largest sizes.

By the end of the seventeenth century great ships had three sails on each mast, the course or lowest sail, the topsail and topgallant-sail. The lateen was still the mizen course, but above it were the two square sails on yards as on the other masts. During that century also it became customary to step a short mast on the bow-sprit end, and on it to cross a yard with a small square sail, the sprit topsail. Thus the six sails of the elementary square rig had become eleven sails, and further multiplication was to follow.

From origins that are little known an entirely new kind of rig had come into use for small vessels, certainly before the middle of the sixteenth century. This was the fore-and-aft rig, seen first as a quadrilateral sail set abaft the mast, with its peak or highest corner extended by a sprit, a spar stepped near the bottom of the mast and rising at an angle. The sprit sail is now seen only in the Thames barges, themselves a rapidly dying class. At the same time, or perhaps a little later, a triangular foresail or jib was set on the forestay, and the fore-and-aft rig in its first form was complete. It would work a vessel to windward better than the square rig, but it was not so good for running before the wind. Owing to its handiness for quickly putting the ship about from tack to tack it was especially valuable for the smaller coasters and such craft as often worked in and out of port and in difficult channels.

Not until the eighteenth century did the men of the big ships begin to appreciate the virtues of the triangular sail set on a stay. Then they began to fit them on all the forward-leading stays that supported the masts when the ship came head to wind. The square sails remained the principal driving power of the large ship, but the fore-and-aft staysails aided her performance when working to windward. At the same time the lateen mizen was converted into a quadrilateral fore-and-aft sail, the spanker, set aft of the mizenmast. So, with the addition of the fine-weather studding-sails (lateral extensions of the courses and topsails), and of small square royals above the topgallant sails, the rig of the nineteenth-century sailing-ship was complete. The sprit topmast was discarded in the early eighteenth century, and the spritsail below the bowsprit in the early nineteenth.

The Navy played the leading part in the development of the complicated later sailing rig, because its ships for fighting purposes had large crews capable of handling the gear. The Navy also built much bigger ships than any merchants, except the East India Company, found it advisable to invest in ; for the merchant was much more concerned with working into difficult anchorages in order to lade his cargoes. Strictly naval ports with dockyard facilities, the world over, were few and far between, whereas in the primitive condition of land transport the merchantman had to pick up her lading wherever it was produced. In this respect the later East India Company resembled the Navy. For various reasons, of which distance was the chief, the largest possible ships were best for the eastern trade, but the Company did not push them into little ports. It relied on the concentration of merchandise into a few places by the native shipping of the Indian Ocean and the China seas—the country ships, they were commonly called—to provide the cargoes for the great liners to take to Europe. The Portuguese had early adopted this principle in the sixteenth century, when their East Indian carracks were the greatest ships sailing the seas. On the coasts of Europe, the American coast, and in the West Indies, with shorter ocean passages entailed, this principle did not apply, and the merchantmen remained small until the nineteenth century. Large West Indiamen were of not much more than 500 tons, and large coal carriers from Newcastle about 400. The smaller colliers which delivered coal on open beaches were round 100–150 tons.

The smaller classes of merchantmen employed in the European trades comprised a very much greater number of vessels, although, in the eighteenth century, much less is known about details. Their names were derived as a rule from the shape and proportions of their hulls, which are for the most part not clearly recorded, or even from the particular trade in which they were used. There are shipwright's delineations of West Indiamen and of large colliers, the latter owing to the fact that four of them used in Cook's voyages were bought into the Navy, when exact records of lines and dimensions were made. But in general the numerous lesser merchantmen are only vaguely described. The names themselves may mean different things at different times ; Cook's colliers were " cat-built barks," but they were not at all like the barques of the nineteenth century ; and the eighteenth-century ketch was completely different from the ketch of our own time. In the nineteenth century it became customary to differentiate sailing-ships by their rig and not by their hulls. The word " ship " then acquired a strict technical meaning as a three-master, square-rigged on all masts. So also " barque " meant a three-master square-rigged on the fore and main, and fore-and-aft rigged on the mizen. In the last generation of the sailing period, when steel construction permitted a great lengthening of the hull, there were four-masted barques, a handful of which were still at work in the period between the great wars of the twentieth century.

In the late eighteenth century the smaller types began to substitute two masts for three. The collier bark became the collier brig, with two square-rigged masts, and brigs were extensively used in the European trades, the so-called home trades, and to some extent in the North Atlantic. Another two-masted vessel was the schooner, with two square topsails on the foremast, but otherwise a fore-and-aft rig, and largely used in the coasting trade. Many schooners worked in the Newfoundland fish trade, and in the fruit trades with Spain and the Atlantic islands. Hybrids of these rigs then appeared, barquentines and brigantines, respectively three- and two-masters, square rigged only on the foremast, and the hermaphrodite brig was completely square-rigged and also completely fore-and-aft rigged, combining the qualities of the brig and the schooner. A single-masted vessel built for speed and not for cargo was the large cutter developed by the Navy for chasing privateers and smugglers. She had a hull of fine lines and an enormous sail area, with two triangular headsails, a gaff mainsail and topsail, and also a square sail for running before the wind. The only weight she carried was her ballast and a few small guns, and a strong crew for handling everything quickly. These cutters were the prototypes of the large cutter yachts owned by rich men in the mid-nineteenth century, who initiated the sport of yacht racing.

The period of the Napoleonic War was the last in which the Channel waters were traversed exclusively by sailing shipping. The smoke of the paddle steamer appeared between Dover and Calais three years after Waterloo, and then the steam tugs began to tow the great ships through the Thames estuary to the Downs and round the Forelands, and the General Steam Navigation Company, using steamers in the home trades, was formed in 1821, while the excursionists to Margate began to go there by steam instead of in the sailing hoys. But for many technical reasons the early steamers were restricted in their uses, and the transition was prolonged. Sail

SAILING SHIPS

and steam overlapped for the rest of the nineteenth century, and
it was not until its ninth decade that the total of steam tonnage
owned in the United Kingdom exceeded that of sailing tonnage.
As late as 1870 there were five tons of British sailing shipping for
every one of steam.[1]

The East Indiamen were the aristocrats of all the merchantmen
sailing through the Channel, as long, that is, as the Company's
monopoly endured. Until 1813 no ships save those of the Company,
and of course the Navy, could legally sail between England and the
eastern seas. In that year the trade with India was thrown open to
private merchants. The Company's monopoly of the China trade
continued for another twenty years, to be ended in 1833. Monopoly
is a bad word nowadays, but in the period of the Company's trade
there was much to be said for it. In southern Asia trade and
politics were inextricably mixed, and irresponsible traders could
create much mischief. This was seen when the Company ceased to
do business at Canton after 1833 : the less responsible and less
experienced competitive firms who succeeded it were soon in
trouble with the Chinese authorities, and by 1839 had embroiled
Great Britain and China in formal war.

The Indiamen themselves were in many ways unique. The
Company, after its re-foundation in 1708–9, did not legally own the
ships it employed. It chartered them from various firms and individuals who had them built. But the ships were built solely for
the Company's trade and were of no use for any other, and the
Company dictated their design, tonnage and equipment. In the early
eighteenth century their usual tonnage was about 600 although, by
playing tricks with the rules of measurement, they were commonly
registered as of 499 tons, the reason being that an Act of Parliament
required every ship of 500 tons and over to carry a chaplain. By
the early nineteenth century the tonnage had risen to 1200. They
had to cope with armed enemies, not only the French in war-time
but eastern pirates at all times, and they were furnished with the
guns of a large frigate, the lids of the gun-ports being picked out
with contrasting paint so that they could be seen and counted from
a distance. Sometimes there were more painted ports than actual

[1] Figures given in R. C. K. Ensor, *England* 1870–1914, Oxford, 1936, p. 108.

guns, but they had the effect of deterring bad characters from closing to fighting range. On one occasion a strong French naval squadron let the China fleet go by because it appeared to be escorted by ships of the British Navy, although in reality they were all Indiamen. Until quite late in the nineteenth century, long after the guns were a thing of the past, British merchantmen in the China trade kept up the practice of painting a row of dummy gun-ports along their sides.

The crews of the Indiamen, outward bound, were Europeans, mostly British. Some died in the course of the long voyage, some deserted in eastern ports, and many were impressed by the East Indies squadron of the Royal Navy, which had no other source of recruitment. Consequently there were not enough left to work the ship home, and Chinese and Lascar sailors were employed, to be returned east as passengers in the outgoing ships. The captains and officers of the Company ranked almost as high as those of the Navy. In time of war the officers could generally be transferred to the Navy at equivalent rank, but few desired to be, for, to the Navy's disgust, the East India service was much more lucrative. The captains and senior officers had extensive private trading privileges, with specified tonnage allotted to their goods. They took out all sorts of luxuries for the British in India, furniture and household goods, clothes and shoes, wines and spirits, harness and saddlery, even horses and dogs, which they sold at fantastically high prices ; and they brought home fine fabrics and silk and chests of tea. After a few good voyages a captain could retire with a handsome fortune, and perhaps a knighthood if he had made a good defence of his ship against the French. But he had first to pay for his command in hard cash to the owner of the ship, or by the political and business influence which his family could exert ; and the Company saw to it that no fools but only talented men rose to command. The Company's service in all ranks, afloat and ashore, was an informal brotherhood in which every man's worth was known.

The shore observer of the new visitor class on the Channel coast had much to interest him if he looked seawards. From Deal he might watch the Downs crammed with merchantmen waiting for a fair wind to go down Channel—on one occasion five hundred sail

were counted there. Dungeness offered usually a lively scene, for
it was a salient into deep water, and the great ships passed close.
On either side of " Dungey," there were recognised anchorages
for shelter against east and west winds respectively, and swarms of
coasters used them, not only in strong weather but in light, when a
foul tide could sweep the vessel back on her course. Anchoring
for tide took place all along the Sussex coast, for the water everywhere was shallow and began to deepen only well to the west of
the Isle of Wight. From the uplands round Hastings on a clear day
there was often a huge concourse of shipping to be seen. Brighton
roads was another inshore anchorage, and Shoreham, where the
coasters waited their tide to go into the harbour. As time went
on the great ocean-going ships did not join these waiting throngs,
for the steam tugs took them clear into the widening Channel,
where they had room for long boards if the wind were not fair.
But all through the peaceful nineteenth century the much more
numerous coasters gave the Channel scene an interest that has now
departed. The coasting trade was slowly but surely eroded away
by railway transport inland, and finished in our time by the motor
lorry. But down to 1914–8 it made a tenacious stand. At St.
Leonards, where the London Road runs down to the sea front, it
meets a continuous line of promenade. Sixty years ago there was
a gap in the masonry allowing carts to be driven down on the beach.
Here the collier schooners, successors of the collier brigs, came
ashore at high water, and as the tide fell the coal carts went alongside
to receive the cargo. House coal in those days was about £1 a ton
in southern England, and the people who supplied it, now a notoriously happy and contented lot, were certainly no less so then.
Until 1849 the coasting trade was reserved to British shipping.
From that year the repeal of the Navigation Acts threw it open to
foreigners.

II. THE FISHING BOATS

The fishing-boats of the coast must go back through unbroken
lines of development to pre-history, but until comparatively recent
times little is known about them. There were deep-sea fishermen
sailing from the Channel ports to the North Sea for cod and herrings,

and westward to Newfoundland for cod. There were inshore fishermen working closer to their homes and changing their methods with the change of the seasons, sometimes trawling for white fish on the bottom, sometimes shooting drift-nets to hang perpendicularly in the water and entrap the shoals of mackerel, herrings and pilchards which visited various parts of the coast, sometimes using baited hooks set on long lines on the bottom, sometimes going for crabs and lobsters with baited wicker traps lowered near the rocky refuges of the shell-fish, sometimes collecting oysters out of their beds in shallow water. These differing activities called ideally for different types of boat, but since most of them endured for only a season of the year the local boats had to be adapted for more than one kind of fishing, and their qualities had to strike a useful average. It has sometimes been stated that trawling was a new invention of the late eighteenth or early nineteenth century and that Brixham in Torbay was its initiator. But this is clearly a mistake. We have noticed a casual reference to trawling in the Brighton visitor's letter of 1736,[1] there are mentions of it in Stuart times, and there is a series of records of trawling at Hastings from 1561. Oyster dredging was a form of trawling, and Richard Hawkins speaks of it in 1583. It must in many places have been the only practicable method of gathering oysters, and they, as we know, had been an attraction of the British coast to the epicures of Roman times. The tropical alternative, of native divers going down and grabbing handfuls, was never thought expedient in our climate. Perhaps the Romans used it, but if so the divers were expendable. Seine netting, whereby a long net managed by several rowing-boats working in concert was drawn in a ring round a shoal of pilchard, was practised in Cornwall within living memory.

It might be thought that in the centuries before good roads and railways were in being, the difficulties of inland transport would have made unsalted sea fish an unknown food to all but the people of the coast. But the zone of distribution was wider than might be supposed. The fish buyers awaited the arrival of the boats at the ports and beaches. They had their markets where they were expected at inland towns and villages and they carried the fresh fish far up

[1] See above, p. 286.

country by light carts or pack-horses. No doubt the farther from the sea the more expensive a luxury was white fish. Both Hastings and Brighton were sending their fish to London in the eighteenth century. For those close to the shore it was a main foodstuff and cheap. London, supplied from the Estuary and the North Sea, sent fish southwards, and there were few parts of Kent, Surrey and Sussex out of reach of some source of supply. Fast-sailing fish carriers collected the catch from the North Sea fishermen, in the manner of sack ships from Newfoundland. Some of the Estuary boats had fish wells into which water from outside was allowed to penetrate, and so brought the fish alive to Billingsgate.

In the drift-net fishery for herrings in the North Sea the boats required stoutly built hulls of large capacity and a moderate sail area, since speed was not called for. They were known as busses. In early times they were square-rigged, with three masts. In the eighteenth century a two-masted English herring-buss had a square mainsail and topsail, a fore-staysail and two jibs on a long bowsprit, and a small mizenmast with one sail.[1] These were the largest English fishing-boats, but probably few were operated from the south coast. They were not suitable for habitual beaching, and could not have been used from such places as Hastings and Brighton.

A large number of different types of boats came into use in the Estuary and on the south coast. The differences were caused not only by the differing methods of fishing but even more by the circumstances of working—whether the boats sailed out of harbour or were launched off beaches. One unique type is to be noted, the Brighton hog-boats. Brighton had a long history of importance as a fishing place. By the close of the eighteenth century it had evolved a large fishing-boat, probably the largest to be normally worked from a beach, for general employment well out in the Channel. The hog-boats were flat-floored, as was desirable for resting upright on the beach, and somewhat box-like in shape. Such hulls would make a good deal of leeway when sailing on the wind, and they were aided against this by the provision of lee-

[1] Model in Science Museum, S. Kensington. In writing this section the author is much indebted to *British Fishing Boats and Coastal Craft*, by E. W. White, 1950, published by H.M. Stationery Office for the Museum.

boards, to be lowered to check drift ; and they were the only large class of south coast fishing-boats to have these lee boards. Their two masts were fore-and-aft rigged, and the mainsail and mizen were extended by sprits, like those of the Thames barges. There are said to have been seventy of these large boats working from Brighton in the Regency period, and they landed a much greater quantity of fish than could have been eaten in the town, growing though it was. The hog-boats had a career of about a century, dying out in the 1880's. Their place was taken by luggers of somewhat smaller build.

Apart from Brighton, the coast was divided between gaff-rigged cutters and ketches, and luggers, at first with three masts and later with two. Local circumstances are generally found to account for the choice between them. The dipping lug was the most weatherly of rigs, and a lugger was more able than any other to beat up to her port with her catch fresh. But the sail had to be lowered and reset every time the boat was put about on a new tack, and this did not yield the quickness in manœuvre needed for entering a narrow harbour. With the gaff-rigged cutter, when the helm was put down and the bows came up into the wind, the mainsail swung over to the new tack without attention. So we find that in the Channel the gaff-rigged boats sailed out of harbours, although luggers did from some, but that for working from beaches, with a wide and easy approach, the lugger was the almost universal type. At sea the lugger had the power and drive needed for dragging a trawl over the bottom, but may have been less handy for laying and picking up the long lines with hooks attached to them. For long-lining the gaff rig was good, and so we find cutters sometimes referred to as hookers, simply because they fished with hooks. For drift-net fishing, for mackerel and for herrings when they came into the Channel, the lugger was able to lower her mainmast into a supporting crutch and lie quietly to the nets until it was time to haul them.

Down Channel, where beaches were fewer and harbours numerous, the lugger was nevertheless, with exceptions, the favoured type in the nineteenth century, probably by reason of her excellent qualities at sea. But it is notable that while the Looe boats were all luggers, those of Polperro, only four miles westward, were "gaffers."

Polperro has a very narrow entrance between jagged rocks calling for the utmost handiness and skill with a sailing boat. Looe has also a narrow entrance, but it has a fairly sheltered anchorage outside in the bay, and the approach is altogether less dangerous.

The biggest west-country exception to the use of luggers was provided by nineteenth-century Brixham. There, from a sheltered harbour, sailed the famous Brixham trawling fleet numbering 300 sail in the years before the first Great War ; and it is true to say that, while Brixham cannot be proved to have invented trawling, it trawled more effectively and on a larger scale than any other Channel port. The trawlers were originally cutters, but in their last half-century were lengthened and rigged as ketches, big boats of well over 40 tons. The mainmast was set well back from the stem, giving space for a large area of headsail. The hulls were fine-lined and deep in the water, and for towing the large trawls they preferred strong winds to light ; and the Brixham fishermen were great seamen. They worked wherever the fishing called, far and wide around the British coasts. Brixham was the last fishing port to keep its sails, but in the 1930's there were less than a dozen of the big trawlers left, and they were being sold off for conversion into yachts. The present writer remembers having seen the diminished fleet of survivors in 1937 sailing westwards along the Devon coast, a sight now for ever vanished ; and, as a counterpart, the harbour of Brixham ten years later filthy with diesel oil.

The three-masted luggers of the eighteenth century began to die out in the nineteenth, and by 1850 a shorter two-masted boat was taking their place. At different parts of the coast they varied in design. At Deal, where the principal interest was waiting on the Downs shipping, speed was the prime quality, and the boats were fine lined with a fairly deep keel. When beached they did not naturally sit upright, and had to be shored up as they were hauled out of the water. The Hastings luggers had a much fuller body and flatter floor and sat nearly upright without shoring. This form made them less good to windward, and towards the end of the sailing era (about 1914) some of them were fitted with centre-boards for greater grip on the water. Elsewhere in Sussex the luggers were of the same general type, and the usual rig was of jib, dipping lug mainsail, standing lug mizen, and mizen topsail. To see dozens of these shapely luggers putting to sea in a long succession for the night's fishing, with the evening sun lighting up their brown sails, was a beautiful thing. They did not all crowd off the beach together because the same shore gang would work at launching several of them, one at a time, and they were strung out as they sought the open sea. The hauling up the steep beach was done by capstans, manhandled at Deal, turned by horses at Hastings ; and here again the boats waited their turns to come in, the horse finishing one job and then going on to another capstan for the next. There are still a few of the sailing lugger hulls on Hastings beach, but they are all driven by engines, and so are the winches which haul them up. Internal combustion has done for horse and sail. The heavy boats are not of course pulled through the yielding shingle : they slide over greased wooden stretchers, and the last stage at the water's edge in launching is assisted by half a dozen men who wade in and put their shoulders against the boat. At Deal, whence the luggers have now entirely vanished, they used to launch bows first and haul off to anchors laid out in the sea. At Hastings they launch stern first.

The west-country luggers using harbours were of the finer-lined type which sailed better. As far west as the Lizard their general shape and rig resembled that of the up-Channel boats already described. The Mount's Bay luggers of the far west were somewhat different in hull form, being double-ended, with pointed sterns instead of the flat transoms used elsewhere and with a raking instead of an upright sternpost ; and they had a sail-plan without the jib. Although sail has gone as a means of propulsion, nearly all the powered fishing-boats up and down the coast retain the small mizen as an aid to lying quietly head to wind while handling the fishing gear.

In-shore fishing, it is generally agreed, has passed its best days, partly because of the superior results gained by the heavily capitalised fishing fleets of the North Sea and the farther north, partly because young men to enter the calling are hard to find and young women prefer husbands not to work at night and come home dirty and wet and smelling of fish. Fixed hours and fixed wages, tea breaks and television, are incompatible with the fisherman's life.

CHAPTER SIXTEEN

Peace in the Channel:
The Coast Resorts

FROM 1815 to 1914 there was peace in the Channel. During all that century not a shot was fired from Kent to Ushant, save for a brief hour in its middle year 1864, when the *Alabama* and the *Kearsarge* fought their duel off Cherbourg; and that was not in a European conflict. In the war of 1870 the French navy was strong and the Prussian so rudimentary that it did not venture westward into Channel waters. The long peace was nevertheless an armed and often apprehensive peace. There were several scares of Anglo-French war and possible invasion. Fleets and coastal fortifications grew in their rival strengths, and until the formation of the *Entente Cordiale* of 1904 the British and French peoples looked on one another as potential enemies, each quick to take offence and see sinister intentions in the other. But it never came to warlike action; and now we may safely say that as between French and British it never will.

Old people in 1815, with memories reaching back through sixty years, would have judged that the English coast of the Channel had been transformed in their time. The idea of the pleasure resort was well established, and the class that fostered it, the money-rich as well as the landed rich, was growing rapidly on the country's industrial progress, which itself did not belong to the southern region in which so much of the profit was spent. Deal, Dover, Folkestone, Hastings, Brighton, Southsea, Southampton, Weymouth, within the radius of comparatively easy travel from London, were all places new in motive and outlook, and others such as St. Leonards, Eastbourne, Seaford, Worthing, Littlehampton,

Bognor and the fishing villages of the Dorset coast were soon to join their ranks. Farther west in Devon there were already Sidmouth, Exmouth and Teignmouth of the earlier standing, with Torquay just on the threshold of a very prosperous new growth out of virtually nothing, and Dawlish and Paignton ready to follow on a lesser scale. Wherever there was an open beach and a cluster of fishing people and good road access, the new rich and the moderately well-to-do were ready to come in the summer to spend their money, and some of them to settle permanently. The majority of the inhabitants were still the descendants of the native coast-folk of the past. The agriculture of the land within the coastal belt was flourishing, but the agricultural labourers were certainly not. Life had grown very hard for them during the long French wars. Food prices were high and wages low, kept down by the Speenhamland dole and all the servility and social tyranny that went with it; and the countrymen of Sussex and Hampshire and Dorset, long deprived by enclosure of their petty properties in the land, lived on starvation diet and yet produced large families to live like them. There was a surplus there of people ready to migrate, and they took the chance offered by the new money on the coastline and swarmed to it to work on building, road-making, shop-keeping, domestic service and all the handmaid appendages to luxurious life. From less localised origins came also the professional people, doctors, clergy, schoolmasters, architects, lawyers, necessary to the new society. As the new age set in the coast acquired not only a new look but also a partly new population.

Yet the old local characteristics long remained, since most of the immigrants came from the adjacent hinterlands. Dialects continued strongly marked until the close of the century, and even to-day after another fifty years varying vowel sounds and intonations remain in the speech of one section and another of the coast except in the larger towns. In them indeed population is now of all English origins. In places like Brighton, Portsmouth and Plymouth the speech of London prevails, and probably a large majority of the inhabitants are not of local descent.

We have seen that the movement to residence by the sea began in the middle of the eighteenth century and was in places well marked before its closing decade. Then the twenty-two years war with revolutionary and Napoleonic France cut off the rich from their old custom of touring on the continent, and this was a powerful aid to the social colonisation of the coast. With the nineteenth-century peace foreign travel began again, but new waves of residents continued to settle on the coast. In spite of all the poverty and distress of the post-war period the country was richer than it had ever been, and the number of people with incomes which they did not personally earn was vastly increased. Road communication between London and the coast grew much easier until, long before the coming of the railways, the more successful sort of City men were able to live mainly on the sea coast if they so desired. We should beware of exaggerating this into a broad generalisation which would not be justified, but there is evidence that it was beginning. Cobbett in 1823 declared that the stockbrokers (whom he hated) were living at Brighton and travelling up to their offices by coach, although it can hardly be imagined that they did so every day. A day return trip at that time would have involved two journeys of about six hours each, with two and a half hours in London between them.

The advantages of coast residence provided varying talking points. Hastings, the old Hastings in its cleft between the hills, was sheltered from cold winds and claimed to be beneficial to sufferers from chest weakness. As the town extended westwards it still had its castle hill to shield it from the worst rigours of the east wind, and the tradition that it was a good winter resort for consumptives lived on to the end of the century. As late as the 1890's people wearing black cloth respirators over their mouths were commonly seen promenading on the sea front. Brighton was breezy and bracing and good for sluggish livers and the generally debilitated. Minerals occurring naturally in the drinking water received much attention. The hard chalky water of the Kent coast was good for soft-boned children threatened with bandy legs. The iron in the water of the wealden coast, especially of Hastings, was thought excellent for rheumatism and anæmia. Southampton owed some of its early popularity as a residential place to a beneficial mineral spring near the Bar Gate which cleared the blood of gouty affections. Later, after the mid-century, the new resort of Bournemouth owed its rapid development to the pine woods whose " balsamic effluvia " were curative of lung trouble. Farther west we hear rather less of the medical aspects. In Dorset and Devon the sheer beauty of the coast, sandy beaches for the children, and boating and fishing for their elders were sufficient attraction. And, of course, sea-bathing was everywhere the primary motive that originated the whole movement.

The result of it all was that before the period 1840–60, when the railways were established and began to show their effects, the social revolution of the up-Channel coast had been accomplished, while that of the down-Channel coast west of the Solent was powerfully begun. In this pre-railway age there was no day-tripper movement save to Margate and Ramsgate by the Thames estuary steamers. The new people were settlers or long-period visitors. They were led by the highest lights in fashionable society. Three royal dukes frequented Brighton before the Prince of Wales followed suit in 1782. The Princess Amelia, daughter of George III, initiated the vogue of Worthing in 1798. The King himself had ten years earlier begun that of Weymouth. The military element was important on the Kent and Sussex coasts in the Revolutionary and Napoleonic wars, and added to the permanent occupation. The Navy brought numbers of residents to Portsmouth and Southsea and to Plymouth, and also had its share in the rise of the Torbay and adjacent resorts. Before the making of the breakwater Plymouth Sound was not always a safe anchorage, and the western squadron often preferred that of Torbay for shelter and minor refit. Retired officers with their families suffered themselves to be grounded on the shores that they knew best. Nelson's wife had a house at Exmouth. Southsea was full of naval officers who after long years at war had lost touch with their places of origin, and settled in the residential town nearest to the great port from which they had sailed and where the interest of their lives still lay. The East contributed its quota. British India was expanding, and its officials came home on long leave in increasing numbers as the century of peace set in. They were not poor, and the prices they paid for their cabins on the voyage home were a large element in the incomes of the captains of the Indiamen. They were naturally attracted by the society and the climate of the

Channel coast. They required expensive houses in the coast resorts, rented for perhaps a year at a time, and when they retired they also settled. They looked for boarding schools in which to place their children, as did the well-to-do Londoners, and the school industry was prominent among the professional elements of the coast. Paul Dombey's Doctor Blimber had his establishment on the sea front at Brighton. The private preparatory school was a coastal institution through the century.

Although geographical circumstances varied, and the coast towns differed in their setting, there were similarities in their social growth. What we may call the aboriginal inhabitants, the fishermen and small tradesmen who saw it all begin, were usually located near the water's edge, but they had no lively appreciation of salt winds and a sea view and were quite ready to yield such amenities to the newcomers who would pay for them. The new towns therefore developed as terraces of tall houses and hotels strung out along the sea front, with other although less desirable penetrations up valleys leading inland. Behind the sea front would lie an area of shops selling good quality wares, and lodging-houses for the poorer visitors. Behind that again, reaching sometimes far inland, would grow rows of meaner streets housing the new working population whose employment depended on the money of the sea front. It was a simple kind of development uncomplicated by industrial factors or past history, and depending on one motive, the sea front with its view, its spacious promenade, and its bathing. These towns therefore very early disregarded the ancient nucleus from which each grew, and spread on the long line of the shore with generally shorter inland extension; but there of course the local topography of hill and vale modified the regularity of growth. By this development Brighton had more than three miles of built sea frontage by 1841, and that year's census counted 46,000 people, including such visitors as were there on a day in June. Hastings by the same census had nearly 12,000 people. But physical obstacles had prevented much coastwise extension, and it was not until about twenty years later that it attained, with St. Leonards, a sea front length of two miles.

In the pre-railway period the occupations of the visiting and idle-resident population amounted in sum to a quiet enjoyment of the physical scene and the social environment. The sea-facing row of buildings had in front of it a roadway and then a sea-wall serving as an esplanade and bordered by the beach. People walked on the esplanade, the sick and the hypochondriacs were towed along it in bath-chairs, the affluent showed themselves on horseback or in carriages along the roadway. There was also driving and riding in the surrounding countryside, and on the beach there were donkey rides for children. Livery stables were interspersed with the shops, as garages now, in the trading belt behind the front. Bathing in summer attracted all who felt fit for it. Circulating libraries sought places on the sea front and were used as informal clubs for conversation and acquaintanceship. The sea itself provided greater interest than it does now. At almost any point on the coast there was a variety of craft to be seen not far out, and their manœuvres and occupations to be discussed. Visitors could go rowing and sailing from the beach, where now they can only roll horribly in motor-boats. The coastal fishing fleets were in full and even growing strength, and the local fish markets at each landing-place were lively scenes, their stalls yielding fish only a few hours caught. Organised indoor entertainment was very moderate. A growing resort would have assembly-rooms for meetings and balls attended by the quality, their selectness defended by the high price of admission. A single theatre would sometimes attract a good London company, and a concert hall performers of real talent. The music hall and such vulgarities were yet in the future, but Punch and Judy were generally in business on the beach. Brighton early produced a promenade pier jutting into the sea, but part of its purpose was the landing of cross-Channel passengers from Dieppe, previously disembarked in boats on the beach. It was not until 1847–8, when the railway reached Newhaven, that Brighton lost its regular cross-Channel steamers.

In the society of the coast and the countryside it was a sincerely religious age, and since it was also class-ridden there was a variety of approaches to the heaven, which, it was vaguely agreed, would be common to all. The sea fronts were predominantly Anglican, although it is rare indeed to see a church allotted one of the valuable sea-front sites. The handsome Anglican churches, together with the more solid sorts of non-conformist chapels, were generally built in the second zone of the shops and lodging-houses. The massed working population inland was largely non-conformist and tended to use the smaller chapels and the occasional less ornate churches of the establishment built in their midst. The nineteenth-century distribution of people into sects ran markedly on the lines of social division. In a time when the aspiring sort of gentleman would not be seen talking to a tradesman in the street—only a " real gentle-man " could do that—the poor person in the resorts was not en-couraged to frequent the fashionable churches unless in the capacity of a domestic servant, when attendance was compulsory. Incum-bents of the new parishes were not as a rule over-endowed, and they sought to attract a congregation which in one form or another paid its way. These very loose generalisations, subject to many exceptions, are put forward to indicate tendencies, which they fairly do. Even so, they apply by no means to the country as a whole. Among the masses of London and the industrial north religion of any kind concerned only a minority, and the large majority of the people were pagans.

On this placidly contemplative scene impinged the railways, roughly in the decade 1840–50. Railway access from London reached Dover in 1844, Folkestone 1843, Hastings 1850, St. Leonards 1848, Eastbourne 1849, Brighton 1841, Worthing 1845. The London and Southampton Railway opened in 1840, and a different line entered Portsmouth from the east through Chichester in 1847. In the western Channel the railway approach was a little later. Wey-mouth received it in 1857, and Torbay in 1848. Dartmouth with its prohibitive topography has never yet been entered by a railway line, but Kingswear on the opposite bank was linked by an econo-mically precarious branch to Torbay as late as 1864. What became the Great Western main line reached Exeter in 1844, and continued through South Devon to Plymouth in 1849. The extension through Plymouth into southern Cornwall began only with the opening of Brunel's famous viaduct across the Tamar in 1859.

As may be supposed, the effects of railway communication were considerable. All the middle classes, and not merely a small nonworking section of them as formerly, began to appear in force and demand furnished lodgings for short-term periods. The family summer holiday by the sea, a month for the family if not always for the father, became a general London custom. The balance of social forces in the resorts was changed, at least in those nearest to London, and the *élite* began insensibly to relax their grip upon the sea front and to seek quiet shores in France or unexploited villages on the more westerly parts of the English coast. But the medical factor remained strong, and the appeal of southern England powerful. Hilaire Belloc fifty years ago wrote of it as " the refuge," and he had in mind mainly Sussex, although he regarded Brighton as a blot to be written off. Many of the " carriage people " therefore did not retire far, perhaps two or three miles up country, where from the rising ground the blue sea still covered the horizon ; and there in fair comfortable houses they dug themselves in for another half-century. Sometimes the retirement was for a brief period coastwise to a flank, as from Hastings to the less vulgar St. Leonards or from Brighton either way to Rottingdean and Hove ; or in the last decade of the century, when a common commonness had enveloped both Hastings and St. Leonards, to the hitherto unregarded site of modern Bexhill, or the hitherto unknown near-coast villages like Angmering, between Worthing and Littlehampton. But such coastal removals were only temporary, for the philistines got wind of them and followed them up.

It did not stop at that, for the railways very soon found a new source of profit in the cheap day excursion, at first run chiefly on Sundays for the irreligious Cockney masses. Before the close of the fifties Hastings was invaded every week by " shoals of Londoners " with wife, children, baby and basket of food, out for a happy day of five hours in the train and nine on the beach.[1] The trippers went to the old-established resorts with the well-known names and a railway station close to the shore. They were highly unpopular both with the older types of holiday visitor and with the tradesmen in whose shops they spent no money. Only the publicans were glad of them, for beer flowed freely, and the tripper party was apt to get slightly or thoroughly tight before seeking the home-bound train. Even

[1] Manwaring Baines, *Historic Hastings*, p. 312.

after the first restriction of hours by Gladstone's Licensing Act of 1872, the public-houses were open all day on Sundays to "travellers," whose legal definition was that they drank their beer at least three miles from the address at which they had passed the previous night. And there was no nonsense then about excluding children : even the baby had his little drop from mother's glass. With the institution of bank holidays about the same time, and the gradual easing of conditions of work in general, weekday tripping set in and flourished, and the resorts became no places for high society in the summer, although some still retained their winter vogue.

With all this, the effect on the coast as a whole was only patchy. There were long stretches of beautiful coastline where the charm of nature was commingled by the centuries with the labours of men on simple natural tasks. In the Victorian age English civilisation was reaching its height, and, had we known it, getting ready to die, like the full-blown rose in its glory. From Ramsgate to Folkestone was such a coast, and from Hythe round Dungeness to Hastings, and then again from Bexhill along the edge of the marsh past Pevensey to Eastbourne and thence over the Beachy cliffs to the Cuckmere river-mouth and on to Seaford. West of the Brighton conurbation (eight miles long by the close of the century), the coast was duller because the Sussex plain was featureless, but between the resorts, small and not yet straggling to overwhelm the villages, as Worthing has now overwhelmed Tarring, the land had its quiet beauty, of lanes where no peril to life dogged the wayfarer's steps, of fishing hutments and boats drawn up the pebble beaches. Littlehampton was a decent little pleasure town with an interesting small port for the sailing coasters, and sands a paradise for children. It might still look like that, but for something that now mars its sea-turned face. Selsey was a small-boat fishing village on a headland related in function to the topography of the adjacent sea, not yet a characterless small town showing no particular aptness to its surroundings. Last point on the Sussex coast was the entrance of Chichester harbour, the spreading basin of the neolithic subsidence, ramifying its channels amid shores of serene, almost desolate beauty, entered by coasters and fishermen, not yet in any numbers by the yachtsmen who are now its almost only users. For Chichester harbour contrived to maintain a psychological defence : its bar was difficult and dangerous. So it was, in the appropriate weather, when all harbour bars are dangerous. But the peril was magnified by repute to the obscuration of the truth that such weather does not occur every day, and is indeed rare in the summer ; and so the taking-over of Chichester as a yachtman's haven was retarded. Between its two entrance points Sussex ends and Hampshire begins.

The fact that the intensive holiday trade right up to the end of the Victorian century did not detract from the beauty of most of the coastline was due partly to the outlook of the holiday crowds and partly to the condition of transport. The month-by-the-sea type of family visitors were content to enjoy lazily their immediate surroundings, the castle-building and cricket on the sands not yet fouled by oil, and the exciting small-life of the rock pools, the smart shops in clean well-kept streets, the theatre and the pier-pavilion and the nigger minstrels on the upper beach, the occasional cliff or country walk for the energetic. Longer excursions were rarer. Pleasure steamers might call at the pier for short trips into the Channel or along the coast. There would perhaps be a few two-horsed wagonettes to carry a dozen passengers apiece to " places of interest " such as castles or beauty-spots a few miles away, and the richer sort would make picnic excursions in hired carriages. But the holiday mood was static and contemplative, a leisurely savouring of the pint-pot without effort to get a quart into it. As for the trippers, they made straight from the station to the beach and stayed there until thirst took them to the adjacent pubs, and the time-table back again to the station. A mile outside that orbit they were never seen. And so the incomparable beauty of the Cinque Port marshlands, and the hilly country behind Hastings, and the downland of western Sussex remained unsullied. The poor man could have it at the price of honest sweat and blistered heels, tramping his twenty miles, resting on some hill-top crowned by a mill with whirling sails, toiling up and sliding down the coastguard path along the undulating cliff edge, free to sing with no one to hear him, feasting his eyes on cloud and marsh and sea, passing thatched and timbered houses not yet self-conscious of being " ye olde," slipping into little churches to commune with the good life of the centuries, drinking beer and eating bread and cheese at the Woolpacks, the Ships and the Anchors that existed to serve real needs. The rich man could have it too, by dwelling in its midst, provided there were not too many of him. And until 1914 there were not too many of either class, or of the literary and artistic people between. They merged into the landscape and thanked God for England as it was. A social balance prevailed, to be destroyed not by individual riches but by the internal combustion engine.

Down Channel, west of the Solent, the nineteenth-century resorts were more widely spaced and not for the most part of the larger sort. There again with the railways the middle-class visitors ousted the upper-class residents as the dominant influence, but the tripper element was small, having no massed urban population like that of London to send it forth. The visitors were chiefly from the western hinterland, itself a civilised land, and not yet, as in later days they were, from the midlands and the north. The high-lying western coast provided fewer sites for resorts to be approached by road or rail, and most of them were cramped sites incapable of holding large towns. Neither roads nor railways could follow the cliff edges of the coastline. Approach to the available places was by valleys down from the interior at right angles to the run of the coast. And since the main line railways ran inland east-and-west, the coast places were generally served by branch lines if served at all. Down Channel there is no long main line in sight of the sea, such as the London Brighton and South Coast Railway built through the length of Sussex from Portsmouth to Hastings.

The west-country branch lines to the coast had to use valleys, and when they used a beautiful river valley they had to keep to the water's edge of the estuary—the Kingswear branch along the eastern margin of the Dart, the Looe branch along that of the Looe river, the Fowey branch on the western bank of the Fowey river. There was some æsthetic loss, but to most minds very little. For the Victorian railway was a comely thing that grew without discord into the Victorian landscape. The lines did not carry many trains, and the stations were small, with a communal-domestic air like that of the market cross in a country town. Railway management in those days knew how to make itself artistically acceptable, and the engines with bright green paint and much shining brass, and the cream-and-chocolate coaches, were a joy to see. The western lines handled a good deal of milk, and there was a pleasant dairy smell about the stations. Reminiscent old noses associate the Great Western, all the way up to Paddington, with that scent. Of course the other railways carried milk : perhaps they did not spill so much.

Bournemouth was different from all the other resorts in that it grew out of nothing whatever, an uninhabited site. Up to 1812 there was nobody there, and in 1841 there were less than thirty houses. The landowner had planted groves of pine trees, and it was these that provided the aromatic air considered beneficial to consumptives. The original congregation of settlers and visitors was select and more intent on health than amusement. There were only 2000 inhabitants in 1861. Ten years later there were 6000, and railway communication had just reached the town.[1] After that its growth was very rapid. It shed the especially invalid association and developed into a residential resort for people with plenty of money, and offered holidays to the quieter sort who were being repelled by the noise and crowding farther east.

Torquay grew during the last French war from a minute fishing village on the northern shore of Torbay, an opening four miles wide and facing eastward, with Paignton in the centre of its arc and the larger Brixham enclosed by its southern arm stretching out to Berry Head. Macaulay, writing of William III's landing, contrasts the bay of 1688 with the scene of the 1840's. To quote his description is imperative : " Since William looked on that harbour its aspect has greatly changed. The amphitheatre which surrounds the spacious basin now exhibits everywhere the signs of prosperity and civilisation. At the north-eastern extremity has sprung up a great watering place [Torquay], to which strangers are attracted from the most remote parts of our island by the Italian softness of the air ; for in that climate the myrtle flourishes unsheltered ; and even the winter is milder than the Northumbrian April. The inhabitants are about ten thousand in number. The newly built churches and chapels, the baths and libraries, the hotels and public gardens, the

[1] The above particulars are from E. W. Gilbert, *Growth of Inland and Seaside Health Resorts, Scottish Geographical Magazine*, January 1939.

infirmary and museum, the white streets, rising terrace above terrace, the gay villas peeping from the midst of shrubberies and flower-beds, present a spectacle widely different from any that in the seventeenth century England could show. At the opposite end of the bay lies, sheltered by Berry Head, the stirring market town of Brixham, the wealthiest seat of our fishing trade. A pier and a haven were formed there at the beginning of the present century, but have been found insufficient for the increasing traffic. The population is about six thousand souls. The shipping amounts to more than two hundred sail. . . . But Torbay, when the Dutch fleet cast anchor there, was known only as a haven where ships sometimes took refuge from the tempests of the Atlantic. Its quiet shores were undisturbed by the bustle either of commerce or of pleasure ; and the huts of ploughmen and fishermen were thinly scattered over what is now the site of crowded marts and of luxurious pavilions." The clear vision of a master. And all this preceded the advent of the railway.

CHAPTER SEVENTEEN

Peace in the Channel :
The Ships and Ports

I. THE STEAM NAVY AND ITS BASES

THE CHANNEL as a highway for trade maintained its relative position in the nineteenth century, for northern Europe was still the focus of the energies of the Western element that dominated the world. But the individual seaports of the English coast of the Channel for the most part receded in relative importance as the age of steam and mechanism developed. This was not true of the Navy's ports, Portsmouth and Devonport, or of Southampton, to which the new conditions yielded a new life greater than any in the past. But it was true of the others, which had little part in the great trades of the ocean and saw even the home trades canalised into tracks that passed them by.

After 1815 the Navy enjoyed a long period of general peace, broken only by short and minor campaigns against opponents of secondary rank. It remained the wooden fleet of full-rigged sailing-ships for the forty years up to the Crimean War of 1854-6. The first phase of steam propulsion was by paddle-wheels, and these were quite hopeless for a fighting ship, since they obstructed the placing of the guns and would have been shot to pieces by the first broadside. Paddle-wheels in the Navy were useful only for tugs and auxiliary craft. Screw propellers, introduced in the forties, were more valuable, and it was early recognised that they could give the traditional battleship a mobility in action that might double her fighting power. But the early engines were extravagant consumers of coal, and the boilers needed large supplies of fresh water, since the use of salt quickly ruined them. Some early boilers did use salt water, and needed to be cooled down and cleaned out after a short period of steaming. Steam power had thus to be reserved for special occasions, and passage-making continued to be done under sail. In the Crimean War some of the battleships had auxiliary steam, and some were still purely sailing vessels. The over-all size of the wooden ships in their last phase showed a general increase, and so did the weight and hitting power of the muzzle-loading cast-iron guns ; and towards the end the guns were firing shells as well as the ancient round-shot. At the beginning of that period one feature of the old Navy faded out : the press gang. After the fall of Napoleon there was no desperate need for large numbers of men. The conditions of service were gradually improved, and the Navy could get all the men it wanted as volunteers. Standards rose, until by the middle of the century it could take its pick of the best seamen the country could produce, catching them young and training them to the special tasks of the service.

In the sixties and seventies armoured iron hulls superseded timber, new methods of gun-making produced heavier weapons of longer range, and compound engines and condensers reduced the coal consumption of the earlier machinery. Slowly it became accepted that passages as well as battles could be achieved under steam, and that the great spread of canvas was no longer necessary. The new great guns, at first mounted on the broadside and then in revolving armoured turrets, were very heavy, and their weight had to be carried as low as possible. An attempt to combine this with the full sailing rig was made with the *Captain*, completed in 1870. It proved to be a fatal error, for the low freeboard did not yield sufficient stability to stand up to the weight and windage of the masts and spars, and the *Captain* heeled and sank in a Biscay gale on her first commission, with the loss of nearly all her company. The error was not that of naval opinion as a whole. From the outset her designer Captain Coles was denounced as a crank. He perished with her. In reaction, the *Devastation* of 1871, another low freeboard ship, was given no sail-plan whatever, and was our first solely power-driven ironclad. But five years later the *Inflexible*, another big-gun turret ship, had higher freeboard with two masts and a square rig. Machinery, however, was improving, and the era of sail for battleships was ending, although the Navy's smaller ships, which had to make long cruises in distant oceans, continued to sail for a few years longer. The last wooden three-decker served with the Mediterranean fleet in 1867. She was the *Victoria* of nearly 7000 tons, with 121 guns, and she had engines and a screw that would be lifted when the ship was under sail. A comparison of her final date with that of the Crimean War shows that in thirteen years what had been the standard type of up-to-date ship had become utterly obsolete.

It was thus an extraordinarily rapid transition, for there were plenty of men still serving in the seventies who had entered the Navy when the wooden three-decker was the highest class of fighting ship. It was carried out with an open-minded alertness remarkable in a long peace, such as in the past had made the fighting services grow hide-bound. But in fact the peace was not profound, and Victorian England was always expecting a new French war. The French were very active in naval improvements. It was they who launched the first big ironclad, the *Gloire*, in 1859, to which the British response was the *Warrior* in 1860. Such revolutionary ships tended to undermine the superior strength of the British Navy, for, with their fighting power greater than that of any previous types, they represented a new departure from scratch in the naval rivalry. And yet the survival of Great Britain depended more than ever on superior sea power. The Navy of Nelson's time had shown invasion to be impossible ; but steam shipping and the rapid concentration of armies by railways had altered the conditions, and the men of the later nineteenth century were by no means sure that they were safe.

The occasions of tension sometimes amounting to danger of imminent war were numerous through the century. The Belgian revolution of the 1830's, whereby the Belgian people dissociated themselves from the Dutch and set up as an independent kingdom, created fears of French intentions to intervene and acquire control, which would have been a *casus belli* to Great Britain. An acute disagreement in 1839–40 on the affairs of Egypt and Syria produced a serious war crisis. French and British went to war in alliance against Russia in 1854–6, but not long afterwards their cordiality again gave place to suspicion. France was from 1851 again ruled by a Bonaparte, Napoleon III. He was personally no enemy of England, but the French army was ready to seek revenge for Waterloo, and the French public of that time was excitable and bellicose. When in 1858 the Italian Orsini, an exile living in England, manufactured a bomb there and with it crossed to France and came very near to assassinating Napoleon III in a Paris street, there was great indignation in France against British laxity in not looking after such criminals, and some lively sabre-rattling by French officers. British opinion was unrepentant and ready to take up the challenge, and even its idol Palmerston was unpopular for the only time in his life because he admitted that the French had a grievance. One result of the scare was the resuscitation of the Volunteers, disbanded after the Napoleonic War, and the Volunteers remained a permanent part of the British military forces until they were merged in the Territorial Army in 1907. Tennyson wrote *Riflemen Form!* a vigorous exhortation to national defence, embodying a decided animus against France and its Emperor. This was the background of the new naval activity expressed by the *Gloire* and the *Warrior*. Through the sixties the suspicion of Napoleon III continued. " Only the Devil can tell what he means," had Tennyson declared in his poem ; and at the opening of the Franco-German war in 1870 many people were anti-French because they expected the conflict to result in another increase of French power.

After the downfall of 1870 France was still the second greatest naval power, and she sought rehabilitation in the founding of a new colonial empire. It led to various collisions with British interests. The year 1885 was particularly a danger period, with sharp disputes over the Newfoundland fishery and the destiny of Burma and Siam. In Newfoundland waters it came almost to shooting, and only the good sense of the British and French naval officers on the spot averted a conflict. In 1898 there was a final crisis over the control of the Sudan, where a French force from West Africa occupied Fashoda. There was again a possibility of war, averted, but leaving angry feelings until the treaties of 1904 settled all outstanding differences and created the *Entente Cordiale*, which has stood the test of fifty tragic years.

Such was, until its last decade before 1914, the century of peace. Looking back, it is evident that peace was preserved by British naval supremacy, built up in the eighteenth century and clinched at Trafalgar. It is also evident that the naval supremacy was not used to promote a world supremacy of British power. French, German, Russian and Italian colonial and imperial expansions proceeded without involving world wars. Tensions between Great Britain and these powers were resolved without coming to blows; and in the colonial disputes Great Britain remained on the defensive and accepted decisions, particularly with Germany, which did her less than justice. It can be claimed that the Navy was used to seek peace, not war, and a fair field for all.

All this had its effects on the Navy's Channel ports. The Mediterranean fleet was the chief guardian of communications with the East, and the chief upholder of British influence in Europe; but the Channel fleet was the defence of the country against the great French army and, after 1870, the great German army. Its bases had to be looked to. Portsmouth was more than ever the chief home of the Navy. In the eighteenth century its fortifications had been those normal at the time, a continuous line of wall and rampart, with bastions and ditch, enclosing an area very much smaller than that of the modern city. The increasing power of artillery in the mid-nineteenth century rendered such defences obsolete, and the system of a ring of independent forts well outside the inhabited area took their place. At Portsmouth the main threat would come from the sea, although the access by land from the interior was not neglected. In the sixties three large circular forts of masonry and armour were built in the shallow water on the sands bordering the approach to Spithead and the harbour entrance by way of St. Helens Roads and the eastern end of the Wight. Approach from the west by the Needles channel was guarded by a series of forts, some at the water's edge [1] and some on the high grounds of the island. The whole of the Solent, Southampton Water and Spithead became one heavily defended area. These hill-top forts on the Isle of Wight have been locally described as "Palmerston's folly," an implication

---

[1] The forts at Hurst and Calshot were built round, and embodied, the castles made by Henry VIII on those points.

that they were of no use because they never came into action in the period for which they were suited. The criticism is flimsy, since it might equally have been applied to the ironclad ships which also never fought an enemy. There was no war. There certainly would have been but for the Navy and its bases.

At Plymouth the main developments were the creation of the breakwater and the growth of Devonport. Rennie's mile-long breakwater, with two miles of sheltered anchorage between it and the Hoe, is a shelving whale-back which foils the seas by causing them to sweep harmlessly up its seaward slope and expend their force without destruction. It was finished after nearly thirty years' work in 1840. Behind its centre was built a large fort to command the approaches through channels left at either end, the western channel being the deeper and more suitable for the largest ships. Gales still sweep the anchorage, but its water remains comparatively smooth. What the area beneath the Hoe could be like without the defence is vividly shown in a print of 1824 [1] depicting coasters torn from their anchors by a south-west gale with a heavy sea, and driven in collision and wreck towards the Cattewater.

Two great architects gave character and dignity to nineteenth-century Plymouth and Devonport, a quality such as Portsmouth has never shown. One of them, Sir John Rennie, designed the Royal William Victualling Yard, which Dr. Hoskins calls " one of the grandest monuments of the nineteenth century in England . . . a vast conception, of Spartan severity : an engineer's architecture suitable in every way for naval affairs and designed down to the detail of the lamp-posts." [2] It is indeed more than a building : completed in 1835, it stands for the eye to scan as creed and articles of the age that followed, solid principle, hard work, thoroughness, permanence. Those things did mean something in Victorian England. The other architect was John Foulston, who planned much of the expansion and eventual union of the two large towns, with the inclusion of the smaller Stonehouse between them. Foulston's work was not only in civic but in domestic buildings, fine and handsome in their age, shabby and grey to-day, when a society

---

[1] In Plymouth Public Library.   [2] Hoskins, *Devon*, pp. 459–60.

with changed values is impatient of their out-of-dateness. Many of his bigger works have been destroyed by the Hun, some by the vandal ; but some remain. The expansion into union is indicated by the census figures : 1801, Plymouth 16,000, Devonport (then Dock) 23,000, Stonehouse 3000 ; 1851, Plymouth 52,000, Devonport 38,000, Stonehouse 11,000 ; 1901, Plymouth 107,000, Devonport 63,000, Stonehouse 15,000. In 1914 all were combined in one city, with a population of 208,000 in 1931.[1]

The island of Portland lies two or three miles south of Weymouth and is connected to the mainland by the prolongation of the Chesil beach. The connection forms a bay sheltered from the west, and it was early used as an anchorage for ships too large to enter the river-port of Weymouth. The Navy found it of increasing value. By 1862 the Admiralty completed a long pier of masonry to protect the anchorage from easterly gales. At the end of the century a northern arm was made to complete the defence against torpedo attack. Portland harbour thus became a protected anchorage for a great fleet, but not a dockyard. R. T. McMullen, in his yachting classic *Down Channel*, under date 1857, remarks : " Went out from Weymouth and anchored in Portland Roads, where there was then no harbour. Neither were the beautiful heights appropriated by the Ordnance Department." Up Channel the closing years of the nineteenth century saw Dover likewise converted into a fleet harbour by great masonry works that enclosed a large area of the bay which had previously been open sea. The work at Dover, begun in 1893, came rather late for its purpose in sheltering the greatest ships, since the conditions of naval warfare were rapidly changing. In the First Great War Dover was a base for submarines and minor surface ships, and of a patrol for preventing German submarines from passing through the narrow Straits. But the great harbour had been designed rather with a view to war against France.

II. SOUTHAMPTON AND MERCHANT SHIPPING

Southampton was the only Channel port to show a great commercial advance during the century. It was time for this to take

[1] Figures from Hoskins, *Devon*, pp. 530, 532.

place, since Southampton had slept since early Tudor days, and three centuries were a rather long sleep. Towards the end of it there had been the period of fashion as a health resort, and for that purpose the double high-water had certainly been an advantage to bathers. Up to about 1830 the town progressed and population increased by reason of the residential attractions. The walls, except some on the waterfronts, were demolished, and some big houses with extensive grounds were built to the northward. But commerce began to awake, and soon caused an alteration of social conditions. The big houses began to be deserted and their gardens to be used as building areas more thickly occupied, and to the eastward the expansion moved over ground previously unoccupied to the bank of the Itchen.

Until the construction of the Royal Pier in 1833 Southampton had no quays that were not dry at low water, and since tidal range is only 11–13 feet this did not permit access at any time to the larger ships of the new century. At the close of the 1830's the London and Southampton Railway and a new Dock Company (subsequently amalgamated) began work on their projects. Through rail communication with London was opened in 1840, and dock accommodation for bigger ships grew through the forties, the docks being pushed out into previously open water to the south-ward. The railway terminus was brought down east of the ancient town close to the dock area. Modern Southampton resumed its medieval function as an outport of London. The Peninsular Steam Navigation Company of 1837 made Southampton its port for traffic with Portugal, Spain and Gibraltar. Its steamers were at first small, well under 1000 tons.[1] It extended its route through the Mediterranean to Alexandria and became the Peninsular and Oriental, with a land transit between Alexandria and Suez to connect with its steamers through the Red Sea and the Indian Ocean to Bombay and far beyond. The Royal Mail Steam Packet Company in 1842 like-wise started its ships from Southampton to the West Indies, and in 1857 the Union line to South Africa. At that date also two great German companies, the Hamburg America and Norddeutscher Lloyd, began to call at Southampton for passengers to North

[1] Its first ship, in 1837, was a paddle steamer of 200 tons.

America. Cross-Channel steamers plied to Havre and the Channel Islands.

The opening of the Suez Canal in 1869 facilitated steam traffic with the East and, although the P. and O. seceded to London in 1875, Southampton's expansion was unchecked. In 1890 the Empress Dock was opened, the only one in the country at which the largest liners could enter or leave at any state of the tide. What did all this shipping carry ? Chiefly passengers for the west, south and east parts of the world, and on occasion the military expeditions of the nineteenth-century British Empire, culminating with the British Expeditionary Force to France in 1914. Export of merchandise was not relatively important, for the heavy industries of Victorian England used Liverpool and the north-eastern ports. But of imports Southampton took a share in the meat, butter, grain and fruit that fed the industrial population. It nearly all came in steamers : modern Southampton was not a sailing-ship port.

The passenger traffic for Canada and the United States went mainly from Liverpool until the last decade of the Victorian period, for Liverpool's steamer interests developed out of her enormous sailing-ship tonnage antedating the rise of Southampton. In 1893 the American Line transferred from Liverpool to Southampton, thereby commencing a big movement south. The advantages of Southampton were that it was nearer London by a hundred miles, that its rail terminus was close to its docks, and that liners could call at Cherbourg for continental passengers. In 1919–20 the Cunard Line and the Canadian Pacific both moved to Southampton, and for freight purposes the P. and O. returned in 1925. Ever more accommodation was called for, and the 1930's witnessed the construction of great docks west of the town along the bank of the Test. The dredging of all the approach channels to a low-water depth of 35 feet provides access for the giant ships of our time.[1]

Falmouth, the westernmost port of the Channel accessible to large ships, developed a new function in the nineteenth century, when the electric telegraph became a new instrument of commerce. The great bulk of Europe's merchandise from all the world arrived in

---

[1] The above dates of developments are drawn from a publication of the Southern Railway Company: *One Hundred Years of Southampton Docks*, 1938.

sailing-ships, which were isolated from all communication during their long passages from Southern Asia, Australasia and Western America. The ships sailed on instructions from home that might be six months stale by the time they neared the Channel, and meanwhile it might have become desirable to alter the destination at which the cargo should be delivered. They therefore made Falmouth their port of arrival, where they picked up the latest instructions from their owners and sailed again for other British or north European ports. " Falmouth for orders " became a common destination for ocean-going sailing-ships until most of them ceased to sail in the early years of the present century. Thus Falmouth, without any important trade of its own, became for a long period, like the Downs, a calling-place for great ships. The Falmouth men, like the Deal boatmen, developed a class of hard-weather sailing-boats with which they went out " seeking " the approaching ships. These were the Falmouth quay punts, of which the last survivors are still sailing in the hands of yachtsmen.

Sea life in the sailing period is also illustrated by another little-known Channel calling. McMullen mentions falling in with a cutter off the Lizard in 1857 : " I learned that their vessel was a tailor's cutter belonging to Falmouth, and their business was boarding homeward-bound ships to supply clothes to those who preferred walking ashore in a new suit to being seen in sea-stained garments." Each century has its own character. In the eighteenth the business of the cutter meeting homeward-bound ships would have been some smuggling affair. McMullen's incident epitomises Victorian respectability.

The merchant steamer began to be seen about 1820, but only on the coast and in the home trades. Not until the 1830's did she begin regularly to cross the Atlantic. It is true that the American *Savannah* crossed from New York to Liverpool in 1819, but her passage took $27\frac{1}{2}$ days, of which only $3\frac{1}{2}$ were under power. For the rest she sailed, so that it was really a sailing passage. Her paddle wheels and 90 h.p. engine yielded only 4 knots in smooth water, and she had the sail plan of a full-rigged ship. The difficulty of all the early steamers was the stowage of sufficient coal, and the coal for an Atlantic passage took up more space than was available for cargo. For example, the *Britannia* of 1840, in which Charles Dickens travelled to America, the first vessel of the Cunard Line, needed 640 tons of coal and could ship only 225 tons of cargo. Until the sixties the steamer did not begin to make a living as a freight-carrier across the ocean, and not even then on the long passages to the East and Australia. It was the opening of the Suez Canal in 1869 that effectively let the cargo steamer into the India and China trades. Until that time it needed first-class passengers and govern-ment mail contracts to keep the ocean liner going, and all the cheaper freight, including most of the emigrants, remained in sail.

The poorer emigrants to North America in the forties and fifties had a terrible time, the passage in sailing-ships lasting for perhaps six weeks, under-victualled, overcrowded, and often carrying on board the infection of typhus and smallpox. The death-roll was frightful, and the hard-hearted shipowner has often been denounced for his villainy in not providing better conditions. But the govern-ing factor was the passage-money. The emigrants could pay only the tiniest fares, and the shipping firms could not give them more than they paid for. If the fares had been raised, most of the emigrants would not have sailed at all. In the mid-nineteenth century it was a hard world for the poor. The peasant from over-populated Ireland had to choose between starving at home and taking his chance in an emigrant ship, and the same applied to the workman of England's industrial towns, in times of depression, and the Scot of Glasgow or the over-peopled Highlands. In the later nineteenth century the industrial advance in Great Britain caught up with its task of supplying human needs, and Ireland's population was reduced to what the land could support ; and the pressure eased. At the same time it was growing more evident in central and eastern Europe, and new waves of emigrants set westward in their turn.

In the mid-century the poorest emigrants went to North America, and sailed chiefly from Liverpool or the Irish ports, and the Channel saw little of them. At the same time there was a considerable exodus going to Australia and New Zealand, and a trickle to South Africa. These voyages were much longer and might have been expected to be more deadly, but in fact they were not. The emigrant to the South had almost a pleasure cruise as compared with his brother going West—unless indeed he went as a convict, which he might do until 1853. The reason was that the southern emigration was of a different sort. The individual had more money behind him and could pay for a better voyage ; and the individuals were moreover organised by non-profit-making societies and companies which looked after their welfare and eliminated the horrors of the Atlantic passage. The mass-outflow to the West was entirely un-regulated until the passing of the first Merchant Shipping Act in 1855. It was almost a blind animal instinct, unreasoning and un-calculating of casualties. That to the South was always under some control, and even the convict ships, brutally as they were run, suf-fered a lower death rate because they were under discipline. The emigration of 1820 which planted the British element in South Africa was under government supervision. That to Western Aus-tralia from 1829 was managed by a syndicate of rich men who were enthusiasts for colonisation and conducted the business at a financial loss to themselves. The same was true of the South Australia Association of 1834, which made financial blunders but planted a successful colony without loss of life. The New Zealand Company of 1839, likewise not a profit-seeker, had a longer career and started colonies at several points on the New Zealand coastline. It made political mistakes and was guilty of some sharp practice in dealing with the Maori natives, but its handling of the emigration was admirable. At the same time a large number of unorganised indi-viduals were going to the senior colony of New South Wales and its offshoots of Victoria and Tasmania. They also did not suffer heavily on the passage out, because they had the means to pay for sufficient accommodation. The length of the voyage barred the poorest from undertaking it, and sent them to America instead.

The Australasian emigration was largely from southern England, with London and sometimes Plymouth as its ports of departure. The agricultural element was strong in it, farmers' sons and men from the little market towns. The various managing bodies were in a position to select their colonists. They required evidence of character and some small financial resource. Some colonists were failures in English life, but had some promise in them. The shiftless Wilkins Micawber was fictitious, but Dickens was a social observer who exaggerated from reality. The farmer's teeming family would equip its younger sons with a stock of tools and the timbers of a hut and see them off to be founders of Adelaide in 1836. The tradesman's son from a country town with a few pounds in his pocket joined the seekers of a promised land on the Swan River. Adventurous Londoners found means to rove southwards. Philanthropic societies equipped and recommended poor boys who promised well, even if, like Dickens's Charley Bates, they had a shady past. When Australian gold was found in the early fifties there was a bigger rush.

Most of this exodus passed through the Channel. A voyage to the Swan river (Western Australia) in 1830, recorded in a private journal, gives a very favourable impression, but may be too good to be entirely typical. The ship sailed from the Thames and waited for a wind in the Downs, and thence got clear away. The emigrants were on the whole a decent lot, men, women and children. They were not overcrowded and were properly fed, although of course some grumbled. The ship's bad character was a drunken Cockney shoemaker, but he did no harm to any but himself. The narrator, a piously brought-up young man, thought there was too much rum in circulation, sold by the steward through the weakness of the captain. The ship touched at Cape Town, where the young man was edified by hearing Dr. Philip [1] preach. And so they went on to the Swan river, without recording a single death on the long voyage. The Swan River colony was a failure in its early years, and most of the settlers moved to New South Wales. The writer of the journal became a sailor, and when he wrote his last letter home was leaving a Javanese port as mate of a merchantman. Thereafter nothing more was heard of him. The first expedition promoted by the New Zealand Company sailed from Plymouth. A stone on the landing-stage at Sutton Pool, standing by the side of the May-flower Stone, records the departure in 1839 of the pioneers of New Zealand in the ship *Tory*. Many other New Zealanders sailed also from Plymouth when the company organised a Devon Colony at New Plymouth in the North Island.

For twenty years before the advent of the screw propeller in

[1] John Philip, the leading missionary in the Cape Colony.

1839 there were numerous small paddle steamers working in the Channel, as tugs, coasters, and passenger carriers on the regular cross-Channel services. They all had a sailing rig to economise coal, and the engine-power was low, the boiler pressures generally below ten pounds to the square inch. For short passages the paddle had advantages, and the cross-Channel boats were mostly paddle-driven to the end of the century. All the early ocean liners were paddle steamers, and they and their screw successors were rigged with sails as late as the 1880's. The first screw steamer on the Atlantic passage was the *Great Britain* of 1843, which crossed west-bound in a fortnight. In her later years she served the Australian gold-rush, but in the capacity of a sailing-ship with auxiliary steam : in fact, in her last years the engines were taken out and she was a pure sailing vessel.

In the 1850's it was too early to run fully steam-driven vessels to Australia. Compound engines and condensers were beginning to economise coal, and boiler pressures were rising, but it was un-economic to run a ship on a passage of several weeks with an initial lading consisting chiefly of coal to be burnt on the voyage. The solution was slowly found by creating coaling-stations on the long routes, where bunkers could be refilled. This provided work and profit for the sailing-ships. Great Britain imported raw materials and exported finished goods, which were in sum less bulky. Thus on some routes the shipping had sailed outward-bound without full cargoes. Coal, the country's greatest raw material, provided a profitable outward lading ; and the great sailing tonnage con-tinued to the end of the century to carry out coal to the coaling-stations for the service of the Navy and the merchant steamers. This was a phase that lasted about fifty years.

Isambard Kingdom Brunel, the engineering genius who planned the Great Western Railway from London to Bristol and designed the liner *Great Britain*, both as links to connect London with New York, thought that the difficulty of steam communication with Australia and India could be overcome by the use of a gigantic ship, whose economics, he believed, would be more favourable than those of the smaller liners already at work. The big ship could be driven at higher speeds than the small one for less proportionate

349

expenditure of fuel. His big ship was to be five or six times as large as the current Atlantic liner. She is known to history as the *Great Eastern*, although some purist at the time objected—heaven knows why—to a name consisting of two adjectives, and proposed *Leviathan*.

The *Great Eastern* was built of iron on the Thames and launched in 1858. Her displacement was 32,000 tons and her length nearly 700 feet. She could carry 6000 tons of cargo and about 4000 passengers. Boiler pressure had now risen to 24 lb. per square inch, and she was fitted with paddle wheels and a screw propeller. She had six masts, two of them square-rigged. The *Great Eastern* was a failure. Brunel was greater as an engineer than as a master of business economy. The capital behind the project was insufficient, and there were long delays in launching and completion. The great ship never sailed East, the voyage for which she had been designed. Not until 1860, after Brunel's death, was she ready to pass round from London to Southampton, and thence she made her first passage to New York. Misfortunes dogged her, chiefly due to lack of working capital, and she more than once changed ownership. Her career as a liner was short and unprofitable, and her vast accommodation was never fully occupied because the traffic stream was insufficient to produce the numbers required on any given voyage. Shipping disasters in the Atlantic were frequent in the middle decades of the century, and passengers were shy of a vessel that acquired a reputation for ill luck. She did her best work in laying transatlantic cables, and passed a long final phase inactive, waiting to be broken up. Not until forty years after her building did the *Oceanic* of 1899 exceed her in length, although not in displacement.

The mass emigration of the very poor slackened in the sixties as British prosperity took an upward turn. But a smaller steady exodus continued through the century. Australia and New Zealand took their share, but railways were opening up Eastern Canada, and many went there. British agriculture was prosperous until the middle seventies, when the American prairies had been opened by trunk railways and began to send grain to Europe at prices with which the old agriculture could not compete. Continental Europe imposed protective duties. The United Kingdom remained free-trade, and her farming men emigrated. The next decade saw the imports of chilled beef and live cattle from America and frozen mutton and dairy produce from Australasia, and the exodus of English and Irish countrymen went on. The Canadian Pacific and other lines opened the Canadian prairie. In the nineties settlers were offered 160 acres of prairie land free, and many went to try their manhood against unbroken Nature. The sailing passage was now a thing of the past, and the emigrants went steerage in the big liners. The hoardings exhibited Canadian government posters offering the free land, and advertisements by the shipping companies pricing the transatlantic passage as low as £5. For that sum the later emigrant travelled in what the unfortunates of 1850 would have described as luxury, and reached his port in a week. Although Liverpool still took much of this traffic, Southampton had a growing share. It specialised also in the concentration of emigrants from continental Europe to Canada and the States. There was a large camp near the railway line outside Southampton, in which the people who arrived from the continent awaited their time to board the liners.

Channel traffic at the close of the century exhibited this growing Southampton business and a steady London stream, partly of passenger shipping but mostly of cargo steamers, bearing foodstuffs and general merchandise up Channel and going away from the Thames in ballast to lade at other ports. Northern Europe, with Germany in the van, owned much of the tonnage using the Channel, where a large increase of steam shipping was noticeable around 1880. The sailing-ships still worked in large numbers, some bound round the Cape for Australia and the Indian Ocean, many for the Pacific side of America, North as well as South. The Cape Horn passage to Pacific America was the last trade route dominated by the sailing-ship, until the opening of the Panama Canal in 1910–14. From about 1870 onwards the tramp cargo steamer, not serving any particular trade but going wherever a cargo offered, took an increasing share of the older commerce. The long experience of British shipowners, greater perhaps than that of most of their rivals, and the low construction and running costs resulting from the free-trade economy, gave this cargo tonnage a great advantage : all shipowners of those times were free-traders. Free trade indeed was killing agriculture, but one could not have it both ways. The shipping interest which had cried out against losing the protection of the Navigation Acts when they were repealed in 1849 was well content with a free field and no restriction forty years later. The Channel procession of the eighties and nineties illustrated the bases of the later Victorian prosperity : cheap imported food from all the earth ; large purchases of raw material ; efficient exportation of manufactures produced at low prices by virtue of those imports ; the exploitation of British coal ; the largest share in the passenger and emigrant traffic. And, behind it all, the Navy.

In that assessment one factor, perhaps the greatest factor, should not be overlooked, the merchant service officers and their crews. The officers (in ocean-going ships) were of all social classes except that of the influential rich who had been prominent in the old East India Company. They all went through the same training. The boy passed the last year or two of his school life in one of the school-ships or training-ships maintained in British ports. Thence, at the age of fifteen or sixteen, he would seek his indentures of apprentice-ship for four years with some firm of sailing-ship owners, the best firms being able to pick the best-seeming candidates. In the sailing-ship the apprentices berthed together in the half-deck, a cabin built on the deck amidships, between the seamen in the fo'c'sle and the officers aft. They learned their seamanship by sharing in all the work of the crew and being handy boys to the boatswain, the car-penter, and the sailmaker ; and the captain, if he did his duty by them, taught them navigation and other things pertaining to an officer's work. Their pay was merely nominal. The firm supported the greenhorn who was worth little at the beginning of his appren-ticeship, and had for almost nothing the services of a good seaman at the end. After the apprenticeship came the Board of Trade examination for second mate, followed at minimum intervals by those for first mate and master. The possession of these certificates did not of itself mean employment in the several ranks. Appoint-ment went by competition in a free market, personal record and reputation being the dominant factor. There were far more men with master's certificates than there were ships to command. The young officer might remain in sail if he saw a prospect of obtaining command. He nearly always so remained until he had his master's certificate, and then he might transfer to service in steamers, which some humorously likened to retirement to a life of ease. Until the Great War of 1914 virtually every captain and senior officer in British steamers of any size was a sail-trained seaman. The crews were probably for the most part British, but there was no restriction after 1849. One categorisation was " Englishmen, Frenchmen, Dagoes and Dutchmen," Dago meaning any southern European, and Dutchman any northern European ; but obviously it was not an exclusive scheme, for other continents and races furnished their quota. The seaman's qualification was his discharge-book, showing in what capacity he had served and with what character he had left his former ships.

In the later decades the sailing-ship was slowly losing its hold on world trade, and no large British full-rigged ships were built after the nineties. The smaller ones continued in strength until 1914. The Channel and its anchorages were lively with schooners, ketches and barges, working the tides, anchoring when wind and tide were foul, entering all the little ports from Cornwall to Kent, carrying coal, minerals, agricultural stuff, china clay, timber, anything on which their freight charges could compete with the railways and speed of delivery was not important. Their title to a living was low running costs, achieved by small crews of hard-working men with inherited knowledge of sails and gear and how to make the most of them.

In this respect the Thames barge was probably the most efficient short-distance carrier ever evolved, with two men able to deliver two hundred tons of goods anywhere on the Channel or North Sea coast or the nearer continent—but only by virtue of hard labour and superb seamanship. How far the technical development of canvas and wooden hull had come may be realised when we remember that a merchantman of similar capacity and range in Drake's time would certainly have had a dozen men to feed and pay, and possibly more. The bargemen kept their vessels sailing at their best speed in all circumstances. In threatening weather a barge might be under full sail as a squall came sweeping across the sea. At the last moment before it struck, down would come the big topsail. And after the squall had passed it took a strong man all that was in him to re-hoist that sail. The anchor work, two men on the windlass, was an exhausting business, and the lifting and lowering of the heavy leeboards every time the barge was put about. As for the skill of manœuvre, it was a sight to see a barge sail at speed into a tiny harbour, such as Whitstable, and round-to in the space of the proverbial pocket-handkerchief, while the bystander awaited an appalling smash which never happened. There are not many left now.

CHAPTER EIGHTEEN

The Past Forty Years

I. THE FIRST WORLD WAR

FROM 1914 onwards wars and preparations for war have bulked large in the history of the Channel. These wars have been so vast that their history, even in summary form, would be quite out of proportion to the scale of this book : one must take them as read and refer by allusion only to some Channel features. In August 1914, for the first time since the Waterloo year 1815, a British regular army crossed the Channel to northern Europe. It embarked at Southampton and landed at Havre, moving up to take position on the left of the French armies facing the invading Germans. More regulars followed, and territorial units as their training became sufficiently advanced to permit of it ; and in the second year the leading divisions of the new army created by Kitchener, of men enlisted after the outbreak of the war. Southampton remained the chief port, indispensable for the heaviest supplies, but as the British army found its station close to the Flanders coast all the up-Channel ports were used for drafts and supplies, and Boulogne became their usual landing-place. As the war went on and great consignments of heavy munitions and such things as railway rolling-stock were required on the Continent, a new war-time port was formed on the Stour at Richborough. Some of its debris remains, and the site has been partly occupied by more recent factories.

Apart from this the war of 1914–18, so near at hand that its gunfire was heard in south-eastern England, left few permanent marks upon the Channel coast. There was not much precautionary fortification, for any large German attempt at invasion was hardly possible so long as the German armies were held in north-eastern

France and the French Channel ports denied them. After the war one saw a few machine-gun posts on such obvious landing shores as Romney Marsh, but nothing as conspicuous as the martello towers of a hundred years before. Destruction by enemy bombers, although it made a great sensation at the time, was as nothing compared with that which the next generation was to experience. When the four years' war began aeroplanes were primitive and their bomb-loads very light. They developed rapidly, but their main targets were generally the opposing armies, and their bombardment of places distant from the military fronts was not very intensive. The great Zeppelin navigable balloons did better as distant bombers, and committed destruction that then seemed large, but later small. Their end came well before the end of the war, when improved fighter planes found them an easy target for machine-gun fire with incendiary bullets.

In the Channel itself the great ships of the Navy were little seen, for the submarine and the minelayer were already able to render narrow waters too dangerous for them. The field of action of the battle fleets was the wider North Sea in its parts remote from the Channel, and the main British bases were far north in Scottish waters. Although the original expeditionary force crossed to France without any molestation, the German submarines soon became active in the narrow seas, taking toll of the merchant shipping that nevertheless continued to enter the Thames by the Channel and from the north. Sometimes in the later stages the minelayers and submarines would interrupt communication with France for brief periods, but always the vigorous action of British small craft based largely on Dover brought the menace under control. Down Channel and far out into the Atlantic the submarines extended their scope, and by 1917 were sinking so many ships that the menace to British continuance of the war became more deadly than that of German success on the Continent. But new measures, convoy and the increase of light British naval forces, adopted perilously late, gradually mastered the danger and the crisis passed. When the United States entered the war in 1917 and sent a massive army across the Atlantic for the climax of the land campaign in the following year, these great forces, aided by the American navy, were able to cross the ocean to western France with little loss. Even at the end the range of aircraft was insufficient to render them an important factor in the war at sea.

II. HOLIDAY-MAKERS TRIUMPHANT

After the war the Channel coast seemed for a short while to be much the same as before. The visitors to the resorts mostly stayed within them. The intervening stretches of cliff and shore remained unvulgarised. The cyclist and the walker could use the roads without much risk. The camper could still find lovely spots in which to pitch without restriction or formality save a direct arrangement with the local owner. But the war had let loose a devil or perhaps antedated his inevitable appearance. Large numbers of people, mostly young, were seized with the desire to get out of town life at every opportunity, and to acquire some refuge in the country or on the coast wherein to spend their time off work. The week-end cottage or its equivalent, if only a shack or a tent, was their aim. The internal combustion engine was their instrument. The small car was still a luxury, but growing commoner. The motor-cycle with a side car served many, and wonders could be done in packing into it a wife and a child or two for the week-end ride to refuge. The monopoly of the railway, which had kept holiday folk mostly to the town resorts, was broken. It was easier to make for some isolated rustic spot than for a town. The war had taught young people not to mind living rough. The first generation of the Boy Scouts were now grown up, imbued with the delights of camping. Surplus war stores included thousands of army tents, sold off at low prices. There was a mania for camping. The old unregulated anyhow and anywhere phase, wherein lay charm, began to pass. Farmers, who had tolerated a party or two and sold them milk and eggs, saw that there was more in it than that. They began to allot one field to a multitude of campers and to charge a weekly rent per tent. And then organisation had to spread to water supply and sanitary matters, and local authorities began to take a hand; and camping as pre-war devotees had known it was gone for ever. It was numbers that killed it, too many people on to a good thing.

It was the same with building. There had been two or three

shack settlements on the shoreline before the war, as at Shoreham and Camber Sands and Dymchurch, the latter unwittingly popularised by Kipling. There had been at least one far back in the early nineteenth century, on the America Ground just west of the old Hastings, where a disreputable community had squatted on the solidified marsh of the Priory Stream estuary, to which no one apparently had a legal title. That was cleared up as Hastings grew, and the land is now the shopping area of the modern resort. The later shack towns were not of the gipsy type, but were cheap holiday resorts with the holiday families owning the little properties. With the lapse of time the temporary buildings became permanent little cottages and bungalows, and another stretch of coastline ceased to be open and natural with only a scant occupation by agriculture and small fishing. The general effect was somewhat mean and ugly, lacking the dignity attained by the nineteenth-century coast towns. They had had a moneyed class in their making, but the new residents were numerous and not rich, and could not aspire to dignity.

The new building did not stop at that. People with a taste for natural beauty began to destroy it by seeking bungalow sites in all the remaining quiet spots. They found them easily enough, for many tenant farmers had thriven on war-time prices and bought their freeholds. With peace the prices of produce collapsed, and the new freeholders were willing to sell for building. As the nineteen-twenties merged into the thirties ribbon developments pushed out along the coastal roads between the old towns and villages, and former farm-tracks became new roads leading to bungalow agglomerations where of old the sheep and the gulls and the marsh birds had lived in possession. Speculative estate developers worked on a larger scale. One of their achievements, and not the worst of them, is a mass of building where the Fairlight cliffs descend to the marsh at Pett Level. It would not be uncomely if only there was room for it ; but the natural beauty of the coast has not room for such things. Down on the Level, by the sea beach, there was an inn called the Ship, the only place of refreshment on the twelve-mile tramp by the coast from Hastings to Rye. Sea defence was neglected in the war and the first years of peace, and the gales drove the beach across the road and destroyed the inn. Two miles farther on, and a mile out of Winchelsea, there is now a new Ship, a smart little pub surrounded by one of the new settlements named Winchelsea Beach. Again, it is a cheerful little spot, but it and its like are eating away the beauty of the marsh. West of Newhaven, on the cliff-road towards Brighton, a development on the grand scale was planned and carried far enough to destroy the landscape. Its promoters proposed to call it Anzac, but Anzac was a sacred word to that war-time generation, and public opinion would not tolerate its use for a business project. So it took shape as Peacehaven, and there it is to-day as a monument of what England could do to its coast. By the thirties the up-Channel coastline as viewed from the sea began to look like a row of houses, save where the cliffs of Beachy Head and the Seven Sisters, in part preserved by the National Trust, remained inviolate.

A further change of social habit affected the holiday people in the large resorts. Many were no longer content to pass the time in rooted contemplation of the sea, and buses and coaches invited them to rove far afield. Tea shops and petrol stations proliferated, and quiet country roads became dangerous to the people who had been their users. Along the whole length of the Channel ancient haunts of peace and beauty, from Rye in Sussex to Polperro in Cornwall, became a noisy pandemonium on every summer day. The invaders in general betrayed no real appreciation of what they saw. They wandered vacantly around for a while, saying " How quaint ! " and then sought a café until it was time to climb into the charabanc once more. They destroyed a phase of English civilisa- tion no less surely and uncomprehendingly than the barbarians of the fifth century had destroyed the civilisation of the Roman Empire. No one was to blame. It was the spontaneous work of free people, and it was going on over all Europe ; and it was better far than a rigid decorum enforced by some cultural tyranny. Artificially pre- served natural beauty, as R. G. Collingwood pointed out, is a con- tradiction in terms.

III. YACHTING

Yachting has its place in Channel history. In the nineteenth century it was in two kinds, the rich man's big yacht with a paid crew, essentially a social appurtenance, the owner and his friends touring the coast in considerable luxury and leaving all the seamanship to their professionals ; and the smaller sailing craft of the true enthusiasts, who might be rich or poor, but did the work themselves and loved it in every detail. The small cruising yacht became common in the latter half of the century. Some were built for the purpose, sound and strong and carefully designed, lasting through long years until they slowly declined into " tore-outs." Some were ex-fishing-boats, sold by the fishermen when they began to decay. Some were even converted ships' lifeboats, not so seaworthy as their name implied, sold by the shipping companies when condemned for their original purpose. The poor man with the true spirit in him could find something in which to put to sea, and the weaker the craft the higher the seamanship it evoked to keep it going. He who preferred to do his repairs and fitting-out himself, or could not afford to have them done for him, learned well and truly the things that the luxury yachtsman never knew. He entered also the brotherhood of those who for long centuries had sailed the coast, with traditions and a lore and life of their own, a community that has been diminishing since our present century set in.

There were two outstanding cruising men of the pre-1914 era, who between them lifted high the practice of their sport. R. T. McMullen, whose *Down Channel* has been quoted in a previous chapter, taught the small sailing yachtsman to equip himself, morally even more than materially, to stay at sea and face whatever came instead of ducking into port at the first sign of trouble. McMullen in spite of his name spoke and thought of himself as an Englishman. He was a London stockbroker who owned in succession various yachts, the largest being a 20-ton yawl in which he employed two paid hands. He was himself a relentless worker and expected the men to be. On one occasion there was so much mutual dissatisfaction that they left him at Cherbourg, whereupon he sailed the heavy vessel back to the Thames single-handed, a feat unprecedented at that time. He was a small man physically, under nine stone, but a giant in spirit. In his later years he sailed alone in smaller boats, and in one of them he died peacefully at the helm in fine weather while on a passage down his beloved Channel in 1891. His writings are a gospel of " how to do it," and at times an unconscious revelation of the rigid Victorian outlook on many things. As McMullen dropped out another master-yachtsman was beginning his sailing career, Claud Worth, an oculist who practised in London. His *Yacht Cruising* covers the thirty years up to the 1914 war, with a short resumption after it. He shared McMullen's passion for perfection in sailing, and also in every detail of construction and fitting-out. Even to-day, when the available materials are very different, the man doing the winter work on his own boat will do well to re-read Worth's remarks on the tasks he has to tackle. As for the sailing, the essence of clear and terse description lies in his account of the great gale of September 1896, which found him single-handed in a 7-tonner between Torbay and Portland Bill. He owed his life to his knowledge of what to do, and to his endurance in doing it.

In the new post-1918 period there was an outburst of new yachting, on an impulse perhaps akin to that which sent the week-enders swarming along the roads to tents and bungalows. Young men in the squalid war had dreamed of the peace of the summer sea, and now many of them sought it. The week-end sail and the holiday afloat appealed to greater numbers than ever before. The auxiliary petrol engine, exasperating contraption though it was, helped the development by ensuring, if it worked, that the becalmed sailor would not miss his Monday morning return to business. The railway managements of that time issued cheap week-end tickets available outwards to one port and homewards from any other, so that the sailing man could work in successive short passages along a considerable stretch of coast. There had always been some women who had shared in this cruising life—even the mid-Victorian McMullen sometimes had his wife with him ; and now there were many more. The small cruising yacht became a family boat, with sleeping accommodation whose content in cubic feet would have roused the horror of slum reformers on land ; and everybody throve healthily in it. The small cruiser, new, cost perhaps slightly more than a new car, but its life was very much longer and its running costs much less. Twenty years old it would fetch a good second-hand price. Yacht moorings began to fill the pleasant small ports from which the fishermen and the coasters were fading out.

All this cruising side of yachting occupied many more people than did the yacht-racing that alone received much notice in the Press. Racing in big yachts with large paid crews had developed through the rich nineteenth century, and continued thereafter, although the actual numbers of the craft and their owners were very small. Although it tested brains and skill and seamanship, there could be no success without money lavishly spent. A momentary fumble in handling a great J-class cutter might lose a mast and a thousand pounds. These great yachts, lovely but fragile, reached the zenith of their fame in the 1930's, and then passed suddenly away with the death of George V their leading patron. In 1936 grim times were in sight and the rich had to tighten their purse-strings. The dead King's beloved *Britannia* was taken to sea, in a sort of viking funeral, and sunk in deep water far out in the western Channel. The other owners laid up their ships or cut down their rigs and used them for cruising. At the Coronation Regatta in Torbay in 1937 there was only one of them to be seen, sailing idly with no one to match her. Tastes change with the changing times, and their like will not be seen again.

A new sort of first-class racing was already well established, not the J-class kind round the few miles of a marked course, but one extending over days on a long passage in the open sea, facing any weather that might come. The Fastnet Race, from Cowes down Channel, out round the Fastnet Rock on the southern Irish coast, and back to Plymouth, was an annual event of the twenties and thirties, and there were others, to Santander, and on shorter Channel courses. At first they attracted the larger cruising yachts, with a handicap to allow for disparities. Of recent years they have become more specialised, with yachts built for the purpose, the expense in many cases spread among a syndicate of ownership. The main differences from the old racing are two : that it is hard-weather work for boats built to stand anything, and that the crews are all

amateurs who need to be fit and tough. Off-shore racing is the
high sport of to-day and the future. With growing experience it is
extending downwards to quite small boats.

There was always much yacht-racing also in classes of smaller
boats, some of them local, some national, some international. In
the nineteen-thirties these classes began to multiply, and since 1945
they have multiplied again. The great development in the present
period of peace is dinghy racing, and numbers of new sailing clubs
hav been formed mainly to cultivate it. It is a specialised form of
sailing, involving capsizes and duckings and acrobatic feats in
righting swamped craft, and is essentially a game for the young. As
they grow old, presumably their blood will cool and they will race
in vessels that will stay right side up.

IV. THE SECOND WORLD WAR

The Channel coast played a greater part in the Second World
War than in the First because air power had become a preponderant
factor in the issue. A threat of invasion developed, much more
serious than ever the Napoleonic schemes had been in 1804, since
the Channel crossing could no longer be barred by sea power alone
and material superiority in the air did not at the outset rest with the
defence. In the pre-war years a few clear-sighted men realised the
danger before the government, whatever it may have thought, was
prepared to take action, and while the people were drugged with
pacifist demonstrations such as the great " Peace Ballot," which
aided the aggressors. Such antics were associated with left-wing
politics, while on the extreme right there was a dangerous disposition to admire dictatorship and connive at its advances. The great
common-sense mass of the people was sound enough, as events
were to prove, but bewildered and looking for leadership which it
did not get. Very late, in the last two or three years before the
catastrophe, defence policies were adopted which were to avert
destruction by an incredibly narrow margin. When the storm
burst with the overthrow of France in the spring of 1940 the
Channel became the scene of events unprecedented in history.

At the end of May, when the military disaster made it necessary to withdraw the British troops from the Continent, and with them a large number of the French who found themselves with their backs to the sea, the Straits witnessed the Dunkirk evacuation. Shipping for the purpose was desperately short, and small craft were essential to take great numbers off the open beaches. The minor ships of the Navy did it, and small merchantmen of all sorts, coasters, fishermen, pleasure steamers, tugs, and the available yachts of the Thames estuary and the south-east coast. Among the yachts-men the word went round by personal communication, and men crowded off to the coast to render service in anything that would cross the narrow sea, anything with an engine, and even some without. The weather by good fortune was fine and calm. Down Channel little was known about its method until it was virtually over. The censorship of news was strict, and perhaps not intelli-gent; for it is a fact that the American people across the Atlantic were informed of what was going on while the bulk of the British were kept in ignorance of the details. The enemy of course were fully apprised and were raining bombs on the beaches and the flotilla throughout the operation. No less than 225,000 British soldiers and half that number of French were taken off. The Dunkirk evacuation was a magnificent feat of enterprise and swift action. By all the rules the British army was lost. Its men, though not its heavy equipment, survived to go back to France in the fulness of time.

After that the German invasion plans took shape, although not without delay. The High Command did not underestimate the difficulty of forcing the Channel passage with a large army and all its fighting gear. The first task was to complete the destruction of the French armies, for only those in the north had been actually eliminated. It was swiftly accomplished, and on 21st June France, the victim of her own leaders more than of the Germans, laid down her arms. For the invasion the Germans had to re-group their forces and provide a great flotilla, mainly of the big power-driven barges used on the continental waterways. The Royal Air Force bombed the assemblies of barges and sank many, but their numbers grew, for Hitler had the whole northern coastline of Europe from Norway to the Spanish frontier to drew upon; and the Rhine and its delta, and the German rivers and the French canals had long been an area of intensive water traffic. Napoleon had had to build his flotilla, but Hitler had only to concentrate his.

To the Germans it was evident that they could cross the Channel only under the cover of superior air power. It was also evident to the British, and in those midsummer weeks before the blow fell they just and only just achieved the minimum strength of fighter aircraft for the defence. Rearmament had been left very late, and mass-production could not yield results at the stroke of the pen. It began to produce the appreciable force only as the German invasion of France took place. If Hitler had not paused to clean up his French victory, and perhaps also to await the British surrender which all the world expected, he would have had a better chance. Meanwhile the machines were coming from the factories, and the pilots, " the few," indescribably few for the change they wrought in the world's history, from the training fields. In the hands of men of ordinary fighting pitch the planes would not have been enough ; but those young men of 1940 were not ordinary, they were super-human, demonic, a flame of fire, as men had once described Nelson in battle. To courage and inspired skill they added an endurance of fatigue that had few precedents. The airmen answered the dictators' gibes about " the decadent pluto-democracy." The fighters destroyed so many German bombers that the attack, intended to crush air resistance and to sweep the Channel clear of British ships, was a costly failure. The people of the coast saw much of it, for the operations were mostly by day. The battles roared overhead, the burning wrecks came down in their fields, and fired cartridge cases fell in their gardens.

These things occupied much of August and September, and at the close of that month the invasion was called off : for the time being, that is to say, since there was always a possibility of its being tried again with improved methods. That winter the German air force turned to night bombing and made devastating attacks on London and the big cities, especially the ports. Plymouth, Southampton, Portsmouth and Dover suffered bitterly in life and material destruction, but nothing could crush the spirit of their people. These were the outstanding victims, but hardly a place along the coast escaped some bombing, and all had the anticipation of more to come. Dover also had the distinction of being under heavy artillery fire from batteries on the French coast across the straits.

The Germans did not announce postponement of the attempt, but the country was steadily getting into better shape to resist a landing if one should be made. In this second war the regular forces were composed of men called up by age groups as training and arming facilities could cope with them, and not of great numbers indiscriminately volunteering as in 1914. It was not that men would not volunteer but that the military authorities would not have them before the set time. But in the month after Dunkirk, when an immediate invasion seemed likely, the cabinet decided to enlist a civilian force of volunteers doing duty in their spare time and organised to resist, each unit in its own locality, the Local Defence Volunteers, afterwards renamed the Home Guard. It contained youngsters not old enough for the call-up, men whose call had not yet come, and older men not likely to be taken for permanent service. Among these latter there was a great deal of military experience, for large numbers over forty had seen service in the first German war. Middle-aged men in general were now physically fitter, age for age, than they had been in earlier times, and they formed the backbone of a useful force ; not that the early Home Guard had any medical examination, for the recruit's physical fitness was accepted on his own statement.

The coastal Home Guard had plenty of duties, training carried out chiefly on Sundays, patrols and watch-posts manned every night, while many of the men, the farm workers in particular, were doing almost double work while the daylight lasted. It was a new phase of a thing old in English history. Sixteen to sixty were roughly the age limits, although over-sixties were in it ; and this force in older days had been the militia of the Tudors ready to meet French or Spanish invaders, and the fyrd of Alfred to resist the Danes. A detailed comparison of the Home Guard with the anti-Napoleonic Volunteers would be interesting. It is likely that it would discern more realism and common sense in the 1940 force. They, like their predecessors were short of arms—four rifles to a platoon was common in 1940 until supplies from America began to arrive ; but

366

they did not grow fractious about it. One guesses also that the oratory was less effervescent—in fact there was none, and certainly there was no hankering after the pompous uniforms of 1803. The uniform at first consisted merely of an arm-band with the letters LDV, and the full khaki kit appeared gradually. But the Home Guard was a protean force of many aspects in the various parts of the country, and there must be very few in a position to speak of it as a whole.

As the war went on both British and Germans created forces of small armed vessels to patrol the coasts and dispute the use of the Channel waters. On the British side the yachtsmen who were prominent in the R.N.V.R. played a great part in the flotilla service, and combats and raids were frequent. The Royal Marines trained bodies of men as commandos[1] to carry out night landings for reconnaissance of the enemy coast. A reconnaissance in force to test the strength of the defences took place at Dieppe in 1942, when several thousand troops landed and remained for some hours before withdrawing after suffering heavy casualties. It was training in what came to be called amphibious operations, a modern version of Pitt's raids in the Seven Years War. On the British side of the Channel there were rumours current of German commando landings, but none of them appear to be substantiated. The British share of the control of the Channel was more extensive than the German, although it was dangerous for large ships of either side to appear in its waters.

When 1943 was merging into '44 there were preparations for the great invasion of Hitler's France. Their scale was unprecedented, and many things were plainly visible. In fact it was not concealed by the allied governments that there was to be an invasion in the summer of '44. But its nature, scope and point of impact were kept substantially secret. Big things like the component parts of the artificial harbours to be placed on the French coast, or the preparations for submarine pipe-lines to feed petrol to the invading armies, were constructed on the English coast. Those who saw them did not know their purpose, and in any case kept their mouths shut.

---

[1] The original use of the word was to denote the troop formations of the Boer republics in the South African wars of the nineteenth century.

There was little blabbing and chattering; after years of war the security habit was highly developed. By night the coastal roads rumbled as fleets of tanks and lorries moved to their concentrations, and by day the civilian came upon them motionless under the cover of trees. He passed on and said nothing, but his heart bounded : at last . . . ! It might be thought that among millions of people enemy spies would have learnt all there was to know. It seems that they did not, and the big secrets were kept. The huge gathering of troops, British, American, Canadian, was ready to embark in the huge flotilla of landing craft and guardian fighting ships collected in the waters round Portsmouth, while the bombers were destroying the German communications in France. That the enemy knew, but he did not know where the blow was to fall, and did not even guess correctly. The Normandy landing was a surprise.

As the spring passed the Home Guard of the Channel coast was on the alert. It was expected that as the invasion day approached the Germans would seek to disrupt the programme by landing airborne troops behind the coastline. Every man so landed would have been sacrificed, but it might have been worth it. The word was that the invading army would not divert its purpose to deal with such landings, but would leave them to the home forces. Arms were plentiful now, and training had made progress. There were practice alarms and sudden night turn-outs to test it, stores of victuals and petrol earmarked for distribution at need. Almost everyone had his humble part to play. But the Germans never tried airborne landings, no doubt considering that their price would exceed their value.

They had something else in preparation, a surprise on their side, but they were a little late with it. Only after the Normandy landing had begun did the secret weapons begin to play across the Channel, the V 1 or pilotless planes that plunged at their appointed range and exploded a middle-sized bomb, and later still the V 2 or rocket with a bomb-head, a more formidable affair of longer range. The V 1's were fired from launching sites all up the French coast. They were mostly directed on London, but some to Portsmouth and South-ampton. They inflicted random damage and many casualties, but they were incapable of accurate aiming, a purely terror weapon such as the German mind delighted in ; and the people they were fired at were past terrorising. The defence lay in anti-aircraft guns and fighter planes shooting them down over the sea or the less populous areas of the coastline. The East Sussex and West Kent region saw most of this. Many were destroyed harmlessly, but many got through. The rocket bombs were a different matter, so swift that there was no warning sound of their approach. Londoners heard the explosion first and the drone of flight after. If they had had more time the rockets could have done enormous damage : they were the missiles of the future. But as the year advanced the Allies drove eastward up the French coast and then into Flanders, and mopped up the nests of these devilish things while yet there was time.

In May 1945 it was finished in Europe. The Channel coast could take stock of its damages : the business centre of Plymouth destroyed, Southampton extensively devastated, in Portsmouth only seven houses in every hundred undamaged, the lower-lying parts of Dover swept by shells and bombs, almost every intervening place along the coast with small or larger scars to show, many villages hit by the numerous night bombers who lost their way and discharged their loads anywhere before turning back. Other things also had left their marks, the airfields of the defence transforming farmland into runways, the tank training grounds, the large-scale practices of landing assaults on open beaches, the firing ranges, the radar masts thick along the coast, the belts of barbed-wire, and the broken-down piers wherever an enemy landing might have been possible. Some of these blots were cleared, others still remain, some look like being permanent.

The post-war rulers of the country, local as well as national, were in a planning mood. The official and the expert were in control, imposing their will and paralysing all other wills : " The gentleman in Whitehall," said one of them, " knows best." That phrase will be quoted in the history books, if there are any, in a hundred years' time. A weary people accepted them. They accepted a plan for a new exotic Plymouth, at variance with all its history. The plan is now sufficiently accomplished for its effect to be seen, a perfect example of the patch of new cloth on the old garment, where the edges will not knit and the contrast of texture and design is grotesque. Southampton has begun something of the sort with a brilliant new main street, bright and heartless to those who remember the old. Nearly all the shops in these new business quarters are held by the multiple-shop organisations that sell exactly the same goods the length and breadth of the country. Local character is going or gone.

The west-country coastline remains beautiful, with changes that are mostly development and not revolution. From the Solent eastward the picture is darker. Southampton Water began to be industrialised between the wars, and the process has accelerated. An emormous oil refinery has covered the hitherto natural area of its New Forest shore, and another is threatened on the Hamble side. The West Sussex resorts link up in new areas of building. The marsh coast east of Dungeness is the especial haunt of chalet camps in which every moment of the holiday-maker's day is planned for him and the painful process of thinking for himself is eliminated. Dungeness itself, we are told, is to be occupied by a nuclear power station with its necessary patch of urbanisation. It is all hopelessly inevitable, for all these things are functions of the society of our time, not only in this country but in others. They are the way of the world we live in. The earlier centuries gave hope of growing civilisation, with an idea of progress afloat, more strongly held in each succeeding generation. The twentieth century offers growing mechanisation with no escape permitted. The individual will soon be the criminal : in many ways he is now. Perhaps it will pass in its turn.

Index

INDEX

INDEX

V. WEAPONS, 368–9
Vectis, 28
Veneti, the, 36–7
Vernon, Admiral, 265, 295
Villas, Roman, 50
Villeneuve, Admiral, 306–8
Volunteers, the, 1803, 305–6

WANTSUM CHANNEL, 30, 44, 71,
    110–12
Ward, John, 224
War scares, 19th century, 338–9
Wars of 20th century, 355–7, 363–9
Weald, the, 49, 68–9, 114
Wennington, Robert, 144–5
Wessex, 64–5
Weymouth, 132, 212, 287, 323
Whitstable, 354
Wight, Isle of, 22, 62, 67; forma-
    tion of, 26–8

William I, see Norman Conquest
William III, 253; invasion, 1688,
    258–63
Wiltshaw, Thomas, 269
Winchelsea, 22, 69, 92, 93, 94,
    102–5, 118, 217; Level,
    358
Winchester, 50
Wine imports, 125, 127, 136
Winstanley, Henry, 277
Winter, Sir William, 178, 184,
    208
Worth, Claud, 361
Worthing, 323, 326
Wrecking, 275–6
Wyndham, Thomas, 182–3

YACHTING, 248–9, 360–3
Yarmouth, Great, 115–16
Yarmouth, I. of Wight, 131

ABOUT THE AUTHOR

James A. Williamson was born in Cobham, Surrey, England, in 1886, and graduated from Watford Grammar School and the University of London. A member of the Royal Historical Society, the Historical Association, and the Hakluyt Society, Dr. Williamson is known as a leading authority on English maritime history and expansion. He is a past Vice President of the Historical Association and was Ford Lecturer in 1939–1940. He has written a number of books on the great English explorers, the British Empire, British expansion, and Elizabethan seamen. In addition to being an eminent maritime historian, Dr. Williamson has, in the course of his life, sailed the whole Channel coast, and has also walked the length of the coast, some stretches many times over.

1   2   3   4   5   64   63   62   61   60